At the Edge
of Existence

At the Edge of Existence

Liminality in Horror Cinema Since the 1970s

BRANDON WEST

McFarland & Company, Inc., Publishers
Jefferson, North Carolina

This book has undergone peer review.

LIBRARY OF CONGRESS CATALOGUING-IN-PUBLICATION DATA

Names: West, Brandon, 1993– author.
Title: At the edge of existence : liminality in horror cinema since the 1970s / Brandon West.
Description: Jefferson, North Carolina : McFarland & Company, Inc., Publishers, 2022 | Includes bibliographical references and index.
Identifiers: LCCN 2021049896 | ISBN 9781476681405 (paperback : acid free paper) ∞
    ISBN 9781476644196 (ebook)
Subjects: LCSH: Horror films—History and criticism. | Liminality in motion pictures. | BISAC: PERFORMING ARTS / Film / Genres / Horror
Classification: LCC PN1995.9.H6 W4335 2021 | DDC 791.43/6164—dc23/eng/20211102
LC record available at https://lccn.loc.gov/2021049896

BRITISH LIBRARY CATALOGUING DATA ARE AVAILABLE

ISBN (print) 978-1-4766-8140-5
ISBN (ebook) 978-1-4766-4419-6

© 2022 Brandon West. All rights reserved

No part of this book may be reproduced or transmitted in any form or by any means, electronic or mechanical, including photocopying or recording, or by any information storage and retrieval system, without permission in writing from the publisher.

On the cover: Wes Craven's *New Nightmare* (1994) aka *Nightmare on Elm Street 7* (New Line Cinema/Photofest)

Printed in the United States of America

McFarland & Company, Inc., Publishers
  Box 611, Jefferson, North Carolina 28640
    www.mcfarlandpub.com

To the memory of Wes Craven

Acknowledgments

Thanks to Drs. Shoshana Milgram Knapp, Charlene Eska, Peter Graham, Nancy Metz, Robert Siegle, Anthony Colaianne, and Thomas Marksbury for their contributions to this project.

Special thanks to my mother, Victoria West, and brother, Kirsten Powell, for helping foster my love of horror, and to Kimaya Thakur for her patient suggestions along the way.

Table of Contents

Acknowledgments	vi
Preface	1
Introduction	4
One—United in Darkness: The Nature of Liminal Horror	9
Two—Shattered Screens and Punctured Skin: When the Fictional Becomes Real	16
Three—Emblazoned in Our Memories: When the Real Becomes Fictional	65
Four—Harsh Realities: Truth Is Scarier Than Fiction	94
Five—Was It All a: Dream(s) and the Liminal Horror Film	125
Six—The Mind's Power: This Is Not Reality	158
Seven—Powers of Belief: How the Mind Writes Reality	206
Afterword	224
Chapter Notes	227
Bibliography	241
Index	249

"Horror films don't create fear. They release it."
—Wes Craven[1]

Preface

"Liminality": the quality of being perched upon a threshold, one foot on either side, a quality predominantly associated with the discipline of anthropology, with some use in depth psychology. It is a rare occurrence when one immediately thinks about "horror" upon hearing "liminality" or about liminality upon hearing "horror." Whereas the horror genre has resonated with feminist, psychoanalytic, formalist, and socio-cultural frameworks (among others), few critics connect horror with anthropology, let alone "liminality," one of the principal concepts of this discipline.

Interestingly, I was unaware of any association between anthropology and liminality until *after* I had already spent years studying the latter concept in terms of horror movies. Liminality, as I understood it without any references to anthropology, denoted the state of being on the margin, on the threshold between two (or more) worlds, neither here nor there. Over time, I began to notice this state of being and not being in horror (maybe because it is my favorite genre); particularly, I noticed how horror films meandered through reality, fiction, and any unspecified states in between. My observations came to fruition during my master's program when, while researching ironic self-awareness in Wes Craven's films, I realized that: (a) liminality in horror was—and could also be—a bigger sub-genre than I had initially conceived and (b) that liminal horror was a largely unexplored topic.

From the scant scholarship I managed to find, I successfully wrote my paper (entitled "A Disrupting Scream in a Postmodern Nightmare: Ironic Self-Awareness in Wes Craven's Horror Films"), and then promptly dedicated myself to conducting a thorough examination of horror movies to understand the scope of liminality. Liminality for me, at this point, simply connoted existing between two or more states or categories of being, and I saw this in horror films that mimicked reality, fictionalized it, professed truth, and, more importantly, obfuscated the boundary between physical and non-physical existences, the actual and the fantastic, until a character (within the horror film) could easily oscillate between these two diverse states of being.

Once I discerned this obscuring—and movement—between the unreal and the real (and vice-versa), my interest in liminality (as it manifests/ed in horror) concretized, and I became especially fascinated with the line that separates fiction from reality. Because, as humans, as thinking beings, we spend so much time engaging in the fictions our minds fabricate, I considered it necessary to investigate how this involvement (and progression) appeared in my favorite genre, horror. Because I was unaware of liminality's interrelation with anthropology even then, my research (and my arguments about liminal horror) developed without any correlation to that discipline. That is, my book surveys "liminality" itself in horror instead of professing an approach that conjoins horror with anthropology. I have, nevertheless, noted liminality's scholarly roots to illustrate the histories of the concept and this project.

Here, I wish to clarify that, though my volume does not bring together these diverse fields, they can be studied in each other's contexts. In fact, I believe anthropology and horror fiction can also complement one another in interesting and hitherto unexplored ways, and my belief stems from reading Victor Turner's elucidation of liminality. As I mentioned earlier, I was ignorant of liminality's association with Turner, or the discipline he helped shape, when I first began researching liminal horror. However, a few months later, I finally came across Turner's seminal piece, "Liminal to Liminoid, in Play, Flow and Ritual: An Essay in Comparative Symbology," and found that, despite the differing natures of our two research areas (horror in my case, anthropology in Turner's), our statements about liminality are similar.

Turner, for instance, avers: "Liminality is a complex series of episodes in sacred space-time, and may also include subversive and lucid events" and "in liminality, people 'play' with the elements of the familiar and defamiliarize them."[1] These claims, especially the latter, resound with my arguments and analyses in Chapters 2 and 3, wherein I explore how characters "play" with fictions, thereby confounding their own realities and existence(s). Moreover, Turner's assessment that "liminality may be for many the acme of insecurity, the breakthrough of chaos into cosmos, of disorder into order, rather than the milieu of creative interhuman or transhuman satisfactions and achievements" connects with several horror films, such as *Scream*, *Found Footage 3-D*, *Urban Legend*, *Sinister*, and *Candyman*, as I illustrate later in this book.[2]

Here, the reader might accuse me of taking Turner's comments out of context, but the following fact is key: though the concept of liminality is primarily associated with anthropology, "liminality" itself can be—and *is*—distinct from the discipline, as demonstrated by its usage in certain aspects of Jungian psychology. What I am trying to convey here is this: that "liminality" (derived from "linen," Latin for "threshold") is in—and applicable to—multiple disciplines, including anthology and (horror) films, just as "synthesis" can be used in the context of literature, philosophy, chemistry, or, "realism" is studied within the diverse disciplines of politics, art, literature, and philosophy.

All this is to say that "liminality"—or the quality of being liminal—is distinct, and as such, is identifiable in multiple topics, so long as its meaning of "threshold" or "margin," or being on a threshold between (two or more) elements/categories/states, remains. That is essentially how liminality is used (and tangentially developed) in anthropology and psychology, and that is fundamentally how I explore liminality in horror movies. As such, liminality in horror can take the form of ambiguity—of characters' states of existence, of a narrative being a myth and/or reality, and so on—brought about by the diminishing of the borders that separate diverse categories, personas, facts from fantasies (amongst other manifestations).

Consequently, what I study in this volume—the negation of the boundary between reality and fiction—is but one facet of "liminality," for liminality is multidimensional and too vast to be comprehensively discussed within a single book. In particular, my exploration of this ambiguous, obfuscated quality as it manifests in horror fiction serves to investigate the nuanced distinctions between the fictional and the real, and the roles horror fiction (horror films, in particular) fulfills for us as a species, especially in the context of human perception, behavior, and psychology. It is my hope that this survey of liminal horror helps develop this sub-genre further, thereby facilitating greater inquiry into it, which, in turn, will enhance our own understanding of how we—humans, as both the creators and the audiences of our fictions—use fantasy to cope with reality. So, without further ado, I will dive into elucidating what I mean by "liminal horror" and analyzing several horror films—from various sub-genres within horror—that exude liminality.

Introduction

This book is about those select horror films whose narratives stand on the threshold between fiction and reality, blurring the boundaries therein on various levels and in a multitude of ways. I call such movies "liminal horror films," and their corresponding sub-genre, "liminal horror." Perhaps the latter term might seem farfetched, or even oxymoronic, for "genre" itself is liminal, with its blurred and often overlapping categories. For instance, the genre of horror can blend with the genres of "thriller," "suspense," and even "mystery," or "sci-fi." Furthermore, horror also includes multiple sub-genres, such as "slasher," "supernatural," and "psychological" horrors. Adding "liminal horror" to this already over-brimming, uncontainable mix might seem like a folly, but the fact is that "liminal horror" is a definable quality that foregrounds all the aforementioned genre types and sub-genres.

This is because, as I demonstrate throughout this book, liminality is inherent to all horror, even if not all horror is *liminal horror*. Though this distinction may seem niche, it is both undeniable and necessary if we are to begin to comprehend the infinite ways in which "horror" operates and evolves in art, culture, and society. Liminal horror, as I evince and substantiate over the next few chapters, stems from the very anxieties and influences of our varied cultures; it draws on—and is fueled by—the cognitive functions of the collective human psyche. An everyday example of this is the various bloodcurdling urban legends (e.g., "Bloody Mary" or "Killer in the backseat"), which acquire power through word-of-mouth and the listeners' resultant conviction that the stories are true.

Such urban legends, especially those that are a mix of myth, superstition, caution, and peril, fall under the genre of "horror." But these very legends *become liminal horror* when they are brought to life, and turn from fiction into reality (and, sometimes, back again), thereby blurring the distinctions between two. Imagine, for instance, that you purchase a skeleton costume for Halloween, despite its tag declaring it "cursed merchandise."

Introduction

You dismiss the warning as a marketing strategy and don the costume, only to find it sticking to your skin, and turning you into a skeleton. What you considered fiction (the "curse") has become your reality, your horrifying liminality. In this scenario, you stand on the threshold between the unreal and real, the imaginary and the actual.

Colloquial though this example may be, it is a simplified and laconic way of elucidating this book's fundamental premise: an analysis and survey of liminal horror, which is that specific gray area, the threshold between the "fictional" (myth, folklore, superstition, film) and the "actual" (what we consider to be empirical reality) *within* the overarching genre of horror. Whereas horror disrupts the "norm" while retaining clear distinctions, liminal horror disrupts the very illusion or perception of a distinction between reality and fiction by muddying the boundaries between the two. To paraphrase this simply by narrowing down on one aspect of liminality in horror: instead of having a proper villain or monster to blame and/or capture (as you would in typical horror), you must determine what, how, or who, exactly, is the monstrosity.

To revert to the earlier example of the skeleton costume: is the culprit the costume, or the wearer of the costume, since now both the costume and the wearer have fused into a third, distinct, entity? These are exactly the kind of nuances—of liminality—that I explore throughout this book by using selected horror films that serve both as examples and propagators of this niche quality that underlies the entire genre. And because this volume is a survey of the sub-genre of liminal horror, it examines liminal horror films from a variety of countries.

To evaluate all horror movies would be a Herculean, if not impossible, task. However, I hope the structurally and thematically varied natures of the films I survey in this book will be foundational for this area of scholarship, for, though liminality is prevalent in all horror, it is sadly overlooked and understudied, a fact I discovered—as I mentioned in the Preface—while researching for a paper I was writing during my master's program. The closest scholarly works I found at that time, which come close to examining "liminality" in horror literature/film, were Alexandra Heller-Nicholas's *Found Footage Horror Films: Fear and the Appearance of Reality* (2014), William Egginton's essay "Reality is Bleeding" (2001), and Jonathan Gottschall's *The Storytelling Animal: How Stories Make Us Human* (2012). These works, though illuminating and innovative in their own right, still do not come close to surveying liminality itself, both in the context of blurring the boundaries between the fictional and the real, and in the genre of horror.

Heller-Nicholas's *Found Footage Horror Films*, for instance, examines the sub-genre of "found footage" movies and argues this sub-genre constructs different versions of reality, if not different realities themselves. In particular, her exploration of the films that "manifest at the intersection between death, film and the real," such as *Peeping Tom* (1960) and *The Last House on Dead End Street* (1977), is especially important, at least in the context of my own examination.[1] Her exploration is limited, however, to the found footage sub-genre, but, I aver that her work *is* relevant to films outside this sub-genre, especially if we scrutinize the "threshold"—the liminality—through (and upon) which this "intersection" occurs, and *how* it occurs, or is *caused* to occur.

Confusing though it may seem, I can clarify my assertion through Egginton's seminal essay, "Reality is Bleeding," in which he explores the "thematic convergence" that blends "the diagetic [sic] reality into other represented realities."[2] Egginton refers to this "trope" as the "bleeding" of reality, and explores its history and occurrence in film, studying such films as *The Blair Witch Project* (1999), *The Truman Show* (1998), and *Pleasantville* (1998), which portray—using different techniques—the "bleeding" between "base reality and a representation of that reality within the already representational reality of the film."[3] While Egginton seeks to study issues that differ considerably from liminal horror (about how such a bleeding of reality affects its philosophical and epistemological notions), he makes several compelling arguments that are applicable to liminal horror as well.

One such claim is how the disruption of the divide between fiction and reality is a destabilizing experience, for the bleeding of reality subverts "the spectator's place and peace of mind."[4] Moreover, he also observes—astutely—that both "'reality' and some other dimension that 'represents' it" are "foundational for a good deal of cultural production," predominantly in the form of "narrative, theater, television, and film."[5] This observation is crucial, and I make a similar assessment about horror films (and, particularly, their obfuscation of the real and the fictional), before delving deeper into examining *why* this bleeding of reality, which brings about the audience's destabilization, is fundamental to the creations of the human imagination. Egginton's analysis helps supplement my postulations about a broader—and more diverse—body of work, thereby aiding in highlighting the manifold consequences that such a subversion causes in horror films.

Likewise, Jonathan Gottschall's *The Storytelling Animal* supports and propels my argument further, for Gottschall, too, avers that the line separating fiction from reality is hazy. His analysis focuses on evolutionary psychology, and he asserts the centrality of stories (fiction) in the human psyche, which—when combined with my own exploration of liminal horror films—enables me to demonstrate the fickle (and ever-changing) nature of the blurry border between fact and fiction. Comprehending the nature of this liminal line between horror fiction and horror reality is, I assert,

Introduction 7

essential because horror serves a didactic function, by often communicating information audiences tend to overlook (or frequently forget). I elucidate this in greater detail (and by using several examples) in Chapter 4, wherein I also scrutinize *why* horror films choose to be liminal and, specifically, liminal in the context of converging fantasy with reality, for didactic purposes.

Heller-Nicholas's, Egginton's, and Gottschall's aforementioned works, consequently, play a substantial role in corroborating and further developing my argument, observations, and analyses; I mention them at various points in this volume, depending on what particular trait of liminal horror films I am discussing in that section or chapter. Each of the works I have referenced (so far) is individually innovative and seminal. However, I would also like to asseverate that combining specific elements from their respective arguments—and incorporating the subsequent psychoanalytical, socio-cultural, and cognitive mix into my own study of liminal horror—facilitates an unprecedented exploration of cultural anxieties that assail us, the audience, thereby highlighting the central function that "horror" itself plays in our corporeal reality, via liminality.

Such an exploration is—unsurprisingly—bound to be extensive and complex, but I have spared no effort in ensuring that it is cohesive, lucid, and comprehensible, every step of the way, by dedicating each chapter—and each section within each chapter—to the discussion of one particular topic that corresponds with—and complements—the overarching theme of this volume. To that end, I discuss the more recondite topics, such as those I mentioned in the preceding paragraph, after first laying out horror's basic traits as they manifest in the context of liminality (in Chapter 1), and then actually depicting the movement between the fictional and real (and back) in Chapters 2 and 3.

It is in Chapter 3, with an examination of how horror films transform the real into fictional (often literally) that I begin to address the more abstruse issues concerning liminal horror, and survey them in detail over the next four chapters and through to the end of this volume. Chapter 4, accordingly, inspects horror's edifying functions, after first establishing its intricate and (im)mutable relationship with reality. In Chapter 5, meanwhile, I evaluate liminal horror's (often therapeutic) role in the context of the human psyche's subconscious/unconscious states. Following in this vein, I extensively explore, in Chapter 6, the function(s) of the human mind in perceiving (or misperceiving) reality, to demonstrate how the human mind often forms its own, subjective (and also misconstrued) realities—and their consequent fictions—which differ from the "objective" truth.

If these arguments seem controversial, my assertion in Chapter 7 will certainly seem outlandish, despite it being a fact: that we, ourselves, create our monsters through our belief (often underlying and unacknowledged) in myths, lore and, yes, magic. One might willfully deny such a claim; empirical reality, after all, does not leave much in the way of horrific legends being brought to life. Or so, we presume, conveniently forgetting that the mind's power renders reality but an illusion. Various psychological and cognitive studies substantiate this, as do several critics and scholars who examine *why* we create fictions and often fictionalize our corporeality in terms of the (ostensibly) unreal. Fact becomes fiction, then, and fiction becomes reality, consequently, because *we* make it so: we can be—and often are—liminal, and so we swim in liminality, regardless of whether we realize it or not.

Horror, therefore, as I observed earlier, is but one medium for exploring and understanding this liminality of our very existence, as well as of the collective human psyche. And, of all the horror fictions, I choose to focus on horror films because the medium of film is—as I demonstrate throughout this book—in itself, liminal in that any given "film" can be simultaneously true and fabricated, and all the variants in between. Moreover, the versatility of film (with film reel, previously, then TV broadcasts, VCRs, DVDs, home videos, and now, with digital cinema) lends itself to being perched on that fine line between the real and the fictional, a fact that several directors, including Wes Craven, acknowledge and exploit. By this reasoning, film can be at once actual and imaginary, and so, can oscillate between transforming reality into fiction, and all manner of fictions into reality. On that note, therefore, I now begin my elucidation of liminal horror, detailing its nature, affect, function, and pervasiveness in our culture and society.

One

United in Darkness
The Nature of Liminal Horror

Liminal horror fiction is unique in that it blends or threatens the boundary between the real and the imagined. It is essential for the reader to understand how the texts I have selected for my exploration of liminality in horror differ from other horror films. After all, a substantial strain of horror criticism has focused on the relationship between the real and the unreal in the genre. Namely, many influential horror scholars have argued that the monsters around which horror films revolve represent an intrusion of the unreal into the real.

Robin Wood, for example, writes that the horror genre's formula is one where "normality is threatened by the monster."[1] For his part, Noël Carroll also argues that the monster is a disturbance of the natural order; at least the natural order as people (e.g., the audience and characters) perceive it.[2] In yet another example, David J. Russell, while presenting his own formulation of the horror genre, cites both Wood and Carroll (as above) and contrives an equation including the categories of *real*, *unreal*, and *part-real*.[3] That is to say that though an exact taxonomy of the horror genre is outside my aim and scope, it is nevertheless useful to note, from the references above, how many horror scholars consider the conflict between the real and unreal (reality and fiction) to be a central part (perhaps *the* central part) of the horror genre.

To illustrate these scholars' arguments and contrast them with liminal horror, consider *Hatchet* (2006), directed by Adam Green. This film follows a group of tourists who get stranded while exploring Honey Island Swamp, Louisiana, and find themselves the helpless victims of Victor Crowley (Kane Hodder). A ghost, Crowley is a local legend, but, as the unfortunate tour group discovers, this particular legend is "true": Crowley prowls the swamp and brutally murders anyone he encounters. He kills all but one of the tourists in the group, and the film concludes with Crowley pulling this lone survivor, this "final girl," out of the water and roaring in her face.[4] The sequels confirm she survives.

Green's *Hatchet* centers on the conflict between the real (the group of tourists) and the unreal (Crowley). When the tourists enter the swamp, they expect a standard tour; they do not expect to encounter a monster, or a ghost doomed to perpetually relive the night of his death (as *Hatchet III* reveals). In other words, the conflict—in this movie and its corresponding series—arises when a mythic figure intrudes into, and thus disrupts, the protagonists' realities. This disruption of the "normal" is precisely what Russell, Wood, and Carroll describe: a disruption arising because the characters' notions of reality are incomplete, due to which they overlook the monster's existence and, hence, get caught off-guard when the monster finally makes its presence known by invading the characters-turned-victims' awareness.

The *Hatchet* series, like most horror films, depicts the distortion of the "norm," of "reality," in such lucid manner, but does so by following the conventions of a slasher film. Contrariwise, if Green's 2006 film were to show Victor Crowley brought to life—transformed into a physical, corporeal monster from his ghostly form—as a result of the tourists circulating stories about him, then *Hatchet* would be a liminal horror film, because it would depict pure fiction becoming reality. That is to say that Russell, Wood, and Carroll's notion of "disturbance of the natural order" as people perceive it does not apply to liminal horror, for liminal horror films not only represent the breaching of the boundaries between fiction and reality

Victor Crowley (Kane Hodder) dismembers Marcus (Deon Richmond) (*Hatchet*, directed by Adam Green. Anchor Bay Entertainment, 2006).

but showcase *how* such a breach occurs. In other words, these films focus on the border that separates the real from the unreal and exhibit how and why that border becomes weaker and weaker until it is nonexistent.

To be sure, the "monster" trope helps unite liminal horror to the overarching genre of horror, however, it is not the only element to do so. The gothic, certainly, has significant overlap with liminal horror, thereby enabling the amalgamation of liminality and horror. For instance, in his *A Glossary of Literary Terms*, M.H. Abrams discusses how the gothic has evolved past its initial conception and moved beyond castles and locales:

> The term "Gothic" has also been extended to a type of fiction that lacks the exotic setting of the earlier romances, but develops a brooding atmosphere of gloom and terror, represents events that are uncanny or macabre or melodramatically violent, and often deals with aberrant psychological states.[5]

Kendall Phillips furthers this notable observation by arguing: "…the gothic has centered around the thin line that exists between the world of day, and with it, reason, rationality, and normalcy, and the world of night, and with it superstition, illusion, madness."[6]

Befitting the gothic's obsession with the threshold between fiction and reality, Phillips also writes that Wes Craven is interested in "the uncertain dividing point between reality and the fantastic."[7] This pronouncement is especially pertinent because Wes Craven's work comprises a substantial portion of this volume. Additionally, both Abrams' and Phillips' assertions are important because scholarship on the gothic provides a useful starting point for my analysis, in general. For instance, it is imperative that scholars of the gothic note how the genre contains a multiplicity of meaning and can be difficult, therefore, to interpret.[8] This is foundational for developing a discussion on liminal horror, regardless of whether a given text is typically "gothic" or not, because of the convergence between the two: essentially, liminality is a characteristic of the gothic, but the gothic, by itself, does not encompass or account for "liminality in horror."

Gothic works may blur the line between fiction and reality, but they often do so by questioning what is or is not real. Contrastingly, liminal horror texts go beyond mere questioning, by making the question itself—of what is real and what is not—revolve around the dividing line that separates the "truth" from the "story." The central texts in this book evaluate, scrutinize, and explore how liminal horror fictions skirt, demarcate, diminish, and even dominate our (the viewers') reality, and even go a few steps further, by making the question revolve around the divide between our tales and our truth.

To rephrase the issue: liminal horror often, but not always and not necessarily, contains gothic elements. Though such gothic fixtures as a conflict between "feeling and reason," settings, journeys, doppelgangers, and supernatural elements are common in liminal horror, and appear throughout this volume, they do not manifest in all works of horror that interrogate the line between fiction and reality.[9] The gothic, therefore, is a useful tool for analyzing instances of liminality in horror, but it would be a mistake to classify all works of liminal horror as gothic. The term "liminality" as I use it (as explained more fully in the Introduction), refers specifically to a blurring of the line between fiction and reality, and many horror films accomplish this task without becoming gothic.

One such film is *Primeval* (2007), directed by Michael Katleman, the poster for which boldly declares it the true story of the world's most prolific serial killer.[10] As I discuss at length later, the film's events are almost entirely fictional. Yet, *Primeval*'s marketing establishes it as a liminal film, one in which the real (the true story) and the fictional (the filmmaker's imagined, inserted elements) co-exist. In a similar vein, found-footage films directors will sometimes try to pass their movies off as real when they are, in fact, fictional. Nevertheless, this marketing tactic primes the audience to consider the ways in which the real and the fictional collide and how flimsy the barrier(s) between the two can be. Of note here is also the fact that both *Primeval* and found-footage films (can) achieve this effect without relying on the gothic, which is primarily why I posit a distinction between these two sub-genres.

While *Primeval*'s protagonists (being from other continents themselves) find Burundi largely exotic, they otherwise find it bears little resemblance to a gothic space. A typical gothic space offers a dream-like atmosphere in which the barriers between fact and fantasy become hazy, and yet there is no such haze in *Primeval*.[11] The land the characters enter collapses no boundaries. And it contains no doppelgangers and, indeed, no supernatural elements whatsoever.[12] Thus, *Primeval* is liminal but not gothic. To gain a comprehensive understanding of reality in horror, it is just as necessary to examine films that blend the real and fictional for the audience as it is to examine films that blend the real and fictional only for the characters. When a filmmaker slaps a label of verisimilitude on their movie's cover, they force audiences to question the boundaries between stories and reality. Conversely, many gothic films do not target the audience this way.

Take, for example, Stuart Gordon's 1987 film, *Dolls*, the plot of which occurs in a notably gothic space, a mansion full of living dolls who murder anyone committing sins inside its walls. This mansion, therefore, has its own reality, in which magic exists and the realm of fantasy intrudes into the protagonists' (but not the audiences') experienced reality. Furthermore, the film's story occurs as if it were a dream, all the events taking place in a single night, coming and going with the rainstorm. *Dolls*, in other words, is both liminal and gothic, but its liminality differs from *Primeval*'s and from that of many found footage films because it blurs the line between fiction and reality with diegetic events instead of non-diegetic declarations.

And while liminal horror shares overlap with the gothic, it also shares some similarities with magical realism, which can, likewise, blend the real and fantastic: "The cohesion of the real and the fantastic is magical realism's 'irreducible element.'"[13] That is to say, like liminal horror, magical realism blurs the boundary between fiction and reality, often by placing characters in a liminal space between the two worlds. Jon Thiem observes: "...textualizations dramatize an interesting psychological puzzle arising from many readers' experience: the state of being in two worlds at once, in the book and outside of the book."[14] Yet, here ends the similarities of liminal horror and magical realism. The fundamental distinction between the two is that liminal horror portrays deviations (i.e., fantastical elements) as dangerous, and characters within liminal horror texts acknowledge these deviations as departures from the norm.

That is to say, characters in magical realism do not always recognize the fantastic to be different from the real, but characters in liminal horror concede this distinction and tend to consider fantastical elements anomalies, anomalies they often greet with skepticism but later accept as cruel, unavoidable reality. On this note, Tzvetan Todorov casts horror as the uncanny (in which the supernatural is explained) and fairy tales as the marvelous (in which the supernatural is accepted).[15] And though fairy tales and magical realism are not synonymous, they do share certain tendencies, such as their reliance on characters accepting, rather than questioning or explaining, the supernatural.

Accordingly, these commonalities make Todorov's analysis useful for illustrating the generic distinctions between magical realism and liminal horror. Because magical realism treats the supernatural differently than liminal horror does, one would be remiss to deem liminal horror a sub-genre of magical realism. Furthermore, because the uncanny is, by definition, unnerving, and the marvelous exalting, magical realism lacks the requisite horror that might enable it to encapsulate liminal horror. Put another way, liminal horror is distinct from magical realism because magical realism is often liminal but not particularly horrific. There is, however, some overlap of the two.

In *Pan's Labyrinth*, for example, Ofelia easily accepts the supernatural's existence (magical realism), but the supernatural is liminal (from Ofelia's storybook, or the special chalk the Faun gives her) and horrific. Additionally, whereas Ofelia accepts the supernatural, none of the film's other characters do. Consequently, *Pan's Labyrinth* exudes qualities simultaneously pertinent to magical realism *and* liminal horror. This, in turn, shows that though liminality can seem akin to magical realism, it is wholly distinct from it.

Finally, another genre with which liminal horror shares characteristics is meta-fiction, works of which refer to their own fictional nature in their narratives, thereby undermining the fourth wall. To be sure, many liminal horror films are meta-fictive. For example, *Scream* undermines the barrier between fiction and reality (thereby becoming liminal) through ironic self-reference (meta-fiction): *Scream* is a horror film that follows a group of teenage horror fans who explicitly refer to the "rules" of horror films and try to follow those rules to save themselves from their real-life peril.[16] Thus, in *Scream*, the fictional (horror films) become real through the use of meta-fiction, thus obfuscating the line between fiction and reality. And so, the use of meta-fiction and/or self-referencing can contribute to the liminality of horror fiction.

Yet, it would be a mistake to conflate liminal horror with meta-fiction, as many liminal horror films are not meta-fictive. For example, whereas *Scream* demonstrates liminality through its various self-references, *Primeval* contains no meta-references but is still liminal. In the same vein, Craven's iconic *A Nightmare on Elm Street*, which blurs the line between dreaming (fiction) and waking (reality), is liminal, but it becomes so without the use of self-reference. Thus, a survey of liminal horror (like this book) will inevitably consider some works of that are meta-fictive and some that are not. Like the gothic and, to a lesser degree, magical realism, meta-fiction shares some overlap with liminal horror and will appear in some of the same works, but the two are not identical. All works of meta-fiction are liminal because they push audiences and creators to consider the boundaries between reality and fiction, but not all liminal works are meta-fictional.

These distinctions make the reader aware that though horror's general traits (like the gothic, magical realism, or metafiction) appear in liminal horror fiction as well, they do not necessarily define liminality; rather, liminality is horror is mutated, manipulated, and so, manifested, in diverse forms through the varied usage or avoidance of these qualities. In terms of liminal horror, therefore, these traits (which can otherwise be regarded as genre classifications) become techniques of emphasizing how reality can be indistinguishable from fiction, and vice-versa, even to the point of creating monsters from one's self.

Consequently, before reading my actual analyses of liminal horror, it will be helpful if my readers lose forthwith the idea that a horror movie must be scary to be (good) horror. Horror's tricks and tropes are aplenty, but they affect everyone differently, based on their individual disposition(s).

Stephen King makes an excellent observation in *Danse Macabre*, wherein he states, "I believe that horror does not horrify unless the reader or viewer has been personally touched."[17] King, therefore, believes horror has a personal element, that not everyone can be touched the same way, and some may not be able to be touched at all.

This claim is especially relevant for my study of liminality in horror, for liminality in horror is but one of the tricks of the encompassing genre and, as such, affects every member of the films' audiences differently. Moreover, as I demonstrate in the following chapters, liminality manifests uniquely in each of the selected films: some manifestations may seem benign (not scary), while others may seem psychologically intrusive to even the most stoic audience, thereby resulting in a stark difference in reactions. However, such subjective views (which are a result of the affects of liminality and horror) do not affect the examination of liminality itself, as it occurs in horror films and blurs the distinctions between fiction and reality.

Two

Shattered Screens and Punctured Skin
When the Fictional Becomes Real

Section One: Initial Blurrings

The sub-genre of found footage films has been popular—and well-studied—for at least the past two decades. The central gambit of films within this genre, that of turning the nature of filmmaking on its head, is especially helpful and relevant to analyzing horror's liminality.[1] This is because found footage films explain, diegetically, the camera's presence, frequently by having the protagonists filming their adventures, and, arguably the most important and seminal found footage horror film is *The Blair Witch Project* (1999), which revolves around a group of "filmmakers" (actors, really) who get disoriented and lost while making a documentary about a local legend—the titular witch—in the forest; the frame narrative of the film is that the "recovered" footage is genuine, the discovered footage of the missing filmmakers.

However, here I must draw attention to a key point that was abstruse during *The Blair Witch Project*'s 1999 release: that though the *Blair Witch* that Donahue, Leonard, and Williams' (the protagonists, seemingly victims, but actors in reality) film seems to be a documentary, *The Blair Witch Project* is actually a made-up film, that is, *not* a documentary. And so, *The Blair Witch Project*'s (dir. Sanchez and Myrick) popularity upon its release in 1999 was based, almost entirely, on its marketing platform, the claim that the "film" was truly the recovered footage of three missing filmmakers. The film's poster proclaimed: "In October of 1994, three student filmmakers disappeared in the woods near Burkittsville, Maryland while shooting a documentary.... A year later their footage was found."[2] And, almost instantly, the film was a hit, making over 200 million dollars after production costs of under 40 thousand.³ It must be noted, however, despite its success, the interest in *Blair Witch* (at least critical interest) focused less on the film itself and more on this phenomenon surrounding it: the film's claim of reality.[4,5]

Multiple scholars—including Alexandra Heller-Nicholas and William Egginton—have already explored both this claim and its corresponding phenomenon. Note, however, the confluence of *Blair Witch*'s appeal to reality and how this appeal manifests itself—or is manifested—within the film. It is precisely on this point (what I call "confluence") that Stephen King writes: "One thing about *Blair Witch: the damn thing looks real*. Another thing about *Blair Witch: the damn thing **feels** real*" (emphasis King's).[6] King, furthermore, states (preempting my argument by two chapters) that because *The Blair Witch* looks and feels real, "it's like the worst nightmare you ever had…."[7] King's assessment is a resounding of both Myrick's and Sanchez's own words, as they have affirmed they found documentaries about the paranormal scarier than horror films. *Blair Witch*, ergo, is their effort of combining the two distinct formats, thereby bringing together paranormal documentary and horror fiction in one seamless film.[8] Based on the reactions to *The Blair Witch*, and King's adjudging words, it is reasonable to say Myrick and Sanchez succeeded.

The success of the film, especially in the context of King's astute observation, is key because it denotes the importance of verisimilitude for creating fear, while also illuminating the defining point of *Blair Witch*: that its claims of being true ("real"), which help generate genuine fear, are the root of its success. This is because, from an aesthetic point of view, the film is amateurish. While the definition and defense of a full aesthetic criteria for film quality are beyond the scope of the present study, I observe, nonetheless, that *Blair Witch* misses many of the marks for a well-done film.

The camera work is shaky, its cinematography low quality, and there is very little plot or action. My point, however, is *not* that these flaws are necessarily bad, but that they are intentional (from the standpoint of the film's makers), thereby making *Blair Witch* a non-traditional film. The early, most dedicated members of the found footage genre really changed the game for what constituted a movie. As King says, *Blair Witch* does not feel like a movie one would ideally watch in theaters, simply (and importantly) because it feels like a true, candid account of events as they transpired. Although the film is not, in fact, real, such is its illusion, and that, arguably, is the marker for brilliance.

The found footage sub-genre is, therefore, uniquely suited to questioning the line between fiction and reality, for it often portrays its material to be reality rather than fiction. Heller-Nicholas makes the following observation about found footage films:

We expect to indulge in a fictional fantasy, but these films make concrete attempts to usurp this belief, hoping the stories will therefore necessarily become closer to our own realities. Filmmakers seek to unsettle and discomfort spectators through this sudden, unexpected proximity shift, milking our suspicions that what we are watching may in fact have actually happened.[9]

In other words, found footage films threaten the boundary between fiction and reality by trying to appear real. However, the reader should note that this sub-genre does not merely rely on its appeal to reality; indeed, as Heller-Nicholas argues, it has largely moved past this technique because audiences have grown wise to it.[10]

The audience's discovery of *Blair Witch* and other such films' deception has forced the sub-genre's creators to develop new techniques to continue being interesting and relevant. Though some critics have kept pace with these developments, hardly any investigation has been conducted into the multilayered interactions between truth and reality—the focus of this book. Conversely, the core films surveyed in this book interrogate the very natures of truth and fiction, instead of merely appealing to truth by portraying fictions becoming reality, or by transforming "real" events or people into fiction.

An exemplary text that bridges and converges these two extremities is the 2017 film *Found Footage 3-D* (released three years after Heller-Nicholas's book). As its name declares, *Found Footage 3-D* is a found footage film. However, it is also a found footage film about making a found footage film, and as such, it leans heavily on the arising meta-discourse. Directed by Steven DeGennaro, *Found Footage 3-D* revolves around a film crew shooting a found-footage horror movie dubbed *Spectre of Death*. The film's crew—as well as the crew of the film within the film—consists of writer/producer/lead actor Derek, director Andrew, lead actress/co-writer Amy, sound technician Carl, production assistant Lily, and behind-the-scenes documentarian Mark.

The opening scenes establish that Derek is in charge. He foists a 3-D production onto Andrew without warning or consulting him, and generally seems uninterested in accepting anyone's advice. Derek is conceited and aggressive, and he believes his 3-D film will be successful, despite its clichéd script and his own lack of experience. He hires Lily as the film's production assistant even though she has no background in filmmaking or production. In fact, the audience can infer Derek recruits Lily only because he is attracted to her—as is evident from their mutual flirtation throughout the film.

Additionally, Derek refuses to recast the film's lead actress: since he and his wife Amy had originally written the script together, with the idea that they themselves would play the on-screen couple, Derek casts Amy as his on-screen wife, even though, in real-life, they are now estranged. Despite her surprise, Amy agrees to the casting, and the crew heads out to their filming location: a deserted, rural cabin in the woods that Amy inherited from her uncle. Soon, however, the team learns that Derek has been hiding the truth from them: that the film's script bears an eerie resemblance to the crew's actual circumstances (under which they are making the film). Moreover, two different scenarios mirror this uncomfortable reality. First, in the script and reality, Derek and Amy (still using their real names) are a couple whose marriage is on the verge of collapse. Second, in the script as in reality, Derek and Amy are vacationing in the cabin Amy inherited from her uncle, a cabin where, in fact, one of her relatives murdered his wife.

Disturbingly, the film's production occurs under the same circumstances, murder and all. When the crew push on despite their misgivings, the script's antagonist, the "spectre [sic] of death," appears on set for real.[11] It possesses Amy, and while they are filming the movie's climax, the specter pushes her to hit Derek with a hammer. Per the script, Amy is only supposed to feign hitting Derek; instead, she smashes in his skull, murdering him. The specter then lashes out at the rest of the crew, killing them each in short order. The film ends after the specter uses Amy to attack Mark, at which point the movie cuts to black, implying Mark and Amy both die.

This summary is to say that *Found Footage 3-D* (*3-D*, here on) disrupts the typical found-footage formula. The film opens on the clichéd expository text one expects from a found-footage film (wherein the movie explains whence the footage came) but then breaks convention by cutting to Andrew and Derek arguing about whether to include said expository in their movie. *3-D*, therefore, immediately banishes the idea that the audience is watching a typical found-footage horror film. Instead, it specifies that the audience is witnessing a found footage film about making a found footage film, and this film-within-a-film construction provides ample ground to explore the sub-genre's tropes.

For instance, the characters themselves readily acknowledge these tropes, and Andrew declares the crew's need to avoid some of the sub-genre's common pitfalls. Namely, he says, they need to justify why the characters are filming, and also why they do not stop filming in the script's third act.[12] Andrew also argues with Derek over how much exposition they should provide about their movie's monster. In this way, the movie foregrounds various concerns about how to effectively communicate with its audience and perform the actions it must then perform. Such generic concerns and conventions, which foreground the film-making within the movie, make the audience more cognizant of the events and actions as they occur, and also help the audience comprehend how the characters' knowledge of the found-footage genre fails them.

Despite his pretensions of knowing the genre, Derek, especially, shows a distinct lack of awareness. Carl criticizes him for putting the crew in danger, predicting the horrors to come: "You don't bring a film crew to a haunted house to shoot a horror movie. Haven't you seen like, you know, every horror movie ever?"[13] He further states: "Seriously guys, you brought us to a cabin that's haunted in the middle of the woods where a man murdered his wife to shoot a movie about a man murdering his wife at a haunted cabin in the woods? For reals? ... That's so dumb."[14] Carl, therefore, is a stand-in for the know-it-all horror movie fan, the one who enjoys pointing out the characters' poor decisions.

Yet, this knowledge does him no service, for Carl dies too. His knowledge, however, showcases the film's multilayered irony. It is ironic that Carl's knowledge fails to help him, but it is also ironic that the other characters fall into the very tropes and clichés they have derided. In these instances, the movie asserts itself over and above its more banal generic brethren, as it explains both why Mark keeps filming (Derek wants a behind-the-scenes documentary) and why he does not ditch the camera when the specter attacks (as he can only see it through the camera and not with his naked eye).

Moreover, the specter is an ambiguous antagonist whose very presence blurs the line between fiction and reality in the movie. Andrew views their movie's specter as the manifestation of Derek and Amy's marital strife, a physical creation of their negative mental energies.[15] *3-D* seems to affirm this reading of the actual specter, as it first appears on the captured footage when Derek and Amy, as characters, are filming a scripted fight that gradually descends into a real fight between the real-life Derek and Amy, the "real" estranged couple. Their conflict appears to beget the specter that their conflict in the film-within-a-film was supposed to beget. Consequently, fiction becomes reality twice over: in the script for *Spectre of Death*, the characters' emotions were to manifest as a physical entity, but *3-D* takes it a step further by manifesting their characters' emotions in exactly the same way that their "fictionally" scripted script predicted it would.

Thus, the film's central conflict is the same as *Spectre of Death*'s central conflict: Derek and Amy's turbulent and disintegrating relationship. The only difference is that they are estranged in *3-D*, but not in *Spectre of Death* (even though they do have significant marital strife in *Spectre* as well). This distinction hints that the couple's circumstances are much worse in reality than in their fictive script, which they co-wrote to create the fictional specter. Almost reflexively, the hauntings in *3-D* are parallel to the movements of Derek and Amy's real and fictional relationships.

Later in the film, while the crew enjoy a breath of levity amid their troubled production, Derek offers to treat them all to a night at the local bar.

All seems to go well until Amy spots Derek flirting with Lily in the scene's background. Amy then throws her drink in Derek's face, and Carl vocalizes the audience's thoughts, asking, "That didn't last very long now, did it?"[16] When the crew get back to their cabin, they find it ransacked. While nothing is missing, everyone but Derek has had their stuff thrown about, scattered, and, in Carl's case, covered in some sort of slime. Amy's frustration with Derek, and the increasing unlikelihood of their reconciliation, manifests as a haunting that slowly, but steadily, grows in power. At the film's end, Amy acknowledges they are living inside the same found-footage film they were trying to create. She tells Mark she "hoped [he] would remember the rule" and then attacks him.[17] The "rule" Amy alludes to is how everyone dies in a generic found-footage film.

The realization that the characters are living in such a film arises before the ending, when Amy says during an interview that "Acting is about finding the truth in the moment," after which she breaks character and asks to film the line again, at which point Derek's flirtations with Lily in the scene's background distract her.[18] Found-Footage is an artifice of reality, a pretending toward being real, and Amy inadvertently makes this clear when she reveals she is manufacturing her "truth in the moment."[19] Fiction and reality, therefore, blend together throughout *3-D*, as the narrative weaves between the constructed and the genuine.

This weave, moreover, loops back upon itself, such that it becomes difficult to disentangle fiction from reality. Note how Amy is trying to nail a pre-rehearsed line about "truth in the moment," thus ironically scripting what she claims is improvised.[20] The behind-the-scenes documentary for which Amy is interviewing purports to give the truth, but Amy's break in character proves the documentary is staged, at least in part. And yet, Amy's actress, Alena von Stroheim, is selling the idea of her being an actress whose real-life husband is flirting with another girl, in plain view, right behind her. Thus, this moment where the film highlights its own fictionality by undermining the artifice of the behind-the-scenes documentary, also allows the film to simultaneously rope the audience in by drawing sympathy for Amy as she struggles to sell a movie and play a character despite being under enormous personal pressure. And so, in the very moment when the film appears to establish its own fictionality, it nevertheless draws the audience in to its fictional narrative.

Such is the paradox at the heart of *3-D*. Ostensibly, the film's acknowledgment of its own conventions should alienate audiences from its core narrative. That is, the film's reminding the audience of a found footage movie's clichés, and then using those same clichés, should make audiences wary of the film, more aware they are watching a fiction. In other words, audiences should lose their immersion. To be sure, whether a viewer loses immersion is a personal question that will vary by individual. Yet, that audiences by and large have not become alienated from 3-D's story hints at the paradox: even when audiences should become alienated, they do not, and those moments that should break immersion fail to do so. In this way, and as I show with other films as well, liminal horror proves unexpectedly resilient and engaging, drawing audiences in when they should, theoretically, become repulsed.

Indeed, liminal horror (and meta-fiction since 3-D fits both categories) often threatens to place audiences in a state of cognitive dissonance whereby they both acknowledge they are watching a fiction (repulsion) and yet remain engrossed (attraction). This state of paradoxically co-existent repulsion and attraction is a quality of the abject, as Julia Kristeva observes in her seminal book *Powers of Horror*.[21] And while 3-D's meta-fiction is not an example of the abject, it is useful to note how this aspect of liminal horror aligns with aspects of horror more generally.

3-D, however, couches this blending of fiction with reality within the found footage genre, meaning it fails to depart fully from Heller-Nicholas's analysis. Yet, other liminal horror films break from this genre to achieve their goal of blurring the line between fiction and reality. Two such films, *Scream* (1996) and *Urban Legend* (1998), both depict fans of scary stories experiencing those very stories upending their lives, albeit in different ways. *Scream*, written by Kevin Williamson and directed by Wes Craven, follows a group of teenagers who find a masked killer is stalking them.

The characters, including protagonist Sidney (Neve Campbell), are well-versed in horror movie tropes and clichés, and, consequently, they actively discuss the murders as if they were being committed in a movie, and project their assessments of film survival strategies onto real-life terror, with mixed success. When the core group is down to only a few survivors, *Scream*'s plot twist occurs: there are two masked murderers, and not one, like the group cognizant of horror-film clichés had expected there to be. The two killers, Billy and Stu, then torment Sidney before she, being the "final girl" that she is, outmaneuvers and overcomes them.[22]

Scream's protagonists are steeped in movie lore, to the point where they explain their real-life in filmic terms. Billy, for instance, even claims that "It's all—It's all a movie. It's all one great big movie," and Randy, the film fanatic, screams that all the information they need to find the killers and survive the massacre is available in the videotapes he holds in his hands.[23] *Scream*'s characters, therefore, use knowledge and strategies garnered from fictional films to try to survive their real-life horrors. Here, it is important to note that this strategy reverses the causal chain movie audiences usually follow. Generally, movie audiences tend to apply their factual knowledge and common sense to the contrived scenarios they see on the screen. A quick internet search, for instance, yields pages of material criticizing the choices fictitious movie characters make.

Subsequently, we, as the real audience of the cinematic fictions, can use our knowledge (or so we think) to make better choices than the movie characters do: build sturdier fences, call the police, and so forth. Conversely, however, what *Scream* gives us is a reversal of what audiences experience and perform in actual life. Instead of trying to apply "real"-istic strategies to their "real"-istic problem, *Scream*'s protagonists (killers as well as victims) turn to fiction. Billy and Stu describe their killing spree as if it were a movie. Billy, for example, references the "perfect ending" they have planned, and Stu says, "We get to carry on and plan the sequel...."[24] All these references to films and the characters' use of films to understand their reality hints at the extent to which fiction shapes the characters' real lives.

Thus, in *Scream*, stories breach the barrier between fiction and reality by influencing characters to reify the films they watch, that is, to make reality of the fictions they enjoy. This obfuscation of the line separating fiction from reality has many profound consequences (some of which I discuss in later chapters). For now, however, one consequence is key. *Scream* is more effective than many horror films partially because it plays on the idea that horror films have the power to influence or entice people into committing violent acts. The resultant fear is evident in those political debates that blame video games for mass shootings, and the kind of public discourse that condemned *Child's Play 3* for the murder of James Bulger, a two-year-old child.[25] *Scream*, therefore, resonates with deep cultural anxieties about the place of horror in our society and its possibly deleterious effects.

The film tries to parry this particular criticism, however, through Billy's emphatic claim that horror movies do not *create* psychopaths, rather they just make psychopaths more creative.[26] Furthermore, Randy, who is arguably the biggest fan of horror in *Scream*, is not one of the killers. Despite demonstrating more horror movie knowledge than any of the other characters, Randy is one of the least morbid. While most of the students at Stu's party rush over to the high school to see the principal's corpse, Randy does not, and he even calls to the departing students that they are going to miss the movie (*Halloween*, playing on Stu's television). He shows no interest in seeing a corpse and is one of the few to not celebrate news of the principal's death. Whereas the other partiers cheer, Randy seems shocked and horrified. Love of horror movies does not, ergo, translate to a propensity toward violence, and *Scream* hereby acknowledges the controversy around horror films while also criticizing those who demonize fiction for what occurs in real life.

Reverting to how *Scream* questions the nature of fiction, I observe that the line between the fictional and the real shifts throughout the film. In the very first scene, Ghostface (probably Billy, though the movie leaves it ambiguous) terrorizes his victim, Casey, by playing horror movie trivia and referring to slasher films such as *Friday the 13th* by name. This move is two-fold: it acknowledges *Scream*'s genre by foreshadowing the events to come, and it simultaneously asserts the film's reality in contrast to the "fictional" movie, *Friday the 13th*.

That is, by treating other films of the slasher sub-genre (to which *Scream* belongs) as fictional, *Scream* implicitly asserts its own reality over and above those films, placing itself closer to its audience, who are presumably familiar with the genre. From the outset, then, *Scream*'s self-awareness complicates readings of it, as it becomes a signifier of both reality and fiction.[27] *Scream*'s references to its own genre make the viewer aware of the film's place within that genre while simultaneously staking out for itself a larger claim to being real, when compared to the others films in the slasher sub-genre.

This first scene (described in the preceding paragraph) interrogates the fictional-real distinction in another way as well. Ghostface's victim, Casey, cowers behind her television. Symbolically, she is hiding behind the protective divide between fiction (television) and reality (killer outside), hoping it will keep her safe. The killer then throws a chair through the window, forcing Casey to flee from her hiding spot. This is an immediate disruption of fiction's protective veil, both for the victim and for the audience. Like the window, the television's screen is made of glass, and the movie killer easily breaches this barrier. The line between reality and fiction comes under threat, therefore, as the events that *Scream*'s characters have seen so many times on the big screen begin to play out in their actual lives.

Billy (Skeet Ulrich, right) prepares to stab Stu (Matthew Lillard) (*Scream*, directed by Wes Craven. Dimension Films, 1996).

During the film's climax, however, the line between fiction and reality relocates from the barrier of glass to the barrier of skin. At this point in the film, Billy and Stu have cornered Sidney, ostensibly the only surviving protagonist. They explain their evil plan to her and seem self-assured of their victory. According to them, all they had to do to execute their scheme and their friends was "watch a few movies, take a few notes," and, now, their plan is reaching its "perfect ending."[28] They are living inside their own film and planning its sequel, and the next step in their plan is to stab each other.[29] By injuring each other with the knife they have used to kill other characters, Billy and Stu are attempting to construct a fictionalized narrative of their lives so they can pass themselves off as victims in front of the police, as well as become the successful auteurs of their shared story. This plan fails, however, as both realize how painful being stabbed is. They cry out, and Stu becomes "woozy."[30]

Despite their perceptions of themselves, their pain brings them back to reality, a reality where they are just as mortal as their victims and where their "fiction" is set to fall apart as Sidney escapes and turns the tables on them. The knife, therefore, lays bare the truth and reveals the flaws in Billy's and Stu's narrative by reminding them of their fragility and making them acknowledge their own status as victims (that is, their mortality). Subsequently, Billy and Stu become one with their victims: as they used the knife to kill other characters, the knife now helps kill them. Thus, what Billy and Stu view as a celebration of their lives—and enduring legacy, as they plan their sequel—is, ironically, the beginning of their deaths.

These deaths, moreover, are gruesome and prolonged. Stu suffers multiple stab wounds before Sidney kills him with his family television. Much like the stabbing, this killing (not murder since Sidney is clearly acting in self-defense) is symbolically significant. Randy has watched horror films on this TV, and it is a small leap to assume Stu has probably done the same. And here, he dies when the instrument he and Billy used to terrorize others (that is, the vector of "scary movies") is turned against him.[31]

Like the engineered stabbing, this turning also takes the form of an attack on Stu's corporeal being. That is, though Stu believes he draws power from the fiction of "scary movies" and, by extension, from his television, the television, like the knife, turns against him.[32] What he thinks is his power, his legacy, becomes an instrument of his undoing. Meanwhile, Sidney stabs Stu's partner Billy with an umbrella before finishing him with a bullet to the head. While Billy's death is not as metaphorically significant as Stu's, it is important to note nevertheless that he dies when some of his would-be victims turn his own weapons (including his costume) against him. The blood drenching Stu and Billy's clothes symbolizes the second reality that their final act brings to the surface, the first reality being the representation of their mortality through pain.

In the horror film, violence often acts as a window into a hidden world, a hidden reality. In her seminal work, *Men, Women, & Chainsaws: Gender in the Modern Horror Film*, Carol J. Clover observes that Franklin in *Texas Chainsaw Massacre* "seems fascinated by the realization that all that lies between the visible, knowable outside of the body and its secret insides is one thin membrane, protected only by a collective taboo against its violation."[33]

Here, Clover hints that the skin is a barrier between worlds, between two realities. It is this reality upon which Billy and Stu stumble when they stab one another. Their wounds cause them to bleed, thereby revealing the world that lies beneath their skin, a world that further unites them with their victims, whose skins they have already ruptured and violated. Thus, the horror film's devotion to bodily injury underscores its interest in discovering new realities and breaching barriers, whether they are physical or, as Clover discusses, socially constructed.[34] I discuss this interest, and the hidden world beneath the skin, further in Chapter 6, but for now, it is

When the slasher villain's knife cuts open a body, we see the body's insides revealed. Here, when the knife slashes open an orange, we see the same: the cut reveals what lies beneath the orange's skin. In other words, the cut reveals a hitherto hidden reality ("Untitled," by Marcus Whaley. Printed with permission of the photographer).

important to note its presence as well as the way in which *Scream* blurs the borders between the real and the fictional.

This same blurring occurs in 1998's *Urban Legend*, directed by Jamie Blanks, which shows stories taking over the protagonists' lives. Whereas the stories in *Scream* are horror films, the stories in *Urban Legend* are, well, urban legends. Merriam-Webster defines an urban legend as "an often lurid story or anecdote that is based on hearsay and widely circulated as true."[35] Examples of such legends include the belief that drinking soda after eating pop-rocks will kill you and the more detailed story of the serial killer lurking in the back seat.

Both legends come up in Jamie Blanks' film, which follows a group of college students at the fictional Pendleton University, where a parka-clad, axe-wielding serial killer begins murdering the group's members one-by-one. The killer bases her murders on urban legends, and the protagonists even begin to guess which legends she will use next, trying to apply their knowledge of folklore to protect themselves. Toward the film's climax, the audience learn the killer is Brenda, one of the core group of students and friend to the "final girl" Natalie (Alicia Witt).

Brenda captures Natalie and reveals her murder spree is actually a revenge plot. Years earlier, Natalie and her friend Michelle, the film's first murder victim, had accidentally killed Brenda's fiancée while trying to reenact an urban legend on the road. Brenda, then, followed Natalie and Michelle to Pendleton and used the latter's ignorance of her identity to instill herself in Natalie's life with the goal of destroying it. Brenda fails, however, as a university security guard, Reese, and a journalism student, Paul, arrive and, with Natalie's help, defeat her.

If *Urban Legend* sounds derivative of *Scream*, that is only because it is. Following *Scream*'s success, a variety of ostensibly self-aware slasher films flooded the horror movie market, *Urban Legend* among them. *Urban Legend* is useful for developing our discussion of *Scream* because its reliance on folklore, instead of cinema, to blur the line between fiction and reality introduces us to a new field of scholarship and to the concept of ostension. In folklore, "ostension" is the behavior of acting out a legend.[36] In *Urban Legend*, the first act of ostension occurs during the first murder. Here, the camera follows Michelle driving through a rainstorm. When she notices her car is low on gas, she pulls into a rural gas station, where she appears to be the only customer. Soon, an attendant (Brad Dourif) with a stutter rushes out and begins fueling her car. The attendant begins to creep out Michelle, as he lures her back into the gas station under the pretense that her credit card was declined. Fearing for her safety, Michelle flees, unable to hear the attendant shouting that there is someone in her backseat.[37] As she speeds away, the person in the backseat, Brenda, reveals herself and kills

Michelle with an axe, thereby acting out the "killer in the backseat" urban legend.

Michelle's murder is an act of ostension, as Brenda takes a popular urban legend and performs it in real-life, thus transposing the legend from fiction to reality, myth to historical fact. Similar movements occur throughout the film, with Brenda enacting more legends, all in response to Natalie and Michelle's original ostension, in which they performed the "headlight initiation" myth and accidentally killed Brenda's fiancée.[38] Hence, Mikel J. Koven writes: "The film seems to be warning young people, the movie and genre's chief demographic, that even seemingly benign forms of ostension, of just playing around *without* murderous intent, can be deadly" (emphasis Koven's).[39] Thus, *Urban Legend* and *Scream* both demonstrate the danger of challenging the barrier between fiction and reality. Natalie, Michelle, Brenda, Billy, and Stu all take stories about death and attempt to make them real, and they all pay the price for the same. Inherent here, in the horror film, is a warning about trying to reenact the horror film. Keep the fiction fictional, it seems to be telling us.

And yet, the message is not that crystal-clear. When Michelle flees from the gas station attendant, she ostensibly performs the smart, self-preserving action. To that point in the film, the attendant appears to be the major threat to her, and we, the audience, likely share her concerns about him. But the film punishes Michelle for her misinterpretation. The attendant is trying to save her, and she dies because she perceives him as a threat rather than a would-be protector. His occupation, appearance, and speech impediment all mark him as an Other to Michelle, and it is this Other-ing on Michelle's part that creates the largest barrier between him and his intentions to save her. This moment is interesting because it enacts (as well as challenges the enactment of) the myth the film is relating.

It enacts the myth because the "killer in the backseat" occurs for real in the film's universe, and also because Michelle's fleeing from her would-be protector mirrors common variations of the legend, in which the protagonist misunderstands another motorist's attempts to save them, as attempts to harm them. This is the same misreading Michelle performs, and, thus, by fleeing the attendant only to fall victim to the killer, Michelle inadvertently acts out the legend. But to conclude that Michelle's death underscores how horror films are warning us about the danger of ostension is to miss the full story. Earlier, I pointed out that *Urban Legend* induces us—the audience—to agree with Michelle about the threat the attendant poses. Indeed, in real-life, most would advise our loved ones to act as Michelle does in this circumstance and flee from the attendant. Yet, our instincts would be wrong if we accept the film's rules. Even so, it is difficult to fault Michelle for her actions since they would generally be correct in real-life.

In other words, though the films provide warnings about ostension's dangers, it is difficult to ascertain the warnings' efficaciousness because the films themselves are inconsistent as to when it is dangerous to violate the (sometimes obscure) boundary between fact and fiction and when it is not. For Michelle to have stayed with the attendant, she would have needed to accept that her instincts were wrong and that the rules of urban legends, rather than real-life, were at play. It is difficult to say both that Michelle should not perform ostension and should also perform ostension. There is no easy way out for her. Indeed, there are rarely any simple answers for horror film protagonists, and that, exactly, is the point.

Straightforward answers and rules make the threat less palpable, as *Scream* highlights when it verbalizes the rules of slasher films and then flagrantly violates them. Both *Scream* and *Urban Legend* not only challenge the dividing line between fiction and reality but challenge it multiple times and in different ways. Billy and Stu apply horror movie logic to their murders, treating their victims as horror movie victims; Brenda does the same with urban legends. In this manner, they try to make the fictional real. They do, however, also do the opposite: they try to make the real fictional.

As I mentioned earlier, Billy and Stu reveal their desire to plan a sequel for their rampage. The later films in the *Scream* franchise vindicate this desire, as other killers step up to fill Billy and Stu's shoes while the in-universe *Stab* film franchise immortalizes Billy and Stu's rampage in fiction. Meanwhile, in *Urban Legend*, college students enshrine Brenda's maniacal murder spree as an urban legend of its own. The film's closing scene shows her, still alive, correcting fellow students at her new university about the finer details of the "killer recreating urban legends" legend. In other words, she edifies them about her own murders, which have become a legend themselves, for the university covers them up like it did with the in-universe Stanley Hall Massacre.[40] Both *Scream* and *Urban Legend*, ergo, hint that stories may not only influence the present but also combine with reality to influence the future. Stories, they suggest, form cyclically.

These films, therefore, show the line between fiction and reality to be permeable, and infinitely so. To truly see how often a film can blur this boundary, consider one of *Urban Legend*'s sequels, *Urban Legends: Final Cut* (2000) directed by John Ottman. The movie follows film student Amy (Jennifer Morrison), who is struggling to plan her thesis film, and finally decides to make a film about a killer who recreates urban legends. As she starts planning and filming her project, however, various acts of ostension occur, as someone, in real-life, begins performing the urban legends to murder the university's film students. Ultimately, Amy's film professor reveals himself to be the killer, whereupon Amy shoots and seemingly cripples him. She then continues to work on her urban legends themed film project.

While the first *Urban Legend* is a film about a killer using urban legends to commit murders, *Urban Legends: Final Cut* (*Final Cut*), is a film about making a film about a serial killer who reconstructs urban legends to commit murders. *Final Cut* also features an actual murderer who kills the people involved in making the film-within-a-film, and this actual killer uses urban legends to do so. From this brief synopsis, it is evident that the sequel's narrative depicts stories frequently oscillating between fiction and reality. To explore this alternation further, one needs only to look where Amy gets the idea for her thesis film.

When walking alone on campus one night, Amy meets Reese, a campus security guard who offers her a ride and tells her the story of the Pendleton murders, a story which, thus far, Amy has regarded as mere legend. As a viewer familiar with the first film will realize, Reese is a survivor of the Pendleton murders and has first-hand knowledge of them. Based on her conversation with Reese, Amy decides to make a thesis film about a killer enacting urban legends. Thus, art imitates life (imitating art) here. Later, when her film professor uses Amy's film as a cover for his own urban legend-based murders (intending to frame Amy for them), he imitates art with life. Hence, life leads to art which leads to life, and so on. But if we consider the legends that inspire the murders in the first *Urban Legend*, we have art leading to life leading to art leading to life.

Consequently, the films seem to suggest that stories propagate themselves over time, and that the border between fiction and reality is not only penetrable but endlessly so. In other words, a tale can pass from fantasy to fact and then back again. *Final Cut* certainly exemplifies this unrestricted movement of narratives from actuality to fabled fabrication and back over time. In other words, a story can pass back and forth between the realm of fiction and the realm of reality, ad infinitum.

Thus, legends are akin to living, organic entities; they are immortal, reborn infinitely with each passage across the flimsy barrier between the worlds of fantasy and truth. This is the cyclical nature of stories toward which *Scream* and *Urban Legend* gesture. A legend, a blend of fiction and reality, influences the present and, thereby, creates a new legend that will also blend fiction with reality. These films suggest, therefore, that narratives can become history or even are, themselves, history. And the narratives people spin, even for themselves, can be as dangerous as any others.

For instance, in *The House That Dripped Blood*, a 1971 British horror anthology film directed by Peter Duffell, the audience meets a writer whose newest story consumes him. In the film's first full story, horror writer Charles (Denholm Elliott) and his wife rent a house away from town so

Charles can find inspiration for his next story. He is experiencing writer's block, and his deadline is fast approaching. He finds inspiration and begins hammering out a story about a strangler named Dominic. He becomes frightened, however, when he sees Dominic in real-life. Fearing he is losing his mind and beginning to impersonate Dominic, he seeks out psychiatric treatment. As it happens, however, he is not losing his mind. Rather, his wife has hired an actor to portray Dominic and gaslight the writer into thinking he is insane. The wife's plan horribly backfires, however, when the actor becomes absorbed in his character and kills her and Charles.

While the contrived twist highlights the movie's cheesy tone, the story itself is useful for understanding how the line between fiction and reality gradually diminishes and, moreover, how a person's own fabrications can consume them. As the segment progresses, Charles sees Dominic becoming more and more real. At first, he describes having seen Dominic in his "mind's eye," whence he gets the idea for the character and begins writing his story.[41] Later, when he fears Dominic is "taking over," he sees the strangler first through a window, second through a mirror, and, third, reflected in a river.[42]

Dominic is gaining physical existence, or so it seems. Charles's psychiatrist explains that "An author's characters are an extension of his own personality," and Charles says after a session: "Everything comes from the inside apparently, a projection of my own imagination."[43] The film suggests a writer's imagination can get so fully submerged in a story that the writer becomes a character from within the story, thereby enabling fiction's transformation into reality through the vehicle of madness. As Charles appears to lose his mind, he simultaneously appears to become more and more like Dominic, his imaginary creation.

Of course, the segment's concluding twist unveils "Dominic" as an actor Charles's wife hired to frame her husband and drive him insane. But the preceding analysis holds because the actor, Richard, becomes so caught up in the role that he believes he actually *is* Dominic. So, he does what his character, a strangler, would do and strangles Charles's wife, killing her. What Charles believed was happening to him, actually happens to the actor: Richard's immersion in a fictional narrative warps his mind until he resembles a character from that narrative. *The House That Dripped Blood* thus makes it easier to comprehend the immersion in fiction that Stu, Billy, and Brenda display.

When one is in the narrative, it makes sense one would be engrossed; it is more understandable that one might take that immersion too far. Note that Stu, Billy, and Brenda are only fans of movies and urban legends, respectively. When *Scream* and *Urban Legend* begin, Stu, Billy, and Brenda have not yet become films or urban legends themselves. They are on the outside, looking into those narratives in which they seek to dwell. Unlike them, however, Charles and Richard are already saturated in the narrative. Charles creates it, shapes it, and it, in turn, shapes him.

Meanwhile, Richard embodies the story, becoming its antagonist. In this way, *The House That Dripped Blood* gives an outlandish warning against method acting, by presenting how purposefully embodying a fiction can make said fiction into a horrific reality beyond the creator's control. Except for (maybe) Brenda, none of these characters manage to exert control over their narratives. In each case, then, these films cast stories as being outside (our) control. Once set free, once told, the story has a life of its own, creator's wishes be damned.

The House That Dripped Blood further addresses pretenses of control over a narrative in the fourth story segment, which is about a veteran horror film actor, Paul Henderson (Jon Pertwee), who plays the lead role in a vampire film entitled *Curse of the Bloodsuckers*. Fed up with the amateurish production, Paul tries to find a replacement vampire cloak for his costume. Discovering a mysterious card for a costume shop in his dressing room, he visits the shop and purchases a black cloak with a red lining. When filming the next day, he realizes the cloak grants him actual vampiric powers after it causes him to bite his co-star, Carla. Paul later apologizes to Carla and invites her to his house for champagne. When she visits, he tries to convince her of the cloak's abilities. Carla then dons the cloak and reveals herself to be a real vampire. She explains that because the vampire community enjoys Paul's performances so much, they want him to become a real vampire and join them. The segment ends as Carla flies at Paul and attacks him.

Here, the film mocks Paul's haughtiness as well as his self-assurance about being an expert on all manner of monsters. He ironically makes the latter assertion in the presence of his vampiric co-star, ignorant of her true nature as a vampire. Later, the film mocks him once more, as it cuts from his statements about his expertise and abilities to portray him kneeling over a toy castle. He inspects the castle carefully; and a change in camera angle reveals it is a model of the film's set. Despite his pretensions of grandiosity, this cut reduces him to a figure who scrutinizes toy castles instead of owning a real castle of his own, as a proper vampire would. His knowledge, then, comes under fire once more when he discovers that his "expertise" neglected the most important fact of all: that vampires exist.

The segment's twist complicates its interpretation. At first, when Paul bites Carla, the implication is that the myth is becoming reality. As Paul sinks his teeth into her neck, he enacts vampirism, moving from pretending to be a vampire (i.e., acting) to being a vampire (i.e., reality). The segment subverts this reading, however, with its revelation that vampires were real throughout its narrative. Thus, Paul's bite is not so much an enactment of a new reality as it is the uncovering of a hidden one. The bite ultimately discloses the concealed truth that vampires are, in fact, real. It does not *make* them real since Carla, unbeknownst to both Paul and the audience, is already a vampire.

In this segment, Paul's misreading of the world around him proves his undoing. Moreover, he predicates his (mis)reading of the situation on his avowed knowledge. Because he is overly confident about his knowledge of monsters, he is blinded to the dangerous reality before him. Like *Scream*, *Urban Legend*, and the first segment of *The House That Dripped Blood*, this final segment shows how stories run amok—and beyond—control. This segment complicates matters, however, because the story's life stems less from the power of fiction and more from the actual being (Carla, the vampire) that the fiction is about.

Nevertheless, one should not underestimate fiction, because fiction itself can also be dangerous, if only because of how it entices people to behave. For example, the classic trope of the self-fulfilling prophecy involves a fiction (the prophecy) that creates a reality by altering a character's actions. Subsequently, it is the character's attempt to prevent the prophecy—or to fulfill it—that then turns the prophecy into truth. Classical literature abounds with examples of such prophecies (see, for instance, *Oedipus Rex* and *Macbeth*), but, then, so does modern film.

For instance, *Darna Zaroori Hai* (*Zaroori Hai*) (2006), a Hindi-language horror anthology directed by Khan, et al., demonstrates one such prophecy playing out. The movie's opening segment follows Satish (Manoj Pahwa), a boisterous movie fan, preparing to go see *Darna Mana Hai* (predecessor to *Darna Zaroori Hai*). Because he is running late, he informs his mother about his intention to use a shorter route, cutting across the local graveyard, so he can reach the theater on time. But his mother implores him not to do so, as she believes it is dangerous to walk through the graveyard that night. She explains: "Today is Friday the 13th and a moonless night.... Because witches venture there on this day."[44] Satish scoffs, and, mocking his mother's beliefs, he asks if anyone has seen a witch, to which she responds: "The person who sees them doesn't survive! But the tinkling of her anklet on such an inauspicious night, everybody can hear that."[45]

Unconvinced, Satish takes the route through the graveyard, watches the film (which he criticizes rudely, throughout), and then heads back home, through the graveyard once again. Only, now, the graveyard has grown darker, more sinister. Consequently, Satish, despite his bravado (in ridiculing *Darna Mana Hai*) and his mockery of his mother's warnings under his breath (when he first entered the cemetery), grows anxious, especially when he hears a clinking sound. This anxiety turns to terror when he thinks someone has grabbed his ankle; in reality, his feet are merely tangled in a tree's fallen branch(es).

In his fright, however, Satish does not consider such a simple solution, and instead, he struggles to get free. It is then that he sees a witch standing outside the cemetery, whereupon he suffers a heart attack. Clutching his chest and gasping for breath, he falls to the ground. Only, as he does, he discovers the source of the clinking sound: the coins in his pocket, which collided together when he walked, even more so when he tried to run. The camera then pans to show the witch, an advertisement poster for another film, *Darna Zaroori Hai*.

Satish's death is highly ironic. Despite her good intentions in giving it, it is his mother's warning about the witch (and her anklet) that kills him. Satish's fear about these parts of his mother's story, augmented by the unease of being alone in a graveyard at night, primes him to panic in circumstances when he might not have, otherwise. His insistence on taking the shorter route through the graveyard certainly indicates his familiarity and so, comfort, with it. It is easy to surmise, therefore, that Satish has traversed this path several times without any trouble. But now, his mother's story renders dangerous some otherwise mundane elements because they conjure images of the supernatural for Satish. These images then terrify him enough to trigger a psychosomatic reaction that overwhelms his heart, killing him. From this description, one can also surmise that Satish would probably have survived, were it not for his mother's warning which primed him for fear. Consequently, his mother's warning becomes a self-fulfilling prophecy.

Moreover, *Zaroori Hai* warns viewers it will fulfill this same prophecy. That is, Satish relentlessly mocks the film's predecessor (*Darna Mana Hai*), but dies upon encountering an image of *Zaroori Hai*'s main antagonist. Satish's death, subsequently, is a statement by *Zaroori Hai*'s creators: a statement that their film will be scarier than its predecessor. In making this declaration, they also warn the audience that the movie to come will be dangerously scary. After all, Satish dies from fright, and, once he does, *Zaroori Hai* proceeds to an introductory song and dance routine, the lyrics of which include "Come, be scared, and die" and "I will scare and kill you."[46] Thus, after depicting a character dying from fear, the film warns the audience that the same fate awaits them. This same fate also awaits the protagonists of *Zaroori Hai*'s frame narrative, in which a group of school children (the protagonists) become lost during a rainstorm and take shelter in a bungalow, wherein they meet an old woman who boasts that her scary stories will frighten all them.

The bulk of *Zaroori Hai*'s runtime follows a simple pattern: the old woman tells a scary story to the children, that horror-themed story plays out on screen for the audience, and the movie then cuts back to the children, one of whom becomes frightened and separates from the group, only to be replaced with a doppelganger. This happens with each child. At the end of the film, the audience learns the old woman has been dead, and the bungalow abandoned, for years. The old woman, her previous caretaker reveals, loved children but never had any of her own. Then, a newscast discusses how the schoolchildren were all found dead, seemingly from fear: "The strange thing is that all five of them died because their heart stopped beating. According to the doctor here, there could be only one reason as to why the heart of such small children stopped beating. Fear. Meaning fright. In simple language, plain fear."[47]

Thus, *Zaroori Hai* does deliver (within its universe) its promised threat: that fear kills. In doing so, it creates a world in which scary stories are dangerous, where fiction can cause people's deaths. Yet, though *Zaroori Hai* establishes this threat, it does not explore it further, let alone in detail. Rather than illustrating the different ways fiction can be dangerous, it merely depicts this threat twice, thereby negating its impact on the audience. Nevertheless, there are several other movies which demonstrate, in diverse ways (and by using different techniques), why fictions themselves can be harmful.

Indeed, *Scream*, the *Urban Legend* franchise, and *The House That Dripped Blood* all portray fictions becoming dangerous through ostension, immersion, and a loss of control. Fictions, these other films suggest, have a life of their own. Some films, however, take this idea more literally. The next section explores that particular category of films: those which evince the perilous nature of fictions by portraying "fictions" (such as myths and legends) that contain malicious living entities.

Section Two: The Ghost in the Frame

The *Scream* and *Urban Legend* films depict characters who consciously attempt to translate fictions into reality. In other films, such as the final segment of *The House That Dripped Blood*, however, the blurring between fiction and reality is unintentional and supernatural, the result of failed ontological understanding rather than of human agency. Other films, however, offer a fuller view of the supernatural.

One such film is 2012's *Sinister*, directed by Scott Derrickson. *Sinister* follows washed-up true crime writer Ellison Oswald (Ethan Hawke), who, in his desperation to write another best-selling book, relocates his family to a new house. Ellison's unsuspecting family is unaware that the house they have moved into was the site of a multiple homicide Ellison wants to investigate in his newest book. He soon discovers a box of old film reels in the attic. The box's origins, however, are suspiciously unclear since, as Ellison realizes, the box is conspicuously absent from police photos of the crime scene.

Having trouble planning his book, Ellison begins watching the film reels, each of which depicts the murder of a different family. Afraid the police will confiscate these tapes, he does not share information about the box—or the records of murders it contains—with them. His motives are desperately selfish. Ellison fears informing the police of such key evidence will prevent him from solving the case, and thereby put an end to his dreams of writing another bestseller to chronicle his masterful investigation.

As he goes through reel after reel and investigates the murders they document, Ellison begins experiencing increasingly bizarre and frightening phenomena related to a character in the films: Bughuul, a Babylonian deity, colloquially known as the devourer of children. Realizing the danger he and his family are in, Ellison abandons his book project and moves his family out of the house. But Bughuul's influence follows them, and their daughter, Ashley, under the deity's influence, films herself murdering the rest of her family. Then, she walks into the image the old projector casts on the wall, joining Bughuul.

The involvement and the role of the supernatural in the film is key, for it highlights the conflict at the heart of *Sinister*, a conflict between two realities: the one Ellison believes to be and the one that really is. Whereas the former is the world of reason, the latter is the world of superstition, populated with supernatural entities.[48] It is in this latter world that Ellison suddenly finds himself. Indeed, Ellison's failure to recognize he lives in the supernatural world leads to his and his family's deaths. When speaking to "Deputy So-And-So," Ellison professes his lack of belief in ghosts and the paranormal. What is significant, however, is how he disavows the paranormal's existence even after he encounters it. Ellison, in other words, denies the paranormal at the very moment when he apprehends evidence for its existence.

To be sure, this denial is in accordance with proper skepticism. But as with Michelle from *Urban Legend* (discussed in the previous section), Ellison's failure to correctly understand the world he inhabits proves fatal. Like Michelle, Ellison (initially) follows the wrong set of rules, believing wholeheartedly in his ability to solve the murders with a secular, investigatory lens. Also, like Michelle, he realizes too late that he can no longer rely on his typical approach if he is to survive his current circumstance.

Here, the genre-savvy reader may note that this conflict between skepticism and belief in the paranormal is central to many horror films.

Although the reader's observation would be correct, the point here is that Ellison's notions of reality and fiction—the very notions most of us apply in our daily lives—prove faulty. What he judges to be fiction (deities such as Bughuul) is reality, and what he considers reality is but an incomplete view. That which Ellison does not see, the part of reality he fails to acknowledge, kills him. *Sinister,* therefore, establishes high stakes by proclaiming that *our* conception of reality is flawed. What reality, then, does the film reveal?

If *Sinister* is portraying a reality different than the one Ellison expects (and the one in which, the skeptic believes, we live) then the film's reality is one where images (fictions) are dangerous. Indeed, it is a reality wherein images can kill, which makes Bughuul an interesting figure for this present study because he derives his power from the image itself. That is, representing Bughuul in any visual medium gives him power, as Ellison (and so, the audience) learn(s) from Professor Jonas (Vincent D'Onofrio). Jonas provides the film's expositional dumps. Only through him does the audience learn how *Sinister's* supernatural horrors function.

Except for the insight Professor Jonas provides, Bughuul's character remains enigmatic, appearing only for the occasional jump-scare but otherwise evading attention and, therefore, any possible explanations. In his final scene, Jonas sends Ellison a handful of scanned images relating to Bughuul, apologizing for their scant number and the delay in sending them. More importantly, he relays that the Babylonians believed in Bughuul's ability to transmit himself through images, and, hence, they destroyed any visuals of him, as and when they appeared. Thus, the exiguous scans Jonas provides are of the only pictures he can find.

Yet, the world of *Sinister* is rife with images. What is a film reel, after all, if not a series of visuals? For it is while perusing the old film reels for clues about the murders that Ellison first encounters an obscure figure in the background: Bughuul. The deity lies, nay, lives, in the images captured on film, and branches out from these to find habitat in Ashley's drawings. He is, therefore, a disease: he spreads like a plague, with the film reels propagating new images of himself that further his aims of "eating" Ashley.[49]

The true danger(s) in *Sinister,* then, lie in the dual categories of seeing as well as failing to see, that is, simultaneous perception and misperception. Bughuul infects families who see his images, and he spreads his infection from one family on to the next. The sequel makes this element clearer, as it shows the children Bughuul has already consumed, forcing his new targets (again, children) to watch videos of his previous murders, preserved in the same Super-8 tapes Ellison finds in the first film. Sight is the cornerstone of Bughuul's power, as he must be seen to gain both power and influence. Therefore, it is the onlooker, the perceiver, over whom he exerts his power.

Bughuul's victims are his audience, and his biggest audience is the one in the movie theater.

The film's concluding shot is the deity's face as he gives one last jump-scare. Symbolically, this shot suggests Bughuul has instilled himself in the movie viewers'—that is, our—lives. Because this is the film's final shot, the last image we see before the lights come back on, it lingers in our minds, seemingly providing an afterimage that preserves Bughuul, spreading him across our vision and memories so we will take him home with us. Indeed, the film also threatens the very notion of "home," as Ellison finds the film reels in his new house and then dies in his old house. From the home to the movie theater, *Sinister* hits and shatters the comfort zone, the "safe space" of the audience. It challenges the notion that one can look without endangering oneself, thereby speaking to the longstanding critical tradition that regards film spectators as voyeurs. Only here, in *Sinister*, we—the audience—cannot be voyeurs with impunity. Our very act of voyeurism, the act of viewing the film, puts us in the monster's sights and opens us to the film's world in ways we do not expect.

This is because the movie-going audience anticipates commonly experiencing a film. The audience certainly does not envision the film transposing itself out into their world from the screen and establishing itself as a threat. Symbolically, however, this is exactly what *Sinister* does. It threatens to breach the pathetic barrier of the film screen and reach out to grip its audience and stalk them. This imperilment sabotages the line separating fiction from reality, as if to question whether the fictional and the real can be distinguished at all. Thus, *Sinister* poses the question: is the very the act of watching a horror movie dangerous? It certainly proves

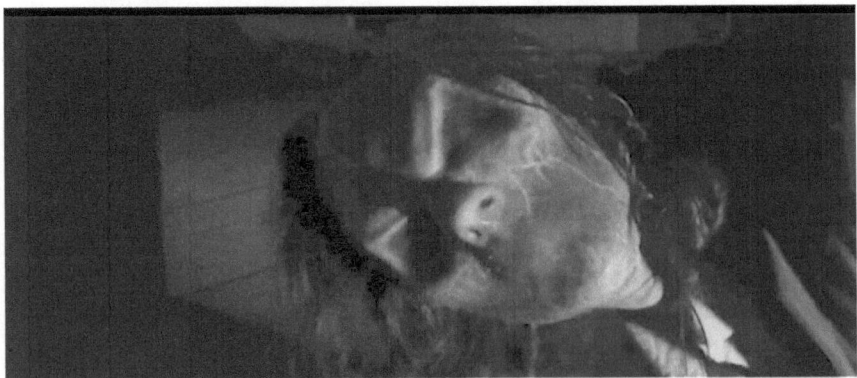

In a blink-and-you-will-miss-it moment, Bughuul (Nicholas King) lunges at the camera, providing *Sinister*'s final jump-scare (*Sinister*, directed by Scott Derrickson. Alliance Films, 2012).

to be so for Ellison, whose life unravels because he watches Bughuul's Super-8 tapes.

If we, as the audience, believe viewing a horror movie is perilous, if we accept (if only for a moment) this analytic leap, then we challenge—if not outright destroy—our tidy notions of fiction versus reality. In such a scenario, fiction becomes not a quick consumable to be imbibed then purged, but rather an infection. It enters the cracks of our being, lingers, festers, and threatens to spill over into our nightmares and hound our everyday lives, forcing us to look twice at every shadow and carefully consider every bump in the night. The success of horror films generally relies on their effectual destabilizing of their audience. If, in addition to this, a film (like *Sinister*) also induces the audience to ponder the perils of simply witnessing it, then said film is much better situated to achieve horror's intended effect.

Ergo, *Sinister* advances further in converging fiction and reality than either *Scream* or the *Urban Legend* films do. Whereas the latter depict characters reenacting stories, the former sees fictions enacting themselves. To paraphrase, the danger in *Scream* and *Urban Legend* is that someone may attempt to imitate fictions in reality, but in *Sinister*, conversely, the peril lies in the images' innate capacity to birth the real from their fictional essences. These images can overpower us. *Sinister*, therefore, presents a notion of fictions as living entities.

I averred something similar about the legends in *Final Cut*. The key difference between these two films, however, is how *Sinister* makes it literal. The images in *Sinister* contain a living, sentient entity which grants them agency. On the contrary, the legends in *Final Cut* are not agents in themselves. Their propagation occurs because people (their audience) propagate them. The legends themselves lack any discernible will, and their power derives from the influence they exert over their audience—an influence that most can resist. After all, few people commit murders based on urban legends. But Bughuul's visuals are harder to withstand, precisely because they proliferate by themselves.

Section Three: Living Stories: Frames That Breathe

That Bughuul's films and images contain an insidious, living (or at least sentient) entity is undeniable. But this inclusion raises a fundamentally problematic question: how did Bughuul come to dwell in the films? Does he predate them? *Sinister* suggests he does. Since Jonas says the images allow Bughuul to spread himself, one can surmise that they are merely his tools, not his birthplace. But because the films never make explicit whence Bughuul came, it is difficult to determine whether the images in which he dwells are his creator or merely the vector of his influence. So, there is no way of ascertaining whether the images themselves are alive if one only considers the film's text. However, it is possible that tracing Bughuul's extra-textual origins can aid in solving this difficulty.

According to *Sinister*'s Facebook page, Bughuul is the brother of the Canaanite god Moloch, to whom the Canaanites would sacrifice children.[50] Even without this post, however, it is possible to connect the two figures. Bughuul and Moloch share geography and avocation. Babylon (whence Bughuul originated) existed in present-day Iraq, an area within the Canaanite region in which Moloch was supposed to dwell. Next, Bughuul is the child-eater while Moloch is the receiver of child sacrifices.

Moreover, both figures share an association with fire. Supplicants would sacrifice children to Moloch through fire, as Leviticus 18:1 declares: "And thou shalt not let any of thy seed pass through the fire to Molech, neither shalt thou profane the name of thy God: I am the LORD."[51] And in *Sinister*, Bughuul spreads himself through Super-8 film reels, the first of which spontaneously bursts into flames after Ellison watches it. It is only after this fire that Bughuul instills himself in the family. To state the obvious, fire is dangerous, and the film reel's catching fire, consequently, foreshadows the danger Ellison's family will face. But more significantly, the fire foreshadows a specific type of danger by hinting at the connection between Bughuul and Moloch, as the latter's mythology directly connects him to fire. Thus, the film implies (if only to an esoteric audience) that Ellison's children will be the ones in danger. If one follows and accepts these connections and the extra-textual evidence, one can conclude that Bughuul predates the visuals he uses to proliferate himself.

This dynamic is vastly common, as most films that showcase an entity emerging from fiction usually establish its existence prior to the current text (or prior to the events occurring in-universe). Consider, for example, Gore Verbinski's 2002 film, *The Ring*. The film's protagonist, journalist Rachel Keller (Naomi Watts) watches a videotape whose viewers invariably die within a week of seeing it. After Rachel's young son also views the tape, she anxiously investigates its origins, tracing it to a disturbed girl named Samara. While she was alive, Samara possessed psychic powers she used to torment others.

Samara's mother consequently drowned her in a well, but not before Samara had already used her powers to instill her spirit in the insidious videotape mentioned above. Rachel finds Samara's corpse, ostensibly putting the latter's spirit to rest. Rachel later discovers, however, that Samara's spirit continues to exist and is still malicious. To save her son, Rachel teaches him how to copy the videotape containing Samara's spirit, since the act of propagating Samara appears to be the only way to assuage her.

Two—Shattered Screens and Punctured Skin 41

The Ring is one of the more influential films I discuss in this book, as its success ushered in a wave of American remakes of Japanese horror films. As such, I would be remiss if I did not discuss *The Ring*, especially since it echoes *Sinister* in some ways. Both films present a malevolent entity using fiction (particularly film) as a medium to propagate itself and hurt more people. The entities have different motives, though. Samara wants others to suffer as she did while Bughuul needs to consume souls for sustenance. Their methods, however, are strikingly similar, and these similarities stem from *Sinister*'s origins, whereby the film's writer, C. Robert Cargill, based it on a nightmare he had after watching *The Ring*.[52] Hence, *Sinister* ostensibly echoes *The Ring* in this case. Nevertheless, it is crucial to perceive that the evil in both films predates the fictions the antagonists later use to spread themselves, especially in the context of comprehending horror's liminality.

It is also beneficial to analyze the media of fictions the supernatural entities choose; Samara replicates herself through VHS tapes while Bughuul does so through Super-8 film reels. These media are integral to—and reflect—the antagonists' goals. VHS tapes are commercial entities that condense films into forms people can buy and take home with them. That is, VHS tapes are a media created to be distributed. Hence, they are a perfect choice for Samara, who wants to distribute—or spread—herself. By using VHS tapes, Samara makes herself a commercial entity to be traded between individuals.

Note, for example, how Rachel and her son only survive because they copy (i.e., circulate) the tapes. In other words, they trade tapes to others or, at least, make the trade possible. One of the film's sequels, *Rings* (2017), makes this dynamic of circulation more explicit, as Samara spreads herself across the internet, and much of the film's plot revolves around having to get others to watch Samara's viral video (pun intended).

Interestingly, *The Ring*'s status as a remake of the Japanese horror film *Ringu* (1998)—adapted from a Japanese novel of the same name—further cements its commercial undertones. The films' (*The Ring* and *Ringu*)'s story first mushroomed across Japan by moving between media, before finally metastasizing to the United States. With each step of this process, the story became more widely known, more influential, and more powerful, as Samara herself would desire. And this proliferation occurred only because the tale was successful (i.e., made money). American filmmakers saw an opportunity to remake *Ringu* for an American audience and thereby make money for themselves. Thus, capitalism became the vector for promulgating Samara's influence across the Pacific.

Hidden within this analysis is also a critique of media ethics. *Scary Movie 3* (2003), which parodies *The Ring*, depicts a news station obtaining Samara's videotape and airing it live. The news station's ruthless quest for ratings (and, by extension, revenue) causes it to risk thousands of lives. This development parallels that of *Rings*, in which a professor digitizes Samara's video and circulates it across the protagonists' college campus. The actions of these fictional characters, of broadcasting Samara's video(s), have also occurred in real-life, as filmmakers have adapted, recreated, and promoted Samara's tale through film. While *The Ring* may not be intended as a critique of a modern media culture which spreads videos and stories with little regard for the ethics of doing so (e.g., of the danger they may pose), its narrative hints at such issues nonetheless. Particularly, it should be noted that the proliferation by today's media relies predominantly on commercial or ideological motives, the same motives that Samara exploits.

By contrast, Bughuul's choice to use Super-8 film reels, as opposed to VHS tapes, aligns with his yearning for intimate, ritualistic murders that mirror the sacrifices he and Moloch desired in Babylonian times. Whereas Samara seeks to expand her influence, Bughuul seemingly targets a single family at a time by placing films of himself in the house of his previous victims. The Super-8 films look like home videos, and this appearance, along with the reels' relative lack of commercial appeal, underscore Bughuul's fixation on the family, which contrasts with Samara's focus on society in general.

Though these approaches differ considerably, they both recognize the power of fiction. Bughuul, for instance, understands (and so, exploits) the value of the home video in the family dynamic. Accordingly, each reel starts with the standard home video recordings of happy memories, though they are filmed from afar, as if by a voyeur. The shots' distance foreshadows the sinister turn where the reels become vectors for Bughuul's corrupting power over children. Here, one must also bear in mind that Bughuul's preoccupation with families stems from his association with Moloch, who, scholars believe, is related to a cult of dead ancestors.[53] Samara, meanwhile, apprehends fiction's (or media's) hold over society, and (un)consciously exploits the globalized world's capitalistic interests in adapting media, since each adaptation furthers her influence. Media sensationalism, trans-Pacific adaptations, and viral videos all aid her in this goal.

One could even say that, to some extent, Samara achieves her goal. Perhaps owing to the successes of *Ringu* and its adaptation, *The Ring*, the trope of a dangerous creature using film as its vector has become somewhat common. It manifests once again, for instance, in the 2008 Thai film *Coming Soon*, directed (in his directorial debut) by Sophon Sakdapisit. *Coming Soon* follows a group of workers at a movie theater in Thailand, where they are screening a new horror film, *Vengeful Spirit* (alternatively translated as *Evil Spirit*).

Desperate for money, the protagonist, Chen (Vorakan Rojchanawat), helps his friend and brother-in-law, Peoll, film a bootleg copy of *Vengeful Spirit*. Peoll disappears, however, without completing the bootleg. It falls on Chen, therefore, to search for his missing friend, allay his wife, Som's, anxiety at her brother's absence, and try to complete the bootleg himself, all while experiencing increasingly powerful hallucinations of a witch named Shomba, the antagonist of *Vengeful Spirit*.

Chen and Som (his estranged wife) begin working together after Som sees the bootleg copy of *Vengeful Spirit* on Peoll's camera. Fearing that *Vengeful Spirit* is the vector for an actual vengeful spirit, Chen and Som investigate the film's creation and discover it is based on a local legend, except that Shomba, while a real person, is alive and permanently hospitalized. This Shomba cannot be the vengeful spirit, and, as the couple soon learns, the spirit is actually the ghost of the actress who plays Shomba's character in *Vengeful Spirit*. This amateur actress died a gruesome death when, during the filming of a hanging scene, a safety wire snapped, and she strangled to death.

The crew, moreover, filmed her death, and this actual, accidental death appears in *Vengeful Spirit*. Realizing that the actress's spirit will attack anyone who watches her real, on-screen, death, Chen and Som hasten to destroy the film reel at the theater. They fail, however, as burning the film traps Chen in a causal loop but destroys neither the spirit nor the movie. Instead, the spirit appears on the movie theater's screen once again, before disappearing from the screen to kill Chen. She also kills Som off-screen; and *Coming Soon* concludes with *Vengeful Spirit* getting a wide release in Thailand as throngs of unsuspecting audience members prepare to watch it.

Whereas *Sinister* concerns a deity who uses images as a way to infect and sacrifice families and *The Ring* shows a malicious spirit who curses those who do not propagate her influence, *Coming Soon* portrays a spirit who is angry at the very film that carries her. The deceased actress (who remains unnamed) seeks revenge against anyone who watches *Vengeful Spirit* because she died in a freak accident while making the film. Were it not for the audience's willingness to watch such a horror film, this actress would not have been cast in the film and would not, therefore, have died when (and how) she did. Thus, she blames the film's viewers for her death and, more so, for enjoying watching her death on the big screen. This is especially evident when, before killing Chen, she asks him: "Want to see me die?"[54]

Coming Soon, therefore, compels the horror film audience to introspect about the consequences of their desire to watch such movies. Not only does the actress die during the film's creation, but her death also becomes the film's central spectacle. And in so doing, it becomes an exaggerated perversion of horror's tendency to make violence, itself, the principal attraction.⁵⁵ Furthermore, the actress appears to blame the audience, not just of *Vengeful Spirit*, but also of *Coming Soon*, for her demise, by asking "Want to see me die, right?" over the closing credits, as if she were talking to the actual film viewer (such as me or you).⁵⁶

On the one hand, forcing the viewers to assume such an introspective position on their own generic preferences opens the potential for *Coming Soon* to make an ethical statement. On the other hand, however, that same statement falls flat. After all, very few horror filmmakers—if any—are callous enough to make money by capturing and depicting real-life deaths on-screen. Such events are, thankfully, the realm of urban legend, and, in reality, watching a horror movie says little to nothing about a person's moral character.

Still, it would be uncharitable to assume Sakapisit is taking such an extreme stance; rather, what he posits is far more nuanced. When Chen is searching for Peoll, the audience sees a reflection of Chen in the mirror, where it appears as if the spirit of the dead actress is riding on his back. Symbolically, the spirit's position represents how audiences carry horror and the fictions they consume with them. Typically, such carrying is mental or emotional (through some horrific image or some feelings of terror or horror). However, *Coming Soon* concretizes this fictive affect and, in part, makes the audience consider how they do not consume fictions in a vacuum. Instead, they carry each story they hear, or each movie they watch, with them, even if only as a fleeting feeling divorced from a concrete source.

Coming Soon further reinforces this reading by having the corpses of the vengeful spirit's victims appear on screen in *Vengeful Spirit*. When the actress's spirit kills Peoll, Chen, and Som, they each become part of *Vengeful Spirit*'s mythos, and so, part of the fictional Shomba's story. Once an audience has encountered a movie, *Coming Soon* hereby alludes, they cannot escape that movie. Viewers give part of themselves to the film, even if that part is but roughly 90 minutes of their lives. Either way, the movie and audience become inextricably linked. Being the audience, the viewers give the movie their time and a reputation, while the movie, in turn, gives its viewers the affect. And, as with any relationship, this one is give-and-take and faces possible ethical concerns.

Vengeful Spirit's posters declare it "based on true events."⁵⁷ But, as Chen and Som find out, the film exaggerates those "events," by inventing a death that did not occur and a ghost that did not exist prior to the film's creation. Ironically, *Vengeful Spirit* creates the same vengeful spirit it purports to document, thereby indicating that, ethically, *Vengeful Spirit*'s creators are, at best, dubious. They inadvertently get an actress killed by forcing her to shoot numerous takes of a dangerous scene.

And if this were all the film's creators had done, the audience might still give them the benefit of the doubt and forgive them. After all, it is quite likely that they did not expect the safety rigging to fail and may not have intended to harm the actress. However, the movie's creators transgress (i.e., act unethically) when they intentionally make her actual death a part of the film. While they do not advertise this fact to the public, they knowingly exploit a woman's death for spectacle and consequent profit in a move most people would denounce as immoral. Furthermore, by concealing the horrible truth, they then make *Vengeful Spirit*'s audience unwittingly complicit in this immoral act.

As I previously stated, in real-life, examples of such extreme audience complicity are quite rare. But real-life instances of on-screen violence do exist, and as *Coming Soon* points out, such actions and films would not prevail if there were no audience for them. Thus, *Coming Soon* insinuates that audiences can become morally culpable for the fiction they consume, more so when such fiction is morally transgressive. I must clarify here, however, that this is a nuanced position, and it does not follow that all fictional portrayals of violence are immoral because, as I observed before, the act in *Vengeful Spirit*'s creation is rather exaggerated.

To connect this discussion of *Coming Soon* (and so, *Vengeful Spirit*) to my greater argument: all the preceding analyses demonstrate that, though fiction is a means to an end for Samara, Bughuul, and, to a lesser extent, the unnamed actress who plays Shomba, none of their corresponding films actually shows a true living story. I aver this because of a few significant details. First, even though they use fiction as their tool, both Samara and Bughuul predate the fictions that contain them. In contrast, while the deceased actress's spirit does not predate her fiction, *Vengeful Spirit*, she only exists as a specter because of the circumstances surrounding the film's creation. That is, for all three of these antagonists, their stories (or their visuals) are not living beings in themselves, but they carry living beings *within* them.

Manifesting a living story while keeping it encased in fiction is difficult, elusive, but there are several films—like those examined in the previous paragraphs—which attempt to do so anyway. The most recent film to purportedly do so is 2019's *Scary Stories to Tell in the Dark* (*Scary Stories*), directed by André Øvredal, and adapted from Alvin Schwartz's book series of the same name. The film showcases a group of kids—including the protagonist, Stella (Zoe Colletti)—who prank, and then flee from, a local bully, Tommy, and then seek safety in the car of a drifter, Ramón. They invite Ramón to join them as they proceed to explore the local haunted house, which originally belonged to the Bellows family. In the haunted house, they discover a secret room, wherein Tommy, who has followed, traps them.

An unseen force releases the kids from the room, however, and they depart, with Stella carrying a story book written by the infamous Sarah Bellows. That night, Stella witnesses a new story being written, of its own accord, in the book, with a red ink resembling blood. The story, entitled "Harold," narrates how a scarecrow comes to life, murders the local bully, Tommy, and then transforms him into an inanimate scarecrow. Stella fears the story may be true, and, upon investigating with Ramón, she discovers a scarecrow dressed in clothes identical to those Tommy had worn the previous day.

And soon even Stella's friends find themselves in similar yet unique predicaments, as new stories seemingly write themselves in the book, each revolving around a different protagonist who corresponds to a different member of the group. That is, on the appearance of each new story, a different member of the group becomes the protagonist, only to disappear—seemingly into nothingness—when that story's monster finds and attacks them. Auggie, for instance, disappears when a zombie with a missing toe grabs him; Chuck falls victim to the pale lady, who ends up absorbing him; and, while Ruth does not physically disappear like Aggie and Chuck do, she is institutionalized after what appears to be a zit turns out to be an insect bite from which erupts a tsunami of spiders.

As these harrowing and traumatizing stories are being fabricated and lived, Stella and Ramón discover that Sarah Bellows is not the monster most believe her to be. Rather, Sarah's family tortured her until she went insane after she tried to expose to the townsfolk that her family was consciously poisoning the town's water supply with mercury deposits. As the film reaches its climax with more monsters, Stella, understanding the injustices Sarah suffered, appeases Sarah's spirit by promising to write—and shed light on—the truth about Sarah Bellows. As Stella begins to pen the true story in Sarah's book, using blood as ink, both Sarah's spirit and the monster chasing Ramón disappear. The movie concludes with Stella resolving to rescue her missing friends, believing they are still alive, somehow living through the stories she believes they are trapped in.

Sarah Bellows presents a sharp contrast to Bughuul and Samara. Of the three, Sarah alone is a tragic character in her own right. After all, both Bughuul and Samara are malevolent. Bughuul, especially, makes no effort to hide his violence, for, as I mentioned earlier, *Sinister 2* (2015) reveals that Bughuul recruits new children by having them watch tapes of previous murders. Samara, meanwhile, may feign innocence, but, as Rachel discovers, she has been malicious since childhood, and the tapes merely provide her with more opportunities to harm others. Sarah, unlike Bughuul and Samara, was benevolent in life and only became evil after her brothers tortured her. In this way, Sarah aligns most with the ghost in *Coming Soon*. Like Bughuul and Samara, however, Sarah also predates her fictions, which means that *Scary Stories*, like *Sinister* and *The Ring*, does not show a true living story.

Sarah's family makes her a monster, and the town she tried to save continues to wrong her in death by perpetuating her family's slanderous lies about her. Her family subjects her to inhumane amounts of electroshock therapy for trying to do the right thing, while the town repays her kindness—albeit unknowingly—by defaming her as a monster when, in fact, she was the least monstrous of her family. Thus wronged, it is unsurprising she becomes a malicious spirit, lashing out at the world around her. Thus, *Scary Stories* demonstrates that the local urban legend of a monster helps create that very monster. It indicates that the tales (rumors, gossip) circulated about Sarah influence her transition from victim to vengeful spirit, for, she remains obsessed with her story. This obsession continues even after she attacks Stella's group, and her spiteful vindictiveness ends only after Stella narrates the truth about Sarah's life.

I use the word "spiteful" because the stories Sarah (or her spirit) writes in her book also blend fiction with reality, as they translate the characters' fears into reality. This appears most prominently with Chuck and Ramón, as the creature that absorbs Chuck is the monster from his nightmares, while "The Jangly Man" that attacks Ramón is a monster from an old campfire story Ramón's brother told him. Yet, it is not clear that Sarah undertakes this same process with every character (each of the new protagonists of her stories). Tommy, for instance, does not appear to be afraid of the scarecrow, Harold. Rather, he strikes it with a baseball bat for sheer amusement.

This discrepancy indicates that Sarah's modus operandi is more inconsistent than either Bughuul's or Samara's is. Moreover, even though the stories Sarah pens play out in real life, almost in real-time, it becomes undeniably clear, throughout the film, that her stories are not, in fact, living fictions. There is a being (Sarah) behind the tales, who is acting as an author and making physical her literary creations, but the narrative itself is not alive. Though it appears otherwise when the red ink (blood) scrawls across the page, it is Sarah's spirit penning the stories; the stories are not writing themselves.

Thus, though *Scary Stories* appears to profess a living story at first glance, a closer examination proves that it does not have one. The film remains useful in the context of this book, however, as it reinforces just how elusive living stories are in liminal horror films. Additionally, *Scary Stories*, in conjunction with *Sinister*, *The Ring*, and *Coming Soon*, helps identify a trait that manifests variedly and conditionally in these films that try to showcase living stories: a character's transformation, by implication, into fiction either via death or disappearance into nothingness.

I specifically clarify "by implication" because these transformations are both erratic and subjective. One need only to look at the differences in the various fictionalizations I have discussed thus far to understand the fickleness of this "trait." For instance, Ellison's family (in *Sinister*) becomes stories contained within Super 8 tapes *after* they die a gruesome death; the amateur actress (in *Coming Soon*) becomes the eponymous vengeful spirit while filming the corresponding fiction; Auggie and Chuck, Stella believes, are trapped in stories (though she says nothing of the sort about Tommy, who, after his death, becomes a scarecrow); and even Samara's victims tangentially (and not directly) become fictional, through the legend of the videotape that kills.

Thus, what I identity as a "trait" is fickle, mutable, and often difficult to discern. Indeed, the fictionalization of once living characters becomes even harder to discern in the 2001 Japanese film *Pulse (Kairo)*, directed by Kiyoshi Kurosawa. *Pulse* presents (non-chronologically) the story of several young adults in Tokyo encountering a supernatural force that infects people via the internet and then absorbs them. One by one, the protagonists see "ghosts," who begin to haunt them, and, one by one, they commit suicide and disappear, leaving black stains on the exact places (or spots) of their deaths. As the story progresses, Tokyo becomes increasingly depopulated. The media reports numerous missing people, and the last surviving protagonist, Michi, flees the country and sets sail for Latin America, where, she hopes, there may still be some civilization left.

Extant scholarship on *Pulse* has focused largely on how the film reflects Japanese sociocultural concerns and the dangers of the digital age. Adam Lovasz, for instance, notes how the film reflects worries about social isolation in the digital age, an observation that Gilles A. Viennot supports.[58] Central to *Pulse* is graduate student Yoshikazi's computer program that (supposedly) models the interactions of humans and ghosts. This program depicts a series of dots floating around on screen before disappearing. Viennot observes that the dots disappear when they are either too far from or too close to one another.[59] Thus, the dots mirror the plight of humans in social isolation: if they become too isolated, they suffer, and if they get too close to others, they suffer because of their anxiety. Either way, their position is precarious.

Viennot and Lovasz provide enlightening readings of this rather arcane film, but their analyses focus on *Pulse*'s sociocultural and sociotechnological aspects. Consequently, there is scope for me to discuss the liminality and ghosts within the movie's story. To be sure, ghosts are somewhat liminal figures in and of themselves since they exist between the worlds of the living and the dead, without fully belonging to either category. This liminality has a clear visual marking in *Pulse*: the black stains

Two—Shattered Screens and Punctured Skin   49

characters leave behind whenever they pass into the ghostly realm.[60] These stains provide passages for the characters.

Kawashima, for example, passes in and out of his stain. That is, characters whom the ghostly realm absorbs can pass in and out of the living world through the stain they left when they got absorbed in the first place. Thus, *Pulse* focuses the audience's attention on the notion of passageways between worlds and, moreover, on the slippage of entities between these different modes of existence: living and dead, physical and digital.

Given the analyses above, I—as well as the reader—would be remiss to not put living and physical and dead and digital on (roughly) equal footing. In *Pulse*, the ghosts weaponize computers against the living, consequently making the consumption of digital media dangerous, and rendering the internet a vector for a pandemic. Technology itself is the passage between worlds in *Pulse*, and connecting his computer to the internet dooms Kawashima to death. However, the film remains ambiguous about Kawashima's actual death, if death implies that one can no longer communicate with the living.

At the end of the movie, Michi says that she is "alone with [her] last friend in the world…."[61] Whereas Viennot argues that Michi is referring to the ship's other passenger as her last friend, it is equally possible that Michi is, instead, referring to Kawashima, whom Michi observes sitting in her ship cabin before he disappears into his stain.[62] Given how she times her statement about her last friend, and given her existent relationship with Kawashima (forged through quick acquaintance during the pandemic), she may well be referring to him and not the ship passenger as her friend. Considering this nuanced possibility—that Kawashima is actually the "friend" Michi is referring to—is important, for it changes the dynamic of what *Pulse* is presenting, which, in turn, reinforces my assessment that the film demonstrates the slipperiness between its different worlds (living and dead, and, physical and digital) and also the ability to cross-communicate between them.

Despite this movement and cross-communication between contrasting yet interconnected worlds, *Pulse* does not showcase a true, living story. Rather, in *Pulse*, ghosts use digital media to affect the world of the living. Though the audience cannot ascertain what, exactly, drives the ghosts in *Pulse*, viewers can still infer that the ghosts are making the internet dangerous and that internet is not inherently hazardous. Thus, as with the other films in this section, *Pulse*'s stories remain vectors for threatening entities. In all these films then, the fictions themselves remain dead, though powerful. That formulation, however, provides a new way of looking at this phenomenon of dangerous fictions. In *Sinister, The Ring, Coming Soon, Scary Stories*, and *Pulse*, fictions contain powerful entities. In other films, however, fictions are, themselves, powerful entities, and this new formulation of fictions as inherently powerful might give us insight into living stories, perhaps the greatest bastion of liminality. A true living story would, after all, dissolve any notions of a barrier between the real and the fictional, the living and the dead.

One promising film is John Carpenter's 2005 entry into the *Masters of Horror* series, *Cigarette Burns*. In it, a cash-strapped theater owner—and rare film aficionado—Kirby Sweetman (Norman Reedus) meets eccentric billionaire Bellinger (Udo Kier), who hires him to track down a copy of *La Fin Absolue Du Monde* (translation: *The Absolute End of the World*). The film is legendary in its notoriety, as, during its sole screening, its audience started rioting and committing homicides. Most believe the film lost and its only copy destroyed. Kirby himself only knows the film by its mythos. Bellinger is confident, however, that the film survives, as he has located one of its cast members, a strange, willowy being (billed as such in the credits) who claims to be connected to the film and, thus, is assured of its continued existence.

Based on this source, Bellinger offers Kirby $200,000, all expenses paid, and the chance for an exclusive two week run of *La Fin Absolue Du Monde* if Kirby can find it. Desperate to pay his father-in-law back, Kirby accepts and begins hunting for the lost print. His journey takes him first to New York, where he finds Meyers, a critic present at the film's one and only screening. Meyers has become insane, however, and spends all his time typing furiously to complete his review of the movie, the pages of which fill the room where he writes. Kirby then goes to Paris, where his friend, Henri, in the French Film Archives confirms, after much prodding from Kirby, that *La Fin Absolue Du Monde* still exists. Though Henri does not have the film, he points Kirby toward someone who might know where it is. Henri warns Kirby, though, that the film is dangerous. He claims he was the projectionist at a private screening, where—once again—the audience erupted in violence and where the fingers on his left hand fused together when he tried to stop the film from playing. He also tells Kirby that the hallucinations Kirby is experiencing will only get worse as he gets closer to finding the film.

Undaunted, Kirby visits the man Henri told him about, a French snuff film director who, like Bellinger, collects memorabilia from *La Fin Absolue Du Monde*. The director tries to kill Kirby as part of a new snuff film, but Kirby manages to mortally wound him in self-defense. With his dying breaths, the snuff film director informs Kirby that the movie's print is with Katja Bakavic, the widow of the film's reclusive director, Hans Bakavic. Armed with this information, Kirby flies to Vancouver and meets Katja, who is sympathetic to Kirby's pain and tells him about how the film drove her husband insane, leading him to slit Katja's throat before committing suicide. As a testament to this event, Katja unwinds her scarf to show Kirby the scar encircling her neck. She then lets him take the film, remarking that Kirby's hallucinations indicate the film has "marked" him and, so, it is too late for him anyway.⁶³

With the print in hand, Kirby returns home, delivers the film to Bellinger, and finds his father-in-law has chained Kirby's theater closed. Before he can contact his father-in-law, however, Bellinger calls Kirby, who rushes back to the billionaire's mansion. There, he discovers that Bellinger and his butler have mutilated themselves in response to watching the film. When he attempts to flee, Kirby encounters his father-in-law, who followed him to the mansion and now holds him at gunpoint. They struggle, and the film cuts to Kirby as he wakes up in Bellinger's private theater and sees his father-in-law watching the end of *La Fin Absolue Du Monde*. Kirby then kills his father-in-law before watching the film and shooting himself in the head. The film closes with the strange, willowy being from earlier walking past Kirby's corpse, carrying the film reels for *La Fin Absolue Du Monde*, and thanking Kirby for retrieving them.

As this summary shows, *Cigarette Burns* alters the formula of the preceding movies by showing a fiction (*La Fin*) that is dangerous on its own accord. There is no monster in *Cigarette Burns*, no creature or spirit living through celluloid. If anything, the celluloid is alive, if unconscious. Its magic is such that it can affect people who have not even seen it, as Katja, Henri, and Meyers all note it has done to Kirby. While the audience does not see any creature contained in the film, they do learn something about the circumstances of the film's creation and why it has such a profound effect on its viewers.

The snuff film director remarks to Kirby: "Something happens when you point a camera at something terrible. The resulting film takes on power."⁶⁴ He further elaborates: "What if you got hold of an angel, a divine being with God's blood flowing through its veins? And what if you sacrificed it on camera? Something that profound, that personal, it changes everything."⁶⁵ Later, Katja adds more details, repeating what Hans told her: "The producers of this film produce many things: chaos, sorrow, suffering, famine.... Evil, he would say, was evil. Does a name really matter?"⁶⁶

With such striking words, both the snuff film director and Katja provide the audience with a clear idea of how Bakavic made his infamous film so powerful: he made a deal with the devil (or some other sufficiently powerful evil entity) who, in turn, provided the film's director with an angel (the willowy being), whom Bakavic mutilated on screen by having its wings cut off. This act of profanity against God cursed the film with a powerful magic that no mortal, not even Bakavic himself, could handle. In fact, this magic is so powerful it transcends the medium of film, as well as the realm of fiction, to reshape the reality around it. Moreover, while the willowy being does claim that its soul is bound to the film, the film itself is not a vector for the being's influence, for the willowy being remains chained in Bellinger's mansion.[67]

Meyers tells Kirby: "We trust filmmakers. We sit in the dark, daring them to affect us, trusting they won't go too far."[68] Bakavic, however, goes too far by creating a film that is so profoundly disturbing it mentally unhinges everyone who watches it. Here, Carpenter takes the opportunity to comment on the nature of film and film-audience relations. Films are an experiential media, designed (at least in theatrical releases) to be consumed in the dark, and in one sitting. In a sense, the movie theater audience is captive. Sitting rapt before the screen as the film's story plays out, the viewers in the theater have no control over the proceedings and no chance to either stop them or turn them off. Here, the viewers are in a vulnerable position, and the filmmaker, if only for a moment, has them cornered. In real life, however, this vulnerability is limited, for the audiences can simply walk out. Carpenter, therefore, exaggerates the real-life situation for dramatic and critical effect.

The idea that a film can contain magic which can kill its audience is certainly liminal, but *Cigarette Burns* goes even beyond that. As Kirby gets closer to finding *La Fin*, he experiences increasingly powerful hallucinations contained in the "cigarette burns" that give Carpenter's film its name.[69] Cigarette burns are a type of flare that occurs on celluloid, and Kirby's employee says they cue the audience that something good is coming.[70] While he searches for *La Fin*, Kirby sees his dead wife, Annie, in cigarette burns that appear in the air around him, as if he were existing on a piece of film. Not only do these burns blur the boundary between Kirby and the movie he searches for, but they also blur the boundary between Kirby and the viewing audience, by reminding viewers that Kirby is but a character in a film, which, in turn, breaks the audience's immersion in the narrative. However, this break in the immersion does not take the audience out of the story; rather, the collapsing border between film and reality ensures that the film travels with its viewers.

It is quite likely that this affect varies from viewer to viewer, but by merely presenting it, *Cigarette Burns* suggests that, despite appearing to be distinct, both the audience and the film can occupy the same ontological space, and that fiction can be reality itself, by being a vector for profane and dangerous truths. Here, I must also note that some audience members might find it difficult to regard this affect with seriousness; after all, viewers are aware that, when they watch *Cigarette Burns*, they are watching a piece of fiction. It may be an exceedingly clever piece of meta-fiction, but it is fiction, nonetheless. There is no *La Fin*. But what if there was?

Two—Shattered Screens and Punctured Skin 53

Whereas *Cigarette Burns*, *The Ring*, and *Ringu* all claim to include films (within them) that kill their viewers, one film actually does: *Antrum: The Deadliest Film Ever Made*.[71] At least, that is what *Antrum: The Deadliest Film Ever Made* promises in its opening minutes, which purport to document the history of a lost cult movie. The narrator informs the audience that: "Since the dawn of cinema, we've been making movies about hell and the devil. And they've been just films, so they've been safe. *Antrum* is not safe."[72] *Antrum*, she tells us, first screened in Budapest in 1988, where the theater caught fire, and a second time in California, in 1993, with horrifying results, including the death of a pregnant woman. Following these events, the film earned notoriety for being cursed, and all copies of it seemingly disappeared—until now, that is. The narrator reveals that the documentary's crew has discovered a print of the film at an estate sale and are now able to play the film for the audience (that is, for us, the viewers). The narrator warns that the documentary's producers want to caution audiences about the film's contents, and a disclaimer flashes on the screen, complete with a timer until *Antrum* itself starts playing. When the timer expires, *Antrum* begins.

The plot of *Antrum* proper follows a pair of siblings, teenager Oralee (Nicole Tompkins) and her young brother, Nathan, who is distraught because he believes the soul of his dead dog, Maxine, is trapped in hell. Oralee, however, informs Nathan that her classmate, Ike, has told her how to redeem Maxine and let her soul into heaven. To do this, the two hike into the forest and set up camp, where they begin digging into the ground. Oralee tells Nathan they are in the forest where Satan landed after God cast him out of heaven, and they are digging at the entrance, or antrum, to hell. Once they dig deep enough, they will free Maxine's soul.

As they camp and dig, however, they encounter increasingly bizarre and frightening images. Nathan, for instance, witnesses a boatman steering a sitting, naked woman across the nearby lake. Moreover, the film itself begins to glitch, showing occult imagery in cigarette burns and—soon after Nathan sees the boatman—cutting to a devilish face that stares into the camera for an extended period. Matters get worse, however, as Oralee and Nathan also discover a cult in an old junkyard in the forest. The cult's two members have a statue of Baphomet atop a fire, and the screams from inside the statue indicate they use it as a brazen bull.[73]

Fearing for their lives, Oralee and Nathan try to flee the forest. Somehow, however, they run in a big circle and find themselves back at their camp, where Oralee admits to Nathan that she fabricated the story about Ike as well as the idea of digging to hell to free Maxine's soul. She confesses she made up the tale—and everything about it—in an effort to make him stop worrying about Maxine. The next day, the cultists track down and tranquilize Oralee and Nathan, who, upon waking up, find themselves in the cultists' junkyard. Oralee is locked in a cage, while the cultists are trying to load Nathan into the brazen bull. Oralee, however, manages to free herself and retrieve a revolver, which she uses to shoot both the cultists, thereby saving Nathan.

Back in the forest, Nathan traces a large chain to a hunting trap pinning the leg of a husky. He frees the dog's leg and smiles as it runs off. Text then appears on the screen, saying "The End," but the film immediately cuts back to Oralee looking for Nathan in the forest. She panics, as she begins seeing demonic figures in the trees surrounding her. After burning the pages of the book wherein she inscribed the ritual for her and Nathan to complete, she hides in their tent, the revolver in her hand. As an exhausted Nathan approaches the outside of the tent, Oralee raises the gun, not sure what or who is approaching. *Antrum* then reaches its conclusion, and the narrator informs the viewers that they "have just watched *Antrum* in its entirety."[74] Some interviews play during the credits, and the movie ends.

The interviews during the credits provide some tools to help the audience understand why *Antrum* is so dangerous. A scholar explains that the sigils appearing in the film's cigarette burns are, in fact, sigils of the demon Astaroth. Alarmingly, these sigils appear over 170 times during the film.[75] The scholar goes on to explain that the sigil is an invitation for Astaroth to enter those exposed to it.[76] Thus, some of the film's danger comes from the demonic force that uses the movie as a vector for its influence, a trope the reader will, undoubtedly, be familiar with by this point in the discussion. Moreover, if the reader thinks this discussion is starting to seem too fantastic to be real, that is only because it is.

Directed by David Amito and Michael Laicini, and released in 2018, *Antrum: The Deadliest Film Ever Made* is a mockumentary that pretends to tell the "true" story of an actual film named *Antrum*, which plays out—in its entirety—during the middle of the mockumentary; the mockumentary acts as a framing device for the "actual film." This, however, is a contrivance, for both the mockumentary and the "actual film" are works of fiction. *Antrum* (the film within) only exists in *Antrum: The Deadliest Film Ever Made* (the mockumentary), and some basic research on the internet confirms this fact.

Antrum: The Deadliest Film Ever Made has its own Wikipedia page, which makes its fictionality clear. For further evidence of this fabrication, one can observe that Nicole Tompkins (who plays Oralee in the film) is too young to have starred in the film back in 1979 (which is when *Antrum* was supposedly filmed); those who disbelieve this can find Tompkins' public profile on the casting site *Backstage*.[77] Still, that *Antrum* can push audiences to ask whether they are watching something real (regardless of what their common sense tells them), is a testament to the power a declaration of reality can carry. This declaration is, in fact, so powerful that one of the top recommended questions about the film on Google search is whether *Antrum*, the film-within-a-film, is real.

Antrum, within its first twenty minutes, announces its similarities to *Cigarette Burns*, even mentioning the latter by name; however, these claims of containing a film that kills fall flat the moment its viewers realize the mockumentary is merely playing on the same tropes several other films use.[78] Yet, I would be remiss to reject *Antrum* here, as it does distinguish itself from similar movies. *Antrum*'s distinction leads me to classify it under—what I dub—the "killer videotape" sub-genre, which lies within the sub-genre of liminal horror. I identify this sub-sub-genre of the "killer videotape" because

i. *Antrum* explicitly references other films in its sub-genre as works of fiction, thereby asserting its reality over and above those other films, and,
ii. the interviews at the film's conclusion reference the phenomenon of binaural beats, which the mockumentary claims can induce hallucinations.

These two aspects indicate that *Antrum* appeals to beliefs in pseudoscience, as well as in demonology, to trick audiences into a state of heightened receptivity to the film's lofty claims.

To paraphrase as well as explicate: *Antrum* professes to show a film that can kill its viewers, and, to make the film more affective (though still nowhere near as affective as a film that can literally kill its viewers), the filmmakers adduce various systems of belief to coax the viewers into believing in the film's power. These appeals can push viewers to think *Antrum*'s power lies either in inviting a demon or inducing hallucinations and/or psychosomatic discomfort. If these warnings (and appeals) can prime the audience to feel any of their corresponding emotions (like fear, discomfort, or confusion), then *Antrum* has achieved its goal (which is evident, as I mentioned earlier, from one of the recommended Google searches for *Antrum* being whether the film is real or not).

Thus, *Antrum* effectively uses its framing device to heighten the horror of its film-within-a-film, that is the "real" *Antrum*. It is highly probable that without its frame narrative the film's power would diminish. In the frame narrative's absence, the viewers would not receive any cautionary warning(s), which, consequently, would (possibly) make the viewers less apprehensive about the film. Moreover, the lack of its frame narrative would also negate the effect of the appeals *Antrum* uses, which, in turn, could make its audience immune to—and skeptical about—its claim to reality.

That is to say, the appeals contained within its frame help ensure the audience regards *Antrum* with seriousness and trepidation. This appears, for instance, in the way the film splits its appeals along the lines of both superstition and rationality. For those who believe in the former, it appeals to demonology and the belief that the spectators themselves can invite demons in. For those who believe in the latter, it appeals to the belief that subliminal sound and messages can worm their way into the audience's minds.

Here, I must note that, though the exact effects of binaural beats are still unclear, there is some evidence to suggest they can heighten levels of vigilance.[79] Such an effect would be useful for a horror film that wants to convince its viewers that they are watching a cursed film that can kill them. What is even more important, however, is that *Antrum* waits until the very end of the film to announce these matters to the audience. It is during the interviews, in the final mockumentary portion, that the film's creators state that beliefs can significantly influence the audience and that fear can make stuff real.[80]

Placing this material at the end of the film is strategic, for it allows the filmmakers to incite the audience into reflecting on the film they have just seen. Typically, the vast majority of audience members will not believe that watching a film can kill them; perhaps no audience members will. But when *Antrum* informs its viewers—through these final, staged interviews—that fear can make beliefs real and that beliefs can be implicit, it compels viewers to think about the film and ponder over how it has affected them. It is quite likely that such a striking move will make the audience regard the film in a new light, thereby making *Antrum* inherently affective and impactful. As the filmmakers hope, the interviews will goad at least some viewers into thinking about the movie long after its conclusion.

Antrum, consequently, is an interesting example of liminal horror because it knowingly situates itself within its sub-genre and keeps destabilizing its audience throughout its narrative. First, the mockumentary frame device makes certain audience members (including myself) curious enough to research whether there was an *Antrum* that predated the documentary (there is not). Thus, in planting this question in the audience's mind, the film transposes its audience from a pure reception mode to an apprehensive, inquisitive mode wherein the audience questions what is to come. It is useful for *Antrum* to keep its viewers in this frame of mind because doing so goads the viewers to cogitate about the film, including the sigils of Astaroth and the binaural beats.

The more the audience reflects on these matters, the more their fascination with the film can grow. And the more their fascination with the film grows, the more their doubt can grow. *Antrum* implants a seed when it suggests the film can hurt even skeptics, and it fertilizes the soil when it raises the aforementioned questions (e.g., about the film's veracity) in the viewers' minds. While *Antrum* cannot create a true killer videotape, it can create an interesting (if very distant) facsimile of one when it spreads its subliminal roots in the viewers' consciousness.

Here, I would also like to point out that when considering *Antrum*, we (the audience as well as I) are considering a film in which the line between fiction and reality is very unclear. The "real" *Antrum* begins on an extreme close-up of a dog's nose, the contours of which appear unrecognizable, as the camera defamiliarizes the audience from what they are looking at. In this scene, the grainy footage, the yellow, washed out, colors, and the bizarre music make the events seem alien, as if to convey to the audience that the film they are watching is, indeed, special. *Antrum*, in other words, wholly embraces the uncanny to make its audience uncomfortable. It induces viewers to think they are looking into a world like theirs but still, somehow, unrecognizable.

This defamiliarizing effect becomes immediately apparent if one questions, for instance, where, exactly, *Antrum* takes place. The film's credits are in a sort of Cyrillic alphabet, which situates the movie somewhere in Eastern Europe. Yet, Oralee and Nathan enter a suicide forest (the most famous of which is in Japan), and they meet a Japanese man, who is preparing to commit seppuku there. These three elements (suicide forest, Japanese man, and seppuku) all suggest the film's location is Japan, rather far away from Eastern Europe. Contrariwise, Oralee, Nathan, and their mother all speak fluent English, the forest's sign is also in English, and the narrator claims the one extant copy of *Antrum* appeared in an estate sell in Connecticut. In contrast to the previous three elements, these three factors indicate the film may be American (the actual mockumentary is).

Additionally, as if only to muddy the waters further, the version of hell Oralee conceives is an amalgamation of various depictions of the underworld. She includes the layers of Dante's *Inferno* (Italian), Cerberus (Greek), and Satan's fall to earth (Judeo-Christian/Middle Eastern). Moreover, the boatsman Nathan sees resembles Charon rowing a departed soul down the River Styx, an image that adds more notions of the afterlife as it appears in Greek mythology. All these disparate elements from different cultures subsequently make it very difficult to pin down where the film takes place. Thus divorced from a readily identifiable cultural or geographic context, the audience flounders with the film's elements and meaning, which progressively become harder to predict.

Overall, therefore, *Antrum* presents an interesting and destabilizing viewing experience that enables viewers to ponder over the role and importance of audience self-reflexivity in liminal horror. Earlier, I observed that

Found Footage 3-D's metafictional elements manage to not alienate its audience, despite establishing the film's fictionality. *Antrum*, however, shows another method of achieving audience retention. Whereas films such as *3-D* and *Scream* get audiences to think about generic constraints, *Antrum* encourages its audience to participate in the breaching of the line between reality and fiction. Unlike *3-D*, *Scream* invites its audience to play by filling itself to the brim with references to the horror genre. *Antrum* takes this idea even further, though, as it not only references its own genre (albeit less playfully than *Scream* does) but also pushes its audience to introspect, an action that may make a reality of—and from—the film's fiction.

And yet, despite its brilliant strategy and showcasing of liminality, *Antrum*, like all the other films in this section, does not portray a true living story. The film-within-a-film, *Antrum*, is the vector, the mockumentary claims, for Astaroth and binaural sounds. The story itself, therefore, is not alive, and this fact places *Antrum* in the same category as *Scary Stories*, *Sinister*, *The Ring*, *Coming Soon*, and even (to some extent) *Pulse*, all of which promise (if implicitly) "living stories" but do not deliver on it (in the sense of actually having stories/fictions that are alive and, hence, real). Furthermore, while the listed above do present entities that occupy fictions (especially after their deaths, transformations into animate objects, or disappearances into nothingness), *Cigarette Burns* and *Antrum*, in contrast, do not illustrate even that, though they effectively portray that fictions can be dangerous.

Consequently, these examples suggest the "trait" of characters transforming into fictions via death is actually fickle and mutable, varying in occurrence between films and characters. Because of its capriciousness, this similarity-based trait is not a definitively characterizing feature of liminal horror films. Nonetheless, identifying and analyzing it thoroughly is vital, for it suggests an inverse movement, that is, a movement from reality into fiction, which is another manifestation of liminality in horror. Moreover, though these instances are both infrequent and ambiguous, they also denote the diverse ways in which certain horror movies create a convergence between the real and the fictional (or unreal), thereby exemplifying liminality in a hitherto unexplored manner. That manner is the supposed "contagiousness" of fiction, which appears in *Videodrome* (1983), directed by David Cronenberg.

Videodrome follows the story of Max Renn (James Woods), the president of a seedy television station. While on the lookout for new material to broadcast, Max discovers the eponymous program (named "Videodrome" in the film's universe), which shows the torture of unnamed prisoners. In trying to decipher and trace the program's origins, he begins hallucinating, which diminishes his ability to distinguish reality from fiction. He does, however, learn the truth. The eponymous program is designed to kill its viewers by causing brain tumors, and this design—Videodrome's purpose—stems from a socially conservative ideology, which aims to end the sort of smut Max airs on TV. To this end, Videodrome (or, more accurately, the people behind it) brainwash Max into murdering his colleagues at the station. Later, he also kills Videodrome's creators before shooting himself in the head, ostensibly committing suicide.

Videodrome proves useful for analyzing liminality in horror because it affords a different perspective into fictions that are powerful enough to irrevocably affect their viewers (as in *Sinister* and *The Ring*), and does so by portraying the fiction itself to be alive instead of merely being a vector for another sentient being (unlike in *Sinister*, *The Ring*, and *Scary Stories*). *Videodrome*'s author mouthpiece (i.e., the figure through which the filmmaker communicates his or her views on the subject) is Professor Brian O'Blivion, an avatar for real-life philosopher Marshall McLuhan, who believes television is our new mind's eye.[81]

O'Blivion states: "The television screen is the retina of the mind's eye. Therefore, the television screen is part of the physical structure of the brain. Therefore, whatever appears on the television screen emerges as pure experience for those who watch it. Therefore, television is reality and reality is—less than television."[82] McLuhan explains this concept further when he elucidates his phrase "the medium is the massage":

> And so the title is intended to draw attention to the fact that a medium is not something neutral—it does something to people. It takes hold of them. It rubs them off, it massages them and bumps them around, chiropractically, as it were, and the general roughing up that any new society gets from a medium, especially a new medium, is what is intended in that title.[83]

Thus, both O'Blivion and his real-life counterpart view fiction as transformative. Fiction (in each of its media) grabs hold of—and molds—its audience, and this effect is more prominent with modern media, which, at the time of *Videodrome*'s release, would have been television and film. Today, one could lump the internet and virtual reality into this category as well.

Videodrome's preferred medium, however, is television, which the movie represents with signals, screens, and video tapes. Max first learns of the eponymous program as a signal, a seemingly illicit broadcast. He then begins experiencing this signal through the mediator of the screen, before finally becoming a literal receptacle for the program's videotapes when a large opening appears in his abdomen. The sequence, like the fiction itself, is transformative, and it gradually concretizes and embodies the electric, the intangible. A signal needs a receiver, and anyone trying to comprehend television signals will require that receiver to get and decode the transmitted signals.

Then, they would need a screen to present the now two-dimensionally solidified image. Even then, though the signal will appear on a screen, the fiction itself will remain out of reach, beyond anyone's physical grasp. *Videodrome* shows this facet through Max's and Harlan's inability to hold the signal for long. Max wants Harlan to keep Videodrome on the screen, but, as Harlan explains, the broadcaster has a "descrambler scrambler," because of which they lose the signal.[84] Signals, therefore, are fleeting. VHS tapes, however, are not. They are solid. They can be grasped and inserted into the appropriate port(s). In this sense, they are the format that most closely resembles that of the human body, a resemblance which appears explicitly in the film.[85]

Like the human body, a VHS tape is a solid, tangible form that contains a world within it. The film tangibly fuses these two distinct media through the deterioration of Max's condition, which opens a large, vagina-like gash in his abdomen. This opening in Max's corporeal form allows the film's antagonist, Barry Convex, to insert VHS tapes directly into Max's body, and therefore, Max himself. These tapes, which reprogram Max's mind and cause him to murder his colleagues, pulsate like living beings. Thus, they fulfill O'Blivion's prophecy of television as reality. Whereas earlier in the movie, O'Blivion's statements carry the weighty air of pseudo-philosophical nonsense, the later revelations of Videodrome's origins vindicate him and his beliefs. Film literally enters *Videodrome*'s protagonist and rewrites his brain, thereby becoming a literal part of him and his mind, per O'Blivion's prediction.

Videodrome, therefore, makes literal that which *Scream* and the rest of my films thus far have only made implicit. Recall how *Scream* hints that the television screen is permeable by having Ghostface symbolically smash through it. *The Ring* and *Sinister* perform similar actions by having their monsters exit out of the screen and enter it, respectively.[86] *Videodrome*, however, shows Max literally entering a television screen when he sticks his head inside his TV. Though this act is, most likely, a hallucination, it nevertheless aligns with the filmic blurring of fiction and reality, represented in the VHS tapes that enter—and pulse within—Max's body when it becomes a VCR.

To be clear, however: though these tapes, these fictions, force Max to murder, it is not the fiction itself that is malicious. Rather, here as in the previously discussed films, fiction is a tool, if still a living one. Despite being named Civic-TV, Max's station (ironically) peddles softcore pornography and other scandalous material. This controversial content makes Max, and his station, the target of social conservatives, who weaponize Videodrome against those they deem are corrupting western society's moral fabric. Barry and Harlan explain to Max how the smut he broadcasts on television makes its viewers weaker and less capable of carrying the mantle of western society. In doing so, Barry and Harlan acknowledge fiction's corrupting power and parrot the sentiments of those who demonize violent fiction in real-life and blame it for societal ills (the likes of whom I discussed earlier while referencing the James Bulger case).

Barry and Harlan's goal, then, is to instill Videodrome in Civic-TV's broadcasts so they can kill off those who consume this immoral material, thereby cleansing western society according to their norms. Here, Cronenberg targets those who criticize horror fiction. And if Barry and Harlan's actions are insufficient for us—the audience—to perceive this critique, we should consider why they choose violent media to communicate the Videodrome signal. They explain to Max that exposure to violence opens one's mind to Videodrome. Thus, violent imagery (and, by extension, the horror genre) is the preferable medium for achieving their socially conservative agenda. Ergo, Cronenberg alludes to the common critique that horror is an agent of the status quo while defending horror itself from the social agenda.[87]

Within the film's universe, Max is, at worst, an unwitting pawn, and not an intentional agent, in Videodrome's design. It is the participants in the political movement behind Videodrome who weaponize horror as a vehicle for social control. Those invested in horror do not perform this act, nor do they seem to agree with it. Max is sleazy, as he enthusiastically peddles smut and flirts with Nikki while being interviewed on live television. However, Max is not as immoral as Barry Convex.

Both Max and Barry perform acts of insertion in the film. Max penetrates Nikki's ear with a needle while they watch Videodrome together, and Barry inserts a VHS tape into Max's stomach gash. The first act seems more violent on its face. It is, after all, an act designed to elicit pain. But the pain it elicits is at the border of sadomasochistic pleasure. Nikki wants Max to do it; in fact, it is her idea. This sexual act therefore underscores who Max is: a man whose dubious morality springs from his catering to people's wants. Max does not tell people what they desire. Rather, he responds to market forces. This is evident, most explicitly, in the marketplace of his sexual relationship with Nikki. Despite initially being averse to the idea, he gives Nikki what she wants; his immorality is performative, done only to satisfy an audience. From this relationship, one gets the sense Max would successfully find a different niche if there were not a pre-existing demand for the softcore pornography he broadcasts.

Barry, on the other hand, is a rapist. When he approaches Max with a tape in hand, Max backs up and cringes, indicating he does not want it

Barry Convex (Leslie Carlson) forces a VHS tape into the gash on Max Renn (James Woods)'s stomach. The violent imagery shows how this is an act of assault by Convex on Renn (*Videodrome*, directed by Daniel Cronenberg. Universal Pictures, 1983).

inside him. But Barry thrusts the tape in anyway. That is, he forcibly shoves an object into the yonic gap in Max's stomach, symbolically committing sexual assault. In doing so, Barry violates Max's bodily autonomy. As the tape overwrites Max's agency, Max loses control over himself and his own body, which Barry exploits for his own ends, further cementing the connection between rape and Barry's actions. It would be difficult, therefore, to read *Videodrome* as approving of Barry's actions and agenda. Still, it would also be problematic to read it as exonerating Max. He may not be as immoral as Barry, but he is certainly not a classic hero.

Videodrome, therefore, is a moral litmus test. It highlights the question of how ethical violent media really is but does not offer a definitive answer.[88] The lack of such a stance highlights the eponymous program's reliance on violence as a means of convenience. That is, the violent content of Videodrome, the program, is a means to an end, and *Videodrome*, the film, is not making, necessarily, a moral judgment. The violence here is a means to multiple ends. For the program, it is a way to make the viewer susceptible to its malign influence.

For the film, it is a way to blur the boundary between fact and fiction while underlining how horror movies tend to achieve this common goal. Notice, for instance, how all the obfuscating, between the real and the fictional, so far in this book has consistently relied on violence. In *Videodrome*, VHS tapes ("television" as the film dubs them) consume Max's reality. He becomes a human VCR, and because this mechanization (this treatment of Max as a VCR) is forcible and, essentially, an act of rape, it is violent.

Similarly, in *Found Footage 3-D*, the specter manifests (i.e., moves from fiction—the script for the film-within-a-film—into reality) through Amy's rage at Derek, attacking at exactly those moments when her distress is most acute. In *Scream* and *Urban Legend*, murderers take inspiration from violent stories and then try to make those stories real. Next, in *Sinister, The Ring, Pulse, Coming Soon,* and *Scary Stories to Tell in the Dark* supernatural entities use fiction as a portal to reach out and murder people. And, finally, in *Cigarette Burns* and *Antrum*, legendary movies are dangerous because of their inherent power, which drives audiences to self-harm and murder.

To conclude, therefore, each of the films in this chapter subverts the divide between fiction and reality, and they do so in their own unique ways that set them apart from the rest of the films. But at their heart, they all share a common affinity for violence and fiction's affective power. Combining these elements—violence and story—enables one to derive a potent cocktail for undermining what people often perceive to be the boundary between fact and fiction. While it is commonplace for horror films to use terror and violence to communicate their message(s), it is striking how consistently they attack and try to sabotage the line that separates fact from fiction.

My analyses in this chapter build a narrative from these attacks to demonstrate how fiction can spur characters to reenact those fictions (ostension) or to use fiction itself as a vehicle for relaying their visceral, living messages. This dualism of reality-blurring affords us—the audience—, first, a realistic critique of fiction's place in our daily lives. *Scream* and *Urban Legend*, among other lessons, warn us about taking fiction too seriously. Not only is it dangerous to try to reenact stories, but it is dangerous to blame them for societal ills, which exist outside—and independently of—them.

Both *Sinister* and *The Ring* reinforce the view of fiction as potentially perilous, but they also highlight a fear of fiction as inescapable, a metaphoric virus. In this manner, they move from a critique of fan culture, and a critique of politicians' attacks on said fan culture, to a two-fold warning about perverse curiosity (which kills cats and characters) and fiction's ability to reach out and touch, contaminate, and influence us. *Found Footage 3-D* picks up this thread and shows the risks of taking fiction for granted. Note how Carl repeatedly criticizes Derek for dismissing horror movie tropes and putting the crew in a hazardous situation. Finally, *Videodrome* cements the narrative of fiction's power by noting fiction's centrality to our worldview. After all, if O'Blivion is correct, television is more real than our perception of reality.[89]

If O'Blivion is correct, then so is Billy: it is all one big movie.[90] And what kind of movie is it, pray tell? Certainly not the one most of us want to live in, I think, for this is a movie of monsters and killers. A dangerous world lies inside the film reel, and, perhaps, as these films all suggest, it would be in the viewers' best interests to respect the divide between our world and the film's. Thus, it is safe to conclude that the movies in this chapter all want us to be aware of—and deferential to—fiction's power: we need not shrink from fiction, but we do need to acknowledge it and its power to overwhelm. Yet, these films have all focused, primarily, on the fictional becoming real. There is, however, another side to this equation: the inverse. That is, sometimes these films portray the real becoming fictional.

Three

Emblazoned in Our Memories
When the Real Becomes Fictional

Section One: Fictive Copycats

One of the obvious instances of the fictional-real inversion lies buried in a film I discussed in the previous chapter: *Scream*, and its corresponding franchise. While discussing liminality in *Scream*, I briefly mention the *Stab* films, a fictional series that exists within the narratives of *Scream*[s] 2–4. *Stab*, and its sequels, are based on (or inspired by), Billy and Stu's murder spree in the first movie installment (*Scream*, 1996). The *Stab* films fictionalize the first *Scream*'s real murders and perpetuate Billy and Stu's legacy across time and space.

Scream 2 (1997), directed by Wes Craven, presents Sidney studying at the fictional Windsor College as the first *Stab* film premieres. Soon, killers in the Ghostface costume begin killing students around Sidney, who finds herself, once more, in the killers' crosshairs. "[K]illers," because yet again there are two murderers working together to target Sidney and her friends: college student Mickey (Timothy Olyphant) and Mrs. Loomis (the mother of Billy from the first film). After numerous struggles, Sidney triumphs over both murderers and survives (again) for the sequel.

Though Mrs. Loomis and Mickey do not make it to *Scream 3*, their characters are interesting because of the differing motives fueling their mutual rampage. Mrs. Loomis's motivation is straightforward: revenge. Sidney kills her son during the events of *Scream*, and Mrs. Loomis wants retribution. Billy himself (very) obliquely foreshadows this event in the first film, revealing that his mother, Mrs. Loomis, abandoned him because Sidney's mother had an affair with Mr. Loomis, Billy's father. This affair, followed by Billy's death, convince Mrs. Loomis she has a bone to pick with Sidney's family, the Prescotts.

Yet, it is difficult to rationalize or sympathize with Mrs. Loomis's decision to murder Sidney for killing Billy—an actual murderer—in self-defense. Frankly, Billy deserves to get shot in the head for attempting to murder Sidney, and for actually murdering her friends. Mickey's incentives, however, are more interesting, as compared to those of his partner-in-crime's, especially in the context of his imitating fiction-turned-reality-turned-fiction. As he readily explains to Sidney, he plans to hire a famous lawyer (mentioning Johnnie Cochran and Alan Dershowitz by name) to defend him, so he can blame horror movies for his actions and plead insanity.[1]

Mickey's rationale, therefore, reflects the overarching theme of the film. As befits the *Scream* franchise, *Scream 2* is a horror movie obsessed with horror movies. Randy, another survivor from the first film, discusses the murders in *Scream 2* as if they were a sequel to the murders in *Scream*, and the first two victims in *Scream 2* die at the premiere of *Stab*. *Scream 2* begins at *Stab*'s opening night, where two Windsor students—Phil and Maureen—encounter Ghostface, who first kills Phil while he is in the restroom, and then enters the theater to sit with Maureen, before stabbing her as well. Maureen stumbles to the front of the theater and dies in front of the audience, who presume she is an actor performing a publicity stunt for the film.

In this scene, Ghostface (whose identity remains unclear) reenacts both *Stab* and *Scream*. Ghostface's costume is an exact replica of the killers' costume in *Stab*, and Ghostface emulates *Stab*'s killers at the screening of the film, bringing the slasher film's events directly to its audience (i.e., from fiction to reality). Through this enactment, Ghostface also recreates the events of the first *Scream*: the killer, Ghostface, is dressed exactly like Billy and Stu were (while on their killing spree), wields a similar weapon (a combat knife), and targets people with names similar to those of Billy and Stu's victims.

Maureen, in *Scream 2*, shares her moniker with Sidney's mother, Maureen Prescott, who was Billy's first victim. On the other hand, Phil's last name, Stevens, closely resembles the name "Steve," Casey's boyfriend in *Scream*, who becomes the very first victim in that movie. This alignment of names becomes a plot point in the film, thereby acknowledging how its killers are aligning themselves with both the original *Scream* and the fictional *Stab*. By emulating the films' killers and their real-life inspirations, and by performing the film's text and title ("stab") in the theater, the killer(s) cross(es) the boundary between fiction and reality multiple times.

Scream portrays fables inspiring actual deeds and reactions, thereby transforming the imaginary into something corporeal. When the *Stab* films immortalize Billy and Stu's rampage, they use bonafide events and fictionalize them for the big screen. This fictionalization (or fiction) then becomes fact once more when the sequel's killers (Mrs. Loomis and Mickey) consciously connect themselves to *Stab*. Thus, *Scream 2*'s text, essentially, focuses on creating a reality from fantasy. Thus, *Scream 2* emphasizes the progression of fabrication into tangible existence, and the inverse occupies but a small part of the text. After all, the film poignantly gives us two characters who base their murders on a single, identifiable event in reality, and a single, identifiable fiction.

Gone here are the vague references to "scary movies,"[2] which now become references to a single work: the *Stab* franchise, the direct reference to which develops further in *Scream 3* (2000).[3] *Scream 3* introduces a new Ghostface (just one of them this time), who targets the cast and crew of *Stab 3*. Ghostface eventually reveals he is actually Roman Bridger (Scott Foley), *Stab 3*'s director. Roman also divulges that he is Sidney's half-brother, born to Maureen Prescott when she was a Hollywood actress. Roman also admits he showed tapes of Maureen's affairs to Billy, and thus is responsible for causing the events in the first two *Scream* films. Now, however, he has resorted to murdering people himself because he is resentful of the fame Sidney has gained from surviving the other massacres.

In this manner, Roman's character becomes thought-provoking because Roman alone occupies the unique position of being able to comment on the stories that immortalize his legacy. He is jealous because others have become famous (or notorious) for the story he created, and he expresses his jealousy at knifepoint. For Roman, the movement of reality to fiction is unfulfilling, even insulting. He views the *Scream* series as his personal story, and consequently regards the *Stab* films, based on Sidney's life (and not his own), as disrespectful to him.

Hence, he sets out to destroy *Stab* (cast and crew) and rewrite his legacy, creating his own fictional account of his life. That is, Roman is less concerned with the idea that reality may move into fiction than he is with *how* others have fictionalized his life. Per Roman's perspective, he is the creator of a narrative which, he believes, other people stole from him, and in doing so, perverted the story of his life. Throughout *Scream 3*, then, Roman attempts to rewrite his fictional legacy, a trait which manifests in the next installment of the franchise as well, *Scream 4*.

Scream 4 (2011) reverts to the format of "two killers" the original film pioneered, and of these two, the main murderer is concerned with constructing her own legacy. The film depicts Roman's nightmare come to fruition: Sidney has written a successful book, is more famous than ever before, and even has her own publicist (Alison Brie). When Sidney visits

Woodsboro, Ghostface plants evidence in her car, and she gets trapped in the town as a new series of murders unfolds. Towards the movie's conclusion, Sidney's niece, Jill (Emma Roberts), doffs her Ghostface mask and, for good measure, also kills her accomplice, Charlie. As she explains to a wounded Sidney, she is jealous of Sidney's fame and wants to become famous by being the lone survivor of the recent massacre. She fails, however, as Sidney survives her wounds and then kills Jill during a final showdown at the hospital.

Fame, subsequently, undergirds almost all the murders in the *Scream* franchise. The first *Scream* shows Billy and Stu's desire to plan their own sequel and be the sole survivors of the original Woodsboro murders. In *Scream 2*, Mickey aspires to hiring a renowned attorney and having a sensational trial. *Scream 3*, on the other hand, depicts Roman's cacoethes to punish Sidney for supposedly stealing his limelight. And, meanwhile, Jill, in *Scream 4*, wants to usurp Sidney's status as the famous one in the family, while her accomplice, Charlie, simply seeks to make his own movie.[4] From this discussion, Mrs. Loomis emerges as the only *Scream* killer who does not seem to covet fame for herself.

The franchise's killers are almost invariably obsessed with movies and, even more so, with the stardom accompanying them. Accordingly, they try to gain this stardom for themselves by enacting the very films they enjoy. That is, they take the fictional from the films and try to make it real. But, in doing so, they are also hoping to complete a movement back into the fictional. Billy, Stu, and Charlie enact films so they themselves can become films.

This is a perversion of an actor's typical quest for stardom. Per the archetype, when an aspiring actor seeks fame, they usually audition for movies and then, over time, become famous after acting successfully in said movies. *Scream*'s killers, though, cheat by attempting to take a shortcut. Instead of working their way up into the film industry, they try to enact movies in real-life to make their lives film worthy. However, by repeatedly demonstrating the failure of such ambitions, the franchise criticizes the all-consuming quest for fame, highlighting its dangers as well as its ability to morally compromise its participants. Thus, the *Scream* series showcases the negative consequences of trying to translate fiction into reality.

Notice, also, that the films tend to cast fame itself as a story. On the one hand, Sidney becomes famous for surviving a gruesome massacre and killing the murderers in self-defense. On the other hand, the films' antagonists try to construct and control their narratives, believing their fabricated stories will be intriguing enough to garner them fame. For instance, Jill murders Charlie because she wants to be the sole survivor, so that she can claim undivided attention and have only the best story to tell. In other words, Jill tries to control the narrative.

The film mocks her efforts, however, as moments after her death, a newscast declares Jill the "sole-surviving hero."[5] This headline indicates that Jill has won (ostensibly), for this is the exact narrative she wants. But this portrayal is destined to be transient, because now, (sheriff) Dewey, Gale, Sidney, and Deputy Judy all know the truth about Jill. One can surmise Sidney and/or Gale will have another book to write after these events, because of which Jill's narrative will gradually fade from the public's eye under the weight of the truth. This is to say that Jill receives her 15 minutes of fame, and no more. Though she enters the pantheon of serial killers to have targeted Sidney Prescott, she, as Billy, Stu, Mickey, and Roman before her, has failed to control the narrative of her life. What Jill tries to convince others about her—her story of her fame—proves to be Jill's undoing.

Thus, the *Scream* franchise moderately depicts the movement of the real into the fictional via the *Stab* franchise and its killers' concerns for controlling the stories of their lives. But the franchise, nevertheless, focuses on the inverse (i.e., the movement of the fictional into the real). This focus, in the texts that demonstrate the real becoming fictional, underscores how rare this inverse movement truly is, especially compared to its opposite (the progression of fiction into reality, as discussed in the previous chapter). This infrequent demonstration, moreover, enables us—the audience—to comprehend the form that the inverse movement usually takes: real events becoming immortalized in stories. Critically, *Scream 3* suggests that this immortalization is incomplete and unfulfilling. This, however, certainly does not prevent its manifestation in other texts, for this same movement occurs in the *Urban Legend* films as well when Brenda's murders become an urban legend.

Section Two: We Are Legend—Becoming Myth

And so, the *Scream* franchise obliquely attempts the movement from reality to fiction, without being entirely successful. However, Bernard Rose's 1992 film *Candyman* completes this movement. Set in Chicago, the film follows a graduate student, Helen, who is trying to research for her thesis on urban legends.[6] Helen becomes intrigued with the legend of Candyman, a specter residents believe haunts the Cabrini-Green housing project.[7] The legend, as Purcell, the condescending folklore professor, informs Helen and the audience, is that Candyman (he receives no other moniker in this film) was the son of a slave. His father, however, became wealthy and raised Candyman in comfort. Candyman, in turn, became a renowned artist, known for his skill at portraiture. When hired to paint the daughter of a wealthy white man, Candyman fell in love with—and impregnated—her, whereupon her father organized a mob to chase Candyman down. They cut off Candyman's painting hand, replaced it with a hook, smeared him with honey, released bees from a nearby apiary, and allowed the bees to sting him to death.

Helen, however, dismisses the story and completes the ritual of repeating Candyman's name five times in front of a mirror.[8] After her testimony leads to the arrest of a drug dealer who uses the name "Candyman," the real Candyman appears before her and tells her: "You were not content with the stories, so I was obliged to come.... I am the writing on the wall, the whisper in the classroom. Without these things, I am nothing. So now, I must shed innocent blood."[9] Candyman then murders a Cabrini-Green woman's dog, kidnaps her infant, and frames Helen. He also kills Helen's friend and research partner, Bernadette, once again framing Helen.

Ultimately, Helen must embrace the legend, as she reenters Cabrini-Green, confronts Candyman, and dies in a fire. At the end of the film, Helen's husband summons her spirit by chanting her name five times in front of a mirror, whereupon she murders him with a hook, echoing Candyman's modus operandi and showing how she, herself, has become a part of the legend.

Candyman is like *The Ring* (discussed earlier in this book), in that they both show antagonists immortalized in fiction.[10] The fictions, their stories, allow them to influence others and spread their madness. Much like *The Ring*, *Candyman* demonstrates this process, but in a more literal form. Samara and Helen are at different stages of the movement from real to fictional. Samara implants herself on the videotapes before *The Ring* begins, and therefore, it is indecipherable exactly how she managed to instill her supernatural powers inside a fictional medium. Conversely, Helen completes her movement into fictionality only at the very end of the film, so the audience can watch her transition whereas they cannot watch Samara's.

Candyman, therefore, demonstrates the complete process of the real becoming fictional (or unreal) as Helen joins Candyman's legend, thereby becoming a Candyman figure in her own right. The process, however, remains nebulous. Samara, in *The Ring*, possesses psychic powers *before* she begins using videotapes as her vector, and, because of her pre-existing abilities, she can project images into people's brains, a power akin to that of fiction. As a film does, Samara implants images into other minds and then uses those minds to achieve different effects, making her lethal to her audience (unlike most fictions). In contrast to Samara, however, Helen has no supernatural powers before she joins the legend; she only gains powers because of her courtship with Candyman.

How Candyman himself gained his powers goes unmentioned, and therefore, remains unclear. At least from what the movie shows, he had no paranormal proclivities when he was alive. Yet, now he "lives" as a story. Thus, he and Helen occupy a liminal space between being and non-being, dubious though its cause may be. Conversely, in *Sinister*, Bughuul lives inside his own nether realm, to which his film reels are a portal. Samara, meanwhile, instantiates herself across VHS tapes and is otherwise divorced from corporeal existence. Candyman and Helen, however, go a step further. Whereas Samara and Bughuul use physical media to reach new victims and prolong their lives, Candyman and Helen appear to have no physical existence left. They have no artifacts except for their (intangible) names. They are no longer located in space. Ergo, *Candyman* posits fiction as a liminal state of being, a way to exist without physically existing, to have life without living.[11]

To frame it differently, the film offers a way to understand *why* one might want to become fictional and cease to be real. Here, stories become an alternative means of existence, a way to escape the bounds of corporeal reality and move into a different world, one which might, also, grant supernatural powers and allow one to pass through the thin veil between the real and fictional worlds, just as Helen does when she murders her husband, Trevor, at the end of the film. The movement from real to fictional may be rare, but it is also powerful, and it affords a useful lens for comprehending the power of stories. The following section discusses one such power, that of containment.

Section Three: Stories as Containment

That is, some liminal horror films portray fiction as containing (i.e., being a means of controlling) real-life fears and entities. One such film is *The Dark Half* (1993). Directed by horror icon George A. Romero, and based on Stephen King's novel of the same name, *The Dark Half* follows Thad Beaumont (Timothy Hutton), a college professor and successful novelist who writes under the nom de plume "George Stark." After a stranger tries to blackmail Thad by revealing he is the real writer behind the Stark persona, Thad decides to get ahead of the narrative by coming clean in a controlled press release. Thad also resolves to use the reveal as an opportunity to retire Stark.

Stark, the persona, however, has other plans. He (also played by Hutton) manifests and begins murdering Thad's associates. He kills the blackmailer, the press release's photographer, and Thad's agent. These events cause Thad to realize Stark has, somehow, become real and that the novels he, Thad, wrote under the moniker "Stark" had, through inexplicable means, contained Stark. Thad also learns from his mother that he was born with a parasitic twin, whom doctors surgically removed from his brain.

All these plot threads finally come together when Stark confronts Thad and, under threat of harming Thad's family, forces Thad to write another Stark novel, this one depicting Stark existing in the real world. Thad never finishes the novel, however, as the two fight and Thad stabs Stark through the neck with a pencil, after which, a flock of sparrows (which the film previously described as psychopomps) appears and dismembers Stark, carrying his soul away.

The Dark Half, essentially, unfolds as a straightforward containment narrative. At the outset, Stark has a physical existence: he is a parasitic twin who causes Thad to experience seizures. His status as a born parasite foreshadows his later parasitic nature when he attaches himself to Thad's stories. This connection also enables the audience to form moral judgments about him. The connotations of "parasite" are decidedly negative since a parasite is a bloodsucker, and, often, can only survive by hurting another creature. And, parasitically, Stark does hurt Thad, at first through the seizures and later by murdering his friends and threatening his family.

Pivotally, Stark continues to have a form of existence after doctors extricate him from Thad's body. At the beginning of the film, Thad has a seizure while a flock of sparrows sits in the tree outside his window. Because the film describes sparrows as psychopomps (spirits which guide to the afterlife the souls of the dearly departed), it is clear the birds are there to carry Stark's soul away. Apparently, they carry it into Thad's stories, as Thad embodies the Stark persona when writing novels under the pseudonym. These novels give Stark a form of life, while simultaneously containing him within their pages. Therefore, when Thad attempts to stop writing the novels, Stark can no longer live through them. He must find another means of existence, and the lack of novels releases Stark back into external reality, at which point the psychopomps return for his soul.

Had the stories not contained Stark, one can surmise the sparrows would have hunted him throughout Thad's life. Given how quickly they corner and destroy Stark during the film, it seems that the novels gave Stark a safe place in which to dwell. They contained and protected him from the sparrows. That is to say, the novels protected Thad from Stark, and Stark from the psychopomps. While Stark is akin to both Bughuul and Samara in that he finds a way to exist through fiction, he is unlike them insofar as the fictions containing Stark protect the outside world from him. The fictions keep him contained (restrained) away from the external world, and so, Stark lashes out only after the stories stop, only after his fictional existence is in danger.

In this vein, he more closely resembles Candyman than he does either Bughuul or Samara. As far as one can tell from their respective movies, neither Stark nor Candyman creates the fictions that contain them and become their vectors. Thus, in a sense, both are the victim: their corporeal existence destroyed, they had no option but to flee into fiction. That is, both Stark and Candyman literally had no other choice, since others—and not they, themselves—created the fictions into which they were able to instill themselves through processes the films do not explicate.

Both Stark and Candyman's stories are, in a sense, memorials. Stark and Daniel Robitaille (Candyman's real name, as revealed in the film's sequels) died through no faults of their own. Stark is a victim of poor genetic luck, as his initial fusion with his twin brother makes him unviable, while a group of racist whites kills Robitaille for committing miscegenation. Stark and Robitaille, therefore, are both victims. The stories that come to contain them celebrate their memories and give them a new existence, a new life.

In this manner, the liminal horror film concretizes remembrance. The stories people tell about dead relatives and fallen heroes perpetuate collective recollections of the dead, allowing them to live through the memories of others. This is a form of existence, albeit not a physical one. These films— *Candyman* and *The Dark Half*—render physical this metaphoric existence, thereby permitting audiences to scrutinize it and its process. Memory, the films remind us, keeps its protagonists alive (in a sense). Further, the stories admonish those who forget the victims of the past. Notice, for instance, how both films punish those who challenge the stories, who undermine the deceased's newfound existence.

This memorializing function becomes clearer through an analysis of *The Dark Half*'s paratextual origins: *The Dark Half* is Stephen King's account of his own personal demon, Richard Bachman.[12] Bachman was a pseudonym (or nom de plume) King used to write several novels, including *The Long Walk* and *The Running Man*. King relates how the media revealed "Bachman is really King."[13] He was miffed they did not consider that King was also really Bachman.[14]

What is interesting here is how King and the press treated Bachman as his own person, a distinct individual and not a fake name King merely adopted. Moreover, this distinction also permeated Bachman and King's respective works. Bachman's work, as King himself relates, is darker. For example, King notes that the ending of *The Running Man* (which shows the protagonist committing suicide by crashing a plane into the main antagonist's office building) is the Bachman version of a happy ending.[15]

The Dark Half depicts the unfolding of a similar (albeit greatly exaggerated and fictionalized) version of this dynamic. There are two writers, Beaumont and Stark, wherein Beaumont represents King, a family man, writer, and professor from New England, while Stark personifies Bachmann, the darker, more violent, more macho version of that same writer. Stark swaggers through life full of pride, whiskey, and a propensity for violence, denoting a complete polarity to Beaumont. Stark is, after all, Thad's "dark half."[16]

And at least one of King's other stories shares this dynamic as well. In "Rest Stop," a short story in the collection *Just After Sunset*, a writer struggles between his two selves, one meek and one powerful, before settling on the latter version, which he then turns against a wife-beater. As *The Dark Half*'s title suggests, King seems to have long struggled with his own dark half, the part of him that wants to be violent, macho, uninhibited. It is an attractive idea, to be sure, that most people probably struggle with at one point or the other during their lives: the possibly never-ending conflict between animal instincts and the rational, civilized mind. Otherwise, this Dr. Jekyll and Mr. Hyde style of narrative would be a rarity, which it certainly is not.

Since *The Dark Half* is King's way of working through his personal problems, its creation and narrative are a therapeutic exercise for King. Moreover, both *The Dark Half* and *Candyman* carry these therapeutic undertones within them. For instance, recall how the ritual to summon Candyman requires the summoner to repeat Candyman's name in front of a mirror. Several real-life myths, most pivotally the "Bloody Mary" legend, share this set-up. They are the "monster in the mirror" legends. In her article, "Ghosts in Mirrors: Reflections of the Self," Elizabeth Tucker applies Jungian analysis to these legends. She connects them and their corresponding games (e.g., saying "Candyman" aloud five times in front of a mirror[17]) to maturing and focuses, accordingly, on college students and their experiences with these legends: "Mirrors tell the truth about aspects of the maturing self that are difficult to acknowledge."[18] Thus, she interprets the mirror's reflective properties symbolically. Mirrors, for her, become windows into one's own consciousness, reflections of the internal self rather than the external self, as it were.

She introduces the Jungian concepts of the animus and anima, the male and female aspects of the self, respectively, and argues that, when one sees an opposite gendered figure in the mirror, they are actually seeing the animus or anima.[19] In other words, a female seeing a male figure in the mirror is, according to Tucker, seeing her animus, the masculine aspect of her psyche. She writes: "Although the mirror provides a different surface, its close connection with identity makes it appropriate for enactment of complex self-perceptions."[20]

Thus, these monster-in-the-mirror myths are, according to her, a process of self-discovery. Here, she briefly uses the example of *Candyman*, arguing that Candyman is Helen's animus and shadow, that is, the male facet of her psyche and the largely negative part of her she is unaware of (at first).[21] Helen's summoning Candyman, accordingly, is an act of self-discovery, of unearthing those parts of her she did not previously see or acknowledge.[22]

Laura Wyrick explores this concept further in her 1998 article, "Summoning Candyman: The Cultural Production of History." Like Tucker, Wyrick argues that Candyman's emergence from the mirror suggests he is emerging from his victims' subconscious minds.[23] Subsequently, Helen's summoning him suggests Candyman is at once Helen's self and an Other.[24] Candyman is a different aspect of Helen's psyche, a part that is alien enough to be "Other," but not enough to be wholly distinct, that is, entirely "Other." Wyrick notes how, in the film, Helen realizes her apartment building's construction is symmetrical to the construction of the Cabrini-Green projects. This symmetry, Wyrick argues, further connects Helen and Candyman[25]: the two are parallel, alike in that they run the same direction, unalike in that they never touch (metaphorically speaking: in the film they do touch). All of this is to say that they are similar yet distinct.

Tucker and Wyrick's articles are helpful here because they highlight the strong connections between Helen and Candyman, which one might otherwise overlook and undervalue. Also, one need not accept the validity of Jungian psychoanalysis to understand how Candyman's smashing through Helen's mirror metaphorically suggests he is part of her psyche.[26] This metaphoric connection suggests that *Candyman*'s narrative is doubly therapeutic: it allows Candyman a measure of revenge on a world that wronged him, and it lets Helen release her frustrations at her philandering husband. Correspondingly, Helen, a scholar of folklore, gets transformed into a subject of folklore.

Similarly, Thad enacts fantasies of violence when he writes novels using the Stark persona. The novels' content is dark, full of the imagery befitting a man who would murder someone, castrate them, and stick their penis in their own mouth.[27] And it is important to note that while writing these books, Thad begins to resemble Stark. Instead of the word processor he uses when writing under his own name, Thad writes Stark's novels with pencil and paper. The scratching of the pencil's sharp tip across the page mimics the action of Stark's straight razor across his victims' throats, thereby underscoring the violence inherent in Stark's writing process. While writing as Stark, Thad also begins smoking and drinking again, despite having quit otherwise.

Thus, memorializing stories become receptacles for both Thad and

Helen's violent impulses, allowing them a space in which to assert themselves. Both are relatively meek in their everyday lives, presenting a sharp contrast to their fictional manifestations. Thad is a mild-mannered writer, far from the intimidating George Stark. Helen is bold enough to confront her husband, Trevor, about her suspicions that he is having an affair with a student, but she is not audacious enough to contradict his denial.

Her willingness to confront yields no results since he continues to be unfaithful to her, a fact Helen learns when the same student moves in with Trevor after Helen is institutionalized. Helen, subsequently, lacks power in her relationship, and this lack of power lies not only in her husband's infidelity, but also the fact that Helen is a graduate student while Trevor is a professor.[28] Thus, their relationship is a mixture of power imbalances, all of which hinder her ability to strikingly affect her circumstances.

As evidenced, the emergence of the dark half is the externalization of one's personal demons, a personal exorcism, if you will. Casting one's personal demon out grants one the power to wrestle with it and try to resolve the contradiction, try to combine the two differing parts of the self into a cohesive whole. For Thad as well as Helen, the resultant combination is a more violent self. Thad, for instance, takes one of Stark's signature pencils, the instrument that prolonged Stark's existence, and stabs it through Stark's neck. Ironically, he chooses a tool of creation and uses it as a tool of destruction.

When Thad uses a pencil to write a George Stark novel, he creates a tangible (and two-fold) entity: a collection of words that form a narrative he can package and sell, and a world in which Stark can safely dwell. Typically, when one tries to stab someone else through their neck with a pencil, the motive is destruction. Yet, when Thad does the same, he not only destroys Stark, but also creates a Thad who is free from Stark's influence.

Helen, meanwhile, resolves the conflict between her two selves when she gets integrated into the Candyman legend and eviscerates Trevor with a hook. Moreover, Candyman, too, embraces the apparatus of his destruction: as a mythic figure, he embraces the bees that stung him to death, and they become an instrumental part of his "Candyman" persona. And though Helen does not destroy Candyman the way Thad destroys Stark, Helen still murders one of her demons after defeating the other. Embracing her id (represented by Candyman), she attains the confidence and power to reverse and end her relationship with Trevor.

She could not control her husband's fidelity or Candyman's assault upon her, but, in becoming a mythic figure through death, she can, and certainly does, end Trevor's infidelity, and conjoins her Helen self to her Candyman self. For this reading of the film to work, a psychoanalytic framework is unnecessary. However, using psychoanalysis makes it easier to express and consolidate the idea. Regardless, it stands to reason that Candyman's emergence from Helen's mirror as well as the symmetry of her apartment and the Cabrini-Green apartments hint at a connection between the two, as do their respective progressions from victims to monsters.[29]

The Dark Half and *Candyman* give their protagonists (and, in the former, the author) a chance to resolve their inner conflicts. Both films also locate these struggles in the annals of history and story. History, hereby, becomes a story told to enable one to make sense of one's self and comprehend their place in the world. *The Dark Half* and *Candyman* both present narratives of self-discovery by showcasing protagonists who must figure out who they are. They do so, moreover, by engaging with the narratives themselves: story and history. Though I distinguish between the two here, the films conflate them and thereby undermine the distinction. *Candyman* implies that Helen is the reincarnation of Candyman's lover, as Candyman tells Helen, "It was always you..." and Helen bears a strong resemblance to a mural of the lover.[30] If true, this implication would indicate Helen has always been part of Candyman's history, a history that indelibly blends with folklore, with story.

Thus, the liminal horror story acts as a therapeutic practice to exorcise personal demons. That is, protagonists in these films must engage with stories to disentangle and settle their personal issues. Their engagement with fictions to resolve personal problems mirrors the actions of real-life authors (e.g., King) who do the same, and the liminal horror story, therefore, and hereby, acknowledges one of the reasons for its own creation.

To further connect the containment narrative to history, look once more to *Scary Stories*. In it, this process of exorcism takes aim at the problem of misremembrance: when the town remembers Sarah, they do not remember her as she was. Instead, they remember her as a monster, and their misremembrance, their twisting of her legacy, motivates her transformation into a vengeful spirit. To appease her spirit, the town people (or, at least, one of them, Stella) must rectify their record, and begin to remember Sarah as she was.

Like Roman from *Scream 3*, Sarah has a vested interest in ensuring others tell her story correctly; she wants exoneration. *Scary Stories*' narrative suggests the truth must come out. The real first became fictional in the film when the true story of Sarah's life, unbeknownst to the public at large, became a (twisted and incorrect) legend about her. Accordingly, for the narrative of vengeance (the story) to end, the protagonist must undo the foremost fictionalization of the real. That is, Stella must retranslate the fictional into the actual, reversing the process.

Thus, each of these three films (*The Dark Half*, *Candyman*, and *Scary Stories*) shows stories as therapeutic exercises that cast out one's personal demons. Thad's novels allow him to contain and ultimately destroy his violent, parasitic twin. Meanwhile, Helen accepts her destiny as part of the Candyman mythos and joins the legend, becoming a mythic figure and attaining power over her unfaithful husband. In the film's final scene, Helen asks: "What's the matter, Trevor? Scared of something?"[31] And in doing so, she turns Trevor's own mocking tone (which he uses on her and on the student who moves in with him) against him. Finally, Stella's rewriting the narrative of Sarah's life finally puts the latter's spirit to rest. Consequently, these films suggest that stories can assuage personal fears and, possibly, even allay them.

What is compellingly thought-provoking, however, is how liminal horror fiction cannot only purge personal demons but can exorcise collective demons as well. No film demonstrates this stimulating power as well as *Wes Craven's New Nightmare* (*New Nightmare*) (1994), directed, fittingly enough, by Wes Craven. This film's plot is highly irregular and layered. In the movie, Heather Langenkamp and the cast of the original *A Nightmare on Elm Street* play fictionalized versions of themselves. Throughout *New Nightmare*, Heather and her family finds themselves stalked by an actual entity who resembles Freddy Kruger, but who exists outside of the *Nightmare* films.

New Nightmare distinguishes this new being from Robert Englund's portrayal of the "fictional" Freddy Kruger in the other *A Nightmare on Elm Street* films, as Englund declares this "real" Freddy to be "darker."[32] Needless to say, this film's multiple layers can be challenging to follow. Though I attempt to do justice to them here, *New Nightmare* is a difficult film for the same reason it is interesting: its endless complexity. The blurring of the boundary between fiction and reality within the film tends to obfuscate the overarching picture and cause the audience's preconceptions to degenerate, thereby thwarting comprehension.

New Nightmare reveals that this "darker" Freddy is a real being whom Wes Craven restrained by means of the *Nightmare* film series. However, now that the franchise has (seemingly) concluded, the "darker" Freddy has managed to break free and invade our, the viewers,' reality (i.e., the reality in which Heather Langenkamp is an actress from the *Nightmare* film series). As the last resort, Craven (also playing a fictionalized version of himself), hands Heather a script, telling her she must "play Nancy one last time" to defeat Freddy.[33] Heather acts accordingly and vanquishes Freddy. In the end, the audience learns the script the fictional Craven hands to the fictional Heather is *New Nightmare*'s actual script. Unsurprisingly, of all the works in this volume, *New Nightmare* particularly resists straightforward summarization.

It also, however, foregrounds the connection between horror and control. By using meta-fiction, the film denotes that horror exists, in part, to help its viewers control their fears. Stephen King writes: "The answer seems to be that we make up horrors to help us cope with the real ones."[34] To substantiate his claim, King demonstrates how horror films tend to follow sub-generic trends that reflect the anxieties of the time. For instance, he points out that the different versions of *Invasion of the Body Snatchers* (1956 and 1978) corresponded with America's differing fears at the times of their releases.[35]

He further writes, "although the uneasy dreams of the mass subconscious may change from decade to decade, the pipeline into that well of dreams remains constant and vital."[36] The documentary *Nightmares in Red, White & Blue* (Andrew Monument, 1999) makes a similar argument by examining multiple decades of American horror fiction, showing how every period of American history produced its own horror films to specifically address the fears of the corresponding period. For example, when the fear of nuclear war pervaded 1950s' America, the horror films of that period often depicted monsters created as a result of nuclear radiation.[37] Craven also espouses a similar sentiment: "[Horror movies are] like boot camp for the psyche. In real life, human beings are packaged in the flimsiest of packages, threatened by real and sometimes horrifying dangers, events like Columbine. But the narrative form puts these fears into a manageable series of events. It gives us a way of thinking rationally about our fears."[38]

The arguments posited by both Stephen King and Wes Craven, and showcased through Monument's aforementioned documentary, all bespeak a key reason as to why we, the audience, we, human beings, like scary stories: we like them partially because they address our fears. Fear is often generated or felt in response to a lack of control. The rat fears the cat because it cannot control the cat's actions. In other words, it cannot prevent the cat from attacking or devouring it. However, once the rat has achieved dominance over the feline, the rat fears less the cat itself, but rather losing control over it. This colloquial analogy is to say that we engage with our fears so that we may control them. Telling stories is merely one such method of control.

When writing about recollecting dreams, Paul Schwenger quotes Maurice Blanchot in saying that we do so "to appropriate them and to establish ourselves, through common speech, not only as the master of our dreams but as their principal actor, thereby decisively taking possession of this similar though eccentric being who was us over the course of the night."[39] Accordingly, one can surmise that we humans create horror fictions partially so that we can externalize and (attempt to) dominate our fears. By vocalizing our fears, we place them, if only temporarily, outside of ourselves, thereby rendering them easier to conquer. A named being like

Freddy Kruger is comparatively not as fearsome as an unnamed, unknown entity. Thus, in a way, these stories help us control our fears.

And Craven is well-aware of all this (as the above quote shows). Consider, for instance, how Freddy in *New Nightmare* is distinct from any of his previous appearances. Both Heather and Robert (who plays Freddy in the preceding films, in addition to *New Nightmare*), call him "darker"[40] thereby proclaiming that this Freddy is not the Freddy they dealt with in the past. This is because, in this movie, Craven wanted to render Freddy's character as terrifying once again, and to do so, he had to distance the new Freddy from the wisecracking persona he had gradually become. In other words, Craven needed to make Freddy an unknown again. He had to destroy the now-familiar character and replace it with a newer version, one that would be "darker," and one whose modus operandi would be unknown and unfamiliar, thereby making it difficult for audiences and characters to combat and control. Without such a drastic transformation, it is quite likely Craven would have struggled to depict Freddy as spine-chilling once more.[41]

Consequently, the real-life inspiration behind *New Nightmare* was to resonate with real-life concerns about subduing and mastering one's fears. Notice, also, how the film's approach is paradoxical: it attempts to threaten one's control while simultaneously providing said control. If *New Nightmare* is more frightening because it upends the audience's expectations, it is also less frightening (than real-life) because, as a film, it provides viewers with a convenient container for their fears. That is, if a person gets too scared while watching it, they can always eject the *New Nightmare* DVD out of the player or hit pause on their computer. The tension here, the horror film's central conceit, is the illusion of losing control. To use a colloquial analogy, moviegoers enter the theater so they can (pretend to) lose control over what is happening to them and thereby experience their fears in a safe, consumable format. Then, they can simply leave and resume their daily lives.

In this manner, the film's narrative metaphorically demonstrates how people use fiction to suppress their fears, as it avouches that the *Nightmare* films contain the real Freddy, the true threat. In other words, Craven uses *New Nightmare* to literally, concretely, render this symbolic psychosexual need horror fulfills. Far from being a personal exorcism, *New Nightmare* is, in fact, about horror's ability to be a cultural exorcist (i.e., its ability to help society wrestle with—and dominate—its collective fears). Craven's diegetic inclusion of the movement from real to fictional affords viewers, perhaps, the best explanation for this particular movement's function: the progression from real to fictional helps audiences allay cultural anxieties. It also enables them to understand that it, the film itself, is doing so. *New Nightmare*, therefore, simultaneously signposts its fictionality and forewarns viewers they are watching a horror movie, thereby altering their perception of its narrative. Interestingly, this specific manner of signposting is also evident in the most common form of real to fictional narratives.

Section Four: This Section Is(n't)— "Based on a True Story"

Though this label has several variants, they all unanimously convey the same basic idea: that the viewer is watching something (at least partially) real and unfabricated. Films bearing such labels claim to take real, historical events and "faithfully" translate or adapt them into a fictional format. They profess an accurate representation of events that actually occurred, while also condensing those events into a digestible form with attractive actors embodying their real-life counterparts. All this is to say that, though these (pseudo-real) movies may exercise—or exploit—creative liberty, they allege fidelity to the essence of the story.

It is unsurprising, therefore, in the light of such appurtenances, that this conceit is problematic. When the audience views these films, they are usually cognizant that they are not going to see raw reality, much as Brian O'Blivion might say otherwise. For instance, they are aware, despite their expectations, that the filmmakers shoulder the burden of choosing as well as discarding elements of the original account(s) to convey an appealing narrative they can also coalesce into the restrictive time frame. As a result, it is incumbent on the audience to understand that these inspired-by-the-truth films may, concomitantly, be fictions. Accordingly, the question is this: exactly how much reality does the audience expect to be mixed with these fictional narratives?

The label, "Based on a true story," or the like is certainly unhelpful. So, what precisely does it mean to be based on real events? Which parts are based on reality? And which parts of the movie are concocted (to varying degrees) by directors motivated to tell an interesting story or by cynical movie producers who only seek profit(s)? Audience response theory (also known as "reception theory") certainly addresses some of these issues. However, that is not an approach I use here, for I am not overtly concerned with scrutinizing the audience's reactions to horror films that are variedly based on reality. Rather, I solely focus on how these claims—and their resultant appurtenances—facilitate liminality by (inadvertently) positioning their corresponding texts on the threshold between the fictional and the real. It is from this standpoint that I analyze several films' claims to reality in this section.

Professing (even partial) representations of truth can possibly add several—and often controversial and/or derisory—appendages to movies. That is why some films, the so-called cinéma vérité, usually try to avoid these issues all together and document pure reality (whatever it may be). But, even as one sets out to make a film of raw reality, they have already failed because the very act of trying to record truth changes it. Moreover, viewers of this documented reality will, most likely, be aware on some level that they are watching a movie and not real life.

And when one tells such an audience that the movie is "vérité," that is, truth, it will only remind them that this particular "truth" is actually a film, and subsequently, an artifice, and not reality. Furthermore, the very act of putting corporeal truth in the frame of a camera fundamentally limits the reality expressed in the resulting footage. The frame is constraining by its nature, for it, by default, spatially limits what the onlooker may observe. Ergo, it is impossible for a film to be raw reality if it aspires to record and reveal only facts.

Here, one might object and assert that the audience's eyes are as limiting as the camera because they, too, cannot observe the whole picture (i.e., behold everything in a 360-degree view) simultaneously. But, unlike the camera, the audience members (in most cases) can certainly control the movements of their eyes. Spectators can choose where to look, what to observe, but the camera, by its very nature, impedes that freedom. It forces the viewer to perceive only a selected picture of reality, instead of the more expansive reality that one can (usually) survey by themselves in real life, without the intermediary of the camera lens.

One should note, also, that this concern has permeated the Western philosophical tradition. For Plato, "all artistic creation becomes a mere imitation, which must always fall short of the original."[42] The inability of representation to move past imitation has led artists and philosophers to arrive at the following conclusion: "For all mental processes fail to grasp reality itself, and in order to represent it, to hold it all, they are driven to the use of symbols."[43] Perhaps because they are aware of this issue, or perhaps because they are simply motivated to tell a different kind of story, but regardless of the rationale, the films I have selected for discussing here do not pretend to be vérité. Instead, they signpost their mixture of fact and fiction.

And the most famous horror films to be "based on true events," in all probability, are *The Texas Chainsaw Massacre* (*Texas Chainsaw*) films (1974 & 2003). The 2003 film is a remake of its predecessor, and both films follow a similar plot in which a group of young adults drives across rural Texas and encounters a deranged hitchhiker. Following this event, they meet a family of cannibals that includes Leatherface, a hulking man who wears a mask made of human skin and attacks the protagonists with a chainsaw among other implements. Eventually in both films, the final girl

Kimaya Thakur takes a photograph of a giraffe while the author takes a photograph of her photograph. In this case, the resulting photograph is a copy of a copy of the giraffe, and something has been lost with each level of mediation between the viewer and the giraffe (author photograph).

(Sally in the original, Erin in the remake) escapes, but Leatherface and his family survive and, presumably, continue their spree of murder and cannibalism.

The original *Texas Chainsaw* plastered its marketing material with claims of being based on true events. It even opens with a text scrawl declaring that the incidents depicted in the film are a true account of what happened to Sally Hardesty and her friends.[44] And the remake further instills allegations of truth into the film, as it opens with handheld footage the narrator proclaims is from the actual crime scene where the film's events occurred. The film then flashes to its main plot, illustrating the events described above. Later, after Erin escapes, the film cuts back once more to the handheld footage, which the narrator again purports to be real. Leatherface, meanwhile, bursts out of the darkness and attacks the police officer the cameraman was following, and the film closes on a still, grainy image of Leatherface, an image the narrator professes to be the only existing visual of "the one they call Leatherface."[45] In this manner, from its promotional material to its text, *Texas Chainsaw* makes claims of authenticity.

If these films' events occurred, three key factors would most likely be present: a massacre (1) in Texas (2) involving a chainsaw (3). This story is, in fact, true, except there was no massacre, it did not happen in Texas, and the killer did not use a chainsaw. That is to say, the films virtually never happened: their narratives are almost entirely fictional. Screenwriter Kim Henkel, in an interview, imparted that he took his inspiration for the original film from the real-life crimes of serial killers Ed Gein and Elmer Wayne Henley.[46]

As Leatherface does in the movie, Gein wore costumes made of people's skin. Meanwhile, Henley's help in abducting young men in Texas vaguely resembles how Leatherface's family abducts and kills the films' protagonists. Thus, though there are elements of truth in the movies, they are especially scant compared with the films' fiction. Though the writer did take inspiration from the news of the time, the plot is almost entirely fabricated: the titular event never occurred.

Yet *Texas Chainsaw* declares its plot to be genuine to heighten its effect. The very thought that a family of cannibals lurks in rural Texas and mutilates innocent passersby is disturbing enough to earn any movie claiming to depict these events a reputation for being graphic. In spite of this reputation, though, the original film shows surprisingly little blood.[47] Clearly, it has achieved its goal: the 1974 film was certainly shocking, for its era at least; and it is quite possible that some of that shock emanated from the audience's belief they were witnessing a faithfully documented narrative of real events.

The "based on true stories" label is, undoubtedly, an easy way to heighten horror's affect because it undermines a film's fictionality. When a film claims to be recounting a true story, we—the audience—generally become primed to encounter the film as reality. Accordingly, this preparation (unconscious and unwilling though it may be) diminishes or at least weakens our barriers: if a film *is* reality, then retreating from it is non-viable.

Typically, the audience is innately equipped with strategies that help them avoid graphic scenes in horror movies, or anything uncomfortable in media, for that matter. They can look away from the screen, pause the movie, take a well-timed break, or use some form of humor. More importantly, the audience can remind itself that what they are viewing is fabricated. True, the movie monster may be scary, and, in all probability, encountering such a monstrous creature in real-life would be terrifying. However, we—the audience—are generally secure, with the knowledge that the monster on screen is not real, and, thus, unable to confront us.

Correspondingly, our ultimate fallback strategy is to constantly remind ourselves of the protective barrier that exists between fiction and reality. Craven himself acknowledges this quotidian habit through a warning in the trailer for *The Last House on the Left*. The trailer cautions that, if viewers get too scared while watching, they can simply repeat to themselves that "It's only a movie, only a movie."[48] *Texas Chainsaw*, however, attempts to remove this strategy from the audience's (that is, *our*) arsenal, because Craven's suggested mantra, that it is "only a movie" becomes useless if the film's events have already happened in real-life. Conventionally, a movie that tells (or claims to tell) a true story is difficult to perceive as "only a movie."[49] The cinephile driving through rural Texas may struggle, indeed, with images of Leatherface, whose family they believe lived somewhere off those same lonely roads.

Yet, this analysis does not exhaust the liminal and narrative possibilities that such labels of truth entail. And other films offer a more complex view of the "based on true events" phenomenon. Directed by Michael Katleman, *Primeval* (2007) presents a war-torn Burundi, where a team attempts to locate and trap the massive, notorious man-eating crocodile, Gustave. Their hunt for Gustave, however, runs afoul of Little Gustave, a warlord who stylizes himself after the near-mythic crocodile. The team records some of Little Gustave's soldiers murdering civilians and must flee when the warlord's other troops chase them down to procure the incriminating footage. Eventually, the two plot threads intertwine, when Gustave eats his would-be successor, and the team escapes from the country. Gustave, meanwhile, survives his wounds from the encounter and slinks back to his lair, free, once again, to continue hunting Burundians.

Primeval proudly declares that it is "Based on the true story of the most prolific serial killer in history."[50] That serial killer is Gustave, and he *is* real. Approximately 20 feet long, Gustave is a male Nile crocodile living in Burundi and boasting as many as 300 human victims.[51] Such a high number of victims would, in fact, position Gustave among the world's most prolific

Gustave surfaces near some smaller Nile crocodiles. Notice how he dwarfs other members of his species and stands out whenever he appears. This photograph's poor quality owes to Gustave's dangerousness and the consequent distance photographers must keep from him (*Capturing the Killer Croc*, directed by Jean-Michel Corillion and Vincent Munié. PBS Home Video, 2004).

serial killers, 300 being more victims than Harold Shipman had.[52] If we, the audience, accept, for the sake of argument, that animals can be serial killers, we more or less reach the end of *Primeval*'s veracity, for the rest of the film is fictitious.

Though there are a few kernels of truth in *Primeval*—that there has, indeed, been at least one expedition to capture Gustave, that that expedition, like the team in the movie, built a cage to house him, and that Burundi was in a state of civil war until 2005—the majority of the film is pure fiction. *Primeval*'s Gustave is a typical movie monster: he chases victims over land, survives a grenade to the mouth, and shows preternatural obsession with pursuing a single group of humans.[53] The real Gustave, in sharp contrast, is a crocodile: he ambushes those people and animals who enter (or stand near) the murky bodies of water that afford him camouflage, and while he has survived being shot, he has never eaten a grenade.[54]

Moreover, though he is massive, his size may actually hinder his ability to hunt prey typical of crocodilians. Gustave's propensity to hunt humans, therefore, may be to compensate for his inability to hunt smaller, faster prey.[55] To be sure, Gustave enjoys a near-mythic reputation in Burundi, and his mystique is great enough to warrant *Primeval*'s creation as well as to spawn the earlier documentary *Capturing the Killer Croc* (PBS, 2004). But *Primeval* takes this mystique and makes it real (or, pseudo-real) within the

Gustave's smaller, more photogenic cousin. The glass separating alligator from photographer makes safe the proximity between the two (author photograph).

film's text. In the movie, Gustave not only has a mythic reputation, but he *is* a mythic monster: his powers transcend those of real animals (especially in the context of masticating a grenade). And, as I explained in the preceding paragraph, this contrast between the real Gustave and his fictional depiction is a gross exaggeration of factual evidence. Gustave is a crocodile, a wild animal; and though he is exceptionally dangerous, he is an animal, nonetheless.

As if to signpost this blend of fiction and reality, *Primeval* seems to change genres as it moves into its more fantastical elements. The first scene is typical of horror movies. A forensic anthropologist examines a mass grave; then an unseen creature attacks, kills, and devours her. This scene establishes the civil war via the mass grave, introduces the monster while maintaining its mystique (a mystique the film later shatters), and establishes the film's life and death stakes. The corpses and the anthropologist's death allow the movie to foreground mortality and its symbols.

Primeval never loses this thread of death, as many characters die during the protagonists' expedition. But the film's horror elements gradually wane as the plot progresses. Gustave moves from being an unseen force, a phantom haunting the film, out of sight but always in mind, to being cartoon-like as he behaves less and less realistically. The film, meanwhile, adopts more elements of action films, as it focuses more on the Burundian civil war than on Gustave himself. In fact, the film holds the war responsible for creating Gustave, as a character surmises Gustave attained his taste for human flesh by feasting on bodies in the river. It is here that the film's focal point shifts. Whereas its marketing material, opening, and expedition all pitch a narrative about the killer crocodile, the film becomes a commentary on Burundi's civil war. Or, at least, it tries to, for most aver it fails on this count.[56]

The film noticeably wavers on the story it wants to tell: the expedition to capture Gustave on the one hand and the war on the other. As a result of trying to portray both stories, *Primeval* ends up spinning an increasingly fictionalized narrative that loses much of its claim to truth. The film also wavers in its stance on Gustave. It rejects Little Gustave's attempts to lionize himself by donning the crocodile's name. And the rejection comes, fittingly enough, from Gustave's own jaws. Little Gustave's death at the teeth of his namesake makes a mockery of his pretense toward power. The warlord is no Gustave, and never will be.

The crocodile is, though, and the film comments precious little on him. Gustave kills (and symbolically mocks) Little Gustave, saves Aviva (Brooke Langton) from getting raped, survives the movie, and remains free to continue eating people. While the film's refusal to kill Gustave does realign it with reality (as Gustave was alive at the time of the film's production), this refusal, combined with the other plot elements, renders Gustave as a kind of anti-hero. After all, he saves the protagonists twice.

Now, it makes sense that *Primeval* takes a more negative view of Little Gustave than it does of Gustave himself, for the former is sapient and culpable for his actions, while the latter is not. Yet, the movie presents the "most prolific serial killer in history" as something of a hero[57] and allows him to pass judgment on a warlord, thereby affording Gustave the moral high ground. Thus, *Primeval*'s failings occur most often when it tries to integrate the real and the fictional. The film drapes itself in a veil of verisimilitude, claiming to be the true story of Gustave, but then moves away from the reality in trying to tell a story about the war in Burundi, thereby converting the true story into a clichéd and confused narrative that is more fiction than reality.

Whereas *Texas Chainsaw* successfully uses its proclamations of vérité to heighten its affect, *Primeval* fails even on this count. If there is anything to be gleaned from this film, it is the folly of the "based on true events" label. Claiming to be real can make a horror story more effective, but doing so also establishes certain expectations. If a story is supposed to be true, the audience will, most likely, approach it with a lower suspension of disbelief than they would a story that professes no such veracity (i.e., that they presume to be fictitious).

Following this strain of expectations, when a narrative such as *Primeval* clearly moves from bearing a pretense of reality to being an outright fiction, the audience, likely, loses their disbelief. This is why a film like, say, *Scream* is more effective than *Primeval*. Merely declaring the story to be true can be a lackadaisical as well as foolhardy way of trying to blur the line between fiction and reality for the sake of affect. The label of truth alone is not enough, and *Scream*'s more comprehensive, narratological approach to blending the fictional with the real makes for a more unnerving, disorienting film than *Primeval*.

Still, I must clarify here that there are more possibilities that the "inspired by true events" label can entail, different than the ones depicted in *Texas Chainsaw* and *Primeval*. And no film treats this label more interestingly than the 2016 Finnish film *Lake Bodom* (*Bodom*), directed by Taneli Mustonen and starring Nelly Hirst-Gee as protagonist Ida. *Bodom* starts with on-screen text giving a brief history of the real events that inspired the film. This text informs the audience that, in the summer of 1960, three teenagers camping at the titular lake (a small body of water outside the city of Espoo, near Helsinki) were murdered, and a fourth member of their group was seriously injured. The murders became some of the most infamous in Finnish history and were never solved.

Following this background information, *Bodom* transitions to its fictional story, which follows a group of four teenagers who arrange to go to Lake Bodom for a camping trip. The group consists of two pairs of friends. The first pair is two boys: the outgoing and sexually active Elias, and his nerdy, Bodom-obsessed friend, Atte. The second pair, composed of girls, includes the confident and sexually active Nora, and the comparatively virginal protagonist Ida. The differences in the four characters' personalities, as well as sexual experiences, become more important as the film unfolds; these aspects play a greater role in the narrative than one might imagine. For instance, the audience quickly learns that Ida has become the subject of controversy at the group's school because, after she passed out at a party, one of Ida's classmates posted nude photos of her online.

Furthermore, divisions quickly appear in the group, as it turns out that Atte has tricked the girls into coming to the lake by not informing them of his plan to stage reconstructions of the infamous Bodom murders. Atte reveals he wants to test his theory that the murders were, in fact, committed by an outside killer, and not by the survivor, as others have speculated. But the rest of the group are uninterested in helping him. That night, Atte and Ida settle into the group's tent while Nora and Elias go into the woods surrounding the lake. Atte broaches the topic of the photos but cannot finish his thought because their tent collapses. Convinced Elias and Nora are messing with him and Ida, Atte leaves the tent—only to be stabbed by an unseen assailant.

Seeing Atte mortally wounded and bleeding profusely from the neck, Ida screams for help, summoning Nora and Elias back to the tent. Together, they try to flee the forest, but Nora twists her ankle and implores the other two to continue without her, rather than allow her to slow them down. Thus, only Ida and Elias continue running toward the group's car. Along the way, they argue about their relationship: the audience, accordingly, learns that Elias and Ida were courting before Ida's nude photos were published; or, perhaps, not published, since Elias insists he has been unable to find them. Ida has trouble believing this revelation, and Elias fails to convince her, as a hooded figure fatally stabs him through the heart.

The figure then removes her hood to reveal herself as Nora, whose ankle is just fine. Here, the audience discovers that Nora and Ida agreed to come to the lake so they could murder Atte and Elias as revenge for (supposedly) publishing Ida's photos. The girls dump the boys' bodies in the lake and discard the evidence of their crimes. As they drive out of the woods in Elias's car, Ida asks Nora about what Elias had insisted before his death. Nora, in turn, confesses she purposely got Ida drunk at a party and then fabricated a rumor that there were nude photos of Ida. Elias, ergo, was correct in maintaining that no photos existed and that all who claimed to have seen them were lying. Worse still, Nora further discloses she created the rumor to nip Ida and Elias's burgeoning relationship in the bud and keep Ida for herself. Nora, the viewers learn, has an unrequited crush on Ida.

Thus, when Ida conveys her displeasure at Nora's actions, Nora hits her in the face with a wrench, causing the two to struggle and crash the car.

When they awaken, wounded from the wreck, they see that a tow truck driver has somehow found them in the remote forest. He tethers their car while Nora and Ida talk to each other. Fearing the man will ruin their efforts to hide Elias and Atte's murders, Nora asks for Ida's knife, assuming Ida stabbed Atte. Ida, however, has no knife, and the two arrive at a terrifying realization: this tow truck driver is the Bodom killer.

He drags their car at high speed behind his truck until it flips, with Ida and Nora still inside. Badly wounded, they are helpless as the man binds them both and places them back in their tent at the campsite of the original murder, exactly where Atte had them camp. The Bodom Killer then kills Nora and leaves Ida alive; the closing narration tells the audience that most blamed Ida for her friends' deaths and that no one believed her when she told them about the man. The film concludes with a group of six new teenagers hiking to the same infamous spot and surveying the expanse of Lake Bodom before them.

As this summary demonstrates, *Bodom* goes further than merely labeling itself "based on a true story." Instead, it follows a group of teenagers who, while trying to dramatize the notorious murders, are caught up in a repeat of the original massacre. Within *Bodom*'s universe, Ida's group unwillingly helps draft a horrid sequel to some of Finland's most infamous murders.[58] Thus, Atte's desire to reconstruct the murders (to act them out as if in a play, a fiction) leads to the creation of a disturbing reality where the murders, in fact, ironically repeat themselves. Subsequently, Atte's fascination with history indirectly makes him a part of that same history: the lake's notoriety would undoubtedly grow if another set of murders occurred on its pristine shores, and even more so if they occurred in the same spot as the original murders.

Thus, history lives as well as interacts with the present in *Bodom*, and essentially only because of its notoriety. That is, Atte would, presumably, have not been so fascinated with the murders if they were not so notorious, so well-known. The coverage through media and word-of-mouth gives the story the chance to move back into the present, thereby psychically scarring a new generation of Finnish youth. Its notoriety is, therefore, self-perpetuating.

The film, itself, hints at this fact when, at is conclusion, it depicts six teenagers standing on the lake's shore. This number, six, matches the number of the Bodom killer's victims by the film's conclusion (i.e., the three original victims in 1960 plus Atte, Elias, and Nora). Moreover, because *Bodom* leaves this shot for the end, it lingers in the audience's minds, long after they have seen it. The shot's strategic placement, coupled with the number of teenagers, makes it a visual marker for the killer's power, history's ability to repeat itself, and the scars etched on the collective cultural psyche from knowing that the murders are unsolved and that the killer may still live.

Nevertheless, *Bodom* simultaneously warns about obsession with a dark past. Atte's stubbornness to solve the murders gets him killed, after all, despite his desire to find "the truth."[59] In fact, when the girls ask why he cares about the murders, he answers: "The killer's still on the loose. Isn't that reason enough?"[60] That is to say, Atte is at the lake because he cannot let go of history, and neither can Ida, which is why she agrees to come to the lake. Throughout the film, different members of the group tell her: "What happened to [her] was horrible."[61] This repetition and her father's furious desire to keep her grounded at home reinforce the notion that Ida cannot escape her history, even though that history never actually happened.

In a similar vein, Atte's constructed history (i.e., his theory) may never have happened either, as the only person formally accused of the murders was the lone survivor.[62] Indeed, though an outside assailant kills teenagers from *this* group, the film does not explicitly confirm that he also killed the original group. It does heavily imply he did, as the film's first shot is of a man sharpening his knife while watching four teenagers frolicking in the lake. Though the shot offers no outright confirmation, it does support the theory that this man is culpable for the original Bodom murders, meaning the film's viewers, like Atte, only have theories and speculations. Such suppositions and concoctions are usually benign; in *Bodom*, however, they are lethal. Atte dies because of his investigation, and Ida is permanently scarred because of her belief in a rumor that sparks her belief in a theory about the culprits of a deed that never happened. In both cases, then, constructed fictions pave the way to real deaths and a perpetuation of history and its mythic allure.

Far from exorcising personal or collective demons, *Bodom* warns its viewers away from engaging in this function of liminal horror. Whereas characters like Helen find some power through horror's therapeutic effects, Atte's and Ida's attempts to do the same prove fatal rather than cathartic. In casting Atte's and Ida's actions in this light, *Bodom* gestures (if, perhaps, obliquely) to its genre, as the presence of danger in horror is unsurprising. And throughout this chapter, various films have shown that the movement from actuality to fantasy tends to be incomplete and/or dangerous. While this movement is more common than it might at first appear, its tendency to emerge as a mere narrative afterthought makes it difficult to thoroughly comprehend. Yet the fictionalization of the real does allow one to examine liminal horror's therapeutic role and understand how it prompts people to reflect on their lives and narratives.

In the context of film itself, nevertheless, one of the primary takeaways from this chapter must be how frequently the foregrounding of this move of professing truth—in some way or the other—can backfire. On the note of its frequency, though, I redirect the reader's attention to this volume's core question: why *do* horror stories blur the line between fiction and reality? All the films in this chapter indirectly offer one answer: reality is scarier than fiction. In *Bodom*, the horror derives from the real-life murders. Without them, *Bodom* would be a generic slasher, bereft of liminality. And so, truth becomes scarier than fiction. But being scary is just the first step. Why, then, do liminal horror films have a stake in trying to scare audiences?

Four

Harsh Realities
Truth Is Scarier Than Fiction

Section One: Horror Films as Didactic Tools

The slasher film sub-genre is, broadly speaking, characterized by a killer stalking a group of (usually young) adults and killing them one by one until the final young adult, typically an attractive and virginal brunette ("the final girl"[1]) defeats the killer and then either survives for the sequel or disappears from the franchise.[2] Slasher films ruled the big screen in the 1980s, when the *Friday the 13th* and *A Nightmare on Elm Street* series were at the zenith of their popularity.

However, with the gradual progression of years, which saw a rapid increase in the number of sequels, the sub-genre became platitudinous and clichéd. Once one has seen a single slasher movie, it can appear as if one has seen them all. Of all the horror sub-genres, the slasher is perhaps the most criticized for its formula. It is from this genre that such beloved horror clichés as the teleporting, indestructible killer, death by sex, and protagonists tripping over their own feet arise.[3] Like any sub-genre, the slasher ran its course and eventually disappeared from the public eye.

In 1996, however, Wes Craven revived the genre with the fresh and deliciously ironic *Scream*, which revitalized the slasher and ushered in a new wave of sequels and imitators. The slasher was back once again, and possibly better than before. It certainly was more self-aware than ever. Like several other horror films today, *Scream* is perhaps most notable for its ironic self-awareness, which it uses to mock horror's clichés. Clichés are frustrating because they imply that the characters are playing by different rules than the audience is. Typically, while watching a film, the spectators may try to identify with the characters and attempt to position themselves in the characters' shoes. However, when said film's characters are clichéd, or even so pseudo-real as to be unbelievable, the audience gets alienated, thereby landing the film in trouble, or marking it as a failure.

And so, a frequent criticism of horror is that it consists of stupid characters who make decisions a realistic and sober audience would not make.[4] As soon as a character in a horror film settles on a course of action that any audience member believes they, or anyone with an instinct of self-preservation, would never undertake, the bond between audience and character shatters. The audience is no longer in the character's shoes, nor do they want to be. Once this connection breaks, so does the audience's immersion, and the story loses its intrigue because the viewer transitions from experiencing the film to criticizing it, which is a fundamental change of perspective. In light of such an estranging scenario, *Scream*, upon its release, was a breath of fresh air, for it represented a step away from clichés. Here, I must choose my words carefully because *Scream* is not quite without clichés, but it is still able to distinguish itself enough to refresh both its narrative and the corresponding sub-genre, while keeping the audience interested.

While Craven introduced the trend of self-awareness, he did so, ironically, not through *Scream*, but rather through *New Nightmare*, which predates *Scream* by two years. *New Nightmare* did not receive as many imitations as *Scream* did, however, and the latter can safely be said to have started the trend toward self-awareness in modern horror, a trend prominently visible in such films as *I Know What You Did Last Summer* (1997), *Urban Legend* (both the original and *Final Cut*), *Feast* (2005), and *The Cabin in the Woods* (2011). Indeed, the former three films deliberately imitated *Scream*. I draw attention to this trend because, though *Scream* is more ironic, *New Nightmare* is the more self-aware of the two. In fact, *New Nightmare*'s relative lack of popularity may, possibly, be due to its multi-layered use of self-reference making its story difficult to follow.

As this discussion suggests, *Scream* is a slasher film fully aware of the relationship between spectator and character. Like most slashers, it stars an attractive cast of young adults. And, like *Scream*'s presumed audience, its characters are fans of the horror genre and, therefore, well-versed in its clichés and nuances. The irony occurs when these characters try to apply their knowledge of horror film rules to their real-life terror, with mixed results. For instance, during Sidney's first brush with Ghostface, she talks about horror film clichés, stating that she dislikes "scary movies" because they always showcase characters making poor decisions, such as running upstairs instead of going out the front door when the killer is chasing them.[5] When Ghostface attacks her, Sidney attempts to flee through the front door, and, finding it locked, must run upstairs. In other words, she must perform the same clichéd action she previously derided: an instance of obvious irony. One should also note that this irony levels a "take that" at the audience.

To develop this point further, one need only look at the film's resident horror guru, Randy, played by Jamie Kennedy. Randy believes he has everything figured out, but, like Sidney, he does not. For instance, while watching *Halloween*, Randy yells at Jamie Lee Curtis, telling "Jamie" to look behind her. As this happens, however, the camera in *Scream* shows the killer standing behind Randy, with his knife raised to strike. Thus, this scene exemplifies an ironic self-reference: Randy, the know-it-all horror expert, is directing Jamie Lee Curtis to turn around, but his use of the actress's name (rather than her character's) is a prompt for the audience to regard Randy not as Randy but rather as his actor, "Jamie" Kennedy. When evaluated in the context of such a cue, this scene essentially depicts Randy telling himself, unwittingly, to turn around, thereby supplying his own character with sound advice.

That the horror expert directs his best advice toward himself, especially when he is completely oblivious to it, is decidedly ironic, and spitefully so. In both these examples (Sidney's predicament with the front door, and Randy's paradoxical situation here), it is evident that *Scream* is pushing back against the idea that any horror fan can survive a horror movie. In doing so, *Scream* indicates that the characters' knowledge does not always help them. Randy's note, for example, that the killer will come back for a final scare proves to be helpful, but his statements about turning around and not having sex prove unhelpful.

On this element, Craven asserts that audiences want to know: "What are the rules? How do you defend yourself?"[6] And viewers try to seek the rules of the narrative and apply them to real life to stave off mortality. *Scream*, however, problematizes this proclivity by asserting that corporeal existence does not abide by a circumscribed set of moral rules. A person may be murdered irrespective of their virginity; sexual intercourse does not necessarily equate death, but, under certain circumstances, it can. And it is this ambiguity that frightens us, the audience. *Scream*, therefore, confronts its viewers with a harsh truth: that you can do everything right, live your life by the book, follow all the rules, and still die at 16. There is no clear guide in real life, and there is none in a self-aware film like *Scream* that purposefully pulls the rug out from under its complacent viewers and characters.

This disruption occurs even within the film itself, particularly in the case of Jamie Kennedy's character. Randy is the group's resident horror fanatic (or so he believes), and he, like the fans he represents, is confident he can solve the mystery behind the film's plot and thereby resolve the situation before more people die. For example, while stocking movies at the local video store, Randy tells Stu: "This is standard horror movie stuff, *Prom Night* revisited."[7] Kevin Williamson, the screenwriter, also takes this opportunity to poke fun at horror fans, as Randy then says: "Besides, if it gets too complicated, you lose your target audience."[8] The irony here is that not only is *Scream* a very complicated movie that did not lose its audience, but it also launched a franchise and revitalized an entire sub-genre.

Seemingly oblivious to this, however, Randy also claims that the police can easily solve the murders if they study horror as he has done. For him, the mystery is easy: "I'm telling you: the dad's a red herring. It's Billy."[9] Here, Randy is right both in acknowledging that the experiences he is living through are akin to those in a slasher film and in recognizing Sidney's dad as a false lead. But he is only half-correct in concluding Billy is the killer. *Scream* famously subverts the slasher film formula by having two killers. And this scene is ironic, as Randy commits (unwittingly) the error of relating his conclusions to the second killer, Stu. This irony allows the film to confront the audience again, as Randy serves as an audience surrogate. Like the viewer, he does not have all the information, and he expects only one killer because, to that time, slasher films typically depicted only one. The film's dual killers, therefore, undermine the audience's expectations by making the traditional whodunit a trick question.

As I indicated while discussing clichés, audiences tend to analyze films not from the character's perspective, but rather from their own, that is, the author's position.[10] In other words, the audience expects film's rules to align with the reality they know. For *Scream*, these presuppositions come alive in the form of genre presumptions. The audience believes it knows what to expect when diving into a slasher film. *Scream*, however, subverts these presumptions and yet, simultaneously, manages to not undermine its sub-genre entirely.

As I stated before, though, *Scream* unfolds as a slasher film, despite playing with the genre's conventions. One should note, for instance, that the virginal brunette survives while her more sexually liberated blonde friend does not. But *Scream* layers such straightforward play with ironic subversion. That is, while it follows genre patterns sometimes, at other times it subverts them entirely. For instance, the scene in which Sidney has sex with Billy is close to the scene with Randy explaining the rules of horror films, including "Never have sex."[11] Sidney, of course, violates that rule, and yet, she lives. Meanwhile, Randy violates the "You can never drink or do drugs" rule and also lives, albeit not through the sequel. On the other hand, Stu makes a show of violating the dictum against saying "I'll be right back," and he dies.[12]

These oscillating examples are evidence that *Scream* does not dismiss its own sub-genre; rather, it acknowledges its conventions and then picks and chooses which generic patterns to conform to and which to subvert, thereby rendering itself unpredictable. Because of its indulgence in self-awareness and saturation in irony, *Scream* becomes a difficult movie to predict and an even harder one to read, as it neither endorses nor dismisses its sub-genre; instead, it demonstrates how merely altering the formula can create an effective film. Here, one should also bear in mind how *Scream*'s very existence relies on formulaic slashers. It needed films to codify the sub-genre so *Scream* could playfully criticize it.

After all, without films such as *Friday the 13th*, *Halloween*, and their slew of sequels, *Scream* would have no precedent to disrupt. The audience's expectations rely on the formulae these preceding films established. And so, employing playful criticism allows Craven to develop the sub-genre further while simultaneously subverting expectations and not discrediting that sub-genre. Moreover, by overthrowing generic presuppositions, Craven surprises jaded horror fans and make his films shocking, if not scary, once again.

As in *Scream*, Craven seeks to defamiliarize and unsettle the audience and the film's characters in his *New Nightmare*. No other film shows the collision between the real and imaginary as explicitly as *New Nightmare* does, and, in fact, no other film shows it as a collision. Unlike the situation in the original *Nightmare*, the "real" Freddy in this film is actively trying to break into the real world and affect the characters.[13] His attempts to breach this increasingly thin barrier are evident, for instance, in Heather's house where the audience sees long gashes open in her wall and on her son Dylan's stuffed T-Rex, whom he regards as his protector.[14]

Note, then, that Freddy begins with an attack on *our*, the viewers,' defenders: we (usually) trust our walls to shelter us from the outside world and its dangers, be they wolves or nightmare demons, just as Dylan trusts that his T-Rex can protect him. Freddy's aggressive efforts, however, prove both Dylan and Heather, and the audience, wrong. In real life, Heather Langenkamp calls the film a "reality-based nightmare."[15] The film is, after all, strangely real: just days after the cast and crew filmed the earthquake sequence, there was an actual earthquake, which also appears in the film.[16] Moreover, countless elements of the story are based in reality. For example, Langenkamp did, in fact, have a stalker and, like her character, was a young mother married to a special effects artist when making the film.[17]

New Nightmare, consequently, is even more meta than *Scream* in the sense that its many layers of reality versus fiction are nigh impossible to keep track of. From Langenkamp, we—the audience—learn that we have our reality. Then there are the film's realities, with all the various characters being fictionalized versions of their real-life counterparts. And all these different layers collide together such that it becomes difficult (if not impossible) to distinguish fiction from reality.

It is important to note, also, that Craven tangentially adds the audience itself to this mix. He states that *New Nightmare* was a precursor to *Scream* and that, while the former was for the adults, the latter was intended for the teenagers, the audience.[18] Whereas *New Nightmare* was a reunion for its cast members, *Scream* is a collection of references for its audience to parse out.[19] These distinctions align with the postmodern notion of play. Specifically, horror hereby becomes a game for the audience to play with the filmmakers.

And Angela Ndalianis supplements this view of the horror film as a game, albeit in the context of another film I discussed earlier. Ndalianis notes that *Blair Witch* performed well in Australia even though the truth about its fictionality was well-known by the time of its Australian release, and states that "pleasure now circulated around both film and extratextual information being about a game of horror."[20] One should, therefore, note that this ironic self-awareness is postmodern in nature and invites the audience to participate, thereby rendering the films fun in an innovative way.

To revert back to the plot of *New Nightmare*, and what I mentioned in the previous chapter, the film has two Freddy Krugers: Robert Englund's "fictional" Freddy and the real Freddy, played by real Robert Englund but not by the character Robert Englund (i.e., the fictionalized version of himself he plays in the film).[21] It takes the wise-cracking Freddy who inhabited the sequels and replaces him with a more serious and dangerous Freddy, thereby changing the narrative.

This change is intentional. As I pointed out earlier, Craven intended to make Freddy Kruger scary again, and this motivation is also (arguably) why Craven relies on self-reference in *New Nightmare* and in *Scream*. Put simply, he wants to unnerve and frighten the audience again. Horror movies, I argue, are more fun, as well as more effective, if they can discompose and terrify the audience outright. *New Nightmare* reinvents its antagonist to make him scary again, and one need only consult the original film to realize that Freddy Kruger was/is, indeed, petrifying. Thus, this push towards self-reference is evidently an attempt to unsettle and frighten the film's spectators by disrupting their ability, as viewers, to predict, and thereby pacify, the narrative.[22]

After all, the fictions people create pale in comparison to real-life horrors. To put this into perspective, one need only contemplate the difference between watching Freddy Kruger on screen and being aware that there is a serial killer prowling one's neighborhood. Which, of these two murderers, is more menacing? Even if Freddy is powerful, he is not real. This distinction is pivotal. Even creators of horror fiction cannot quite compete with such a harsh truth, and the reason why is obvious: the serial killer prowling around someone's neighborhood might actually murder them tonight. On the other hand, Freddy Kruger is incapable of doing so because he lacks physical existence in *our* reality. If one fears one's mortality as most humans instinctually do, the former is surely the bigger threat and greater source of fear. A movie, by contrast, is merely a fiction. Thus, one can escape, combat, ignore, or overcome it more easily than they could any tangible threats. Given this incompatibility of fiction, then, it is unsurprising that so many movies proclaim "truth" (as I discussed in the previous chapter).

To further substantiate *how* "true stories" are scarier—or at least more effective—than imagined ones, take Conor McPherson's *The Weir*, a play consisting of multiple stories steeped in the supernatural, with paranormal entities such as fairies and ghosts. *The Weir* is also useful here because it demonstrates that reality is more effective for evoking most emotions (e.g., sadness), rather than just fear. While *The Weir* is the only non-cinematic of my central texts, I include it in this volume because it validates my point about evoking emotions better than any other work I have identified, cinematic or otherwise.

The play's plot revolves around a group of men in rural Ireland, sitting in a bar, narrating stories to an outsider, Valerie, the only person there not used to the setting, the stories, and their characters. The men begin telling stories to entertain Valerie and reminisce. It is evident, in fact, that Valerie is their audience, for they address their stories to her. Most these tales are horror stories, which harken back to old Irish folklore and bygone terrors. Jack's tale, for instance, involves fairies, or rather the hint of them.

In the story, a family sits around their house late at night; per local legend, their house is on a fairy road. They hear a knock on the door, except that the knocking sounds lower on the door than any of them would expect, certainly lower than a person would knock. Subsequently, they hear knocking on other doors and windows, but the mother refuses to let her daughter investigate. Instead, the mother lets the fire in the hearth die, rather than braving opening the door and going outside for more wood.

While the presumed fairies show no malice, this tale is unnerving nonetheless, for it exhibits a typical urban legend or paranormal encounter: unverifiable, creepy, pulling on older traditions, and infringing on the audience's notions of reality. As it does with any other urban legend or myth, the question of veracity hangs over the play's stories. Indeed, one of the play's characters addresses this question with ambivalence. Whereas Valerie represents the audience, Finbar represents the skeptic, and he is quick to provide logical explanations for all the paranormal phenomena in these stories. He says of Jack's tale, "You're not bothered by that, are you Valerie? 'Cause it's old cod, you know? You hear these around, up and down the country."[23] Valerie, however, responds: "Well. I think there's probably something in them. No, I do."²⁴ Valerie's apparent belief is important because, of all the stories within the play, her tale is arguably the least terrifying but is certainly the most believed by her audience. None of the men place much stock in the folktales they tell, attributing them to sickness and alcohol.²⁵ But then, Valerie narrates her own story, shifting the play's narrative.

To this point in *The Weir*, the stories have been frightening, albeit to varying degrees. In contrast, Valerie's story is sad: though it maintains the supernatural element, it perceptibly affects the group's emotions, and the play shifts from debatably scary folklore and humor to somberness. The tale Valerie narrates is about her getting a phone call from her dead daughter, which is less frightening and more depressing, and Valerie's narration makes her emotional and solemnizes the party. Her audience is less skeptical of this story than they are of the other tales. Though Jim and Finbar attempt to rationalize the events for a moment, they relent in the face of Valerie's belief. She is adamant about her experience: "It's something that happened."²⁶

The audience never learns if Valerie believed in the paranormal before this encounter, but it is evident she does now. Moreover, she takes comfort from the other stories, which denotes an important fact: that these stories affect people irrespective of whether they are true or not. Finbar says, "no one knows about these things, sure, they're not real even … there's usually some kind of explanation for it."²⁷ Despite this logical claim, however, Valerie's story affects her, and everyone around her, even though it is unclear if the narrated event actually occurred, or if Valerie is merely convinced that it did.

This impact that Valerie's tale has—on herself and her audience—is key, for, as far as humanity's perceived and empirical "reality" demonstrates, a dead person is incapable of dialing a number or speaking on the phone. Realistically, it is implausible that Valerie's dead daughter could call her, and this, in turn, indicates that, logically speaking, her story is untrue. Yet, the fact remains that Valerie wholeheartedly believes it, and that her audience believes in it enough that they are discernibly affected. And it is this response, this belief, that is also key: the authenticity of her tale matters not to either Valerie or her fellow storytellers, for their conviction overpowers (their need for/understanding of) verity.

The response Valerie's narrative evokes, despite its questionable validity, connotes the stronghold of belief in one's mind that can be compelling enough to negate the reality, be it preconceived or empirical. This negation of the "real," subsequently, thwarts the generally perceivable facts of corporeal existence, thereby permitting the influx of the fantastic. To paraphrase this simply, the power of one's belief in the fictional can becloud reality, which is already often blurry, indistinct, and confusing. I explore this concept at length later, but it is apparent that "truth" becomes obscure in *The Weir* due to the strength of its characters' convictions. This observation, however, is debatable, for the play itself does not reveal if Valerie's story actually took place or not. Due to this lack of information, one could argue that, within the play's universe, Valerie did receive a phone call from her deceased daughter, thereby having a supernatural encounter.

This is to reiterate that (as I have indicated over the past few chapters), trying to impose the rules of "our" reality onto fictional realities is an inherently flawed enterprise. The men in the story corroborate this by accepting Valerie's tale as the most credible of all the paranormal stories, but, due to the lack of verifiable evidence, I am inclined to disagree with readings that presume Valerie's story is real. This is because, for one, her audience refrains from cross-examining her about the story as much as they do with the other folktales; though the story *appears* credible due to its lack of fictional entities such as fairies and monsters, the men do not prod further into parsing her tale for logical and reasonable explanations.

Perhaps this is because Valerie is virtually a stranger to them, and so, they are not as comfortable contradicting her as they are with each other. Or it is also possible that, because Valerie herself is her sad tale's protagonist, the men are uncomfortable doubting such an emotional story and countering it with rational thought, lest they cause her more distress. If this is indeed the case (since the play does not betray a single reason for the men's acquiescence), one can insist that they are tactful enough to not probe the subject. If Valerie wishes to believe this unrealistic supernatural encounter did take place, they let her, instead of hurting her further.

Compared to the group's preceding stories, Valerie's story is sorrowful, and the possibility that it may have actually happened (its veracity solely reliant on the teller's fervent belief), makes it tragic. Following Valerie's narrative is the play's concluding story: Jack's seemingly realistic account of losing his girlfriend for reasons he cannot quite fathom. Unlike the tales before his, Jack's story does not have a single paranormal element in it, but, like Valerie's narrative, it is clearly a tale of loss.[28]

This tale, combined with Valerie's, ends the play on a sobering note, as both these stories affect the other characters more than the earlier, discernibly fictional stories did. That the characters respond more to these two seemingly realistic narratives (regardless of whether they are actually true) gestures toward an important human characteristic: the more we believe something aligns with reality, regardless of how much it necessarily does, the more effective it (that particular "something") will be. *The Weir*, therefore, evinces how tales of loss, especially when told by those who experienced them, are stronger, more striking, and more affective than any fictional scary stories.

The example of *The Weir*, consequently, aids in explaining *why* a movie might advertise alleged claims to truth: it is because every ounce of reality a film can claim makes it seem more real, and therefore (in the context of horror movies), more threatening. Robert Egginton writes: "Given that the loss of reality is a priori one of the most unsettling feelings one can have, it should come as no surprise to learn that bleeding came into its own as a technique peculiar to horror films."[29] This is why a film about a serial killer terrorizing *your* (the audience's) particular neighborhood is more relevant and more poignant than a pure fiction like *A Nightmare on Elm Street*. As compared to Craven's film, the former can and has happened, and, therefore, is less far-fetched. In other words, when a film can stretch that fine boundary between fiction and reality, it can reach out and touch (impact/change/move) the audience, and horror stories, in particular, *want* to touch audiences.

Horror functions by making its audience tense and/or afraid. Accordingly, filmmakers will use any technique they can to achieve this goal. In fact, the audience may hold them responsible for this task—and this quality—of horror fiction. But that still does not answer the question: why do horror authors seek to scare us at all? And as I noted before, there is no "single" answer to this pivotal query because it questions the existence of an entire genre, which is as expansive and diverse as any other. Consequently, such an inquiry, which is central to the genre's conception and continuation, defies a sole, all-encompassing answer and favors varied, multilayered, ever-mutable explanations.

One of the many explanations is, of course, Stephen King's assessment, which I discussed earlier in this book. As King avers, horror reflects contemporary fears and lets audiences control them. Though I agree wholeheartedly with King, the answer I propound (and which I briefly identified earlier) goes a step beyond King's: that not only does horror aid in controlling (or combating) fear(s), but in the very process of doing so, it educates. Horror, as I asserted before, is didactic and teaches audiences by frightening them.

Perhaps my asseveration may seem farfetched to the reader, but it certainly is not unfounded. Craven, a master of horror, also espouses a similar thought when he asserts that: "Horror films talk about the bare bones realities. We are corporeal beings. Rich, poor, whatever we are, someone sticks a little piece of metal in us—we can die right there. Our existence comes to an end."[30] Amalgamated with Craven's pronouncement about horror movies and rules (available in this section's discussion of *Scream*), it becomes clear how, exactly, Craven thinks horror films enlighten viewers.

For instance, one only needs to consider all the Craven films in this volume: *A Nightmare on Elm Street*, *New Nightmare*, and the four films of the *Scream* franchise. All these films, in their own unique ways, question the line between fiction and reality, thereby providing a glimpse into Craven's philosophy. If horror reflects reality, what is the reality these movies depict? Clearly, it is a reality where fact and fiction blend together, where creatures from dreams can reach out and kill, where belief is dangerous, and where stories can come true.

That is, if horror is indeed about reality, and includes all these elements, the conclusion is inevitable: reality *is* blurred. Like the line that separates fiction from fact within these stories, the line distinguishing truth from tale, in (*our*) real-life, is not dichotomous: as much as we—the audience—would like to deny it, the fact is that we live in an obscure, nebulous reality. Quite possibly, we may (frequently) overlook this fact, but horror fiction endlessly tries to bring it back to our attention, and it always has. On this point, Egginton writes:

> What Craven and Carpenter realized was that cinema had a heightened capacity for frightening its viewers owing to its tendency to coerce them (without their noticing) to adapt a certain point of view—to accept, in other words, new coordinates for the experience of what we are calling base reality.[31]

In other words, by moving viewers to a new reality, horror films make them reflect on it.[32]

As Craven points out, we viewers tend to think we can survive our corporeal existence if only we are cunning and prudent enough to learn the rules.[33] Accordingly, an audience seeking (to learn) the rules would be, initially, at home in *Scream*, which readily supplies the guidelines in a convenient list. The film's subversion of the very rules it provides would, however, shatter the audience's false sense of security. Craven's ultimate effect—if not intention—therefore, is to fracture the audience's complacency and force viewers to confront the stark realization of their own mortality. Consequently, Craven's horror films become exceedingly confrontational, forcing us to encounter the reality of our weakness(es) and our own vulnerability(-ies). Attempts to hide behind the screen of well-established rules, *Scream* asserts, are in vain, because one can die anytime and for very little reason. After all, "motives are incidental."[34]

It is precisely this confrontation, this directive of coercing one to encounter one's shortcomings, that renders horror films didactic: they do not allow anyone to take cover behind the superficial safety of rules, or hide beneath the protective veil of either genre or fiction. Horror films force you to face reality as it is, if only for a moment, which further denotes an essential truth: that horror is confrontational. Another master of horror, David Cronenberg, elaborates: "I think of horror films as art, as films of confrontation. Films that make you confront aspects of your own life that are difficult to face. Just because you're making a horror film doesn't mean you can't make an artful film."[35] What Cronenberg is saying, therefore, is that horror compels its audience to apprehend their corporeal existence as it is, often through strange (and possibly defamiliarizing) lenses: that they are all mortal and can drop dead at any time. And, as Craven and Cronenberg assert, horror makes its audience aware of this immanent truth.

As a result, therefore, horror makes one reflective. It compels one to come to terms with the times, or even with one's own impending death, if only for a short period. But because the experience is temporary, the audience can confront their mortality while watching the movie(s), and then leave the movie(s), happy.[36] That is, the audience tackles their own death by proxy, but then leaves the film with their tensions released. Craven, therefore, builds tension in his audience to enable them to challenge their mortal shortcomings. He achieves this feat by employing self-awareness to surprise viewers, and then prompts them into releasing that agitated surprise through laughter and screams, making it all seem "okay" or "normal" because it is, after all, only a movie.[37]

Craven's consistent attempts at defamiliarizing us—his audience—however, indicate we still have much to learn from the knowledge horror films offer, which brings me back to my assertion about horror being didactic. Regardless of whether we actively use that knowledge, and regardless of whether we even believe or accept that knowledge, horror conveys social norms that can, depending on the context, become (seemingly effective) survival skills. Perhaps it is because of this tendency that many consider horror an agent of the status quo.[38] For instance, consider the slasher sub-genre, which, at one point, popularized the idea that sex kills.

This is a puritanical notion: do not have premarital sex or you might be brutally murdered. Popularized by the slasher genre through direct implications, this notion seems akin to a public service announcement printed on pamphlets handed out in 1950s' high schools. Clear evidence for this appears in *Scream*, wherein the horror-film know-it-all, Randy, readily points out that practicing abstinence is, in fact, a "rule" for surviving horror films.

Except for a few notable exceptions, including *Scream*, sexually active characters do not survive to the end of most horror films. This, in turn, leads to the charge that horror is a means to maintain society's moral status quo, and adding in *Scream*'s second rule—about not using drugs—only strengthens this claim. But whether horror is an agent of the status quo or not is beside the point here: because regardless (and irrespective) of its upholding (or overturning) of the status quo, it is apparent that horror attempts to educate its audience. If the slasher genre is about propagating puritanical morality, then ensuring promiscuous characters die enlightens the audience to the "fact" that sex kills. This is didactic, and so is the inverse. That is, even if horror films subvert the status quo, or depict that any concerns or fears about sexual intercourse are unreasonable or exaggerated, they are still teaching their audience something, conveying a message through the films. That, too, is didactic.

When issues at hand are as critical as the matters of life and death, as is frequently the case within horror movies, it becomes easy to understand and learn the proffered lessons. Note, for example, Craven's averment about learning rules. The audience, essentially, turns to horror films to learn how to survive, and the films, therefore, are uniquely suited to imparting various lessons (e.g., about morality).[39,40] Fiction may also be particularly well-suited to this role, as it holds a powerful sway over the human mind: "If the storyteller is skilled, he simply invades us and takes over. There is little we can do to resist, aside from abruptly clapping the book shut."[41] Moreover, Jonathan Gottschall writes: "But the land of make-believe is less like heaven and more like hell. Children's play is not escapist. It confronts the problems of the human condition head-on."[42] Accordingly, one can infer that a fiction full of problems is more likely to educate than one that is merely tranquilizing. The creatures in one's imagination, therefore, are threats to combat and overcome, for only by facing one's demons does one truly understand themselves and their reality.

Per this acknowledgment of the power of fiction, and horror fiction in particular, it is undeniable that horror has infinite precepts and (harsh) truths to impart to its audience, to us. Scaring us, therefore, is simply a means to an end sometimes, for like the texts in any other genre, not *all* horror stories actively strive to teach us anything. However, many of them do, and in doing so, they enlighten the audience about the world in which the audience lives. Furthermore, because horror—by itself—tends to be dark and grim, it is uniquely suited to teaching its audience—us— the uncomfortable and sobering lessons we might otherwise prefer to not learn, such as lessons about nightmares, death, tragedy, and trauma, lessons that are crucially pertinent to our reality.

Section Two: The Folklore Horror Film as Moralistic Tool

Horror wants to teach, and it can often use "strange" lenses to do so. One such lens is that of folklore, as apparent from *The Weir* (discussed earlier). This connection between horror cinema and folklore is well-established in horror studies. Clover, for instance, writes: "…the fact is that horror movies look like nothing so much as folktales—a set of fixed tale types that generate an endless stream of what are in effect variants...."[43] Koven further refines this connection in his essay, "The Terror Tale: Urban Legends and the Slasher Film," wherein he defines multiple kinds of legends, one of which he calls the "terror tale," an urban legend meant to arouse terror rather than disgust.[44] In this volume, I, likewise, have focused on the "terror tale," and establishing how the horror films I analyze herein are akin to folkloric terror tales allows me to grant the reader a better understanding of folkloric horror films, and, specifically, their moralistic implements.

In his famous work, *The Vanishing Hitchhiker: American Urban Legends & Their Meanings*, renowned folklore scholar Jan Harold Brunvand writes: "Legends can survive in our culture as living narrative folklore if they contain three essential elements: a strong basic story-appeal, a foundation in actual belief, and a meaningful message or 'moral.'"[45] It is the last of these three that interests me the most here, for though the majority of the horror films I focus on in this book are not folktales in themselves and, often, lack a "foundation in actual belief," they nevertheless share some essential characteristics with folktales, thereby rendering Brunvand's analysis valuable (both in general and in the context of my argument).[46]

In Koven's analysis of the "terror tale," he observes that each legend belonging to this genre has four central components: an interdiction (i.e., a warning), a violation of the interdiction, ensuing consequences for the violation, and the protagonist's attempt to escape these consequences.[47] This formula applies to the slasher film a little too well. In *Scream*, for instance, Randy declares that horror movie characters must retain their virginity if they are to survive. This, in essence, is an interdiction Sidney violates when she loses her virginity to Billy. Consequently, Billy and Stu explicitly reference how Sidney must die since she is no longer a virgin (ensuing consequences), only for Sidney to fight back against them in an attempt to survive (escape the consequences).

A more archetypal slasher film, *Friday the 13th* (1980), fits this mold even better. In the film, a group of counselors assembles to reopen a long-abandoned summer camp, and despite warnings from the locals that the camp has a "death curse," the group decides to stay (interdiction and violation).[48] As night approaches, an unseen assailant begins murdering the counselors one-by-one (ensuing consequences). When Alice, being the last member alive, becomes the final girl, she must fight for her life against the killer, Mrs. Voorhees (attempt to escape).

These are but two instances, and though it would be fun to continue demonstrating the manifestation of this folkloric formula in the slasher genre, the examples above effectively prove the point. In both these films, the interdiction and its violation are key: the protagonists cannot come to harm if they have done nothing "wrong." It should be noted here, however, that "wrong" is explicitly in the eye of the beholder: the slasher film often finds fairly innocuous activities as grounds for death. Nevertheless, a warning and a willful ignoring of that warning are prevalent themes in most of the horror films I survey in this volume.

One can discern these themes, for instance, in a previously discussed text: *Urban Legend*. Though I have already analyzed this film in Chapter Two, I would be remiss if I do not examine this film in the section dedicated to folkloric horror films, more so because *Urban Legend* wears its roots in plain sight. Beneath the obvious references to—and ostension of—urban legends, the film incorporates subtler folkloric elements. Namely, *Urban Legend* foreshadows each of the main protagonists' deaths. The first of these foreshadowings is evident before Michelle's murder, as she listens to "Total Eclipse of the Heart," a song which repeats the lyrics "Turn Around." Much as Randy directs "Jamie" to look behind her in *Scream*, Michelle is now (virtually) telling herself (she sings along with the music) to do the same. The implication here is that if she had heeded this warning, perhaps she would have seen the killer hiding in her backseat.

More importantly, however, this moment primes the viewer for what to expect. The song, along with a glimpse of Brenda's hoodie in the backseat, and the subtle cue of the gas station attendant glancing into Michelle's car, warn the viewer about where the danger lies. When Brenda's axe crashes through the window on the driver's side (and, presumably, through Michelle's skull), the viewers experience a moment of vindication: it is through that moment that the spectators know they correctly understood (or not) the cues foreshadowing Michelle's death. Thus, in an anti–*Scream* fashion, the film espouses the belief that a horror fan's knowledge of horror stories can protect them from real-life dangers.

The foreshadowing portending Michelle's death continues throughout the film, but more subtly. Before Natalie and Damon leave to talk in the woods, the camera moves upward, following the line of trees on Pendleton's campus. A few minutes later, Damon is hanging by his neck from a tree. At first glance, these two moments might seem unrelated, but the transition between scenes connects these two trees in the eagle-eyed viewer's mind. In fact, it was only after several careful viewings of the film that I noticed this moment and its minute attention to detail.

Another instance occurs before Tosh's death, when Natalie and Sasha flip through an encyclopedia of urban legends and the camera pauses momentarily on the "Aren't you glad you didn't turn on the lights?" legend. The pause is so brief it is easy to miss. But if the audience catches it, they are prompted into being apprehensive of Tosh's prospective one-night stand, which is akin to the earlier focus on the trees, a focus suggesting (to the viewers) how Damon's death will be connected to the trees surrounding him and Natalie.

A later example is that of Parker carrying his dog and a funnel through his party. Following this, Brenda uses the "dog in the microwave" legend to make Parker rush to the bathroom so she can ambush him and use the funnel to pour drain cleaner down his throat, thereby killing him. Finally, before she leaves for the radio station, Sasha speaks to another student (at the same party) about how the scream recorded in the song they are listening to is, in fact, a real scream from a 911 call. As this discussion foretells, Sasha's death occurs while she is live on air, and her screams and whimpers broadcast much as the scream in the 911 legend. In fact, this scene is so steeped in the legend that the partier whom Sasha was speaking to believes she is performing an "art piece."[49]

Thus, these numerous occurrences of foreshadowing are too consistent to be unintentional, and yet, the foreshadowing itself is still weaker than one would expect. The connection between the trees and Damon's hanging is, perhaps, a little shoddy, and Parker's death at the hands of the dog and the funnel is odd, to say the least. It is only upon repeated viewings that most audience members can connect the cues to the respective deaths in these cases. In other words, it is hard—at times—to even realize the film is providing multiple cues portending its characters' deaths. On the other hand, there is a clear correlation between some deaths and their foretokens, such as the scene wherein Natalie and Sasha read the legend in the encyclopedia, which prompts the audience to expect Tosh's death in a certain way, as well as the conversation between Sasha and another partier, wherein her manner of demise becomes obvious. This is to say that the foreshadowing in *Urban Legend* is consistent in its presence but inconsistent in its strength.

Yet, there are times when it is absent altogether. For instance, Professor Wexler, the janitor, and the dean all die, with the latter two even meeting their ends according to urban legends. The janitor dies when Brenda runs his car off the road after he mistakenly plays along with the "flashing headlights" legend, while Brenda murders the dean by reenacting the "killer hiding under a car and slashing the driver's Achilles' tendon" legend on him. However, the film does not foreshadow any of these deaths, at least not in the thematic, folkloric way it uses to foreshow the students' (the protagonists') deaths. Perhaps this absence of foreshadowing (in the context of the dean's and the janitor's deaths), indicates that some of these elements do not fit well together. From an out-of-the-film perspective (that is, a critical point of view), this absence can make it seem as if the storyteller does a poor job, adding extraneous details and outlandish elements that confuse the narrative and dilute its underlying themes.

There may, however, be an alternate, in-universe explanation for the discrepancies. Shortly before the film's ending, Natalie muses that Brenda's rampage will become a legend.[50] Following this, the film fades into a fire, out of which the camera moves to face a group of students, one of whom relates the tale of Brenda's murders. Brenda, however, contradicts the student for relating the details incorrectly, and then offers to provide an accurate narrative of the events herself. The implication of this "correction" and the ending fade is that the film *Urban Legend* is actually a student's flawed recollection of the story, and not the narrative of the events as they actually occurred. This inference (if accepted) helps explain some of the film's outlandish elements, such as Brenda's apparent super strength. This inference also lets the audience (that is, us) understand for whom these warnings exist: they exist solely for the hearer of the tale, as the teller weaves them directly into the narrative, so as to make the listener apprehensive about what occurs next.

Since urban legends thrive on repetition, it seems logical for a film based on them to have subtle cues one might notice only upon repeated viewings. An attentive audience member could, as Craven suggests they are wont to do, recognize the foreshadowing in the narrative and feel vicariously vindicated because they would not have died as the characters did, owing to their correct interpretation of the signs. Thus, it is certain that the film is warning its audience, but it is difficult to determine precisely what it is trying to teach them. One may venture that perhaps the film's moral is about the danger of overconfidence and misperception, of failure to heed warnings. Even so, the interdictions remain unclear.

This is apparent from how, though there are numerous examples of foreshadowing throughout the film (as I describe earlier), the victims-to-be are rarely in a position to actually act in accordance with the warning signs or even to recognize them as such. A "Keep Out" sign is a clear warning of danger; but one's roommate briefly glancing at a legend, the reenactment of which leads to one's death, does not immediately portend danger. In Tosh's case, especially, she is not even the one receiving the forewarning (as oblique as it is). This contradiction, subsequently, leads to two possible readings of the film. On the one hand, the film could be interpreted as a confused production that fails to impart a clear moral. Conversely, the confusion could be the storyteller's fault, if only one accepts the entire film to be his (the student whom Brenda contradicts at the end)'s flawed recollection of, possibly, a third-hand tale. Consequently, though *Urban Legend* is insightful in that it illustrates folkloric foreshadowing in horror films, it is ineffectual in showing any didacticism in horror (at least in an explicit manner).

The next film, however, addresses that purpose and fulfills it perfectly:

Dolls (1987), directed by Stuart Gordon. An obscure movie, *Dolls* transports the audience to the English countryside, where a young girl, Judy (Carrie Lorraine), is traveling through a storm with her despicable father, David, and her ignoble and vicious stepmother, Rosemary. On the way, however, their car gets lodged in the mud, and they seek shelter in a nearby mansion. Breaking in, they encounter the homeowners, an elderly, toy-making couple named Gabriel and Hilary Hartwicke. The couple welcomes the family into their home for the evening and extend the same invitation to a second group of three stranded motorists, naïve Ralph, and the hitchhikers he met on the road, Isabel and Enid. Upon getting settled in the hospitable couple's mansion, however, these various guests reveal their true colors: whereas Judy and Ralph are kind, their companions are most certainly not.

Throughout the night, the duplicitous characters fall victim to the Hartwickes' dolls, which are not only alive and sentient, but also violent. They kill Isabel and transform her into a doll, trick Rosemary into jumping out a window to her death, and fatally shoot Enid. The dolls also begin to attack Ralph, but stop when Judy leaps to his defense and calls him her friend, upon which the dolls confer amongst themselves, and, as Judy reports, deem Ralph to be sufficiently childlike and innocent to spare. Ralph, they believe, is a child in spirit despite being an adult physically.

Meanwhile, David discovers Rosemary's dead body and, believing Ralph responsible, attacks him. After he overpowers Ralph and Judy, David fights one of the dolls and destroys it. At that point, the Hartwickes appear and reveal themselves to be a wizard and a witch who view toys as the heart

The dolls prepare to shoot Enid to death (*The Dolls*, directed by Stuart Gordon. Empire Pictures, 1987).

of childhood. Accordingly, they frequently allow visitors to stay overnight in their mansion and punish those who fail to change their reprehensible ways (e.g., people like David, Rosemary, Isabel, and Enid). David, however, in his rage, tries to attack the couple, who promptly turn him into a doll.

Awakening the next morning, Judy and Ralph find themselves alone in the house with the Hartwickes, who state that the two bleary-eyed guests merely dreamed the previous night's events and that the other four guests have already left. Gabriel and Hilary then read a letter which, they claim, David wrote. In it, "David" acknowledges he has been a poor father and tells Judy to go live with her mother in Boston. Accordingly, Judy and Ralph leave for Boston together, while the camera moves to reveal (to the audience) that their former companions—David, Rosemary, Enid, and Isabel—are sitting on the Hartwickes' mantle, as dolls. The film concludes with another car full of motorists getting stuck in the mud (in the same spot as before), implying the cycle is about to begin anew.

As this summary suggests, *Dolls* is a fairytale in film form, though possibly darker in some ways. Perhaps the most easily recognizable fairytale trope appears at the very beginning of the film, through the character of the evil stepmother. Rosemary openly dislikes Judy, and even throws Judy's beloved Teddy Bear away while they are stranded out in the storm. As befits the evil stepmothers from conventional fairytales (like "Cinderella" or "Snow White"), Rosemary is cruel and nefarious, and an audience familiar with the traditional tales can easily draw this connection between the two. Consequently, Rosemary is more a trope than a character. Narratively, her function is three-fold: first, her presence clearly marks the story as a fairy tale, thereby establishing audience's expectations; second, she serves as the perfect contrast to congenial Judy; and third, her death is karmic, thus allowing the film to become a morality tale.

The audience learns everything it needs to know about Judy merely by comparing her to Rosemary: whereas the former is outgoing and friendly, the latter is spiteful and hostile. More importantly, Rosemary is a jaded adult, but Judy is only an innocent child. One must note here how all of Judy's qualities mark her as pure, the perfect fairytale heroine. Moreover, it is quite likely that the characters' names also play significant roles: "Judy" derives from "Judith," a Hebrew name meaning "Woman from Judea."[51] This translation connects her to the Israelites and, by extension, Jesus. Symbolically, her name suggests her innocence and morality to the audience, while simultaneously establishing her as the character viewers should support and laud.

Thus, the film wants to align its audience with its most moral character because, as a fairytale, it is supposed to impart morality. Scholar Jack Zipes writes:

>...the world of the fairy tale has always been created as a *counter-world* to the reality of the storyteller by the storyteller and listeners. Together, storyteller and listeners have collaborated through intuition as well as conscious conception to form worlds filled with naïve morality. Fundamental to the feel of a fairy tale is its moral pulse. It tells us what we lack and how the world has to be organized differently so that we can receive what we need.[52]

Here, it is the film's propagation of a moral message that codes it as a fairytale. That is to say, the film is not moral simply because it is a fairytale and fairytales are generally moralistic; this argument would be circular. Rather, the film's morality is a trope that helps the audience determine that it is, indeed, a fairy tale. After all, as Zipes' observations (quoted above) demonstrate, morality is a central component of such stories.

And the film's moral message is obvious. David and Rosemary alternate between berating and neglecting Judy from the moment they first appear on the screen. Likewise, Isabel and Enid appear beside the sputtering, nervous Ralph, and the disparity between the characters' ages, attire, and manner, suggests to the audience that the girls are exploiting Ralph's good nature. *Dolls* affirms these differences when it discloses that Isabel is planning to steal Ralph's car and wallet before she leaves.

Discontent with stealing from just one person, she also sets about exploring the mansion to find items she can pilfer. And while Enid does not share her friend's enthusiasm for theft, she is still complicit in Isabel's actions. These actions, like David's and Rosemary's, are immoral. As a result, the dolls target these character, slaying Isabel, Enid, and Rosemary. The eponymous dolls do not kill David, but the Hartwickes transform him into a doll, a karmic comeuppance for his destroying Judy's doll, Punch. The other three miscreants also become dolls in similar karmic moments.

Thus, at the most basic level, the film's narrative (or the Hartwickes' plan) punishes bad behavior and rewards good behavior. Didactically, the film preaches the distinction between immoral and moral acts, and upholds standard moral behavior by penalizing its opposite, the immoral. As is apparent, it is a straightforward morality tale thus far. But *Dolls* goes even further, as it is not only concerned about basic morality: it also depicts anxiety associated with growing up and the loss of innocence. Pivotally, Judy, the film's most moral character, is a child, and the dolls refer to Ralph, the only other traveler the Hartwickes spare, as childlike. Their childish natures save Judy and Ralph from the dolls' wrath. Conversely, it is because the Hartwickes view toys (e.g., their dolls) as the heart of childhood that they punish reprobate visitors by connecting them with children and turning them into symbols of that which they left behind: innocence and youth.

Dolls, subsequently, preoccupies itself with the loss of innocence that can accompany age. It does not go so far as to deem all adults immoral since it spares three adults within its universe: Ralph, who is childlike, and the Hartwickes, who are nurturing toward children. The film's cyclic nature further underscores this reading of the film. At the end, a new group of motorists gets stranded outside the Hartwicke family's mansion. Their arrival, coupled with the Hartwickes' explanation of how they test their guests, suggests the film's events will occur again. Moreover, the sheer number of dolls in the mansion indicates the Hartwickes have been performing this ritual for a long time, and on many different travelers/motorists. Thus, the film begins where it ends and ends where it begins: with a group of characters moving into an otherworldly realm that tests their ethics.

This cyclical narrative structure connects the film more strongly to folklore; as explicated earlier, the repetition of shared tropes is one of folklore's key characteristics. The cycle also makes the film an allegory for human society. As a young girl, Judy represents society's youngest generation. Her elders die when they fail to uphold societal standards, and Judy survives to carry the mantle herself, to be the bearer of virtue. Later, as she passes out of the audience's view, and metaphorically into the future, a new generation (the new group of motorists) arrives. With this new arrival, Judy is no longer the youngest generation, and now a new group must face the Hartwickes' test.

The Hartwicke mansion, wherein the elderly couple evaluates their guests' morality, is a concrete symbol for the coming-of-age narrative. The mansion becomes a litmus test to determine whether characters have successfully held onto their ethics or forsaken them. And as each group passes back out of the mansion, back away from that liminal space magic pervades, a new group, a new youngest generation, must arrive and take their place. Thus, society marches on, youth giving way to age, each generation passing the baton to the next. As a tool of moral instruction, the fairytale is ageless. It carries and propagates societal values across time, reaching each new generation as they come of age.

Rosemary's name, especially, reinforces this reading of *Dolls*. Her name derives from the herb, which represents remembrance,[53] and what is it that the audience is supposed to remember through Rosemary's example? The film's moral lessons, those same lessons each generation must learn if it is to carry on its society's values (e.g., do not steal and do not disrespect your hosts). *Dolls* is, therefore, an intensely didactic film, aimed at moral instruction and enlightenment. While not all horror films are as moralistic as *Dolls*, all the movies I discuss in this volume are didactic to different degrees. For a more implicit approach to morality, one may consider a text that, at the first glance, deceptively seems to be a fairytale movie: Guillermo del Toro's 2006 film, *Pan's Labyrinth* (*El Laberinto del Fauno*).

This acclaimed Mexican-Spanish co-production takes place in 1944's fascist Spain, where protagonist Ofelia (Ivana Baquero) moves to a remote location in the woods with her heavily-pregnant mother, Carmen, so they can be with Ofelia's new step-father, the vicious Captain Vidal. Acrimonious toward the captain, Ofelia embraces a life of fantasy, which begins when she sees a "fairy" in the forest near her new home.[54] Ofelia later follows the fairy into the woods, to a labyrinth, where she meets a faun, an ambiguous creature who claims Ofelia is actually the reincarnation of the fairy princess, Moanna.[55] He further says she must complete three tasks to prove her heritage and earn the right to join her father, the fairy king. A fan of fairytales, Ofelia accepts the faun's tasks, which require her to retrieve a key from a large toad under a tree, to fetch a dagger from a child eating monster, and to shed innocent blood on an altar.

Running parallel to Ofelia's mythical quests is a narrative about Spanish fascism. In this story, Captain Vidal struggles to eliminate rebels living in the remote forests around his home. Vidal is brutal, and his methods Draconian, which is evident when he executes two starving men, merely on the suspicion that they are helping the rebels. He kills them personally, even taking the time to bash in one man's face before shooting him. What makes his act truly atrocious is how he kills the men even before he finishes inspecting their bag, the contents of which include two dead rabbits, appearing to confirm that the men were, indeed, mere hunters and not the traitors Vidal executed them on suspicion of being.

Vidal does, however, battle an actual rebel contingent in the forest. These rebels have been receiving help from Vidal's servant, Mercedes, and from the local doctor, who has also been attending to Carmen. During his battle, Vidal discovers Mercedes and the doctor's treachery, executing the latter and threatening to torture the former. After killing the doctor, the captain also finds a mandrake root Ofelia has placed under her mother's bed in an attempt to cure her illness. Enraged, the captain storms out, and Carmen, consequently angry at Ofelia, burns the root, whereupon she collapses in pain. She soon dies giving birth to her and Vidal's son, Ofelia's half-brother.

Meanwhile, Ofelia completes her first two tasks and then takes her infant brother into the labyrinth to complete the third task. There, in the maze, the faun tells her she must shed innocent blood (her brother's) on the altar, and Ofelia must make her choice against the backdrop of the rebels' direct attack on Vidal's forces. Ofelia refuses to harm her brother but unwittingly completes the faun's task when Vidal shoots her, causing her (innocent) blood to fall upon the altar. The rebels then kill Vidal and take his infant son into their care, while Ofelia—now physically dead—enters the fairy kingdom and takes her place at her parents' side.

Though my inclusion of *Pan's Labyrinth* may seem somewhat strange (after all, many do not regard it as a horror movie), the film does contain several elements of horror, as critics such as Laura Hubner and Jack Zipes have observed.[56] For example, Ofelia's new family occupies a precarious position, at the edge of civilization and surrounded by a wilderness full of hidden threats (the rebels). They also occupy a place on the edge of two different worlds: one with human monsters and one with mythological monsters. Perhaps the best example of both the film's monsters and the film's horror movie elements is the Pale Man, a grotesque, child-eating beast.

Like a depraved serial killer, he surrounds himself with images of his sins, as paintings of his child-eating encircle the room where he sits, apparently waiting for children to enter his domain. Like the witch from "Hansel and Gretel," he entices children with food and then consumes them. Moreover, the paintings suggest he celebrates this behavior and wants to bask in the glory of his child-murders. The Pale Man, therefore, cuts the figure of a horror movie villain, and his presence codes *Pan's Labyrinth* as, at times, a horror film.

Furthermore, as I discussed earlier, central to gothic horror is the slippage between a world of reason (e.g., fascist Spain) and a world of superstition (e.g., Ofelia's fairy tale world).[57] The presence of this slippage in *Pan's Labyrinth* is obvious and well-documented.[58] Thus, *Pan's Labyrinth* contains enough elements of the horror genre to justify its inclusion in a volume on horror films, and, more importantly, it is a liminal enough work to warrant its inclusion in a work on liminality. This intermingling of two states of existence within *Pan's Labyrinth* also appears in Hubner's work, as she contends that the forest outside Ofelia's home is a liminal space, a place that is at once primeval and enlightening.[59] For the most part, however, the extant scholarship on *Pan's Labyrinth* has extensively analyzed the film's gender politics and sociopolitical commentary on fascism and Spanish national identity.

Such matters are crucial to a comprehensive study of the movie, but they also fall outside the scope of this volume, wherein I primarily focus on liminality in horror, and, to a lesser extent, the didacticism of liminal horror. Though *Pan's Labyrinth* is not as intensely moralistic as *Dolls*, and not as rife with foreshadowing as *Urban Legend*, it nevertheless contains a moral center, particularly in Ofelia's fairytale storyline. While Ofelia's first task goes smoothly (notwithstanding the captain's anger toward her), her second does not. Before Ofelia enters the Pale Man's lair, the faun warns her not to eat from the Pale Man's table (interdiction). When she sees the feast, however, Ofelia gives into temptation, waves away the fairies who try to stop her, and eats two of the Pale Man's grapes (violation). Her act of eating the fruit awakens the Pale Man and forces her to run for her life, as she narrowly avoids dying (consequences and attempted escape).

Later that night, the faun returns to her and becomes incensed when he learns about her actions. He proclaims that since Ofelia has broken the rules, she can no longer join the fairy king and will never see him, the faun, again. Though the faun does not keep this promise, it is unmistakable that he is threatening to punish Ofelia for gluttony, a motif that resounds throughout the film. In *Pan's Labyrinth*, the local villagers are subject to the fascist government's stringent food rationing. This is first evident, for instance, when Vidal kills the two farmers on suspicion that they are working with the rebels. These farmers are thin, and they tell Vidal they were hunting because they need food. As if to reinforce the theme of famine, the film's prop department even makes the two rabbits the farmers kill quite skinny, as if the rabbits, too, were starving.

Another instance of this occurs when the film shows a line of villagers forming outside Vidal's home so that they can exchange their ration cards for provisions (which Vidal's soldiers guard). This rationing of food and necessities is intentional, unequal, and hypocritically exploitative. While Ofelia is completing her first task, the captain hosts a dinner party. There, one party member ladles food from a platter while listening to the other party goers' discussion about the necessity of rationing food; in response, this man remarks that rationing will be fine so long as they are careful.[60] That is, he abuses his position of privilege and plenty by saying they will need to ration while, ironically, indulging in a feast. Put another way, "they," the poor villagers, will need to ration, but he will not.

Ofelia, moreover, occupies the same social class as this man. Though she shares a mutual disdain with him, Ofelia is Captain Vidal's stepdaughter and, therefore, a privileged member of the area's highest social class. She will not want for food, shelter, or medical care, unlike the villagers and the rebels in the forest. Thus, her eating the grapes from the Pale Man's table is an act of gluttony, of greed: she does not eat because she is starving, she does it because she cannot resist the temptation. Accordingly, when the faun threatens punishment, he is threatening Ofelia for her moral transgression. As I previously mentioned, however, the faun does not follow through on his threat, and he returns to offer Ofelia the third task after all.

For this final task, Ofelia must take the Pale Man's dagger and her infant brother into the middle of the labyrinth, where the faun commands her to shed her brother's (innocent) blood. Ofelia refuses to harm her brother though, and, in doing so, passes the test. As the film reveals, the actual test was whether Ofelia would refuse to harm an innocent and sacrifice herself instead, which she does, when Captain Vidal shoots her and causes her blood to spill upon the altar. Thus, the faun punishes Ofelia for indulging in one of the seven deadly sins, and then tests her moral judgment by tempting her toward harming an innocent. Though Ofelia fails when she eats from the Pale Man's table, she succeeds in her refusal to hurt her baby brother. Consequently, *Pan's Labyrinth* does espouse a lesson in morality, though it is implicit as compared to the explicit moral didacticism of *Dolls*.

Though *Dolls* is the most inherently moralistic text I have discussed so far, I must note that the other horror films discussed within this section are, nevertheless, edifying and, thus, demonstrate some of the forms that liminal horror's didacticism can take. The messages didactic liminal horror conveys differ from movie to movie: sometimes these films teach their audience the distinction between appropriate and inappropriate behaviors, but at other times, however, their lessons concern something else entirely.

Section Three: Blurred Reality

As this book has shown, liminal horror films undermine the boundary between fiction and reality, albeit to varying degrees. Some films are subtle about it (for instance, *Primeval*) or merely depict troubled individuals using stories as inspiration for their heinous acts (such as the *Scream* franchise or *Urban Legend*). Others, however, go a few steps further and destroy that boundary all together. And these films help to better illustrate why horror stories (liminal horror stories, in particular) are so obsessed with questions about what is real and what is not.

One such film is 1994's *In the Mouth of Madness*, directed by John Carpenter. The protagonist of the film is an insurance investigator, John Trent (Sam Neill), who—while discussing a potential investigation with a colleague over lunch—is attacked by a man with an axe. The man asks if Trent reads Sutter Cane (a famous horror novelist), before a police officer fatally shoots him, saving Trent's life. Soon, Trent learns the man with the axe was Sutter Cane's agent, and also that Trent's new investigation job (which he was discussing before the attack) is to find the missing Sutter Cane and recover the manuscript to Cane's latest novel. According to Cane's publisher, the eccentric writer is missing, and his novel is due. Undaunted by preceding events, Trent accepts the job, suspecting that the publisher himself has staged Cane's disappearance as a publicity stunt to promote the new book.

Nevertheless, Trent, along with Linda (Cane's editor), begins searching for Cane. The duo follow Trent's hunch that the writer is in New Hampshire, residing in that part of the state that most closely corresponds to the location of Hobb's End, a fictional town Cane likes to use as a setting for his stories. Despite the seemingly weak evidence, based on the designs of Cane's book covers, Trent's hunch proves correct, and while driving through the night, he and Linda arrive in Hobb's End itself. The town is apparently real, and it bears an uncanny resemblance to the town in Cane's novels.

Trent, however, is still skeptical, for he believes the town is also a complex ruse to increase the mystique around Cane and his horror stories. Linda, conversely, grows worried. She admits that, initially, Cane's disappearance was a publicity stunt but denies any knowledge of the town. While Linda encounters Cane in a church, Trent encounters a mob of deformed, monstrous people, whereupon he tries to flee Hobb's End in his car. However, with each escape attempt, he simply finds himself teleported back to the town. After crashing, he wakes up in the church, discovering Linda and Cane.

There, Cane informs Trent that the public's belief in his novels has allowed a race of monsters to walk the Earth. Cane also claims that Trent is one of Cane's fictional characters, a character doomed to deliver Cane's final manuscript to the publisher, thereby ushering in the end of the world. Following this revelation, Trent manages to truly escape Hobb's End, and, immediately upon his return to reality, he burns the manuscript, to no avail. On visiting the publisher, Trent learns, to his surprise, that he went alone to find Cane (the publisher disavows all knowledge of Linda), and that the manuscript is already published, with a film adaptation of the book in post-production.

Leaving the publisher's office, Trent finds a man on the street who is reading Cane's new novel, the very book Trent was supposed to find. After asking the man if he is enjoying the book, Trent kills him with an axe. Later, as Cane's monsters ravage the world, Trent walks the deserted streets before watching the book's film adaptation, *In the Mouth of Madness*, alone in a theater. He first laughs, then cries, when he sees himself on the screen and realizes he is the film's main character.

If this summary seems confusing, it is only because Carpenter's 1994 film is, itself, inherently confusing, and on multiple different levels. For instance, where does the reality end and the fiction begin? Despite Trent's declaration that his experience is reality, the film's ending suggests otherwise.[61] But if one follows that thread and regards Trent's existence as fictional, then, why (and how) does the publisher remember Trent and treat him as a real person? Apparently, Cane has literally written Trent into reality, overwriting the publisher's memory. Or, possibly, there is another explanation that remains elusive. This is to say, it is difficult, if not impossible, to separate the layers of fiction and reality in this movie. Perhaps the most useful approach to comprehending this film is its connection to the work of Howard Phillips Lovecraft (a.k.a. H.P. Lovecraft), a highly influential American horror writer from the early 20th century.

Lovecraft's horror often revolves around the incomprehensible, the alien horrors whose very appearance can drive a person to madness. His story "Pickman's Model" involves paintings so horrific their painter, the eponymous Pickman, becomes a pariah, and the story concludes with the narrator viewing a photograph of Pickman's titular model, a real-life creature the painter attempted to capture on canvas. Pivotally here, Pickman can paint horrifying monstrosities only because he has seen such monstrosities in real-life. His paintings are a pale representation of actual horrors. Forming but one small part of Lovecraft's opus, this story feeds into the recurring pop culture narrative that Lovecraft perceived something horrible.

By using the term "pop culture," I mean to convey that *In the Mouth of Madness* is not the only work to suggest that Lovecraft (or an avatar of him, such as Sutter Cane) truly encountered some cosmic horror. Television series such as *Chilling Adventures of Sabrina* and *Supernatural* also depict similar events. So, *In the Mouth of Madness* is part of a broader cultural conversation about Lovecraft's horror and its origins. However, none of this is to say Lovecraft himself encountered the supernatural or that the writers of these various pop culture works believe he did. Rather, because Lovecraftian horror so often places the locus of terror in the real world, wherein it dwarfs fictions and overwhelms understanding, Lovecraft has become an interesting fixture in the Western cultural lexicon. He is, essentially, a shorthand for the notions of real-life terrors and the madness they can cause. Quite simply, for Lovecraft, real-life is indeed scarier than fiction.

This same dynamic carries over into the film, where Sutter Cane's new novel (which bears the same title as the movie) is a paradox. Not only does the novel seem to write the film's events into place, but it also writes the film itself within the film's universe. Consequently, when Trent goes to see *In the Mouth of Madness*, the audience learns that the film Trent is watching, alone in the theater, is the same *In the Mouth of Madness* that the audience has been watching. Cane's novel, therefore, not only bends the reality around itself, but also writes the reality around it. Confusing though this may seem, the very existence of Cane's novel alters the way the audience—we—perceive(s) the film's meta-layers.

To phrase it in a simplistic yet undeniably perplexing manner, how is it possible for Cane's novel to write reality and then to represent the very film that *I* am watching in the external world, a film that stars the character *I* have been watching for the past hour and a half? None of this makes for easy comprehension, which, precisely, is the point: the film's blurring of fiction and reality renders it virtually unfathomable. Much like a Lovecraftian horror, it mocks attempts to understand it and threatens audiences with madness if they even try.

Madness is, of course, central enough to the film to be in its title. This is abundantly clear in the narrative when Trent becomes institutionalized. It is apparent, again, when Trent breaks down while watching the movie alongside the audience. An interesting (and maddening) point to note here is how Trent is watching *In the Mouth of Madness* at the same moment the audience is as well. Since the audience and Trent are engaged in the same activity, they are temporarily aligned with each other. Here, I would like to observe that films operate on connecting us—the audience—with their protagonists. On this point, Garth Jowett and James M. Linton write:

> The object of the moviemaker, then, becomes one of persuading the viewer to cross the distance that separates the viewer from the screen, and to imaginatively enter the space of the screen world to experience vicariously the events that occur within that world.... This intense vicarious involvement in the flow of events is brought about because of two principal factors. This first is displacement of attention ... the second is identification with stars, characters, story types, and situations.[62]

In the context of Carpenter's movie, this means that the line between film and audience becomes even thinner, thereby strengthening the spectators' connection to Trent. Accordingly, the viewers find themselves closer to the narrative that inspires the madness consuming Trent. The conceit of films—the goal of making spectators connect with protagonists and experience their stories vicariously—gets the audience closer to Trent's madness than would have been possible otherwise.

As a result, this moment threatens to allow the film to break into the audience's (our) reality, adding yet another layer to the already complicated obfuscation and obscuration of the fictional and the real occurring throughout its plot. *In the Mouth of Madness,* therefore, is an exercise in instability: it destabilizes the viewer at every turn, by forcing them to question what is real and what is not while they are trying to make sense of a story that makes little sense. The instability, moreover, is akin to the madness Cane's book inspires in the film's universe. Implicitly, *In the Mouth of Madness* threatens us, its audience, by telling us a truth prominent in Lovecraft's work: that there are certain truths better left undiscovered.

The film's cyclical narrative further underscores the connection between real-life and its fictionalization. For instance, at the beginning of the film, an axe-wielding man attacks Trent because of Sutter Cane's novel. Toward the end of the film, however, Trent becomes an axe-wielding man attacking another because of Sutter Cane's novel. Thus, Trent completes a full circle. Likewise, the film's frame narrative depicts Trent in the hospital before he recounts his story and then after he has recounted it, thereby coming to a full circle once again. In both the cases, the circle shows the beginning of a story and then the story's aftermath. Taking a closer look at the events that concern Trent (occur to him or around him) can make this clearer.

In the beginning, for example, Trent has his run-in with Cane's axe-wielding agent even before he agrees to investigate Cane. The agent, therefore, knows Cane's story when Trent does not. Meanwhile, it becomes apparent that Trent's story with Cane has only just begun. He enters the story proper when he commences his search for the elusive writer. At the end of the movie, he is in the agent's shoes, aware now (like the agent was), of Cane's story.

Such a similarity happens again at the very start of the film when Trent is beginning to tell his story. At the film's conclusion, it appears he has narrated it. In the interim, as Trent (and, consequently, the audience) is ignorant of Cane's story while investigating him, the audience, too, is ignorant about Trent's own story at the commencement of the frame narrative (i.e., when Trent starts telling his story of his search for Cane). And this paralleled ignorance further connects the film's audience with its ill-fated protagonist. The spectators experience the story alongside Trent, and they know all the film's secrets only by its conclusion, which is when Trent discovers them as well.

Like Trent, the audience is swept up in a world wherein reality and fiction are virtually indistinguishable from each other. Since one of the film's primary conceits is that fiction can be dangerous, the audience must ask themselves, at the movie's conclusion, whether they have made a mistake in watching it. We, the spectators, question what is real and what is not, and even if we only ask these questions about the events within the film (and not about our own lives), *In the Mouth of Madness* still successfully compels its audience to reflect on the delineation of the story from the truth by narratively aligning us with a mad character for whom the very border that separates fact from fiction remains hazy.

Interestingly, *In the Mouth of Madness* achieves liminality through a strategy that no other film I have discussed so far in this volume has used. Namely, it distorts time. One of the difficulties in analyzing the film lies in its refusal to adhere to a linear chronology. As I noted before, the film favors a cyclical narrative rather than a straightforward one the audience could more readily apprehend. These temporal distortions, moreover, undermine the law of cause and effect, thereby disrupting the audience's ability to comprehend the narrative. In fact, to make sense of the story, it would seem the audience needs to consider the film as a film, a fictional artifact whose story is supposed to be confusing. That is, to impose logic upon the story, the moviegoer must refuse to meet the movie where it is and must align not with the characters, but, rather, with the filmmaker.

Still, for all its incomprehensibility, *In the Mouth of Madness* does not go as far as *Videodrome*, which attacks the very practice of delineating fiction from reality. At stake in *Videodrome* is the threat of reality becoming television. Recall, for instance, how O'Blivion believes television to be more real than reality itself. Consequently, prior to the film's events, he acts on this belief and records hundreds of videotapes of himself. Together, the tapes form a library O'Blivion's daughter curates.

She informs Max of her father's belief that *we* (the audience, or the inhabitants of the film's universe) will come to live through television. What this implies is that if O'Blivion was right in his belief, then he is still alive. His daughter confirms this leap of logic as she continues to speak of him in the present tense, as if he were still living, as if the tapes were his body. The corpus of tapes, therefore, become O'Blivion's new corpus, which is why the tapes Convex inserts into Max pulsate as if they are breathing.

Television is, in *Videodrome*, a new reality that is in the process of supplanting our current, corporeal reality. As if to hammer this point home, Max utters the film's final lines right before shooting himself in the head: "Long live the new flesh."[63] This "new flesh," according to O'Blivion's philosophy, is television.[64] Max's suicide and final words reify the belief that our fictional media allow us to live beyond our physical death, that they can encode us into a new reality. Here, one might object (and rightly so), by pointing out that Max says the aforementioned words (quoted above) while under the influence of O'Blivion's daughter. The words, therefore, might not be his. However, the film supports the notion of this new, mechanical flesh when Max's gun fuses to his hand, thus becoming part of his skin.

While this fusion of man and machine could be another of Max's hallucinations, it reinforces the trope whereby *Videodrome* dissolves the barriers between humanity's corporeal existence and the apparatuses we create. Apparatuses, *Videodrome* suggests, become part of their users. German philosopher Martin Heidegger concurs, reasoning "that since we don't consciously think about our fingers while tying our shoelaces ... in some sense we 'fuse' with our most familiar, functional tools. They become part of us...."[65] If Heidegger's words apply intrinsically to the film, they reveal that *Videodrome* is unique because it does not merely blur the border between fiction and reality: it also questions whether the border is even important. Accordingly, if a digital existence is more real than a corporeal one, then death is but an inconvenience.

If one follows this train of thought the movie proposes, it indicates that what one takes to be real is the dream, and one's fiction is actually the means of waking up. Fiction, consequently, not only becomes reality; fiction *is* reality. And the reverse, of course, is also true: "reality" is but a fiction. At this point, I would be remiss if I did not say that perhaps this, exactly, is the liminal horror film's primary lesson: if horror is didactic, horror films that challenge the distinction between fact and fiction highlight how similar and, at times, indistinguishable the two truly are. While *In the Mouth of Madness* and *Videodrome* are fictions (i.e., they are not real), they nevertheless hint at this truth: humanity's collective, common sense notion of reality is but a fiction, an artificial construction to keep the terrors (or the real monsters) at bay. In real-life, fiction and reality overlap in ways most overlook.

Five

Was It All a
Dream(s) and the Liminal Horror Film

Section One: Waking States and the Fuzzy Border at the Edge of Sleep

Dreams are liminal states if one comprehends that, despite being "fictions" the mind weaves as one sleeps, dreams are not easy to distinguish from reality. In other words, the line between waking and dreaming is thin. Indeed, E.B. Gurstelle and J.L. de Oliveira have proposed a phenomenon called "daytime parahypnagogia," an experience in which waking individuals experience fleeting dreamlike episodes, of which they are aware.[1] Accordingly, their work demonstrates that one can pass from waking to dreaming quite quickly.[2] This finding seems to track with everyday experiences, wherein people traverse in and out of daydreams. Furthermore, Gurstelle and de Oliveira discuss the passage from waking to sleeping and corroborate that there is indeed a liminal space between these two states, where it is difficult to judge oneself to be either awake or asleep.[3]

In early sleep stages, the mind can begin to dream, and yet, conscious thought can still intrude. Upon this intrusion, the dreamer might jolt awake, only to realize they had, however briefly, lost consciousness, that they had slipped into another world without being aware of it. When a person dreams, they often do not know they are dreaming, and, consequently, they think their dreams are real as they unfold. It is only later, with the benefit of hindsight the waking state affords, that they realize their nightly experiences were a fiction, a disembodied figment of their active imaginations. It is quite possible, therefore, that at least for a short period of time, they are convinced that their fictions are reality. Equally probable is that whenever they hear sleep's siren song, their corporeal reality can give way to fleeting episodes of a dreamed existence, regardless of whether they permit it to do so.

Perhaps the most famous and lauded film to illustrate these dynamics is *A Nightmare on Elm Street* (1984). Wes Craven wrote and directed this film, in which a group of teenagers realizes they are having similar nightmares in which a horribly burned figure is chasing them. After a few members of the group die in their sleep, the protagonist, Nancy, begins to put the pieces together. She realizes that this monstrous figure is Freddy Kruger, a child murderer who, after being executed via vigilante justice, is exacting revenge by slaying his killers' children in their sleep. Freddy succeeds in killing most of the group, and Nancy must face him by herself. She ultimately defeats Kruger when she realizes his power relies, principally, on her fear. Thus, she defeats Freddy by turning her back on him, declaring that she is "tak[ing] back every bit of energy [she] gave [him]."[4]

A Nightmare on Elm Street (*Nightmare*) makes the line between dream and reality increasingly hard to distinguish as its story progresses. At the beginning of the film, the audience can easily tell what is a dream and what is not. When Nancy dreams in her classroom, the events are outlandish, nightmarish. The audience, therefore, understands them to be part of a nightmare, as does Nancy, who screams toward Freddy (but probably also to herself) that "It's only a dream."[5] Nevertheless, one should note that an element of doubt pervades the film. Tina, for instance, has trouble telling whether she is awake or not, and Nancy checks the wall above her bed after dreaming the wall is moving. This doubt, though almost negligible at first, grows greater with time.

After she pulls Freddy out of her dream, both Nancy and the audience experience bizarre imagery. When Freddy kills Marge, we (the moviegoers as well as Nancy) watch her body disappear into a storm within her bed. This clearly appears to be dream imagery, and yet, to this point, the audience has been led to believe Nancy is awake. Thus, at this point in the narrative, it is nearly impossible to distinguish dreams from reality. Then, after Nancy banishes Freddy, the audience witnesses a sudden cut to the film's last scene, where Nancy exits her house, with her (dead?) mother following, and gets into a car with her (dead?) boyfriend and friends.

The film's conclusion is notoriously difficult to analyze. Ideally, the last scene should be one where Nancy is awake. Yet, the blurring of the background, the overly bright light, and the out of place, unacknowledged jump-roping little girls all point to the contrary. They indicate this scene is a dream, as do the other inexplicable phenomena concerning the car and Freddy's pulling Marge through the door window. All these events cannot—and do not—make sense if the scene is not a dream. Even so, this scene *should* not be a dream, given the narrative to this point.[6] Essentially, the scene is a conundrum, but it is useful in that it demonstrates, perfectly, the difficulty in distinguishing dreams from reality, thereby reiterating that dreams, themselves, exist in a liminal state.[7]

The film gradually blurs this line even further, so my preceding point—about the movie's ending—is, at most, a nuanced criticism. There is a famous shot (one of many for such an iconic film) where Nancy's phone rings, and upon answering the call, she hears Freddy on the other end, who tells her he is her boyfriend now; then, Freddy's tongue extends from the phone and licks her.[8,9] If the film's conclusion is a conundrum, this moment is a build-up to it, for this scene is tricky to analyze—in the context of the film—because, so far as the audience can tell, Nancy is not asleep when this event takes place. She is attempting to contact Glenn to wake him up.

Accordingly, here, the movie pushes the audience to—once again—acknowledge that the line between waking and dreaming, reality and fiction, is not only blurred, but blurred by degrees. Put another way, this dividing line can become increasingly strained. As *A Nightmare on Elm Street* progresses, this border becomes harder to navigate, with dream "fictions" beginning to crossover into the "real world." The strain, and its illustration, is such that the film challenges the very notion of distinguishing dream from reality, postulating also that, sometimes, the states can coexist, as happens with the incidents of Marge and the bed and Nancy and the phone.

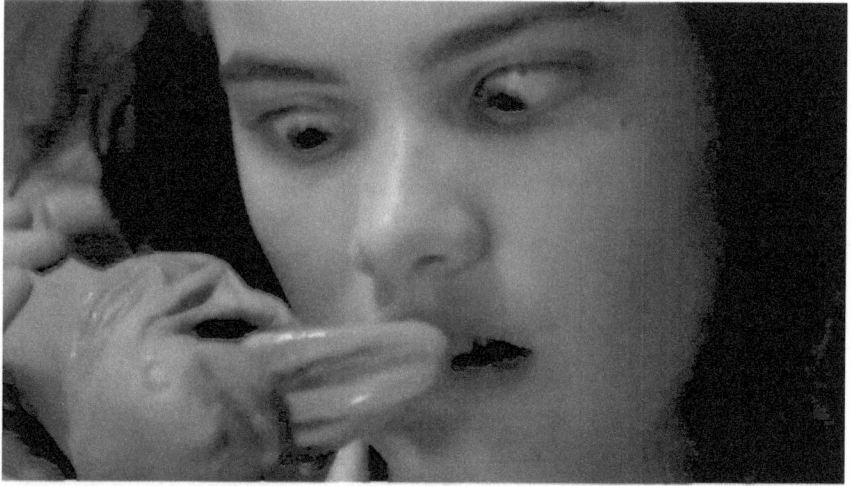

Freddy's tongue extends from Nancy (Heather Langenkamp)'s unplugged telephone (*A Nightmare on Elm Street*, directed by Wes Craven. New Line Cinema, 1984).

Thomas Metzinger describes a related (albeit un-identical) phenomenon: "You can have dreams in which you are not only aware of the fact that you are dreaming but also possess a complete memory both of your dream life and your waking life, as well as the phenomenal property of agency on the level of attention, thought, and behavior. Such dreams are called *lucid dreams*" (emphasis in the original text).[10] The audience, while watching *Nightmare*, can never be certain that Nancy ever lucid dreams; what they can certainly perceive, however, are dreams overlapping with waking reality when Nancy asks Glen to watch her sleep. During this scene, Nancy walks around in her dream but is still cognizant enough of the waking world to inquire of Glen whether he is still watching her, and she experiences his answer in her dream, wherein he appears to give her a confirmation, before disappearing again.[11]

This scene, however, does not quite prove that Nancy can lucid dream, as she seems only somewhat aware of her external circumstances. That is, Nancy can only partially access reality. She predominantly remains in the dream and must confirm with Glen that he is awake and still watching her; additionally, her ability to perform even this action diminishes as she drifts further into the dream. Still, the phenomenon of lucid dreaming enables the audience to comprehend—to a certain extent—the mixing of dream and life during the film's climax, more so because the inability of Nancy (and the viewers) to differentiate dream from real-life strongly resounds with the phenomena of lucid dreaming *and* day dreaming, both of which intermix the states of sleeping and waking in real life, thereby blurring and negating the distinctions between the two.

This trend appears in some films I have already discussed in this book. Candyman, the legend, for instance, is initially content to let Candyman the criminal keep his name alive, and he only appears to Helen after this proves insufficient. It is from there that the charge of Helen's delusion begins.[12] Before the real Candyman's appearance, however, the audience has no reason to believe he is real in the film's universe. Such a perception is, in fact, reasonable, and we—the external audience—have to only extend the skepticism with which we regard everyday ghost stories to the film's narrative to understand why Helen and Bernadette believe Candyman is merely a legend. Once the film's spectators see him, though, they have a reason to accept that Candyman may be more than a legend, that he may actually be real.

From this moment on, it matters less and less that Helen becomes increasingly delirious and seems to faint whenever she is around Candyman. Regardless of whether Helen is a delusional murderer or the prey of a legendary vengeful spirit, the intrusion has already occurred: legend has already breached onto reality, and consequently, *our* distinctions (as the audience) between fiction and reality become obfuscated. The audience must start asking what is real and what is not. And this obscuration of the real and the fictional reaches its peak with the film's conclusion, when Helen becomes her own Bloody Mary-esque spirit, thereby espousing the fact (or fiction-turned-fact) that legends evolve to encompass a truth that would not exist, if not for the pre-existence of the legend itself.

In fact, this gradual blurring is a natural extension of plot structure and story development: usually, movies tend to accelerate as they near their climaxes. If this general rule applies to horror films, we—the audience—perceive that the threat(s) to the movies' protagonists, particularly the central protagonist(s), become more palpable as the story develops. In one way or another, the violence escalates as the horror film approaches its climax. To use a previously discussed, straightforward example, in slasher films like *Friday the 13th*, the killer begins by lurking in the shadows, targeting individual characters as they separate from the herd. Once a significant number of characters are dead, however, the killer emerges to engage the final survivor in a life-and-death chase.

This is, in fact, an escalation: whatever trends the movie uses and establishes until that particular point become exaggerated toward the end. It is therefore natural that these "reality bleed" films gradually escalate their blurring of fiction and reality.[13] In *Scream*, the overt film references become discussions of life as if it were a movie. Billy says to Sidney, "It's all—It's all a movie. It's all one great big movie," and Sidney quips "Not in my movie" after shooting Billy in the head.[14] In other words, the references to horror films and the treatment of life as if it were a film get more explicit as *Scream* progresses. At its conclusion, the characters refer to their own movies, thereby taking ownership of the narrative and staking their own claims to it. The film's characters, therefore, increasingly acknowledge the film's events as *film events* unfolding based on the role each character plays.

Likewise, in *New Nightmare*, Freddy's incursions into the real world become increasingly explicit, and the line separating fiction and reality all but dissolves. Freddy reaches down out of the sky to move Heather's son on a highway, and Heather ends the film itself by reading the film's script, written by Wes Craven's character (played by Craven himself). This is to say that when a film seeks to increase the tension, the dramatic stakes, it can attack the line between fiction and reality, using techniques of meta-discourse, and, more importantly, liminality via the fictionalization of the real and the realization of the fictional. Revealing to the audience that the line dividing the two states is porous is merely a tactic to prime the audience for an all-encompassing assault, with fiction and reality violently blending into each other. That this blend is violent hints at horror's unique ability to confront this subject matter.[15]

Accordingly, the first—and most pivotal—fact that we, as the audience, must comprehend about the liminal horror film's inclusion of dreams is this: that the line between waking and dreaming is actually blurry and permeable in real-life, just as it is in fiction. Moreover, the dramatic escalation I observe here mirrors the escalating distress of one stuck in a nightmare or fever dream. Thus, liminal horror films such as *A Nightmare on Elm Street* depict uncomfortable truths about the moviegoer's reality, a reality in which people can traverse back and forth between the waking and the dreaming states without being aware of it. This reality, disconcerting though it may be, is, in truth, a world wherein nightmares can act as the mind's personal psychiatrist.

Section Two: Slaying the Dream Demon— Nightmares as Therapy

The Oxford English Dictionary (OED) declares that the word "nightmare" started life in 1300 as an actual mare of the night, meaning "A female spirit or monster supposed to settle on or produce a feeling of suffocation in a sleeping person or animal."[16] By 1562, however, the word had evolved to signify a bad dream.[17] Simply put, then, a nightmare is a dream whose primary content is emotionally charged and negative, and that often (though not always), concerns a supernatural entity pursuing the dreamer.[18]

Neurologist Patrick McNamara finds this to be a recurring and significant aspect of the nightmare. Not only is a nightmare negatively charged, but its negative charge focuses on this creature, the being who does not belong and who attacks the dreamer. Ergo, conflict is central to the nightmare.[19] For example, when examining a woman's long-term dream journals, McNamara observes that "The nightmares were high in 'striving.'"[20] In other words, nightmares are goal-oriented, and their goal is inseparable from their affinity for the unfamiliar, which takes form as the aforementioned creatures/monsters.[21] The nightmare's conflict, then, revolves around a creature the dreamer's mind has created.

McNamara points out, however, that a creature formulated by one's own mind must, therefore, have its thoughts and actions readily available to the dreamer.[22] This postulation suggests that the creature in one's dream is less an outside force and more an aspect of oneself.[23] To phrase it simply: the monster is the dreamer; each person is the monster haunting their own most spine-chilling dreams. Consequently, the nightmare conflict, that same chase sequence most dreamers have run before, represents not self versus outsider but rather self versus self. It is a representation of one aspect of a person's identity contradicting another aspect of their identity so that the two clash. McNamara substantiates this notion by showing that anxiety about identity is, in fact, a reliable trigger for nightmares[24]; additionally, he notes that nightmares become more frequent at key transitional periods during childhood development, when a young person is fundamentally reshaping or defining their personal identity.[25]

Accordingly, the crux of McNamara's work is this: that nightmares tend to involve a conflict between the dreamer's self and another, monstrous, part of themselves that then threatens the dreamer's sense of identity. Consider, for instance, that the dream character is actually the dreamer's avatar, a symbol of their identity. If one applies this consideration to some of the previously discussed nightmarish characters, then it becomes evident that creatures like Freddy Kruger threaten not so much the dreamer's life as they do the dreamer's sense of self, threatening to erase or override it with another part of the same psyche.[26] To further demonstrate the validity of this asseveration and stress the important role nightmares play in liminal horror films, I discuss five works in this section: Henry Fuseli's painting *The Nightmare* (1781), Craven's *A Nightmare on Elm Street*, *Jacob's Ladder* (1990, directed by Adrian Lyne), *Gothic* (1986,

The Nightmare by Henry Fuseli (1781).

directed by Ken Russell), and *Der Nachtmahr* (2016, directed by Achim Bornhak).

The first of these texts, Fuseli's *The Nightmare*, is a famous painting that depicts a sleeping woman reclined on her bed with an imp sitting on her chest and a horse looking on.[27] Both in title and content, the painting invokes nightmares.[28] Specifically though, the painting showcases the night hag, a phenomenon in which the dreamer cannot move but is aware of a malevolent entity's presence, can feel the pressure of the entity upon their corporeal person, and feels a sense of dread, all while maintaining an awareness of their surroundings.[29] In other, simpler, words, Fuseli chose to capture not a fictional example of a dream or nightmare, but a real world experience many have encountered. Unfortunately, most readily available sources on the night hag are, to put it lightly, less than reputable for a scholarly work, but the phenomenon itself is well-documented as an extant experience.[30]

In a similar vein, Christopher Frayling writes: "The critics seemed to agree that Fuseli had personified an idea. The question was, what exactly *was* the idea?"[31] As I have argued, however, Fuseli portrays one notion of nightmares themselves: i.e., he presents one type of nightmare occurrence.[32] And that Fuseli chose to focus on a real-world phenomenon, the original nightmare itself, simply heightens its relevance for my discussion. *The Nightmare* compels one to perceive the image of a malevolent entity weighing down a dreamer, a motif that reoccurs throughout the central works in this volume. The image of the tortured dreamer, trying to escape the creature at their heels or attempting to free themselves of the weight on their chest, is pivotal to further comprehend the common, everyday desire to escape one's nightmares. Indeed, an understanding of this aspect of Fuseli's famous work helps one understand the connotations of many other nightmare fictions. *The Nightmare* is a legacy by—and in—itself.

For instance, the painting appears in *Gothic*, a film it inspires and that takes place almost entirely on June 16, 1816. On that day in history, a group of writers including Percy Bysshe Shelley, Mary Godwin and Lord Byron convened at Byron's estate, Villa Diodati. Supplemented by lurid tales, their circumstances in the haunted summer stoked their imaginations into dark fires of fantasy, and they set about creating their own ghouls and creatures. The group read ghost stories and then challenged each other to craft scary tales of their own, the most famous of which became Mary Shelley's *Frankenstein* (1818).

Directed by Ken Russell, *Gothic* is a modern spin on that night at Diodati. The movie shows Percy Shelley, Mary Godwin, and Claire Clairmont joining Dr. Polidori at Diodati, on the shores of Lake Geneva. The group settles in, and, that night, they read German ghost stories and hold a séance wherein they project their worst fears onto a skull. However (or as one might have guessed from such an introduction), the night soon takes a turn for the bizarre and horrific, as characters begin acting strangely and experiencing bizarre events. As this happens, the characters realize they have brought a creature to life that is the amalgamation of all their fears, the very fears they projected onto the skull. The increasingly unhinged cast joins, once again, to hold a second séance, hoping to banish the creature they created. Mary, however, smashes the skull, and becomes even more desperate, which, in turn, leads her to attempt jumping down from the villa's balcony. She is, however, saved when Percy intervenes, and Mary awakens the next day to find everyone unfazed.

Though she wakes up, Mary does so with a heavy heart, for the last bit of her nightmare, the creature—which nicely fits McNamara's point that all nightmare monsters are reflections of the self—has her stuck in a room full of doors.[33] Each door she opens gives her a prophetic vision of impending doom. She sees, for instance, Percy's drowned body, and, as the film's final lines disclose, eight years after the events at Diodati, all the members of the central cast are dead, except for Mary and Claire. Thus, Mary's visions come true. The dream world punishes her for trying to escape, ending its surrealist horror on a poignantly real note. Consequently, when Mary awakens, she must carry with her the knowledge of what is to come. Though she then joins Percy at play, it is clear she has reservations, and she is justified in her concern. Thus, despite being awake, she fails to escape the nightmare, for its power is not confined to the dream world, a phenomenon to which moviegoers are also susceptible.

That this phenomenon is true becomes clear when one considers how many people feel compelled to relate their dreams in some form; if a nightmare's power was restricted to its fictional world, people would not feel the need to express either their dreams or nightmares, in narratives, art, film, and so on. Paul Schwenger writes in *At the Borders of Sleep: On Liminal Literature* that telling (framing or narrating) one's dreams is "a project of control."[34] Furthermore, Schwenger quotes Maurice Blanchot to state that people tell dreams "to appropriate them and to establish ourselves, through common speech, not only as the master of our dreams but as their principal actor, thereby decisively taking possession of this similar though eccentric being who was us over the course of the night."[35]

What this evinces is how dreams exert power over their dreamers, even outside the dream world. While I suspect this is not a shocking revelation, it, nevertheless, helps validate the worry Mary feels in *Gothic*, even after she is awake. This is especially true when the last vestiges of reality's protective veil fall away and the dreamer (or, in the case of the film, Mary) becomes exposed to fiction's scorching rays, or finds themselves at the mercy of figures from their nightmares, the very creatures with the power to hurt them.

This leads me to note that the parallels between *A Nightmare on Elm Street* and *Gothic* are strong: both take place, primarily, in the dream world, and both involve their protagonists ultimately breaking out.[36,37] Both films depict a supernatural being tormenting the protagonist, which (as I have stated before) is a hallmark of nightmares.[38] As the films progress, though, the conflicts develop further and become more nuanced, and the protagonists get pointed advice about what they must do to escape. For instance, Nancy's boyfriend and her mother both tell her she must abandon her fear. Glenn informs Nancy about the Balinese way of dreaming, claiming that they know one must turn one's back against the dream monster to defeat it. As for those who do not turn their backs, he says: "I guess those people don't wake up to tell what happens."[39] Similarly, her mother says, "You face things. That's your nature. That's your gift. But sometimes you have to turn away too."[40]

In *Gothic*, meanwhile, Byron gives Mary the solution to escaping her nightmare. When the group is frantically trying to hold the second séance with the hopes of banishing their abomination back into their minds, Mary refuses to participate. She and Byron argue over whether it is, in fact, possible to slay a nightmare, and Byron echoes Percy's earlier sentiment ("What we have created with our minds, we can destroy with our minds") by saying that "We can wipe it away like waking from a dream."[41] Contrarily, Mary replies: "No, thoughts are immortal. Thoughts can't die."[42] Thus, Mary does not participate in the séance, and despite Percy's assurance that "The storm is over," the next morning she reflects, "We are dead. It showed me the torture it has in store for us."[43]

Consider the advice that these two distinct characters receive in two different texts: Nancy is directed to overcome her phobia, and Mary is told she must confront her fear, project it back onto the skull, and destroy the horror she created, the embodiment of her unborn child. And how do Nancy and Mary use this advice? How do the films end? *A Nightmare on Elm Street* reaches its conclusion once Nancy defeats Freddy: this is possible only after she turns her back on him and refuses to be afraid of him any longer. She tells him, "This is just a dream. You're not alive. This whole thing is just a dream."[44] She literally turns her back on him, whereupon he lunges at her only to disappear as Nancy terminates the source of his power: her fear. Thus, she is successfully able to escape the dream and defeat the villain by following the advice she has received.

In *Gothic*, Byron's advice to Mary is quite similar. As I noted earlier, Marge and Glen both instruct Nancy that she must abandon her fear if she is to overpower Freddy. Meanwhile, Mary initially embodies her worst fears, which provide fuel for the creation of *Gothic*'s nightmarish monster. Then, she learns she must project her fears again, this time to contain them. Accordingly, the second séance is about control. The first séance is Mary's subconscious bringing her fears to light so she may face them, and the second séance is her opportunity to defeat said fears—which she fails to do. Unlike Nancy, Mary does not follow the advice, and consequently, she fails to take a step toward self-realization, a step that (these works suggest) is pivotal for escaping nightmares. Nancy overcomes her nightmare, and were it not for the slew of sequels, the audience might believe her ordeal has ended. Mary, on the other hand, remains haunted by her dream, a dream she did not escape so much as outlast. While she cannot sleep forever, Mary cannot, at the same time, run forever.

It is here that Fuseli's painting becomes applicable to Mary's predicament in *Gothic*; *The Nightmare*, being a frozen image, presents its spectators with the moment of the nightmare but affords them no clue about how to escape from it. That is, Fuseli illustrates the nightmare's phenomenology but not its escape route. So, this painting becomes a road map to the nightmares of the haunted summer, as for the fictionalized Mary, there is no escape. As with Fuseli's character, she stays weighed down and tortured in her sleep, and whatever reprieve she finds is fleeting, a temporary respite from a demon that will not stop visiting her.[45]

That the film's director, Russell, included Fuseli's *The Nightmare* in *Gothic* is apposite since the painting enables the audience to comprehend the film's story. Russell delivers to his audience a Mary who cannot overcome her fears, possibly because the woman in the painting can never overcome her fears either: a painting—unlike a film image—never moves, never changes, thereby presenting a poignant and pertinent juxtaposition, emphasizing that nightmares are, even in reality, inescapable.

Thus, *The Nightmare*, *A Nightmare on Elm Street*, and *Gothic* all demonstrate three similar treatments of nightmare fiction and how we, the audience, may (or may not, ever) escape it. The resultant scenario is bleak indeed. The nightmare's beating hooves pursue Mary well past the dream state, through the unhallowed halls of her darkest fears. In comparison, *A Nightmare on Elm Street* proves useful, then, because it unveils a protagonist who succeeds in the same trial Mary fails. Presumably, it indicates to a critical observer what would have happened if only Mary had confronted her fears.

Thus, different characteristics of nightmares come to the forefront in nightmare fiction, where the blurring (of reality and fiction) mimics the details available to the dreamer: the liminal states (e.g., between life and death) prevail, logic falls by the wayside sometimes, and escape proves easier said than done. The prevailing trend here is that people (e.g., characters and audiences), generally, wish to get out of—escape—their nightmares, but that doing so is difficult. Mary fails to escape her nightmare, while Nancy undergoes significant trials before she finally succeeds at ending her torment.

We—the audience as well as the fictional characters—want to be able to say: "It's only a dream," a statement Craven echoes with *The Last House on the Left*'s mantra of "It's only a movie."[46] Nancy, too, yells the very same at Freddy but manages to escape that particular dream only by burning herself on a pipe. Thus, the cries of "it's just a dream" often prove ineffectual. The nightmare continues, and moviegoers recurringly see this image of tormented dreamers crying out, hoping to escape.[47] This is because, seemingly, there are only two ways to escape the nightmare, escaping being the trapped character's earnest hope.

The first method is evident when one tries to impose an external reality to overcome the nightmare's internal reality; that is, when one attempts to wake up to escape the nightmare. This can work, sometimes, because when the subject becomes aware that they are dreaming, the dream world often collapses. As *Gothic* demonstrates, however, this is only a partial answer: it is akin to slapping a band-aid over deep-running, psychological wounds. McNamara's averment about nightmare conflicts validates this comparison since, as he notes, waking up is merely a superficial and temporary relief, for the real battle is never between the subject and the monster: it is between the subject and their own selves.

That is, nightmares are confrontations people experience between what they *presume* themselves to be and those facets of their selves they have not yet explored. Thus, when they have a nightmare, they are not fighting literally for life and death but rather the preservation of their self-identity, which is a metaphorical life and death combat. When they flee from such a fight (as Mary does in *Gothic*), they leave themselves weak and render their identities tenuous. What is key, consequently, is that to overcome the nightmare, one must face its monsters head-on, confront one's weakness of self and resolve the inconsistencies.

Reviewing the three texts discussed so far in this section, however, one may realize, with some close observation, that at the end of each of these three texts, the protagonist's escape is apparently incomplete. Note, for instance, how *A Nightmare on Elm Street*'s final scene appears to take Nancy back into the nightmare. Even if one interprets the film (as I largely have) as if it had preserved its original ending, the audience has no way of knowing, precisely, how the experience has affected Nancy because she does not receive much screen time after (ostensibly) defeating Freddy.

Even though she overcomes her fear, she continues to be angry at

Freddy, and the film does not reveal (explicitly) if she finds happiness when she (apparently) exits the nightmare. The lasting impression, therefore, is one of ominous ambiguity, which does not seem encouraging in the context that Nancy did defeat the monster that was an embodiment of her own alien self. Thus, to end this section on a high note, it would be useful to examine a film that illustrates a complete escape (and puts a more positive spin on this form of narrative). That complete escape appears at the end of *Jacob's Ladder*.

The film's eponymous protagonist, Jacob Singer, is a Vietnam war veteran suffering from horrific hallucinations of demons and other bizarre entities. As his mental health deteriorates, Jacob experiences frequent flashbacks to the day in Vietnam when he was bayoneted in the stomach, and so, the audience watches as American forces discover and medevac Jacob from the battle. Contradicting all these events, however, the film's conclusion reveals Jacob died in Vietnam, as the bayonet wound proved fatal. Consequently, the film's main narrative, and the scenes in the city, were all Jacob's dying dream, as well as the demons and the monsters in his final nightmare.

It is this last part of the movie, which discloses that the entire film was, in fact, Jacob's dying dream, that links together all the texts in this specific section. Wes Craven initially intended for *A Nightmare on Elm Street* to end similarly. He wanted the entire film to be Nancy's nightmare, with all the character deaths, and, indeed, the entire narrative, being a single dream. The film's title was supposed to be literal, with the entire movie being one nightmare, *a* nightmare on Elm Street (where Nancy lives), as it were. The film's producers, however, saw its potential as a franchise and changed the ending accordingly. This alteration begot the film's famously difficult final scene.[48,49]

And so, here there are three central film texts that either are or were supposed to be a dream (Fuseli's *The Nightmare* differs from these three movies in that it depicts an external view of a dream and not the narrative playing out in the dreamer's mind—the actual dream). However, as I have established thus far, even these three films are not identical. There are three different protagonists—Mary, Nancy, and Jacob—with three distinct outcomes: the first assuredly fails to fully escape her dream, the second seemingly fails as well (though it is ambiguous), but the third successfully flees from his nightmare.

Like *A Nightmare on Elm Street*, *Jacob's Ladder* takes place primarily in the dream world and involves its protagonists ultimately breaking out of their nightmare, in some way or the other. Another similarity is the one I have already observed with regard to *Gothic* and *A Nightmare on Elm Street*: that both *Jacob's Ladder* and *A Nightmare on Elm Street* present their protagonists struggling with supernatural beings, which are, once again, hallmarks of nightmares.[50] As these two films progress, however, the conflicts evolve, and (as with Mary and Nancy) both Jacob and Nancy get pointed advice about what they must do to escape successfully. I have already discussed the advice Nancy receives, so I focus here on directives Jacob gets from his chiropractor, Louie.

Louie describes Jacob's circumstances with remarkable (almost prescient) accuracy, informing him: "If you're frightened of dying and holding on, you'll see devils tearing your life away. But, if you've made your peace, then the devils are really angels freeing you from the earth."[51] Louie, one should note, is decidedly angelic. Jacob compares him to an angel in a scene where Louie stands over him, clad in white, and framed with bright light at his back. He may be foulmouthed and aggressive, but Louie is clearly Jacob's angel.[52]

Given his poignant advice and guidance to a dying man who is hesitating to move on, Louie can also be regarded as a psychopomp, much like the sparrows in *The Dark Half*. Moreover, the instructions Louie imparts to Jacob are comparable to those imparted to Nancy: where Nancy must overcome her fear, Jacob must make his peace (i.e., be ready to die). And they defeat their nightmares by doing exactly that, as the movies' conclusions show: Nancy defeats Freddy only once she turns her back on him and refuses to fear him any longer, while Jacob makes peace with his death by accepting that he is dying.[53]

As mentioned, *Jacob's Ladder* is almost entirely Jacob's final dream (or nightmare), and the audience realizes Jacob did witness all the events, the dream sequences, depicted to the spectators, as one of the army doctors presiding over him after his death says: "He looks kind of peaceful, the guy. He put up a hell of a fight, though."[54] In other words, Jacob struggled against dying longer than he needed to, past the point where such a struggle actually mattered. That struggle led to his struggling with the devils Louie mentions. To achieve the "peaceful" look, Jacob had to confront his demons and come to terms with his impending death, and, in particular, also accept his son Gabe's young death.[55]

Gabe, as the viewers learn, was hit by a car while walking his bike across the street, and yet, Jacob sees images of Gabe and his bike throughout the film. For instance, Jacob spots an out-of-place bike with a spinning wheel in the hospital, when doctors are taking him in for an "x-ray."[56] This scene is one of several that code the film as a nightmare, as the hospital has bloody body parts strewn about the floor, an open mental asylum somehow on the way to radiology, and an empty, dilapidated hall with random bicycles. The imagery is out of place and horrific, as befits a nightmare.

However, as the final scene of the main narrative (city) portrays, Jacob and Gabe meet, and Gabe says to his father, "Come on. Let's go up."[57] The two ascend the stairs, hand in hand, disappearing into an increasingly bright light. The ascension, the blinding light, and Gabe's name (an allusion to the archangel Gabriel) all combine to indicate Jacob is going to heaven. He is going to attain rest and peace, which contrast with the torment he has experienced throughout the film. It is only after this scene that the army doctor—who corroborates Jacob's struggle with death—appears and the movie discloses Jacob died in Vietnam and that all the film's other events took place in his head. Following Louie's suggestion, Jacob makes his peace so he can move on, out of his hellish dying dream and into the light with his likewise dead son. Tormented in his dream, Jacob dies at ease.

What is striking about these three films (*Gothic*, *A Nightmare on Elm Street*, and *Jacob's Ladder*) is also the theme of this section: their similar portrayal of an equally comparable conflict, that of escaping the nightmare. Each of these three films substantiates how the nightmare liminal horror film presents another opportunity for liminal horror to act as personal therapy. All three protagonists (Mary, Nancy, and Jacob) find themselves trapped in nightmares, and all three must resolve their inner conflicts if they are to successfully escape the dream world and, thereby, reengage with external reality. Interestingly, external reality is a moving target, and not all nightmare films require protagonists to move back into it and out of the nightmare.

One such film is director Achim Bornhak's 2015 *Der Nachtmahr* (*The Nightmare*). This German film follows a young woman, Tina, on the cusp of her 18th birthday. Tina spends much of her time partying with her friends, but, one night, she begins experiencing frightening imagery. One of her classmates shows her a picture of a disfigured fetus on her phone and then uses an app to morph a photo of Tina into the picture of the fetus. Another classmate then shows her a video of a car striking a bikini-clad girl in the middle of the street. Tina wanders away from the party to urinate, only to see the fetus in the bush. Shaken, she convinces her friends to take her home. When they go to the car, Tina finds her necklace has somehow fallen into the middle of the road. So, she walks over to the necklace and kneels to gather its pieces, only for a car to strike her.

Strangely enough, she wakes up as if these events did not happen and finds herself back in the car outside of the party, with her necklace safe around her neck. Once she is back home, Tina sees the fetus again, but her parents assure her she was merely having a nightmare. After this event, disconnected scenes occupy the film, as its flashes between scenes of Tina partying, speaking with a therapist, and being threatened with institutionalization, as her parents (and classmates) think she is having a psychotic breakdown.

Tina has another encounter with the fetus as it raids her family's refrigerator. The next day, she also discovers she and the fetus are physically linked. When the fetus cuts its tongue, her tongue also bleeds. Unable to escape the fetus, Tina accepts it. Once she does, however, her parents see the fetus for the first time, as it sleeps in Tina's arms. They attack it and call animal control, who tranquilize and remove the fetus, placing it in the hospital. With the fetus gone, Tina attempts to readjust to school and normalcy, but finds the fetus remains on her mind. She also discovers her friends have quietly disinvited her from her own birthday party.

The night of the party, Tina stubbornly dresses, breaks the fetus out of the hospital, and crashes the party, even passionately kissing her crush, Adam, for the first time. Her parents track her down, and they stand awestruck with the rest of the partygoers, watching as Tina picks up and embraces the fetus. Her father, however, snaps out of the seeming—yet shocking and unusual—idyll, and appears to bludgeon the creature to death. Then the film rewinds itself, until Tina wakes up in a car the fetus is driving down the road (the same car shown in the film's opening shot). Tina climbs from the backseat into the passenger seat beside the fetus, and, with that, the film abruptly ends.

If this summary seems confusing, it is only because *Der Nachtmahr* is a strange, borderline incomprehensible, film. In fact, the director says he intends for viewers to lose their sense of what is happening while they watch the movie, thereby forcing them to arrive at their own individual interpretations of it.[58] Disorientation, therefore, is central to *Der Nachtmahr*'s mission. It even starts with a disclaimer that warns of intense strobe lights (likely a warning for viewers with epilepsy), isochronic tones, and binaural frequencies. "[A]nyway," the disclaimer concludes, "this film should be played loudly."[59] This is interesting because, as I noted during my discussion of *Antrum*, the science on binaural frequencies remains unclear, even though there is some evidence to suggest they can unnerve audiences. The case for isochronic tones is similar, as the two are related phenomena.[60]

Moreover, the use of these destabilizing effects aligns *Der Nachtmahr* with the effect of an actual nightmare that forces the dreamer to wrestle with unclear logic and non-linear stories. *Der Nachtmahr*, in other words, aims to be an experience rather than a story, and underlying this aim is the story's structure: the film's narrative is a circle that mirrors the sleep-wake cycle. The story opens on a car driving down the road, and it closes, as I mentioned earlier, on the same car on the same road. The film reinforces this notion of cyclicality at other times as well. For example, the fetus haunting Tina is the same fetus in the picture Tina's friends show her, and the video Tina sees—of a girl being hit by a car—perfectly matches the incident when Tina herself is hit by a car. These two moments hint at the film's underlying structure, whereby the end becomes the beginning, and events keep repeating themselves.

This structure is akin to that of the sleep-wake cycle because that cycle is also one of repeated events, wherein a person lies down, sleeps, dreams, wakes up, lies down, sleeps, dreams, and so on, until the moment of death. In this sense, the title *Der Nachtmahr* is meta-referential for the film because it denotes how the film is supposed to encapsulate a nightmare and be like a nightmare in itself: an experience the dreamer has to make sense of. However, since by watching the film unfold, it is the viewers who are watching *Der Nachtmahr,* it becomes their responsibility to parse the film in an attempt to comprehend it.

Here, one should note that film scholars have likened the act of watching a movie to the act of dreaming, because movie theaters offer dark, oneiric spaces in which images appear projected onto a screen, much as dream images appear projected onto the mind's eye.[61] And because *Der Nachtmahr*'s plot mirrors not just the sleep-wake cycle but also the film viewing cycle (enter theater, view movie, leave theater), the film becomes even more complicated than it might appear at first glance. To analyze it, one would do well to keep both these cycles (sleep-wake and movie viewing) in mind. Consequently, as the film's director, Bornhak, intends, each viewer will, quite likely, interpret the film differently and so, infer different meanings from it. Accordingly, here, I present what I understand from the film. Upon watching *Der Nachtmahr,* I was able to discern two apparent readings: a coming of age narrative and a narrative about mental illness.

As the film's events occur on and around Tina's 18th birthday, the day she becomes a legal adult according to German law, it is natural to read the film as a bildungsroman.[62] More details from the film augment this reading. First, Tina childishly squabbles with her romantic rival, even lashing out when the other girl acts friendly toward her. Second, she is also an inexperienced driver, as she stalls her parents' car the only time she drives during the movie. Third, and finally, not only does Tina still live with her parents, but she runs to them for safety when the fetus frightens her. Thus, in many ways, Tina is still a child, and the film, consequently, becomes a tale about Tina slowly reaching maturity and entering adulthood when she is not entirely ready.

To be sure, she is an adult in some ways. For instance, her appearance is mature enough that one could take her for an adult. In another instance of her physical maturity, she dabbles in drugs; her intellectual maturity, on the other hand, is evident from her insight into William Blake's poetry (during the one class she attends throughout the film). Accordingly, the film seems to insinuate that, though Tina may be considered an adult physically and intellectually, she must still accept responsibility and attain emotional maturity. In addition to Tina's contrasting levels of (im)maturity, the fetus further reinforces this insinuation about Tina.

As a fetus, the creature concretely connects to childbirth. Meanwhile, as a young adult, who is emotionally immature yet physically capable of reproducing, Tina faces the threat of becoming a teenage mother. While she does not have sexual intercourse in the film and appears to struggle with acting on her feelings toward Adam, the metaphoric connection is clear. Moreover, the fetus acts akin to an infant when it explores the world with its mouth. That is, it focuses on eating and tasting whatever it can reach, including Tina's razor, which cuts its tongue. As a fetus, the creature would be part of its mother's body, and the film does connect it to Tina's body on numerous occasions. For example, whenever someone attacks the fetus, Tina also gets hurt. Thus, if one follows the film's metaphorical presentation, the implied meaning becomes clear: the fetus is Tina's, gestating in her womb.

This reading is strictly metaphorical, for there is no explicit evidence in the film to prove Tina is pregnant. Nevertheless, it is significant that Tina's ability to overcome the extreme stress she experiences due to the fetus's presence directly correlates to her accepting and embracing the fetus. At her birthday party, she stands across a water fixture from her classmates, as she alone has the courage to approach the creature. Not only that, but when she picks it up, she carries it as a mother would a young child, balancing it against her hip. The film seems to treat this as a triumphant moment for Tina, for here, she is confident, bold, and dares anyone to challenge her about her fetus. In a sense, she has embraced motherhood, which, traditionally, is symbolic of emotional maturity and responsibility.

The film further reinforces this attaining of maturity and responsibility when, in the concluding scene, Tina climbs from the backseat to the passenger seat, so she can sit by the fetus. Tina, therefore, is no longer a child riding in the backseat of life, allowing others to steer her. Instead, she is now asserting herself and taking a position of rough equivalence next to the driver who, at least metaphorically, is part of her. Tina has gained at least a modicum of control over her life, and she has done so by accepting that the fetus is essentially a piece of her now. This acceptance does not (necessarily or exhaustively) mean Tina is embracing pregnancy or responsibility, for there are several other possibilities—any of which she might be accepting.

She might, for instance, be embracing a mental illness. The film cuts rapidly between different scenes that often differ significantly from one another. One scene might show Tina speaking with her therapist, and a rapid cut might then show her dancing in a neon-lit club. The rapid cutting between these scenes often accompanies some discussion of Tina's mental state, whereby her parents and therapist believe she is suffering some sort of psychotic breakdown, including hallucinations of a creature (the fetus) and high levels of anxiety manifesting in self-harm. Her parents believe, for instance, that she has cut herself when her mouth begins to bleed after the fetus tries to taste her razor. In this sense, then, the film may be about Tina's struggle with a newly manifested mental illness that makes it difficult for her to differentiate fiction from reality. Indeed, Tina's symptoms do seem to indicate she is struggling with some psychological issue.

Psychologists tend to assess abnormality according to the criteria of the "Four Ds": danger, distress, deviance, and dysfunction.[63] And, as the film demonstrates, Tina fulfills all four of these criteria. If one reads the embryo as a hallucination or metaphor, then Tina's actions with the razor may be self-harm, which means she poses a danger to herself (thereby meeting the first "D"). The second "D" is clear from Tina's distress throughout the film, as she struggles against the fetus and also against being institutionalized. Finally, the third and the fourth "Ds" are apparent in that Tina's behavior clearly deviates from the norm, and, also that she misses a month and a half of school because of her issues, which, in turn, indicates she is suffering from dysfunction.[64] Consequently, from this reading, one can conclude, reasonably, that Tina is suffering from some unspecified mental illness(es) during the film.

Mental illness, moreover, is a personal struggle, a battle with one's own psyche, and, as I have illustrated throughout this chapter, nightmare horror fiction tends to externalize this sort of battle, rendering it concrete and monstrous so that the protagonist can defeat it. *Der Nachtmahr*, however, takes a different approach. Whereas Freddy Kruger is a dangerous force Nancy must defeat, the fetus does not threaten Tina, and she does not defeat it. In fact, the fetus shows some level of attachment toward Tina and acts more as an infant toward its mother, or a cat toward its owner, than as a monster toward its victim.

Unlike Nancy's struggle, therefore, Tina's battle is not about defeating her dream demon; it is about living with it, the way one sometimes has to learn to live with a mental illness, a part of their being that modern medicine cannot dissolve or destroy. Indeed, Tina's therapist also alludes to this inability when he says: "Our brains are the biggest mystery on earth, trust me. And sometimes they play tricks on us."[65] Thus, one can read *Der Nachtmahr*'s narrative arc as a tale of self-acceptance, of coming to term with one's own abnormality. And while the film certainly connects this struggle to that of the mentally ill, one could also read it as the struggle to accept and embrace one's true identity. This struggle is part and parcel of the bildungsroman.

As a young woman on the threshold of adulthood, Tina is still figuring out her place in the world, a conflict the film highlights through Tina's "friends," who show little concern for her well-being. For instance, early in the film, Tina's two friends sit next to her while she is listening to music on her phone. They then take her ear buds out of her ears and even take her phone, showing little respect for her and her belongings. Significantly, the film's other characters mostly react to Tina when her actions become inconvenient for them. Toward the end of the film, on her way to her birthday party, Tina sneaks into the hospital and rescues the fetus. The hospital workers do not notice her when she enters but do notice her when she leaves with the fetus in her arms. In other words, they notice her when she is causing problems for them by taking their patient out of its hospital bed.

Likewise, her parents, despite their clear affection for her, focus on her problems to the extent that they discuss them with their guests at a dinner party. Even though Tina is present with them, her parents speak about her as if she is not there. Her friends ostracize her and do not invite her to *her own birthday party* when she is dealing with personal problems. Throughout the film, therefore, the people around Tina try to legislate normalcy and enforce their ideas about normal behavior. Socially isolated, struggling to figure herself out, and on the cusp of becoming an adult, Tina is thus pulled in various directions and subject to extreme levels of stress which, consequently, cause her anxiety and distress. According to horror film logic, then, Tina must struggle against a monster to unite the sides of her divided self, and, like Jacob, she does so by accepting another part of herself. Accordingly, just like Jacob, she ends the film by moving to be beside the other half of her, the part she struggled to accept.

That acceptance, however, does little to clarify the film's layers of fiction and reality. That is, in my discussion about *Der Nachtmahr* so far, I have not specified (or even analyzed) exactly which events take place in Tina's dreams (the titular nightmare[s]), and which occur in real-life. I have done so because the film does not offer any legend that would permit one—including myself—to navigate the events it depicts. Though the film's cyclical narrative is a useful symbol of the film's connection to the sleep-wake cycle, it makes the movie uniquely difficult to read. One might ask, for instance, "How can Tina's classmates show her footage of an event that has yet to happen?" One possible answer could be that the footage is not of the car hitting Tina but, rather, of a different hit and run. This answer, however, is speculative; the film offers no concrete evidence either way. Accordingly, if the film is indeed one nightmare, as the title suggests it is, it is difficult to determine when the nightmare begins.

One might, for example, be tempted to guess the nightmare starts when Tina gets sick at the party, during the film's beginning. This reading would make sense because the film does show Tina becoming ill at this time, and even possibly hallucinating twice: first when she sees the fetus in the bushes and, second, when the car hits her. Thus, it is quite likely that Tina starts dreaming during this scene. Perhaps she is experiencing a vivid, hellish, fever dream from her illness, or maybe she is witnessing a dying dream after the car hits her. The film, however, offers no concrete evidence to support the first possibility; the second possibility (that of a dying dream), meanwhile, makes little sense in the context of the film's ending where all the film's events rewind and Tina wakes up in the car the fetus is driving.

That is, though the film's rewinding—in its entirety—before the viewers' eyes is more reminiscent of a dying dream (the "life flashing before a person's eyes" trope) than the rest of the film is, it still does not account for *Der Nachtmahr*'s concluding shot. After all, Tina appears to be in the same car that struck her, which would fit the film's cyclical nature but would fit less well with the idea that Tina is seeing her dying dream. If Tina was in the car that struck her, then causality in *Der Nachtmahr* would be non-linear (similar to the causality in *In the Mouth of Madness*), so it would be difficult to justify claiming the entire narrative is Tina's dying dream.

Then again, though, maybe Tina's dying brain is picturing her inside the car that killed her. Yet Tina's dying so early in the film would render her character arc moot. And the film's cyclical nature is, itself, reminiscent of a nightmare (reinforcing a view that the film is offering a non-linear type of causality), with its non-linear chronology and unclear logic. Accordingly, since *Der Nachtmahr* wants to disorient viewers, it follows that the film wants to make it difficult for viewers to tell where reality and fiction begin and end in the film's narrative.

Thus, the films in this chapter affirm that dreams are the battleground of the psyche: they are the arenas wherein we (characters as well as audience members) act out internal struggles, and this holds true for both fiction and reality. Here, the liminal horror story is disturbingly real. It shows the real-life dynamic of nightmares in hyperbolic, visceral detail. And while this section's first three films ultimately submit to careful analysis, *Der Nachtmahr* reveals that other movies more closely resemble dreams, because they evade, and even thumb their noses at, any attempts at concrete rationalization. These are the stories of dream logic.

Section Three: This Makes No Sense: Dream Logic and Abandoning Rationality

The narrative of a dream is often one of confused, convoluted logic. Most the films in the previous section contain a coherent story, the likes of which many dreams lack. This is because a dream may switch plot lines randomly or adjust itself to accommodate the sleeper's changing circumstances. To use a colloquial example, if the dreamer is cold, it is quite likely their dream will change to explain why the dream-self is cold (e.g., by having them appear in the arctic). This is to say that dreams, essentially, are fluid.[66] To dream is to let oneself drift in a changing current, for resisting the flow may cause the dream to sour or to end.

To use the examples from the previous section, Mary, Nancy, and Jacob struggle against their dreams (at first), fighting the demons within. Mary refuses to participate in the second séance, Nancy clashes with Freddy, and Jacob refuses to accept Gabe's death. These characters, therefore, are as swimmers paddling against a powerful current: their task is futile. The best evidence for this futility appears when Mary's dream haunts her even after she awakens. It is possible (in the film's story) that she could have prevented her companions' deaths if she had banished the nightmare monster; but regardless of whether such an occurrence is viable or not, Mary is troubled when she awakens. She cannot be free of the dream because she did not fulfill its story.

Particularly, within the dream, Byron tells her to participate in a second séance. And McNamara's analysis provides a basis to read Byron as a part of Mary's self, just like the monster (that is, if one reads that night's events as Mary's nightmare). Hence, by going against Byron, Mary is fighting that very part of her that knows what she must accomplish to overcome her nightmare, the same part compelling her to overcome her fear. Similarly, Nancy struggles to conquer her fear and accept that the various elements of her consciousness telling her what she must do are, in fact, correct. Nancy, unlike Mary, ultimately listens, and she emerges less scathed than her counterpart in *Gothic*.

I specifically say "less scathed," as opposed to "unscathed," for the latter term would be inaccurate and inapplicable given *A Nightmare on Elm Street*'s conclusion; however, the third installment in the franchise confirms Nancy survives the first film. In other words, Nancy and Jacob succeed in resolving their dreams because they play along with the dream's (seemingly random) narrative. They accept their fates and go with the current rather than against it. Inherent to the dream narrative, therefore, is a message of letting go.

Letting go may, in fact, be a key message in Bernard Rose's 1988 film *Paperhouse*. *Paperhouse* is the story of 11-year-old Anna Madden (Charlotte Burke) who, suffering from a glandular fever, seeks refuge in drawing. When she dreams, she finds herself inside a house she has drawn. On waking up, she adds to that drawing, and when she dreams again, she finds the house has changed according to her alterations. The most important change is a boy, Marc, who resides in the house Anna has drawn. What is interesting though, is that Marc, like Anna, is a real-life person, and that these two sick children are patients of the same doctor. After she learns Marc cannot leave the house, Anna tries to improve his time there, but her attempts at playing God backfire. In attempting to make a helper for Marc, she accidentally creates a monstrous facsimile of her alcoholic father, whom she and Marc later defeat. Following this, Anna recovers from her illness, but Marc dies. He reaches out to Anna at the film's conclusion, inviting her to join him, but she cannot.

From this summary, one may ask: how did another living person, Marc, enter Anna's dreamscape? Also, how did she gain god-like powers over that space? And how, finally, did Marc reach out to her at the film's conclusion? The movie does not answer these questions. My compulsion, therefore, to dissect this film as I have *Gothic*, *A Nightmare on Elm Street*, *Jacob's Ladder*, and, to a degree, *Der Nachtmahr* feels out of place and futile, for *Paperhouse* appears to mock any attempt at rational analysis. I believe, however, that this thwarting of a cohesive reading is intentional and, arguably, *Paperhouse*'s most important effect.

Roger Ebert writes that *Paperhouse* "is not a movie to be measured and weighed and plumbed, but to be surrendered to."[67] It is a dream film, an experience. On the surrendering front, *Paperhouse* is a movie that effectively hooks the viewer into a mystery: how does Anna's drawing contain a real person, and will her drawings be able to help or even save Marc? As they are in most dreams, the answers are inherently elusive here. As for comprehending the film and drawing deductive conclusions, it would seem Anna and Marc are linked in their illness and doctor. One can surmise (without hard evidence from the film, however) that these two connections enable them to share a dream space, of which Anna is the architect.

Nonetheless, as many a would-be lucid dreamer has discovered, taking control of one's dreams can prove quite challenging, as Anna finds out through her struggles to control the dream and provide for Marc. Her powers, it appears, are limited to the dream world. And though the dream world increasingly intrudes into her waking life, she never seems capable of gaining (or exerting) power over the waking world. This is especially apparent when the film implies, at its conclusion, that Anna would have died had she fallen off the cliff.

Paperhouse, consequently, is unique among the films in this chapter because it does not portray the characters in Anna's dream as extensions of herself. Marc is distinct from Anna; he is not part of her mind. Yet, a careful observer can still decipher a message the dream carries for Anna: she must let go. Anna's attempts to better Marc's circumstances almost invariably backfire: the more she tries to save her terminally ill friend, the more harm she does. Likewise, she almost dies because she perseveres in trying to join Marc despite the danger in doing so.

Anna's final encounter with Marc occurs after she has woken up—by which time Marc has passed on. Having apparently gained powers like Anna's, at the end of the film, Marc becomes a helicopter and welcomes Anna to climb aboard and be with him once again. He hovers near a set of sea cliffs, and Anna's attempts to reach him make her teeter precariously at the edge. It is only when she abandons trying to climb aboard and join Marc that she can move back into safety. Despite her many failures throughout the film, Anna exits her fever dreams with her persistence intact. Once she returns to reality, however, she lets go and relinquishes her quest to save or join Marc. That is, she learns to say goodbye.

Though they are well-intentioned, Anna's efforts to rescue he who cannot be saved cause her significant trouble. Subsequently, *Paperhouse* pits its young protagonist in a struggle against death, a struggle that, unfortunately, she is fated to always lose. Her only choices are to surrender or to lose; to accept defeat or to merely be defeated. Here, I would be remiss to paint Anna's attempts as purely unsuccessful; she does succeed in providing Marc with companionship during some of his final days. This indicates, ergo, that Anna fails when she tries to do what is beyond her power. Her dream abilities appear god-like but are, ironically, a torture mechanism, whereby Anna's dream repeatedly forces her to acknowledge that which she cannot change (such as Marc's death). This interpretation, however, does not account for Anna's father.

After Anna and Marc defeat the warped, dream version of Anna's father, and after Anna recovers, her father actually reappears in her life, and he even wants to work through his marital problems with his wife, Anna's mom. Given this scenario, how does he fit into the overarching narrative? The film ostensibly suggests that Anna's father reappears because she defeats his monstrous side. In doing so, Anna (apparently) changes something outside her control, but that seems unlikely given how her dream powers mock her whenever she employs them to help Marc. Thus, on the one hand, Anna must learn to let go. On the other, she must also fight. This double-edged message is unclear, unless one presumes that Anna must go with the flow no matter the circumstance, perhaps understanding and accepting the difference between that which she cannot change (Marc's condition) and that which she can (her feelings about her dad).

Anna's dreams, ergo, betray her lingering paternal anxieties. The dream version of her father exudes only his negative traits. For instance, he is aggressive and menacing, and rather than running to his embrace, Anna runs away from it, her movements contradicting those a father would normally wish for from his child(ren). The dream father is clad in shadows, his features indistinct, like those of a face conjured in a faded memory, which may reflect the reality where he is distant from Anna; this distance is apparent even in his booming, echoing voice. Resembling that of an adult yelling at a small child, his voice is overwhelming and seemingly inescapable.

By ripping her dad out of her drawing, however, Anna overcomes her lingering anxieties, cleansing them (albeit inadvertently) in fire. Nevertheless, it would be overly simplistic to say Anna has only antipathetic feelings for her father; after all, she adds him to the drawing because she thinks he can help Marc. That he turns out to be convoluted and aggressive exhibits Anna's own ambivalence towards him. She wants to view her father as a helper, a powerful figure upon whom she can rely, but, deep down, she subconsciously worries about his unfavorable qualities.

This dream logic becomes apparent in *Paperhouse* when Anna's symbolic purge of her issues with her father somehow brings him back into her life. It is, of course, quite likely that Anna's dad, concerned about her health, arrives while Anna is asleep. After all, Anna's mother tries to make a call while Anna struggles through her fever dream. But, once again, the film retains its ambiguity on this matter: because the audience experiences the movie's events almost entirely through Anna's eyes, they obtain little knowledge about what occurs *outside* Anna's (admittedly limited, and biasing) vision. This limited frame, in turn, constrains how the audience experiences the film, and forcibly pulls them along for the journey, much as a riptide draws in the unwary swimmer. Like Anna—and because of her—the audience is caught in the narrative's current and cannot escape.

However, once we—as the audience—cease struggling against the film (by trying to fully rationalize it), we become capable of observing the beauty around us, as well as in the film (and, perhaps, in this case, the dream) for what it essentially is: but an experience. Consequently, we must surrender to the dream because the dream's logic will consistently defy our (attempts at) understanding and codification. Unlike Nancy, who explicitly articulates what she has learned, Anna utters no morals. She has quite an ordeal with a hyper-realistic dream, but it cannot be affirmed that she regards the dream as a lesson so much as an experience, a time to be with her new friend, Marc, in his final moments. What this emphasizes, yet again, is that despite varied and multifaceted attempts, *Paperhouse* defies rationalization: the film cannot entirely be explained using logic and reasoning.

What is key here is how liminal horror films about dreams (or nightmares) are surprisingly realistic portrayals of dream phenomena. These films explicitly demonstrate dreams reaching across the gap between the real and the fictional, a phenomenon evident even in real life, regardless of whether one accepts it or not. But, as one learns from *Paperhouse*, it is better to accept reality (that which one cannot change) than to swim fruitlessly against the current. In other words, denying reality does not change it.

These films signify dreams as a form of personal, self-conscious therapy, another phenomenon psychologists recognize. Equally crucial is that these films emphasize how dreams often make little sense, which is yet another nod to reality. These factors, consequently, mean that, at every step, these liminal horror films are simply exaggerating reality, by illustrating, through a multitude of techniques, that the line between fiction and reality is truly liminal: that people exist inherently in a state between the two.[68] Unbelievable though it may seem, lucid dreaming further exemplifies this liminality.

Section Four: Mixed States: Lucid Dreaming

Nowhere is the border between the states of reality and fiction harder to discern than in the experience of lucid dreaming, the practice of being aware that one is dreaming and, so, taking control of the dream. There are some practitioners of lucid dreaming in actual life; some, on the other hand, are wary of it. In fiction, however, nowhere is lucid dreaming clearer than when the practice of it becomes a major plot device in Romain Basset's English-Language, French, film *Horsehead* (2015). In this film, Jessica (Lilly-Fleur Pointeaux), a student of lucid dreaming, travels home for her grandmother's funeral; she has not been home for some time, for she experiences mutual tension with the women in her family. Upon her arrival, Jessica receives warm greetings from her stepfather, Jim, and the family handyman, George. Her mother, Catelyn, however, gives Jessica only a curt acknowledgment and makes Jessica sleep in a room beside her grandmother's room.

Jessica wonders about this arrangement, as she had never been close to her grandmother and, furthermore, she senses that her family is concealing something from her. Because of this, she begins investigating the truth through lucid dreams, where she encounters a younger version of her grandmother, Rose, who warns Jessica about the Cardinal, a male, horse-headed figure in clerical clothing, who carries a religious scepter. The

Cardinal then captures Jessica and crucifies her while she is naked. Awakening from this nightmare, Jessica searches through Rose's belongings and finds drawings of the Cardinal and of a wolf that Rose told Jessica about in the dream. Subsequently, Jessica's grasp on reality weakens as she begins to sleep more and more, and the doctor diagnoses her with the flu.

Sleep brings Jessica more dreams, wherein she encounters a young Rose again, only for the Cardinal to attack Jessica and slice her cheek with his scepter. Upon waking, Jessica discovers a fresh cut exactly where the Cardinal struck her in the dream. She does not stay awake for long, however, and dreams next of her mother; in the dream, Catelyn is having sexual intercourse with a man whose face remains blurred. Jessica wonders whether this man is her father, as Catelyn has never revealed his identity to Jessica.

Waking again, Jessica questions her mother about the conversation she witnessed between Catelyn and the Cardinal (albeit not the horse-headed version of him), and her mother's reactions seemingly confirm this conversation happened. Catelyn avoids giving Jessica clear answers, however, obliquely hinting instead that the place in the dream, where the Cardinal threatened to take Catelyn, was Saint Winston, a scary chapel that her father, Winston, would threaten Catelyn with as a punishment.

Jessica, however, falls asleep again before she can get any more answers, and, in her dream, she follows the wolf toward the town's church, where she encounters the horse-headed Cardinal again. As the Cardinal and the wolf fight, Jessica runs towards the church, and, after a brief skirmish, the Cardinal impales the wolf with his scepter, seemingly killing it. Concurrent to this dream-world battle, Catelyn, in the real world, speaks to her doctor and learns from him that Jessica is pregnant. In the dream, meanwhile, Jessica retrieves a key from the wolf's scepter wound and enters the church where, apparently, her grandfather was a priest.

There, Jessica watches Catelyn gives birth while Rose and Winston look on. The baby is stillborn, which does not surprise Winston (for, as the film shows, he stabbed Catelyn in the stomach earlier). However, when Catelyn unexpectedly gives birth to a second, living, child, Winston rejects Catelyn and her newborn daughter, Jessica. Catelyn had not expected twins and had only named Jessica's sister, Lucy.

With these revelations about her dead sister, and her own unexpected birth, Jessica tries to awaken herself from her lucid dream and head toward the attic, where, she believes, she can use the key she found in the wolf. However, she struggles in the dream with Catelyn, who informs her that Jessica was the daughter she never wanted. Jessica, therefore, offers to rid her mother of the baby she never wanted by stabbing Catelyn in the stomach. Then, she staggers onward toward the attic. However, the horse-headed

Cardinal intercepts her, and Jessica uses her lucid dreaming strategy to transform the key into a copy of his scepter; she spears him with her transformed key and, apparently, kills him.

Meanwhile, in the real world, Catelyn and Jim cradle an unconscious, convulsing Jessica who, in the world of her lucid dream, opens the room in the attic. She watches as a nude figure—who bears a striking resemblance to Jessica—claws her way out of an embryonic sac and looks up at her. The figure (who seems to be the dead sister, Lucy) and Jessica hug each other; in doing so, their forms combine, and Jessica gazes upward, her eyes having become heterochromatic.

Several films in this book are difficult to summarize; even so, *Horsehead* is particularly difficult to preview in a few short paragraphs, because its plot is disjointed (as befits a nightmare) and avoids answering the questions it raises. Perhaps one may understand *Horsehead* more via the critical scholarship on it, but, unfortunately, there are no extant scholarly works on this obscure film.

And in this film (as in others), dreams are a battleground for the psyche, a place, in both reality and fiction (and in-between), where the dreamer can work through their inner conflicts. In *Horsehead*, however, Jessica uses her dreams to navigate her family's secret history. Unlike Nancy, she is not fighting a purely external threat, and unlike Jacob, she is not fighting a purely internal battle. Rather, Jessica's dreams mix her internal and external quests for discovery in an arena (that of lucid dreaming) that collapses her internal and external worlds together. The resulting space, wherein her conscious and purposeful dreaming takes place, is difficult to navigate, and it confounds any logical, reasonable attempts at reading the film. Moreover, this in-between (or liminal) space also gives Jessica the room she needs to figure out why her family is so dysfunctional.

The film itself hints at the issue when it depicts Sean, Jessica's mentor, reading a passage from his book while Jessica listens through headphones: "During the exploration of dreams, we encounter many symbolic patterns. You see, the horse is one of them. Carl Jung sees in it one of the archetypes of the Mother...."[69] Following this, Sean says that the horse may also be a symbol for the ferryman.[70] Here, the film provides two views the audience can use to understand the narrative as well as Jessica's actions: interpreting the horse as a symbol of either the mother or the ferryman.

Interestingly, though these views differ from one another, the film still lends credence to both. For instance, at the film's conclusion, it appears (since the film provides no explicit confirmation) that Jessica is dead and has reunited with her twin sister in the afterlife, which, in turn, renders the horse-headed Cardinal a sort of ferryman who ushers Jessica from one world into the next. On the other hand, interpreting the horse as the mother makes sense as well, in the context of how Jessica is trying to figure out her issues with her mother and grandmother. From this perspective, the mention of Jungian views of the horse as a dream symbol for the mother foreshadows Jessica's relationships with her female relatives.

Another interesting aspect is that the film itself is steeped in Jungian symbolism. Indeed, many dream-based horror films resonate with psychoanalytic readings, perhaps because psychoanalytic thought has permeated Western popular culture enough to influence the films' creators. Referring to the horse, Jung writes: "It is evident, then, that 'horse' is the equivalent of 'mother' with a slight shift of meaning. The mother stands for life at its origin, and the horse for the merely animal life of the body. If we apply this meaning to the dream, it says: the animal life destroys itself."[71] Here, Jung connects horses to three major forces: motherhood, sexuality, and death, and, accordingly, each of these becomes an important, interlocking force in *Horsehead*. Perhaps the film's most disturbing element is its combination of the three, which manifests in how Jessica negotiates her relationships with Rose and Catelyn through sexual fantasies.

Jessica, in the libidinous space of her dreams, tries to reconcile herself to the women in her life, and, more importantly, to the mothers in her life, a group she is (perhaps unwittingly) soon to join. In this manner, Jessica's search for reconciliation is kairotic in that, to be a better mother herself, she must discover the source of mother-child conflicts in her family. This journey begins with an inverted shot, about 12 minutes into the film, showing Jessica lying naked in a bathtub. Between the inversion, the tub's milky texture, and Jessica's sensual writhing (the source of which remains unclear, though it may possibly be caused by the pleasant feeling of the water), the tub becomes a yonic space, a symbol the film reinforces with quick cuts to both the horse-headed Cardinal and the person in the embryonic sac (who, in all probability, seems to be Lucy, but the film does not affirm it).

With these depictions, consequently, Jessica's bathtub becomes a space rife with images of reproduction. Furthermore, it is into this space that a young Rose enters, when she and Jessica's dream avatar share a bath, as if they were lovers. Rose caresses Jessica's naked body before the two flee, underwater, from the horse-headed Cardinal, who stabs the water and cuts Jessica's cheek (as previously mentioned) with his scepter. That is to say, the male religious authority figure disrupts a lesbian coupling and uses his phallic scepter to pierce a sapphic space (the water). This phallic disruption, in turn, is emblematic of the influence Jessica's grandfather has over her family, even after his death.

In Jessica's next dream, she moves to another sexually coded space, the bed, which she shares with her mother, Catelyn. The two kiss passionately until Catelyn breaks contact, slaps Jessica, and shames her for the kissing. The dream then cuts to Catelyn having intercourse with a man whose face is blurred out, because of which Jessica cannot identify him. It is possible Jessica is getting a vision of her conception (or, at least, a coupling between her mother and father), and because she does not know anything about her father, the man's face in the vision remains indistinct. The film hereby implies, but never confirms, that Jessica and Lucy were the result of Winston raping his daughter, Catelyn.

Certainly, Jessica's incestuous fantasies buttress this reading, as does another dream Jessica has, wherein Winston takes a communion wafer from his mouth and places it into his daughter's. Here, what is supposed to be a sacred act becomes inappropriately sexual. Subsequently, this inappropriateness hints at the possibly illicit nature of Winston's relationship with his daughter, a relationship that would, if present, poison Jessica's family for generations. Thus, it is little wonder that Jessica negotiates her relationships with her family through sexual fantasies, given how her family apparently has a history of incest.

In another instance, when Jessica heads to the cathedral, she wears a red cape and hood and receives guidance (and protection) from a wolf. Both these visual elements (wolf and red hood) cue the film's Western audience to recognize Jessica as Little Red Riding Hood, a character who, several folklorists argue, is on the precipice of puberty.[72] Accordingly, in this reading, the hood's red color becomes a symbol for menstrual blood.[73] Hence, when Jessica fights the Cardinal and he snatches her red hood from her, he is metaphorically stealing her blood (i.e., ending her menstrual cycle). This is an act of rape, as is his act of stabbing Jessica's cheek with the scepter, for in doing so, he not only penetrates Jessica's lesbian union with Rose, but also breaches the water (symbolically) of the womb.

Here, I connect the water in the tub to the water of the womb because the film explicitly shows the aftermath of Winston stabbing needles into Catelyn's pregnant stomach in an attempt to abort her fetus; he kills Lucy in the process. In two cases, then, Winston uses a blade (a phallus) to attack one of his granddaughters. The snatching of the hood, therefore, further reinforces the perspective that Jessica is, actually, the product of incest, an original sin that has, unfortunately, cast a long shadow over her life. This shadow, moreover, is akin to that of the night-mare itself, symbolized in the Cardinal's equine features. He is, literally, Jessica's night-mare, the weight on her chest she cannot shirk; it is what weighs upon her body and psyche at night. Here, *Horsehead* recalls Fuseli's painting, and the inspiration is clear.

That Winston is the metaphorical night-mare who bears down Jessica becomes clearer when George, the family handyman, notes that this was one of Winston's tendencies: "Let's just say that your grandfather was an old testament type of man to the grave. Even after his death, he threw quite a big shadow on Rose."[74] From the drawings of the horse-headed Cardinal in Rose's notebooks, the audience can conclude Rose saw Winston even in her dreams, where he served as her night-mare as well. And given Catelyn's behavior, and the incestuous undertones of her relationship with Winston, it is apparent he is her night-mare too. So, Winston, the night-mare, becomes a phantom who haunts characters as they sleep and live. The past, consequently, becomes inescapable for Jessica's family.

In *Horsehead*, therefore, dreams are not only the space for personal therapy (an arena in which to slay personal demons); they are also an avenue for discovery. Pivotally, the revelations Jessica gets from her lucid dreams continually align with reality. She dreams about Rose seeing a horse-headed Cardinal and a wolf, and then she finds Rose's drawings of a horse-headed Cardinal and a wolf. Indeed, Jessica's dreams so align with Rose's that her family remarks on the similarities and Catelyn believes Jessica must have seen Rose's drawings first, and then dreamed about them, rather than the other way around.[75] Jessica also dreams of Winston threatening her mother with "Saint Winston" and telling her mother to "Keep praying," both of which Catelyn appears to have actually experienced.[76]

Thus, dreams in *Horsehead* are an avenue to the truth about one's family history: they are a way to learn about external reality. As a result, in *Horsehead*, the line between the sleeping and waking states becomes so indistinct that the latter state occupies an epistemic reality that we (characters and audiences) typically reserve for external reality. Despite this, the plot of *Horsehead* is not as far-fetched as one would probably expect, because research into lucid dreaming has shown that, during this phenomenon, one can both dream and be conscious simultaneously, thus occupying both a sleeping and a waking state.[77] The line between sleeping and waking, therefore, can collapse entirely, a fact appearing in both *Horsehead* and *Der Nachtmahr*; the latter film also illustrates the collapsing of yet another kind of border.

In *Horsehead*, when Jessica's dream avatar fights her way to the attic while simultaneously watching her real body have a seizure, just for a moment, the two different avatars of Jessica appear to occupy the same space. *Der Nachtmahr*, however, takes this phenomenon a step further following Tina's second encounter with the fetus. In her attempts to avoid the creature, Tina loafs around town; meanwhile, music plays in the background as the camera pans across the city. The film then cuts to Tina sitting alone and listening to music on headphones, and the audience realizes she is listening to the same music they have been listening to. This sequence, in other words, takes non-diegetic music and makes it diegetic, thereby collapsing the non-diegetic and diegetic spaces together.

This collapse, in turn, forces the viewer into Tina's position: lonely, isolated, and wary of the fetus that they (Tina and the viewer) are doomed to reencounter. This is because, while listening to the (ostensibly) non-diegetic music, the audience believes that they have knowledge the characters do not, or even that they are having an experience the characters are oblivious to. The revelation that Tina is listening to the same song, however, undermines the viewer's comfortable position of power and places them on the same level as Tina, with the same amount of knowledge she has.

From a filmmaker's perspective, this is an effective technique to boost audience engagement, consequently making the film more unnerving. Unlike *Scream*, however, *Der Nachtmahr* aims not just to surprise the audience but also to place them in a liminal state of dwelling: for a brief moment, in the moment of the collapse of the borders, the audience is situated in the filmic space. *Der Nachtmahr* is supposed to be a nightmare, a haptic experience, and accordingly, this collapse unbalances the audience, thereby placing them—virtually—in the film itself. In doing so, it harkens back to the early cinema's experimentation with externalizing the film experience.

Whereas William Castle would release a fake skeleton in the theater to bring the film experience into external reality, *Der Nachtmahr* relies on its narrative to break down the fourth wall and bridge the divide between the film and audience.[78] Yet, while the two works may share similar desires, their effects are quite different. Castle's antics allowed him to reach out to his films' audiences. *Der Nachtmahr*, however, grabs the audience and puts it into the movie. When the diegetic and non-diegetic spaces collapse together, the audience finds themselves sitting in the film beside Tina. Consequently, the effect of dissolving the border between fiction and reality becomes more effective in the liminal horror film than it was in the early cinema's attempts to accomplish this same dissolution. Nevertheless, this—along with Castle's antics—demonstrates that the desire to reach into the audience and allow fiction to permeate into reality has been prevailing for a long time.

Tina, therefore, like Jessica in *Horsehead*, straddles the line between fiction and reality; she lives in both the spaces simultaneously. Whereas the gothic usually relies on the movement of one between the two spaces, Jessica and Tina dwell in the boundary between them, by existing in that liminal space where both worlds exist and are equally real. That is, both *Horsehead* and *Der Nachtmahr* showcase how the line between fiction and reality is hard to define and difficult to discern. Moreover, just as the border between waking and sleep is hard to perceive, so, too, is objective truth. The mind itself has the potential to distance and defamiliarize one by employing mechanizations akin to optical illusions. It is time, ergo, to examine the trouble inherent to the very act of perception itself: the mind's function in differentiating real from unreal.

Six

The Mind's Power
This Is Not Reality

Section One: Perceiving and Misperceiving: How Our Senses Steer Us Wrong

This section examines three types of (mis)perception: misreading, mirrors, and hallucinations. This chronology of misperception is important, for each type is more removed from objectivity than the last. Thus, this section's sequence will gradually build to more and more flawed, subjective experiences of reality.

Sub-Section A: Misreading

Just as interdictions (i.e., warnings) are central to many horror films (e.g., *Scream* and *Urban Legend*), so is characters' failing to apprehend these interdictions or misreading them. Indeed, such misreading is key to 1973's classic *Don't Look Now*, directed by Nicolas Roeg. The film depicts a couple, John (Donald Sutherland) and Laura Baxter, who, after the death of their daughter in an accidental drowning, go to Venice, where John has accepted the job of restoring an old church. There, the couple meets a pair of sisters, one of whom is a blind psychic. Laura believes in the medium's powers, but John does not.

And while the couple wrestles with their grief, a serial killer terrorizes the city. Throughout these events, however, John keeps sighting a figure in the distance, whose small frame and red coat resemble those of his dead daughter. Toward the end of the film, he is finally able to chase after the figure, only to discover said figure is not his daughter but rather a female dwarf responsible for all the murders in the film. John too gets murdered, as she slashes his neck and kills him.

This summary, which is sufficient for providing an accurate overview of the film, is insufficient in conveying how *Don't Look Now*'s plot inherently revolves around the themes of perceiving and misperceiving.[1,2] The blind psychic, Heather, foresees John's death, as does John himself. For instance, about halfway through the movie, John perceives his wife riding a ferry with the two sisters; later, this same ferry reappears, with his wife and the sisters aboard, only this time, it is the hearse bearing John's corpse. John, therefore, has a premonition of his death, but his staunch refusal to accept the existence of psychic abilities (as evident in his dismissal of Heather's powers) causes him to misinterpret the vision. Instead of a premonition (the future), he believes he is witnessing the present itself, and he acts accordingly: due to his (perhaps willing) misinterpretation of the message he cannot (or will not) act upon its warning, and so, he chases the dwarf, ultimately to his own demise.

Quite ironically, *Don't Look Now* casts sight as blindness, and blindness as sight. Echoing the Western tradition of blind prophets spanning from Tiresias to today, Heather's lack of physical sight grants her another form of visual perception. She can see in ways others cannot, and because she recognizes the danger John faces when he does not, her sight may even be considered superior to his. On the other hand, John's perception appears impeded by his physical ability to see: his eyes allow him to spot the red-coated serial killer while his mind's eye tries to warn him about the danger she poses. Conversely, Heather does not see the killer but does perceive the danger. Were John unable to see the killer (whose appearance has an eerie resemblance to his late daughter's), he would not be inclined to chase after her, and if he had not chased her, he would have survived.

Despite this, regarding physical sight as hindering and/or useless would be farfetched, for sight has its own purpose. Indeed, the Italian film *All the Colors of the Dark* (1972), directed by Sergio Martino, demonstrates how sight can be exceedingly useful at some points and utterly useless at others. The movie begins with Jane Harrison (Edwige Fenech) experiencing unsettling nightmares and seeing a blue-eyed man following her around the city. These nightmares result in Jane having difficulty sexually performing with her partner, Richard. Yet, some crucial events occurred before the film's timeline. As the plot later reveals, Richard, while driving Jane to the hospital as she went into labor, crashed into a tree, causing Jane to lose the baby.

The knowledge of these past events helps the audience understand what Jane undergoes in the film, for, now, in the film's current time, she sees images of the crash in her dreams alongside the nightmares of the blue-eyed man stabbing her. These images bleed over into her waking life whenever she tries to have intercourse with Richard, rendering her frigid. She struggles to find the right remedy for her condition. Richard, a pharmaceutical salesman, gives her vitamins he instructs her to take every night. On the other hand, her sister, Barbara, wants Jane to see the psychiatrist for whom Barbara works. Yet another potential solution emerges when Jane meets her neighbor, Mary: that of attending a black mass. Though Mary does not use the term, the ceremony's nature becomes clear when Jane attends it.

After the mass, Jane finds herself capable of being sexually intimate with Richard once again. But she remains haunted by visions of the blue-eyed man, who seems to stalk her. She attends a second black mass, where she sleeps with the high priest and the congregation forces her to kill Mary, who throws herself upon a dagger in Jane's hands. Horrified at this turn of events, Jane soon discovers her situation is even worse than she first thought: the blue-eyed man is, in fact, a member of the cult, and when she tries to flee from him, he uses dogs to chase her down.

Following this revelation, Jane wakes up as if the preceding events were a dream, but she still bears bite wounds from the dogs. So, she goes to her psychiatrist for help, and he sequesters her with some friends of his, whom the blue-eyed man murders the next day. The blue-eyed man also slays the psychiatrist when he returns for Jane, and he tries to murder Jane until Richard intervenes and stabs the man in the back, killing him. Richard also kills Barbara, as he determines (correctly) that she is the culprit behind the attempts on Jane's life.

Even then, however, Jane's dreams remain troubled, and she dreams of the high priest ambushing Richard in their apartment building's stairwell. When she awakes, Richard and some inspectors he called comfort her and assure her the dream was just that. They also inform her about the cult and how they have arrested all its members except for the high priest, who remains at large. When Jane and Richard return to their building, Jane predicts the high priest will appear, and, indeed, he does. Eventually, Richard manages to push the priest off their apartment building's roof, and the priest plummets to his death.

Slightly convoluted (and possibly confusing) though this summary may be, it evidences how "sight" has a mixed record in *All the Colors of the Dark*. For the most part, in this film, vision serves to disorient the viewer. The title refers to what people cannot see: the colors of the dark. Darkness is the absence of light; it does not grant the beholder the ability to perceive any colors. In this sense, darkness is the negation of color itself, and, from this standpoint, the film warns the audience, from the outset, that its narrative transcends the limits of human vision. If the film is the colors of darkness, then its story is one the audience can approach only indirectly, incompletely, and the audience—we—can perceive this same notion reappearing throughout the story.

For instance, the film opens with one of Jane's dreams: a fractured, erratic nightmare overlaid with shrill, discordant music and consisting of horrific imagery, including Jane's own stabbed and deceased nude body. The camera offers a kaleidoscopic view of both Jane and her dream, and this kaleidoscopic effect recurs as the film progresses, always disorienting the viewer by multiplying the number of Jane(s) on the screen. The resultant effect is akin to the viewer (seemingly) having a drunk, and, therefore, unstable visualization of the film's narrative. Accordingly, when the audience's—our—perception of Jane has to pass through the filtering medium of the kaleidoscope (which resembles that of "drunk goggles"), it becomes difficult for us to locate her in space: how are we to ascertain which of the Janes present is the real one? In this manner, consequently, vision in these scenes becomes an impediment to perceiving reality, for it disorients the viewer in space.

This disorientation becomes more powerful through the film's editing techniques. An example of this occurs in the scene before Jane attends her first black mass, wherein she finds the blue-eyed man stalking her and flees from him. After she jumps into her car, she frantically searches for the man, trying to determine if she has managed to lose him or, at least, where he is. Here, the camera follows Jane's hurried glances, as it cuts from the front of the car to the back, and so forth, repeatedly. The rapid editing of cuts mirrors Jane's eyes as they dart around her. Because the camera follows Jane's eyes when she is disoriented (trying to find the man, the landmark against which she defines the safety of her position), the viewer also becomes disoriented.

Like Jane, the spectators cannot be sure of the man's location, and, therefore, cannot ascertain whether they are safe or not. This is key, because being the audience of the film, they cannot control the direction of their gaze (in the context of the events occurring within the film); their gaze, in this aspect, is controlled entirely by the camera. The viewer's loss of control, combined with the ensuing confusion, aligns them with Jane. This connection grows stronger when they later learn Barbara is manipulating Jane, for this demonstrates that Jane, like the audience, is not in control. In particular, Jane must wonder whether she is still the master of her own mind. Note, for instance, how she asks her psychiatrist if she is crazy. So, this cinematic disorientation of the viewer cultivates viewer sympathy for Jane, as it puts them in her shoes.

The film also hints at the visual distortion the audience experiences when it follows Jane after her first black mass. Jane and Richard sit in a café, and the camera zooms in on them through the window they are sitting next to. The zoom completed, the camera cuts to the inside of the café. Significantly, though, the audience's gaze needs to pass through the window to reach Jane and Richard, which means that the audience gets a distorted view of them, a view mediated through both the window and the camera's lens, the latter of which the film has already established as untrustworthy via the earlier kaleidoscopic effect. At almost every instance, then, *All the Colors of the Dark* gives the viewer an incomplete visual record, and it often highlights that it is doing so.

By introducing the kaleidoscopic effects as well as the frantic editing that undermines the viewer's ability to follow the action (i.e., to correctly perceive all that is happening), the film primes the viewer to expect visual distortions. In other words, the film warns us, the audience, to question our eyes and wonder if what we are seeing is real or not. Jane, herself, articulates this anxiety when she cries to Richard: "I don't know what's real anymore."[3] As it does with Jane, the film forces the viewer to question which of the film's events occurred and which did not, and, consequently, which side of the line between fiction and reality they are really on.

Despite all this, as I stated earlier, vision is not only an impediment in *All the Colors of the Dark*: not only does sight become Jane's greatest tool against the cult, but sight is also a kind of weapon throughout the film. The blue-eyed man's looking at Jane, for instance, becomes an act of violence, underscoring his menace and status as one of the film's primary antagonists. For most of the story, he does nothing to Jane other than follow and look at her. But those two actions are potent enough to establish his threat in the minds of Jane and the audience. If eyes are indeed the windows to the soul, then one can have no doubts as to the malice lurking in the blue-eyed man. One should furthermore note that the eye is also the cult's symbol. The high priest wears a necklace with an eye painted on it, and the cult members tattoo eyes on their bodies as part of their initiation.

The problem with weapons, though, is that they work both ways. To use a colloquial example for clarification, if you can use a knife against your enemy, your enemy can also use that knife against you. In the context of the film, the cult would have done well to keep this lesson, this double-edged nature of weapons, in mind. A perfect example of this would be when Barbara's eye tattoo betrays her to Richard: as soon as Richard spots it, it lets him know she is in the cult and behind the attacks against Jane. The symbol of her status ironically undoes her. Undeterred at first, however, she says she wanted Richard to see the symbol, and she tries to seduce him while surreptitiously reaching for a pistol. This pistol kills *her*, though, and not Richard, as he turns it against her and shoots her with it.

Thus, her weapons of subterfuge, eye, and gun all prove disloyal, as Richard harnesses all three to kill her. Emblazoning one's members with an eye tattoo symbolically asserts that the group's members have some power of sight or can harness the eye in ways that others (presumably those not in the cult) cannot. But Richard's eyes allow him to spot Barbara's tattoo, and so, Richard's power of sight leads to Barbara's death. Barbara's second refuge is in tricking Richard, but Richard only pretends to play along, and he sees her reaching for the gun, once again proving sight is a double-edged sword.

A similar dynamic occurs with the high priest as well. During the black masses, the priest wears a set of knives on his fingers that make it seem as if he has claws. That is, in wearing those knives, the high priest is pretending toward having power he does not really possess. Much as the claws might suggest otherwise, he is not an animal, and he lacks the raw physical strength and dexterity that the animals he tries to emulate have. Moreover, the cult embraces the animal, as they force Jane to drink dog's blood during the first mass. In a parallel move, the cult also appears to embrace an animalistic identity when they frame their rituals in overt sexual terms.

The two masses Jane attends involve the cult surrounding and forcibly kissing her. In the second mass, it even appears she has intercourse with the high priest while he wears the knives on his fingers. The cult, therefore, pretends to a high degree of power and carnality, as associated with the animalistic. But all of this is a pretense, as the cult does not appear to have any actual supernatural abilities. At the end of the film, the police arrest all but the high priest, whom Richard kills by simply punching him off a roof. One can safely conclude, through all these examples, that the cult's powers are superficial and unimpressive.

Jane's, on the other hand, are not. When she and Richard return to their apartment building after the police arrest the members of the cult, Jane realizes the dream she had in the hospital was, in fact, prophetic. Accordingly, she can warn Richard in time for him to block the high priest's ambush attack. Thus, with this act, Jane becomes a seer. Whereas the film has hitherto cast sight as the cult's power, Richard's and Jane's abilities, now, suggest otherwise. That Richard and Jane can use sight as a weapon against the cult members suggests sight is their power and not the cult's. The dynamic has reversed, and the cult's erstwhile weapon now belongs to Jane and Richard, the ostensible victims. Sight, the film suggests, may be untrustworthy insofar as the disorientation it causes, in both the film's characters and the audience. However, the film also indicates that sight can be the most potent weapon, if only one understands its strengths and limitations.

For Jane to become a seer, for her to gain mastery over vision, she must recognize her dream for what it really is: a premonition. She must understand that her conception of sight has been flawed. In other words, she not only must reorient her relationship with reality, but also with the tools she uses to perceive it. Ironically, it is the blue-eyed man who (unintentionally) informs Jane about all this, in his attempts to destroy her confidence: "You've crossed the boundaries of reality, Jane. You can't go back. You know the whole truth now."[4] But what truth, exactly, has she learned?

She has learned that the stark divide between premonitions and reality is a myth. Jane has also learned her visions of the blue-eyed man stabbing her were actually premonitions: of her later encounter with him, and his ultimate attempt at murdering her, wherein he tries to stab her with the same dagger she has seen in her visions. To reconcile herself with reality, "the whole truth" as it were, Jane must understand that she now sees with her mind rather than with her eyes, and that it is the mind's eye she needs to trust, for the mind's eye grants her the power to fight back against the cult.

Mary actually insinuates this to Jane earlier in the film, when she, Mary, tells Jane that fear has a meaning and that Jane must find out what Jane's fear means if she is to conquer it.[5] Here, note that Jane was already using this power to some extent, when she acted on her fear of the blue-eyed man, which the mind's eye had cultivated in her; but she did so without recognizing her power. Once Jane recognizes the power, however, she can harness it as a weapon in self-defense. *All the Colors of the Dark*, therefore, hints that the reality one perceives is not the only reality there is; but that there may be, in fact, a more real "reality" beyond the pale of physical sight, a reality one may often overlook.

As if to drive this point home, the film attacks our—the audience's—sense of hearing as well. While the film's primary focus is on the power and failings of sight, its soundtrack augments the movie's disorienting effect. This effect occurs, for instance, when Jane enters her first black mass, and the music (apparently non-diegetic) becomes overpowering. The viewer has trouble hearing much over the discordant voices comprising the music, and so, the audience's sight and hearing fail them simultaneously. Because of the combination of the overpowering music and distorted visuals, in this scene at least, the spectators cannot rely on either sight or audio to ground them.

Instead, the film emphasizes the mass's carnality to suggest the audience may rely on touch. The touch between the cultists and Jane gives Jane a way to ground herself in the moment, to orient herself in space where she is so often disoriented. For the movie viewer, though, this revelation is of little comfort, because for all its ability to attack the viewers—us—via multiple senses, *All the Colors of the Dark*, for the most part, fails to reach out and physically touch its audience (i.e., to communicate with the audience through touch). Perhaps this is for the best since the spectators, generally, do not wish to experience all the tactile sensations a horror movie character does. As Billy and Stu attest, getting stabbed hurts.

This analysis does, however, leave something out: even though horror movies cannot directly assault touch, they can still *indirectly* assault it. The body responds to sensory input, and a viewer can feel their body's response even when the film is not actually touching them: the viewer can feel the changes in their pulse, or they can feel themselves cringing away from disturbing imagery. Here, *All the Colors of the Dark* points out the disconnect between the audience and Jane even as it further cements their bond with her. On the one hand, the viewer realizes they cannot share Jane's corporeal experience, the tactical sensations she relies on in the moment, and on the other hand, the viewer is almost as disoriented as Jane is, and so the viewer empathizes with her and aligns themselves with her position.

Because the movie's viewers still have an embodied experience of the film alongside Jane, they can remain connected to her even at the precise moment when their rationalization reminds them about the untraversable distance between themselves and Jane. Here, as with its title, the film attacks the idea of rationality, telling viewers to rely on feeling, gut instinct, rather than on logic or empiricism. To understand a film such as *All the Colors of the Dark*, therefore, one must embrace it as an experience rather than an intellectual exercise (as is also the case with *Paperhouse*, discussed earlier), or so the film seems to suggest at times. This discussion, however, focuses only on misperception, even though there is more to the picture, such as arriving at the wrong conclusions.

While *Don't Look Now* and *All the Colors of the Dark* show the dangers of misperceiving, there are other films which focus, instead, on misunderstanding (which, in itself, is a different type of seeing incorrectly). *Halloween* (2018) is one such film, and it affords the audience a different, less traveled path to perceiving the role of misunderstanding in horror.[6] Directed by David Gordon Green, the film is a sequel to the original *Halloween* (1978) and is set forty years after that night's events. It depicts Laurie Strode (Jamie Lee Curtis) still living in Haddonfield; psychologically, she remains stuck in that night when Michael Myers killed her friends and almost killed her. Living as a hermit, she fortifies her home, collects firearms, and struggles with alcoholism. She is obsessed with Michael and with killing him. When Michael escapes from a prison transfer bus, the town faces his rampage once again, and Laurie tries to hunt him down.

As Michael carves his way through Haddonfield, the audience learns his psychiatrist, Dr. Sartain, helped free him from the bus because he, Sartain, wanted to see how Michael would react to being back in Haddonfield on the anniversary of his murder spree. Sartain's obsession proves deadly, as Michael thwarts the psychiatrist's attempts to psychoanalyze him and smashes the doctor's face in by stomping on it. Michael then follows Laurie's granddaughter to Laurie's home. There, Laurie, together with her daughter and her granddaughter, catches Michael in a trap of her own design and then sets him ablaze.

Michael Myers, as a character, is fascinating. For 40 years, he has captivated America's movie-going audience, spawning a massive and successful horror franchise. Despite the sequels' relative lack of success, there was still enough demand for a new *Halloween* to bring about 2018's revival movie. One should note, however, that Myers appeals not just to film audiences, for the characters in the *Halloween* films likewise remain obsessed with him, to the point that, in 2018's *Halloween*, they help bring the killer home once more.

The movie opens with a pair of podcasters going to the asylum where Michael is imprisoned so they can interview him. Here, the readers and audience familiar with the franchise will immediately spot the obvious problem: that Myers is one of the two quintessential silent slasher film villains, with Jason Voorhees being the other. Throughout the franchise's history, Myers has never spoken. Yet, these two podcasters think they can get him to speak. They bear with them his iconic mask, the same mask he wore during the original Haddonfield massacre, hoping that seeing it after the long interim will elicit some reaction from Michael. And, indeed, it does: Michael turns his head slightly to look at the mask. That is it. Despite Aaron's shouted demand for him to "Say something!," Michael remains silent.[7]

Immediately following this shout, the film cuts to the title sequence overlaid with Carpenter's revised *Halloween* theme song, for such is Myers' mystique. By pairing Aaron's futile command with the title sequence and theme song, Green suggests that silence is part of Michael's allure, that spectators (within and outside the film) are drawn to him because he is mysterious, an observation the original film supports. In the original *Halloween*, characters frequently refer to Michael as the boogeyman; his exact nature and motivations remain unclear.

While some of the later sequels do attempt to explain these matters, the 2018 *Halloween* film only treats itself and the original film as canon. Because the latest installment in the franchise dismisses all but the original film and itself, I do not review the remainder of the *Halloween* movies here; the original *Halloween* and the 2018 *Halloween* are sufficient for both elucidating my analysis and for the reader to comprehend it.

Michael's mysteriousness, when considered in the context of Dana and Aaron's (the podcasters') actions, informs the audience about one of the film's undercurrents: the characters' attempts to make sense of Michael. Dr. Sartain carries this torch later in the film, after Michael murders Dana and Aaron, and, in so doing, regains his mask. Sartain saves Michael from deputy Hawkins, who stands poised to shoot the incapacitated killer, by stabbing Hawkins in the neck, seemingly killing him. Then the mad doctor explains to Allison, Laurie's granddaughter, that he is interested in seeing how Michael will react to being back in Haddonfield again. Sartain is obsessed with understanding Michael and Michael's motivations. To that end, he is conducting an experiment to test his hypothesis that Michael views himself as an apex predator and that losing to Laurie has disrupted his worldview and become a lingering source of anxiety.

Like Dana and Aaron, Sartain is fixated on hearing Michael speak. In forty years of continuous incarceration, Michael has never uttered a single word, and his silence presents a barrier to Sartain's desire to diagnose and understand him. Allison capitalizes on this desire and almost tricks Sartain into releasing her by lying and claiming Michael has spoken to her. Sartain demands to know what Michael said, and even offers a possibility: "Was it the sister's name? Judith?"[8] Sartain is so desperate for an answer he not only risks innocent lives (and, ostensibly, takes one such life himself) but also risks getting false data by biasing an eyewitness. Feeding Allison a potential answer to his question makes for poor research practice, as it increases the chances of getting unreliable information. After all, Allison could now give a plausible answer without ever having heard Michael speak (as the audience knows she has not), and the answer will be the one Sartain appears to want, especially if it frees her.

That is, Michael's silence has corrupted the doctor. Ironically, Sartain's attempts to get into Michael's head have had the opposite effect of letting Michael into Sartain's head. As a psychiatrist, it is Sartain's job to figure Michael out, to diagnose him, and determine, perhaps, the factors or events that made him a murderer. However, as Sartain fruitlessly beats his head against Michael's wall of inscrutable silence, his job transforms into a mission: he continues chasing, with greater and greater zeal, the remote possibility of understanding Michael, which culminates in his going mad and becoming a(n) (attempted) murderer himself. As a doctor, Sartain is supposed to normalize Michael or, at least, make it so that the broader public can understand him. In other words, his responsibility is to make Michael better. Instead, it is Michael who makes Sartain worse, thus ironically inverting (and perverting) the psychiatrist-patient relationship.

Sartain's obsession is so central to his character it is evident in his name itself: Sartain means "certain."[9] And it is the search for certainty, Sartain's unwavering pursuit of answers he cannot have, that gets him killed. Sartain never abandons his attempts to understand Michael. His last words, which he speaks as Michael moves to kill him, are "Say something."[10] Michael promptly answers by stomping on Sartain's face and smashing it in. In doing so, Michael rejects Sartain's attempts to understand him, while simultaneously also rejecting Sartain's hypothesis about him and his behavior.

Yet, because the film offers no other answers about what drives Michael, viewers cannot be sure Sartain was incorrect; perhaps his hypothesis was right. The point is that neither the audience nor the characters can know for sure. No one has the answer to the enigma that Michael is: he remains something of a boogeyman, a mysterious figure who lurks in the shadows, haunts people's dreams, and defies their understanding.

But why does this lack of understanding drive Sartain to obsessive madness? Why do even Dana and Aaron wish to prod Michael into speaking? Because as a culture, American viewers want to know what makes serial killers tick. A brief search on YouTube, for instance, yields hours upon hours of interviews of, and biographies about, murderers. These clips—videos, documentaries—ask such questions as why these people committed their crimes and whether they were merely born to kill. Thus, Sartain (and, by extension, the American movie audience)'s obsession with Michael is like the real-life obsession with getting answers, with trying to make sense of the surrounding world in a way that is plausible and does not disrupt one's sense of security.

But as Sartain's, Dana's, and Aaron's fates portray, one cannot always have the answers one wants, and, therefore, the world does not always make sense. Furthermore, believing one has the answers when one does not is a foolproof recipe for disaster. As John and Sartain find out, ignoring warning signs is a very bad idea. Many unfortunate people have suffered and even died because of these two mistakes, of believing they know more than they actually do, and blatantly ignoring interdictions: they misread a situation, or are overconfident in their abilities, or they ignore warnings, and consequently, they end up in trouble.

To provide a colloquial example, here is a scenario. A young man walks to the edge of a swollen river. Beside the shore, a crooked wooden sign reads "No Swimming: Dangerous Currents." The man, however, is assured that he is a capable swimmer (perhaps he swam on his high school team, or perhaps, he has been swimming regularly for recreation, for several years), and he is confident he can reach the other side. The currents *appear* strong, sure, but not so strong he cannot handle them. What he does not know is there are stronger currents running beneath the water's turgid surface. Thus ignorant, he dives in. Soon, he finds himself swept up in a series of conflicting currents that overpower him, and he drowns.

This, of course, is not a true story, in the sense that I have made it up here for illustrative purposes. But, unfortunately, similar scenarios have played out innumerable times, as a quick Google search will evince. Real-life is full of dangers, and one mistake in judgment, one moment of ignorance or overconfidence, can prove fatal. The movies in this sub-section, *Don't Look Now, All the Colors of the Dark,* and *Halloween*

(2018), therefore, speak to a very real anxiety: they demonstrate how one can misread a situation and thus land oneself in irrevocable danger. And while they exaggerate these dangers, the films are, nevertheless, highlighting real facts and real threats. While one may not have psychic powers, one's vision still provides a flawed record of external reality. Furthermore, these films illustrate how one can make one's dangerous situation even more perilous, by not comprehending that what one sees is not reality but, instead, a reflection of it.

Sub-Section B: Mirrors

While writing about Dario Argento's Italian horror classic *Suspiria* (1977), Alexandra Heller-Nicholas observes how reflections warp the line between fiction and reality: "Increasingly lost in her own reflection, it is through Suzy that the film seemingly appears to be questioning the veracity of the real and unreal as the camera zooms in slowly to the reflection of her face...."[11] Heller-Nicholas further writes: "Even the mere mention of the witches has the power to shatter the boundaries that distinguish reality from the fantastic."[12] This shattering, moreover, takes the form of the camera's zooming in past the characters toward the reflections in the windows behind them, and, in this manner, *Suspiria* locates the fiction-reality distinction at the border of the mirror's surface.[13]

Though *Suspiria* helps the audience understand this border's existence, it offers little in the way of exploring the border because mirrors are but a motif in the film; they are not the central idea. Mirrors are, however, central to Mike Flanagan's 2013 film *Oculus*, which revolves around two siblings, Kaylie (Karen Gillan) and Tim. As children, Kaylie and Tim witness the corruption of their parents' minds and their parents' slow descent into madness, caused by a mirror their father bought to decorate his office. The mirror warps the family's perception, creating hyper-realistic hallucinations they mistake for reality. The mother begins to act like an animal, and the parents attack their children. Tim kills their father in self-defense (when, in a moment of lucidity, the father gestures for him to), and the police arrest him for the crime. He spends the next 11 years incarcerated.

After his release, Tim reunites with Kaylie at their childhood home, where she has reacquired the antique mirror. In hopes of exonerating her brother, Kaylie has arranged for them to study and document the mirror's abilities. If they can prove it has supernatural powers, she hopes, they can clear her brother's name. This task, however, proves difficult, as the mirror begins to warp the siblings' perception once more. As the night progresses, they find themselves trapped under the mirror's influence.

The mirror supplies Kaylie with visual hallucinations through which her fiancée, who is merely checking in on her, looks like Kaylie's mother. The mirror also blocks the siblings' attempts to call for help by making them believe, through auditory hallucinations, that another person is using the phone. Following this, the mirror forces Kaylie and Tim to relive some of their childhood nightmares. Desperate, Tim finally triggers the kill switch (that Kaylie previously set up) to destroy the mirror. Only, he discovers, to his horror, that the mirror has warped his perception once again so that, this time, he does not see Kaylie standing in front of it. The anchor she has set to smash the mirror impales and kills her, but the mirror remains exactly as it was. The police arrive on the scene and arrest Tim again, now for his sister's murder. As they drag him to a parked cruiser, Tim shouts in vain, as he did when he was a child, that the mirror is to blame.[14]

Mirrors are ostensibly designed to aid the user's vision, to render visible the normally unseen, such as one's own face or eyes, or the vehicles behind one's own car on the road. However, they can also frustrate one's attempts to perceive reality. An everyday instance of this would be when one looks into the mirror: when you glance in a mirror, you see a reflection, that is, you perceive a reflection of reality and not an objective view of reality as it is. Most obviously, mirrors flip perception, reversing left and right such that attempts to understand reality through them can become more difficult. Just like *Suspiria* before it, *Oculus* takes this undeniable fact that defines mirrors and hyperbolizes it.

Thus, the goal of *Oculus* is to disorient the viewer. Moviegoers use sensory data to orient themselves in space, as do the characters in the film. As a direct consequence of this crutch, the mirror's powers are very difficult to counter because they remove the ability to rely on one's senses. When the mirror can distort (if not outright control) one's abilities of sight and hearing, it can warp one, and so, it can also appear unbeatable. For instance, Kaylie, in the film, takes a lot of precautions when she designs her experiment.

She sets timers to inform them how much time has passed (in case the mirror warps their sense of time as well). She sets up the kill switch as a failsafe. She also asks her fiancée to check in on her, and she sets up a camera to document what really happens. Kaylie takes all these measures so she and Tim can double-check their memories against an objective record; she truly believes she has planned against any adversity the mirror may cause through its distortions, and given her extensive—and logical—efforts, the audience is led to believe so too.

Ultimately, however, it does not matter: the mirror overcomes all her safeguards, and, despite them and Kaylie's knowledge of its abilities, the mirror still wins without sustaining any damage. Given this outcome, one criticism the audience can level at the film is that the mirror is too powerful:

the film's protagonist is far more prepared than any average horror movie protagonist, but despite all her preparations, she still fails. Even worse is how she does not get close to winning. It is unclear what she could have done differently to defeat the mirror. But, then again, such is the power of perception: the mirror's powers make it a particularly challenging adversary because all the senses it can warp (and does warp) are the same ones Kaylie (and viewers) would have to rely on (ideally) to try to defeat it. The film's director, Flanagan, indicates this effect was intentional. He says: "Evil in the world doesn't have an answer" and that the mirror is akin to a Lovecraftian monster in "that if you even were to try to comprehend it completely it would drive you mad."[15]

Oculus, therefore, intentionally thwarts the audience's efforts to parse it in any logical manner: like *In the Mouth of Madness*, it mocks attempts at understanding and explaining it. And yet, *Oculus* is easier to follow as a story, especially when compared with the story of *In the Mouth of Madness* (discussed in Chapter Four), which makes little sense, even to its protagonist, Trent, who can hardly comprehend it. By contrast, the story of *Oculus* is comprehensible, even though Kaylie and Tim have trouble understanding it. Though the film wavers between flashbacks and the present, the audience is nevertheless able to construct the two plotlines without much difficulty.

Oculus's disorientation, then, is diegetic, affecting more the characters and less the audience, except, that is, for the hallucinations; the hallucinations make both the characters and the spectators wonder what is real and what is not. When Kaylie appears to bite a lightbulb instead of an apple, we—as the audience—believe, at first, along with Kaylie herself, that the hallucination is real. Likewise, we later learn, alongside her, that it is not. This simple tactic of placing us, the viewers, in a position of questioning what is real and what is not as the story unfolds, disorients us (albeit to a far lesser degree than films such as *In the Mouth of Madness* do).

What the audience perceives in *Oculus*, along with the movie's characters, is less actual reality, and more a distorted reflection of the real. A mirror's function is to reflect rays of light to let the beholder see. The film's mirror, though, takes those rays and corrupts them such that they reflect a reality that is non-existent but that the characters will then act upon. It gets them to fight phantoms and each other. When gazing into a mirror, a person beholds the reflection of the reality behind them. Thus, even though the mirror is not quite a projector, it still casts a perverted reality around the perceiver: it creates a world in which the perceiver then dwells so long as they look into the mirror. In *Oculus*, however, the mirror's constructed reality continues to exist even when the characters (and, therefore, audience) are no longer looking into its glass. By ironically perverting the mirror's role, *Oculus* gives the audience a reason to pause and take stock of how the underpinnings upon which they rest their conception of reality can, in fact, prove faulty or even be turned against them.

Likewise, the mirror can become a passage. If one stares into a mirror and then turns and walks away from it, from the mirror's perspective (or the perspective of a camera recording the mirror's surface) the observer is entering the mirror's contorted reality: they are walking further into the mirrored world. Accordingly, when Kaylie and Tim look into the mirror and then turn away to begin their documentation process, they unwittingly enter the mirror's space. Because they looked into the mirror and they beheld their reflection (the reality the mirror distorts), they entered its world and so became subject to the mirror's powers. Here, one should note that it is not entirely clear from the film whether one must look into the mirror for the mirror to affect them, and so, it is quite likely that in *Oculus*, the mirror's powers extend beyond those I have analyzed thus far. Nevertheless, my analysis is a plausible reading of how the mirror exerts its influence over people and controls them (or, at least, their perception, and so, their actions).

It is interesting to note, furthermore, that similar notions of mirrors as a passage occur in *Candyman*. The monster in the mirror myth hints that a mirror can be a portal into another world, and, in particular, the world of monsters. Within *Candyman*, both Helen and Candyman use mirrors as doorways into the other's world. For instance, in Cabrini-Green, Helen crawls through a mirror-turned-passageway and into an adjoining, abandoned apartment. Around the portal is a painting of Candyman, with the passage standing in for his gaping mouth. Symbolically, in this scene, Helen is entering Candyman's world, as represented by the painting on the wall as well as the candy and razor blades on the floor. Later, Helen (as I discussed earlier, in Chapter Three) finds that her apartment building's construction parallels that of Cabrini-Green's. Thus, her bathroom mirror, once removed, reveals a passage into a vacant neighboring apartment.

Candyman also uses this mirror as a passage into Helen's apartment. After she returns home following her arrest, Candyman smashes his hook hand through the mirror and begins swinging at Helen through the hole. It is important to remember here how these events occur *after* Helen has passed through the mirror-passage in Cabrini-Green. While the mirror itself is missing, its passage remains, which, in turn, propagates the understanding that there is an indisputable connection between the mirror and passage. Conclusively, the point stands that Helen encounters Candyman *after* she has passed through the mirror into his, the monster's, world, which is to say that she is living a reflected, and thus distorted, reality.

Helen (Virginia Madsen) looks through a passage in Cabrini-Green where a mirror used to be. Around the entrance, we, and not Helen, can see a painting of Candyman (Tony Todd). Soon, she will move through the passage, symbolically entering Candyman's world (*Candyman*, directed by Bernard Rose. TriStar Pictures, 1992).

Through my discussions thus far, it is evident, at various times in this volume, that the screen is permeable. In *Videodrome*, for instance, Max hallucinates that he is literally sticking his head into the television screen. I draw attention to this here because the mirror, like the television screen, is made of glass and seems to reveal an inner world. As evident in *Videodrome*, the screen acts as a passage between two places, between two states of existence. Subsequently, through this reasoning, the mirror becomes permeable as well: it contains, within it, a reality hidden insofar as many often ignore its larger implications. While many recognize that the mirror flips their horizontal perception, they do not necessarily think about how—consequently—the mirror constructs a separate reality, a reality that is perhaps best revealed when one positions two mirrors so that they are facing one another. The infinite number of reflected mirrors reveals the infinities within the reflection; they reveal something of the world behind the glass or even within it.

One film takes this notion literally: *Into the Mirror*, a 2003 Korean film directed by Kim Sung-ho and starring Yoo Ji-tae as Wu, a former police detective who now works as the head of security for a shopping center. Wu's employers are preparing to reopen the shopping center after a significant fire damaged the building. This reopening comes under threat, however, when someone starts killing the employees. These murders prompt a police investigation, and the officers reveal Wu's backstory: he quit his job as a detective after he accidentally caused his partner's death during a standoff. Despite being a skilled marksman, Wu mistook a gunman's reflection for the genuine article, the missed shot leading to his partner's death.

Wu, meanwhile, goes back to his roots to begin investigating the deaths and starts seeing an ethereal woman in purple around the shopping center. The woman appears to be an employee who died in the fire. Upon researching more into her life, however, Wu discovers the ethereal woman is actually the dead employee's twin sister, Lee Ji-hyun. Together, they investigate her sister's death and discover she was actually murdered; the fire that significantly damaged the building was merely an attempt to cover the crime. Furthermore, it appears the sister's spirit has been using mirrors as a passageway between worlds so she can kill her murderers in revenge. To help her spirit attain peace, Wu and Lee sneak into the shopping center and break the mirrors until they find the sister's corpse, hidden in the wall behind one of said mirrors.

At this point, however, the sister's murderer, Choi, appears and tries to kill Wu and Lee to hide his crime. He shoots Wu, who crashes through a mirror and has a conversation with his own reflection, wherein Wu resolves to overcome his anxiety (about shooting a gun) and kill Choi. He fails, however, as he merely wounds Choi with a grazing shot. Choi then struggles with Lee until the sister's spirit emerges from a mirror and kills Choi, thus completing (and so, ending) her quest for vengeance. Later, Wu wakes up, recovered from his gunshot wound, only to discover he is now trapped in the mirror world; he is able to see, but not interact with, the real world beyond it.

Into the Mirror, therefore, provides two distinct views of the mirror-world. The first view becomes apparent when Choi shoots Wu through a mirror in the shopping center, whereupon Wu finds himself in a dark, void-like space filled with mirrors, one of which reflects himself. His reflection speaks to him, accusing him of being too afraid to kill Choi. Here, the mirror operates as a manifestation of a split mind, allowing Wu to externalize his inner conflict and interact with it, as if his anxiety were a separate entity distinct from him.

In this moment, *Into the Mirror* invokes the age-old trope of the doppelgänger, a hallmark of the gothic tradition.[16] The reflected self becomes a manifestation of the reflected person's psyche; that is, it becomes their double, a fact the film makes explicit when Wu's psychiatrist friend informs him that: "Once you start thinking your reflection is someone else, at any moment, two egos and two worlds may appear. Self-hatred, caused by a massive shock, causes a personality to split.... The person is psychologically divided in two."[17]

Thus, Wu's quest in *Into the Mirror* is akin to Nancy's quest in *A Nightmare on Elm Street*. Both Nancy and Wu must reconcile two parts of themselves by slaying their fears/anxieties. Whereas Nancy accomplishes this task by terminating Freddy's source of power, Wu does so by shooting his reflected self, thereby committing a form of suicide. What is troubling, however, is the question of which Wu killed the other. That is, it is unclear from the film whether the mirror-world version of Wu shoots and kills the real self or if the real self shoots and kills the mirror-world version of Wu.

One reason it is difficult to tell which version of Wu kills the other is the film's rapid cuts, which make it hard for the audience to follow the unfolding action. Certainly, from the events that transpire, it seems as if the real Wu shoots his reflection; after all, the audience sees him point a gun at his reflection in the mirror. But if that is indeed the case, then why does the film's conclusion depict Wu trapped in the mirror world? And if the mirror self shot the real Wu, then why is Wu surprised when he finds himself in the mirror world at the movie's end?

All this is to say it is difficult for the audience to determine which persona of Wu dies and which survives. As a result, it is challenging to conclude whether Wu actually reconciles the two halves of himself. While he does manage to overcome his anxiety and shoot Choi, the film's ambiguous conclusion makes it appear that, to conquer his anxiety, Wu had to commit suicide by ending his life in the real world (regardless of which version of Wu fired the fatal shot). Thus, compared to all the films I have discussed so far, Wu's quest for reconciliation with his doppelgänger is unique because Wu, alone, appears to fail his quest.[18]

By associating one's mirror reflection with a psychological division, *Into the Mirror* implies the world in the mirror is akin to the world of the mind.[19] Subsequently, because the film's conclusion shows Wu trapped in the mirror-world, one can surmise Wu is now stuck in his own mind, which, in turn, can be an indication that he has not completely defeated his anxiety. The film seems to be saying, therefore, that those who fail to reconcile their two selves risk being trapped in a world of their own mental isolation. This, essentially, is the second view of the mirror-world that *Into the Mirror* provides: a horizontally flipped version of one's own external reality.

Symbolically, this full-scale world within the mirror represents how the mirror allows one to inspect themselves and thereby embark on quests of self-discovery. When someone looks into a mirror and, for instance, finds a mark on their face they have been unaware of, they have discovered some fact about themselves. This colloquial example is to say that mirrors, in the real world, allow for some limited degree of self-exploration, a fact

Into the Mirror exaggerates but, nevertheless, alludes to. Though this allusion is explicitly clear, it is also incomplete, because *Into the Mirror* does not explore this second world at length; instead, the film only provides a brief glimpse of this world at its conclusion. Fortunately, at least in the context of this book, *Into the Mirror* is not the only film proclaiming the existence of a world mirroring reality.

The Sender, an obscure 1982 horror film directed by Roger Christian, offers an interesting view of this world (as well as an additional world). The film stars Kathryn Harrold as Dr. Gail Farmer and Željko Ivanek (in his feature debut) as John Doe #83. Dr. Farmer is a psychiatrist working at a mental hospital, and she receives a new patient, a suicidal young man rescued from a local waterway (he had filled his pockets with rocks and tried to drown himself). Because he does not seem to remember his name, the staff dub him John Doe #83.

Dr. Farmer tries to help Doe, but she finds doing so difficult, for he remains amnesiac and suicidal. Even worse, he has the power to project his dreams into other's minds. Thus, Dr. Farmer finds herself experiencing powerful hallucinations stemming from John Doe's imagination. These hallucinations tie her to him and give her the chance to start helping him. At the end of the film, she even saves his life, by rescuing him from a house fire after he has left the hospital.

Though my summarization does not emphasize it, mirrors occupy but one revealing scene in *The Sender*. When John Doe #83 is slashing his wrist with a shard of glass, Dr. Farmer gets a vision of the mirrors in the staff bathroom cracking and then bleeding. This vision warns her John Doe is attempting suicide, which, subsequently, allows her to save his life, thereby connoting the vision's narrative function. What, however, is its symbolic function? What would it mean for a mirror to bleed?

To state the obvious, mirrors reflect. They project back a representation of reality, a representation one believes to be accurate, even if flipped. To state the obvious again, blood allows one to live. Therefore, there are two crucial objects here: the mirror, which one uses to see reality (distorted though it may be), and blood, which is essential for one's survival. The mirror's surface is a border between two realities: the one people experience and the one the mirror reflects to them. This surface is typically smooth and impermeable.

But, as the aforementioned scene demonstrates, when a mirror's surface can crack, and, furthermore, when blood can ooze from this crack, the barrier between the two realities is no longer impermeable; suddenly, it is penetrable—it can be breached, and indeed, it has been breached. Blood contributes to this scenario of a cracked and bleeding mirror because such a mirror is most closely akin to one's skin. Skin, like the mirror in the scene, bleeds blood when cracked. Thus, the film hereby connects the surface of a mirror with the surface of one's skin.

In particular, the surface of skin is interesting here because it reminds the audience about horror's carnality. When analyzing *Scream* earlier in this volume, I observed how the knife in that film reveals a hidden truth to Billy and Stu. A gash in the skin unveils the world beneath it: the human body's inner workings, of which blood is a part. Following this observation, I can reason here that a bleeding crack in a mirror is suggestive of the reality hidden beneath the mirror's surface. Consequently, if there is a world concealed inside the human body, there is a similarly concealed world inside the mirror. And this conclusion, in turn, begets the question: what type of a world is it, exactly? Given my film analyses to now, it is clear this new world is one with the power to negatively affect, and render troubling, one's conception of the external world.

One of the obvious difficulties here, however, is that this world the cracks expose remains difficult to fully perceive. To explain, in a simplified manner: a cut not only reveals a reality but also causes a new reality to burst through, and a gush of blood intrudes into the external world, rapidly mixing these two worlds into one. Nevertheless, I would be remiss to claim that these slashes only have a revealing function, because blood both reveals *and* obscures. As a fresh cut fills to the brim with scarlet, the blood frustrates the onlooker's goal to see inside the cut, beyond the liquid veil, and into the anatomical workings of the body, which is another reality. Thus, when Ghostface wishes to see what Casey's "insides look like," blood impedes him,[20] which, in turn, reinforces the notion that the exposed world, the world the cracks unveil, still remains beyond one's grasp and, therefore, beyond one's comprehension.[21]

This is all to say that no matter how one slices it, perception becomes frustrated, and borders and barriers abound. Blood, therefore, hints at a hidden world and offers a glimpse of it, but it simultaneously masks that world from view, thereby becoming a symbol for a deeper (physical and metaphorical) truth one cannot perceive with one's regular sight. The blood's presence reveals one's success in peeking beneath the veil as well as one's failure to fully apprehend the new world. And so, by combining the imagery of blood and mirrors, *The Sender* indicates how an object—in this case, mirrors—can offer both tantalizing and incomplete glimpses of reality (the world in which many people believe they live).

Though the film does not explicitly state this, it does hint, at various points, that the viewer's world is liminal, that viewers occupy a liminal— an in-between—state between a variety of overlapping realities.[22] It further suggests that the apparatuses viewers use to distinguish between these realities often fail to let them do so, and more importantly, that they do not always know when they have failed to determine the exact reality in which they are dwelling.

Sub-Section C: Hallucinations

And so, sometimes one's experience of reality can be entirely fictional (i.e., hallucinatory). Hallucinations can warp a person's perceptions of the real and make them lose their sense of stability. André Øvredal's 2016 film, *The Autopsy of Jane Doe* (*Autopsy*), delves into this phenomenon, while also exploring the secrets the body reveals and conceals. The film takes place, almost completely, in the Tilden family morgue. The Tildens are father, Tommy (Brian Cox), and son, Austin.

Tommy is a small-town coroner, and the local sheriff asks him to autopsy the corpse of a Jane Doe police found buried in a local basement. Austin backs out of a date with his girlfriend so he can help his father with the autopsy, and the two soon make strange discoveries: though her body bears no outward signs of trauma, her wrists and ankles are broken, and her lungs are blackened, as if she has been through a fire. They also find one of her teeth placed in her stomach and wrapped in a ceremonial cloth, whereupon the lights go out and the morgue's other corpses vanish.

Following this, Tommy and Austin attempt to flee the morgue but find themselves trapped. Surmising Jane Doe does not want them to figure out the truth about her death, they resolve themselves to solve the mystery and, hopefully, escape thereby. Accordingly, they continue the autopsy, and find, surprisingly, that the activity in Jane Doe's brain cells indicates she is still alive despite laying on the table, sliced open. Also, further inspection of the cloth from her stomach reveals references to the biblical book of Leviticus, particularly to a passage concerning witches. The cloth also has the Roman numerals for the year 1693, the year of the Salem Witch Trials.

From these discoveries, Tommy and Austin decide Jane Doe was possibly an innocent woman burned at the stake on suspicion of witchcraft. They believe that, from being thus wronged, she developed actual magical powers she is now using to exact revenge on the world around her. Based on these conclusions, Tommy begs Jane Doe to punish him and spare Austin. Following this request, Tommy's wrists and ankles break, and Austin mercy-kills his father before trying, once again, to flee the morgue. He finds himself trapped, however, as the door still refuses to open. He then sees a vision of his father's corpse, and, startled, he falls backward over a bannister and dies. The next morning, the sheriff arrives to find a crime scene: both the Tildens are dead, and Jane Doe is laying on the autopsy table, untouched.

Like *Oculus*, *Autopsy* warps the audience's perceptions of real events versus hallucinated events to simultaneously destabilize both the viewers and characters. Although, unlike *Oculus*, *Autopsy* provides some probable answers about its antagonist's origins. The destabilization in *Autopsy* hooks the viewer into a mystery. That is, the film compels spectators to find out more about Jane Doe and the bizarre circumstances of her death and injuries. Like the Tildens, the audience, too, asks questions about Jane Doe and the seemingly inexplicable nature of her corpse. And like Tommy and Austin, the viewers want some answers to these questions. To avail themselves of these answers, the Tildens must continue the autopsy, and the spectators must continue watching the movie to its conclusion. In this manner, *Autopsy* plays with the audience's—our—curiosity as viewers and entices us to go on a journey with its characters to see what knowledge the Tildens might unearth.

In another vein of similarity, *Autopsy*, like *Oculus*, can be difficult to comprehend, for both films consciously occlude the audience's ability to determine what is real and what is not. For instance, even when I first watched *Autopsy*, I found myself repeatedly wondering which events were real and which were hallucinated; it was difficult to determine the distinguishing line between the two (actual and hallucinated events) if not next to impossible. This difficulty and confusion are due, in some degree, to Jane Doe's ability to create illusions.

For instance, when Austin tries to flee the morgue, he finds the door blocked and hears the sheriff's voice speaking to him. The end of the film, however, reveals that not only was there no storm on the night of the eponymous autopsy, but also the sheriff was not there that night and no tree had fallen on the door and blocked the exit. The fallen tree and the sheriff were illusions, and, from this, the audience can also determine Jane Doe fabricated the storm, which allowed her to explain how the door was blocked and what caused the power outage.

Thus, when the police find Jane Doe's body unharmed at the end of the film, the audience might—especially in the light of these earlier instances—conclude the autopsy itself was a hallucination. That is, perhaps Jane cast illusions to make the Tildens think they were slicing into her when, in fact, they were not. One of the main side effects of giving a character (in any story) the power to warp perception is that the audience may forever question which events (or even characters) in the story were real, and which were illusions. Perhaps, some viewers will even claim the entire story is, itself, a hallucination, or even a dream, by questioning whether the eponymous autopsy ever occurred at all.

Countering such claims and questions, however, the film itself provides some good reasons to validate the occurrence of the autopsy. First, Tommy and Austin's reading of Jane Doe's motivations seems plausible, more so because the strange occurrences escalate as the two get closer to figuring out who she is. When they discover her tooth and the cloth that leads them to Leviticus, Jane Doe appears to blow out the lights and raise the corpses around her. The dramatic way in which she raises the stakes suggests Tommy and Austin are right in surmising Jane Doe does not want them to complete the autopsy. After all, it appears she is repeatedly attempting to stop them from doing so.

Another piece of evidence emerges in Jane Doe's obvious ability to heal herself; the strange nature of her injuries does not make sense otherwise. For instance, despite significant internal damage ranging from charred lungs to broken bones, she has no outward signs of trauma, and, hence, to make sense of these discrepancies, one need only look at how Jane recovers from injuries she sustains throughout the film. Her autopsy wounds heal as Tommy's body contorts and damages itself in parallel to Jane's injuries, and the remainder of the damage she sustains during the film disappears at the end, when she dispels her illusions.

Though one can argue, using the second healing's coinciding with the dispelling as evidence, that the autopsy is entirely an illusion, such a reading remains more implausible than the reading that she wants to stop the Tildens' investigation. Since there is proof enough to demonstrate Jane Doe can heal her wounds anyway, it negates the necessity for presuming she feigns all her injuries as well. Put another way, though she creates some illusions, her injuries are not a part of them; she can heal the injuries she sustains, meaning she has little reason to fake them.

Revisiting the moment when Tommy makes his deal with Jane provides further evidence about how Jane's healing may work: the cuts on her body close as she inflicts on Tommy the pain the inquisitors probably inflicted upon her during the witch trials (if the Tilden's inductions are accurate). Thus, for her to heal, she must harm others, and she ritualistically reenacts the mode of her torture so she can regain her power. Inflicting the torture on others gives Jane Doe the position of power she lacked during the witch trials. When she burned at the stake, she was powerless, possibly a victim. (Whether she was a victim or not depends on how one reads the film, and on whether she got her powers after she was burned, as the Tildens believe, or if she always had her powers, which led to her burning.)

If one believes the Tildens' reasoning, it becomes apparent that when Jane Doe destroys others as her persecutors destroyed her, she reverses the dynamic: now, she is in the position of power to inflict pain and judgment upon others. Through this move, the film inverts the witch trial, as the witch tries the people around her. Jane Doe's theme song, "Open Your Heart and Let the Sun Shine In," also substantiates this shift, wherein she transforms from a victim into an offender. The song is religious, and it extols the power of prayer to push the devil away. The "sun" "shining in" is God's glory, which keeps the devil at bay. As a "witch" burned at the stake, in the name of God and in accordance with Leviticus, Jane was—at least in the eyes of the Church—against God. Therefore, it is ironic that Jane chooses this song to play over the radio since, ostensibly, she connects more with the devil than with God.

Jane, however, seems to associate herself with sunshine, and vice versa. During her autopsy, for instance, she creates the illusion of a storm and blows out the morgue's lights, thereby bringing in darkness. But once the autopsy is over, she dispels the illusion, thereby bringing back the light. Moreover, in the film's final scene, when the audience sees her move slightly, it is daylight outside and the song plays again, indicating it is Jane's victory tune. Her movement of her big toe, the only motion she makes throughout the film, is vaguely reminiscent of her tapping her foot to the music. For a serial killing witch to appropriate a Christian song for her own ends is for that same witch to profane the sacred, to make a mockery of God and his glory. Consequently, it becomes difficult to give her the benefit of the doubt here, as, again, she has evidently murdered multiple people, and seemingly celebrates that fact.

Here, when Jane reverses her position—from that of a victim to that of an offender—the ritualistic nature of this transformation, of *how* she heals her wounds (through murder and rejoicing in that murder) connects her to folklore, the haven of the witch, as well as the realm of magic.[23] Magic then provides the film's final shot, as well as an explanation for it: Jane Doe riding in the back of an ambulance, her big toe moving slightly, which indicates she is getting stronger. That she becomes more powerful after she destroys Tommy further reinforces the idea that she must harm others, just as she was harmed, to regain her abilities, including her ability to move.

This gradual increase of strength is also evident—to some extent—from the repetition of certain events within the film. For example, at the film's beginning, there is a scene depicting multiple dead bodies of victims who were trying, apparently, to escape. The movie later repeats this scene with the Tildens in the morgue, who are attempting to escape as well, and who also fail. The stark similarities between these two scenes (and crime scenes) indicate Jane has enacted some version of the film's events at least twice, and this repetition contributes to her strength, if only in small quantities.

Here, one can even argue that this slow increase in her power, as well as her seeming willingness to harm others, is suggestive of her having been a witch all along. Contrariwise, it is also possible Jane Doe is willing to hurt others because she suffered an extremely painful death and has been trapped, immobile, in her body for over 300 years. The film does not convey which of these readings is true; the decision is left up to the audience and what they think is more probable.

Nevertheless, regardless of which of these two readings the viewer prefers, the cyclical nature of Jane's actions underscores the film's folkloric roots. If we, the audience, perceive the film from this perspective, the warning signs in *Autopsy* become easy to spot. For instance, the very first murder scene is easily decipherable as the first warning: as the body is already connected to multiple deaths, it is, in itself, a warning sign of danger, even if it is a weak one. The corpse's mysterious nature further reinforces its dangerousness, as does the death of Stanley, the Tildens' cat. The Tildens, however, push forward regardless, thus ignoring the signs and putting themselves in harm's way.

Here, I would like to point out that the Tildens' actions make sense: if such events were to happen in the real world, most would undoubtedly want the coroners to pursue their investigation and find some answers. Moreover, one should also note that the Tildens do decide to abandon the autopsy at a reasonable moment: once they can no longer deny the supernatural, they choose to run. Given the actions of most horror film characters I discussed earlier (such as Michelle from *Urban Legend* or Ellison from *Sinister*) Tommy and Austin's actions stand out, especially in the context of self-preservation. Most horror movie protagonists (including those in *Scream*) could learn a thing or two from the Tildens about when to flee and save oneself.

Despite this, the point still stands that they ignore the initial warning signs and forge ahead on their quest for discovery. Though this ignorance, this overlooking, is slight, it is sufficient to sign their death warrants. The investigation they conduct is essentially a quest for answers; an autopsy, the process by which a coroner discovers how someone died, is an investigation in itself; it is a search for truth. In *Autopsy*, this pursuit for truth plays out across and within Jane Doe's body. In this case, however, Jane Doe is still alive, as her brain tissue (which shows neural activity) and the movement of her toe in the final scene, wherein a bell attached to her toe jingles as the film cuts to black, evidence. Earlier in the film, Tommy reveals that coroners attach these bells to the toes of corpses to ensure they have not (accidentally) classified a living person as dead. Since comatose patients can appear deceased, coroners need to pick up on the smallest signs of life, such as the wiggling of a toe.

And so, Jane Doe shows signs of life, both through the movement of her toe, and through her neural activity, both of which are qualifications enough to deem her as "alive" (at least per the coroner's regulations).

Consequently, because Jane is still alive, the film's titular autopsy is a misnomer. The term "autopsy" refers to the dissection of a corpse, not of a living body. The dissection of a living body is a vivisection. Thus, the film's title is ironic. Once the audience has watched the film in its entirety, they become aware it does not contain an actual autopsy. The film's title, therefore, not only hints that the audience's perceptions (or presumptions) about the events contained therein are incorrect, but in doing so, it helps the viewers understand both Jane and the film better. That is, like *The Sender*, *Autopsy* concerns the investigation of a living body's inner workings, instead of an actual postmortem.

The eponymous autopsy reflects the attempted postmortem investigation, which is supposed to help the police discover Jane Doe's identity so they can solve the case of her death as well as those of the victims at the film's beginning. However, what one needs to bear in mind here is that as an ostensible corpse, and as a mute trapped, and immobile, inside her own body, Jane has lost control of herself. Her very sense of identity diminishes inside her corporeal prison. Observe, for example, how the very name "Jane Doe" is but a placeholder police give to unidentified bodies and persons. "Jane Doe" is not the witch's (or the woman's) real name. Moreover, the body is the site of the self, and as I observed, Jane Doe has no control over this site, though it encompasses her own self.[24] Thus, deprived of both her name and body, Jane's sense of self, her sense of her identity, becomes weakened and imperiled.

This imperiling, this endangering of Jane Doe, becomes even more pronounced when the Tildens begin slicing into her, for not only are they wounding her, but they are also threatening to discover an identity she has lost for herself. As coroners, and as motile beings, Tommy and Austin have a mastery over Jane Doe's body that she herself does not possess: she can certainly heal her wounds, but she shows no ability to manipulate her limbs (before the film's ending, that is) or to even open her mouth (or skin). She cannot lay her secrets bare the way the Tildens can.

From this perspective, consequently, the viewer can regard Jane's attempts at thwarting the autopsy as her efforts to safeguard her fleeting sense of self. Jane's body, like that of John Doe #83's, is seemingly open for investigation. However, as *Autopsy* demonstrates, blood is not a complete impediment to the process of discovery: once dead and exsanguinated, the body is open for exploration. Nonetheless, because these two criteria are necessary for one to plumb the body's depths and thereby complete this exploration, one must, as Tommy and Austin do, come face to face with death. In this manner, therefore, *Autopsy* goes further than either *The Sender* or *Scream* does, by venturing beyond the mere exposure of blood, which the latter two movies portray as an impediment.

As the sublime counterpart to life, death is, practically by definition, that which eludes humanity's understanding.[25] Death is that which defies language and understanding because there exist no methods through which characters, and more importantly, the audience—its potential target—can apprehend and control it; as living creatures, death is beyond moviegoers, and yet it is also inevitable. That is why, even though they may be afraid of it, they feel compelled to study it, to approach it, all while being cognizant of their inability to ever truly comprehend it until they experience it for themselves. At that point, however, their understanding may cease all together.[26]

This inability, on the viewer's behalf, to truly apprehend the specter of death is, perhaps, most apparent from Jane Doe's cloudy eyes in the film. Early in the autopsy, the Tildens aver that Jane's eyes indicate she has been dead for at least several days. Clouded over, her eyes are those of the deceased (though she does not belong to that group herself). Popular folk knowledge takes a person's eyes to be the window(s) to their soul. Even in everyday life, if one looks closely into someone else's eyes, one can see oneself reflected in them; one can see what the other person's eyes are seeing. In this manner, the eye acts as a mirror. In contrast, however, Jane's eyes reflect little of the sort, as their occlusion hinders their ability to reflect. Consequently, upon looking down into them, the Tildens barely see themselves, leading them to conclude she has been dead for several days.

Jane Doe's eyes are the eyes of ostensible death, which offer little reflection, and hence, provide no way of perceiving oneself in relation to them. To elucidate: a mirror with a clean surface typically allows a reflected person to successfully orient themselves in any given space, but a clouded

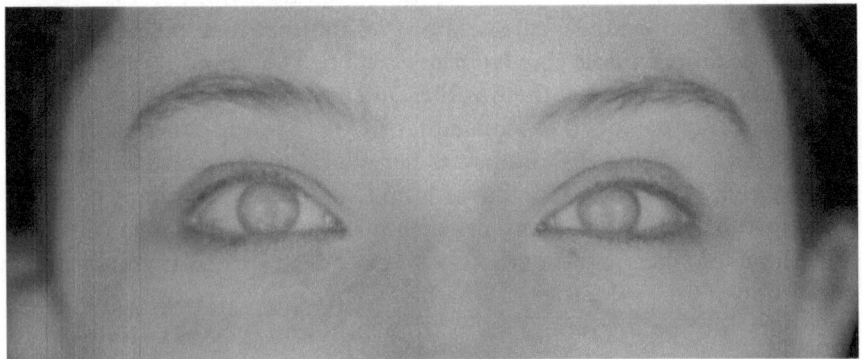

Jane Doe (Olwen Kelly) lays motionless after the Tildens open her eyes. Her clouded eyes give but highly imperfect reflections of the lights above her (*The Autopsy of Jane Doe*, directed by André Øvredal. IFC Midnight, 2016).

mirror fails to perform this task; it offers no bearing, no way of perceiving, and so, no way of understanding themselves as they are reflected in it. Fog (or any other source of opacity) on a mirror transforms the mirror from a passage to an abyss: its depths now conceal, rather than reveal, themselves. Accordingly, searching Jane Doe for an understanding of death is a fool's errand.

By extension, so is searching the film for answers to its mysteries. Neither the characters nor the viewers know who Jane Doe is: they do not know her motivations, her history, even her name, and hence, they are ignorant about where her powers stop and reality begins. In this way, *Autopsy*, like *Oculus*, offers mere hints instead of definite answers. For the rest, it leaves the audience—us—in the dark and Jane Doe in the light. Knowledge is hers and hers alone.

Moreover, Jane resembles a blind prophet in that, while she lacks sight herself, her supernatural powers still revolve around seeing. Namely, Jane can alter her victims' perceptions, including their sight, making them perceive what is not really there. This power of hers relies on making others look where she wants them to. She needs them to see the illusions she creates (or, pertaining to other senses, to hear or feel them). Thus, like the mirror in *Oculus*, Jane directs people on where to look, on what to perceive. And the film camera does the same. When the camera zooms in, it limits the reality on screen: the perceived world narrows, thereby reducing the possibilities. The camera's frame is a limiter the film director inevitably places on reality: a camera has a defined outer edge, and so, it cannot show what is beyond its scope, what falls outside the area the lens can capture. In an expanding universe, a finite screen can never capture everything. Film crews must, therefore, choose which parts of reality they will present to the audience, and determine what to omit; this is the filmmaker's primary and most difficult task.

Consequently, what a movie does not show is, perhaps, even more important than what it does portray. Each of the films I have discussed thus far in this chapter demonstrates the presence of some sort of truth that evades the audience by being outside the camera's frame, and so, beyond their field of vision. The absence of these varied truths—especially when considered together—becomes conspicuous: just as the body's inner workings remain elusive, so do complete understandings of how the films' supernatural elements operate. This lack of answers, and the resultant lingering mystery, exists for two reasons.

The first reason is that mysteries are intriguing. The lack of easy answers entices the viewer to look deeper and find some answers for (and by) themselves. Mysteries—untold truths, in this case—grab the viewer's attention and help retain it. The second reason is that a film cannot disclose all truths, not only because the camera cannot capture everything simultaneously, but also because some truths cannot be apprehended. Note, for instance, how Jane Doe's eyes and, by extension, death, defy explanation and understanding. That is, because human understanding is limited (at least for now), no film can reveal every possible truth. Instead, these horror films gesture at truths they cannot showcase, pushing viewers to consider questions that currently lack answers. Scholar Roger Shattuck reinforces this observation when he states: "One of the basic givens of humanity is final ignorance about ourselves and those closest to us. But we cannot help kicking this aspect of human condition, wanting to know what we can never know."[27]

Moreover, by inclining the audience to consider the camera's role (in forcing the audience to look where the filmmaker wants), these films incite the audience to consider how films operate much like the mirror and Jane Doe's powers do. Both the mirror from *Oculus* and Jane Doe herself rely on controlling where others look, and what these others perceive (be it real or unreal). They, therefore, mimic the film camera's main effect so they can gain power. Thus, all films rely on the warping or controlling of human perception, in some way or the other. In this way, fiction can operate as a (very) low-grade form of mind control, which directs audiences into assuming a certain perspective, a certain belief, as well as a particular way of feeling and behaving. This is where understanding liminality in horror becomes essential, for the didactic nature of the liminal horror film encourages viewers to think more deeply about the nature of perception, film, and fiction. It induces them to consider how each of these is flawed, how each can bias their conclusions, and, in doing so, make them misperceive the reality around them.

Furthermore, the films' varied use of hallucinations and premonitions (i.e., perceiving what is not actually present in the external world) prompts the audience—us—to realize how liminal reality actually is: even in real-life, hallucinations can reveal hidden truths that, in turn, indicate that fictions (in this case, illusions—those things that are not, externally speaking, real) can also be truths. That is, the border between fiction and reality is porous, even outside the dream state. One need only think about hallucinogenic drugs to understand how liminality functions in everyday life. Writing about such hallucinogenic substances, Jennifer Ouellette observes that the patterns one sees when tripping are actually the patterns of the brain itself:

> Since there is no external input when the eyes are closed, that pattern should reflect the architecture of the brain, specifically the functional organization of the visual cortex.... "You are not seeing the cells themselves, but the way they're organized—as if the brain is revealing itself to itself."[28]

What Ouellette's observation connotes, in the contexts of mind, fiction, and reality, which the films in this chapter explore, is this: that changing our perception of reality presents us with those realities which would otherwise remain hidden from us.

Accordingly, instead of being mere fictions, hallucinations can, in fact, be real. Reality, therefore, is multi-layered. We, as both the audience and characters, dwell in a state hinging on the borders of various layers, a state that moves across those different borders early and often. Far from being mere fictions, the liminal horror films I have discussed are, consequently, more real than we (as the audience) tend to give them credit for. Didactically, they are teaching us lessons about the world in which we live: a world where our senses are truly untrustworthy, and where hidden realities exist all around us, often beyond our scope of comprehension. Thus, we live in a world that also defies our attempts to taxonomize it, and liminal horror films simply enlighten us to this fact.

Section Two: Flawed Memories

As the movies I discuss in the previous section demonstrate, our (i.e., humanity's) senses are flawed. And people construct their memories from the data these senses provide. It follows, then, that our memories are flawed as well. Not only does a binary view of reality (as being wholly distinct from fiction) ignore the obvious power of fiction and the human mind, but it also ignores the fallibility of memory. We humans (often unconsciously) filter reality through our memory, which we trust to provide us with an accurate account of real-life. However, memory is not nearly as good at this job as most believe.

For instance, whenever someone tells him "I know what I saw," Yale neurologist Stephen Novella has a habit of saying, "No you don't."[29] Novella is right to counter such a claim because human memory is notoriously unreliable. Indeed, psychologist Elizabeth Loftus has conducted seminal research on human memory and found that human memories are malleable.[30] Loftus, in her research, can make people believe they remember events that did not actually happen (such as being lost at the mall when they were children) or could not have happened (for instance, seeing Bugs Bunny, a character who does not belong to Disney, at Disneyland).[31] Reviewing these experts' testimony, skeptical podcaster Craig Good puts it bluntly: "We are a story our brain tells itself. And our brains are habitual liars."[32]

This unreliability of memories, in turn, denotes the issue of personal realities. That is, two people will experience and remember the same event differently. As a result, it can be difficult to judge what is real and what is not, what actually occurred and what did not. While exploring this very issue in fiction, Heller-Nicholas turns to the found footage film *Home Movie*, in which the parents and children of a dysfunctional family produce dueling—or conflicting—home videos. The children, Heller-Nicholas writes, "construct their own version of reality, but their story is strikingly different from the upbeat version that David [their father] has presented."[33] Different authors, she notes, produce different versions of "reality," as do different spectators: "'The Jack and Emily Show' therefore argues that home videos are not a straightforward documentation of reality. They can construct a range of realities, which in the hands of different authors present diverse narratives about what are sometimes incomprehensible secrets."[34] If one couples this assertion with Good's quotation in the preceding paragraph, fiction's function—in shaping one's memory, and so, one's reality—becomes evident.

Understanding the role of fiction in shaping reality is essential, for we live inherently fictional lives, by constantly crafting narratives (either consciously or unconsciously) that suit our own ends. That is, your life *is* your story, not only in sense of having a beginning and end, but in the sense that you are creating a fiction for yourself, per your own needs. Hence the famous aphorism: everyone is the hero of their own story.[35] Pertaining to this fabrication of one's self and memory, Novella writes: "You have a distorted and constructed memory of a distorted and constructed perception, both of which are subservient to whatever narrative your brain is operating under."[36] Jonathan Gottschall agrees with Novella on this point: "We tell some of the best stories to ourselves. Scientists have discovered that the memories we use to form our own life stories are boldly fictionalized."[37] This is all to reiterate that the line between fiction and reality is hard to decipher and judge because our memories are fallible and our brains prone to spinning their own stories, those fictions we then believe are reality.

While an unfiltered, objective reality may well exist (John Doe either committed the crime or he did not), we do not encounter it. Rather, each person experiences their own, subjective, reality, where truth is a question rather than a tangible object, and where they view events from their own self-centered perspectives. Humanity's fictions, Gottschall notes, affect our realities: "In laboratory settings, fiction can mislead people into believing outlandish things: that brushing their teeth is bad for them...."[38] He corroborates his observation by using fear as an example: "Take fear. In a 2009 study, Joanne Cantor showed that most of us have been traumatized by scary fiction. Seventy-five percent of her research subjects reported intense anxiety, disruptive thoughts, and sleeplessness after viewing a horror film."³⁹,⁴⁰ He later adds, "In fact, fiction seems to be more effective at changing beliefs than nonfiction...."⁴¹

These different scholars and their strikingly similar arguments further evidence the didactic nature of horror, and in particular, liminal horror. Thus far, I have argued that horror fiction educates its audience about their own mortality. Tangentially, horror also teaches audiences about their lived reality. Because everyone constructs their own narratives of events, they therefore experience "realities" different from the "realities" those around them experience.

While these subjective realities do not overwrite objective truth (when it does exist), it is our responsibility to acknowledge that truth itself is not always objective. Namely, the senses we use to construct our notions of truth and the memories storing said notions are both imperfect and biased. They do not construct objective records of what is, but rather flawed, self-serving narratives of what we perceive (an incomplete view) or what we want to believe there is (the story that presents the remembering person in the best light, and the others as villains).

A person's memory is *their* record of *their* experiences, and records, like memories themselves, can be flawed and/or wrong. An instance of this occurs in *Oculus*, wherein the police arrest Tim twice, and both times, for crimes he did not really commit. Per the record, Tim has killed his father and sister. But according to the objective "truth" the movie's audience perceives, Tim kills his father in self-defense and at his father's request, while he kills his sister by accident. In both these cases, the mirror warps the perceptions and characters of the people around it and compels Tim into committing acts which we, as the audience, cannot be sure he would have committed otherwise.

However, the police do not know this, and we cannot blame them for not considering seriously the "killer mirror" alibi. While the film does not show the aftermath of Tim's second arrest, it implies society (in-universe) will deem Tim a mentally unhinged murderer; they will not see him as a victim of supernatural forces. In other words, the collective record will be wrong. Just as the individual's memory can be an inaccurate record, so, too, can society's memory (i.e., history) be imprecise and unreliable.

For instance, history presents the Salem Witch Trials as (partially) the result of socioeconomic tensions in Salem.⁴² In contrast, *Autopsy* (discussed in the previous section), raises the specter of actual witches in the colonial village. Different groups, therefore, have different histories. Jane Doe and her inquisitors remember the events in Salem very differently, and it is the latter group that chronicled the trials in society's history books. A similar dynamic is evident in *Candyman*, where Helen's colleague, Dr.

Purcell, understands the Candyman myth quite differently than the residents of Cabrini-Green do.

For him (and, initially, for Helen as well), it is a myth based in historical fact, a myth the Cabrini-Green residents then use to explain their daily strife: living in a wretched slum, they make a boogeyman of an historical victim. This boogeyman, they claim, is responsible for their suffering, or so Purcell and Helen think. For the Cabrini-Green community, however, the story is different. Namely, it is more of a reality than a myth. For them, Candyman is real, not a mere specter who haunts their memories, but a tangible entity who can emerge and interact with their world.

Thus, though Purcell and Helen are correct in believing the myth to be based in history, they fail to fully apprehend how the myth works in Cabrini-Green. The two communities, therefore, construct different histories along socioeconomic lines. Both these histories carry some truth, but neither forms a fully objective record of reality. Note, for example, how Candyman only reaches out and interacts with Helen's middle-class, white society *after* she crosses the socioeconomic divide and enters Candyman's domain, or, as Purcell calls it, "Candyman country."[43]

Consequently, regardless of the responsible factors and causes, the distinctions persist, and these distinctions ensure that we do not—that we cannot—encounter the unfiltered, objective truth. This, in turn, negates the possibility of unfiltered and objective memories as well. As the various psychological studies (referenced earlier in this section) and the examples of *Autopsy*, *Oculus*, and *Candyman* demonstrate, individual memories are largely fictional, and so are the memories of society at large. Thus, our record of the real is as flawed as the tools we use to gather the information to build the record (that is, our senses).

Here, and over the past few pages, I have specifically been using collective personal pronouns like "we," "us," and "our," to lead the reader into contemplating the very nature of the word "we." This word, along with, e.g., "I," "me," and "mine," are more problematic than most of us probably take them to be. And they are problematic because the concept of self they represent is far more complex and nebulous than many of us acknowledge.

Section Three: The Self as Fictional

It is my central contention that the self is a slippery product of the mind and that none of us has a stable, singular "self" but, rather, many different selves. To use an everyday example for explaining my assertion: think about how you talk to the various people in your life. Does your nature/personality stay the same throughout all your interactions, or do different people bring forth different versions of you? More importantly, think about how these different personas of yourself compare with the person you are when you are alone, or in public, or even while you are at work.

The point is: we constantly present different versions of ourselves every day, from hour to hour or even from minute to minute. And these variations in one's self (or selves) are a common rhetorical strategy. For instance, in a job interview, one ideally presents oneself as formal, respectful, and intelligent. In contrast, some of these niceties can disappear when one is in the company of their closest friends, only to reappear later when one is at work or on a business trip. But then, which of those versions is the real version, the true manifestation of one's Self? Which of these different personas is the real person?

The answer may well vary depending on the individual, but I contend that all these different variations are real, for each of them represents a part of one's personality, but not all of it. Humans are complex creatures, with wavering motivations and emotions that make it difficult to generalize or completely comprehend them. Everyone is more a collection of various individuals than a single, discreet entity.

This is all to explicate that "I," "you," and even "we" are more concepts than actualities. What we often take to be the "Self" is never truly a singular entity: it is, in fact, the amalgamation of various smaller "selves," various traits that get expressed more or less depending on the situation. "Self," in other words, is fluid.[44] It expands to incorporate new aspects. In chapter four, for example, I referenced Heidegger's view that our minds grow to include our tools. Cognitive scientist Anthony Chemero concurs: "You're so tightly coupled to the tools you use that they're literally part of you as a thinking, behaving thing."[45] Sometimes, this multiplicity of self becomes even more literal.

"We" see this, for instance, in the case of split-brain surgeries. As a last-resort treatment for epilepsy, doctors may sometimes sever the corpus callosum, the part of the brain joining the left and right hemispheres. The results of this procedure, however, are interesting: the right and left hands operate independently of one another, as their corresponding hemispheres can no longer communicate. That is, if you present the name of an object to the right side of the body (controlled by the left hemisphere), the subject will be able to both pick up the correct object and correctly explain why they picked it up: because they were told to do so. If, however, you present the name of an object to the left side (controlled by the right hemisphere) and try to do the same, the subject will be able to pick up the correct object but will not provide the correct explanation. Instead, the subject will spontaneously tell a plausible, though incorrect, story.[46]

The left hemisphere controls language. Thus, when the right hemisphere must grab something, the left, once they are separated, does not know the real reason, but it knows how to fabricate a story. This further reinforces the argument that the human mind is a creative storyteller fully capable of deluding itself. Gottschall writes: "The storytelling mind is allergic to uncertainty … [it] is a factory that churns out true stories when it can, but will manufacture lies when it can't."[47] In contrast, CGP Grey, an educational YouTuber, argues that this disassociation, caused by separating the brain's hemispheres, is evidence of a separate consciousness within ourselves. The two parts of the brain operate independently and seem to even have differing views, disagreeing on choices the person makes.[48] "You," Grey states, "are two."[49] And Nobel Prize winning psychologist Roger Wolcott Sperry similarly observes: "The presence of two minds in one body, as it were, is manifested in a large number and variety of test responses…."[50]

While Gottschall does not go this far, he does agree that split brain surgeries teach us about the intact brain: "But this research has important implications for how we understand ordinary, intact brains. The storytelling mind is not created when the scalpel cuts into the corpus callosum. Splitting the brain just pins it down for study."[51] Consequently, the more we study psychology, the more we realize how much there is to this idea of the blurred and multiple self/selves. You may be two, but more likely, you are many. In this context, I suppose, we are legion.

Furthermore, as the referenced scholarship (in the preceding paragraphs) shows, we are also stories—the stories we tell ourselves and the stories that others tell about us: "Everyone finds their own way to create meaning out of our allotted time on this Earth—an evocative metaphor, a personal philosophy, a belief in an afterlife, anything that shapes the ups and downs of our lives and inevitable deaths into a story that makes sense."[52] In fact, the memories we use to construct our notions of ourselves can often mistake stories to be experiences: "Nor does the brain distinguish much between reading about an experience, or listening to a description, and actually encountering it."[53] Thus, despite our claims of truth and reality, we inherently understand ourselves through fiction. But how does this fiction affect the notion of the "self": is the "self" an entirely fictional construct? That is, does the "self" even exist?

M. Night Shyamalan's 2016 film, *Split*, provides a unique perspective on this question.[54] The movie stars James McAvoy as a man suffering from Dissociative Identity Disorder (D.I.D.), popularly referred to as Multiple Personality Disorder. McAvoy's character kidnaps three teenage girls and takes them to the underground compound where he lives. The girls soon notice his disorder, as he changes clothes, personalities, mannerisms, and voices. At different times, he is different people, and he even answers to different names corresponding to those personas/people. Running parallel to this main narrative of the girls' kidnapping is the story of Dr. Fletcher, the therapist treating McAvoy's character. Through her scenes, the audience learns the antagonist has 23 personalities, and each personality is highly distinct, with its own ticks and aversions. Some are even deviants (e.g., Dennis and Patricia, the two who orchestrate the girls' kidnapping), whereas others are not.

Through these two overlapping storylines, we, the audience, learn Dennis and Patricia are trying to summon a 24th personality, whom they call The Beast. If Dennis and Patricia are perverse, The Beast is a monster. The former two manage to manifest him, and The Beast promptly begins murdering and eating people, including Dr. Fletcher and all but one of the kidnapped girls. Moreover, The Beast possesses superpowers: he has super strength, can climb walls, and can easily shrug off being shot with a shotgun. At the film's conclusion, he spares one of the girls, Casey, and it is revealed the events of this film have occurred in the same fictional universe as Shyamalan's earlier film, *Unbreakable* (2000). This ending subsequently changes the film's dynamic because it reintroduces the audience to David Dunn, *Unbreakable*'s superhero protagonist. Thus, *Split* is actually a supervillain's origin story, and this revelation explains the extreme escalation during the film's third-act, as well as its genre shift from psychological thriller to supernatural horror film.

My summarization of *Split* may seem odd to the reader, for it heavily downplays Casey's role as the story's protagonist, and because it does not name McAvoy's character. However, these narrative choices are intentional. I do not focus more on Casey's role in the film (to the point that my summary does not portray her as the protagonist) because though she is an interesting character in her own right, she does not suffer from the fractured sense of self, which is the main reason I discuss *Split* in this volume. As for not naming McAvoy's character, I do so because his character lacks a single name: instead, he has 24 different names, and because he switches between these names (and their corresponding personalities) throughout the film, the actor's name, McAvoy, becomes easier to use as a referent.

Indeed, *Split* derives its title from the term "split personality," a reference to the D.I.D. from which McAvoy's character suffers. McAvoy's character was born Kevin Wendell Crumb. The Kevin personality is the original of the 24, and this personality manifests just once in the film, when Casey manages to bring him forth. Here, Kevin is horrified at what his other personalities have done, and he begs Casey to kill him, even telling her where his shotgun is. He disappears, however, as the other personalities fight him for primacy, with the nine-year-old child personality, Hedwig, emerging as the winner. Kevin, therefore, is at war with his various selves. For him, the concept of multiple selves is frighteningly concrete, and there is no single, core identity. I remarked earlier that all of us are possibly legion, containing a multitude of selves within us. This is especially true for Kevin, whom the media dub "The Horde."[55]

This notion of the self as legion (or "The Horde," according to the film) appears in *Split* like a series of cracks across a mirror. When one stares into a cracked mirror, one finds their self fractured. Each part of the mirror operates as a mirror all its own, reflecting at the single corporeal observer multiple versions of themselves. Symbolically, the cracked mirror reveals the multiple "selves" hidden within a single mind, a single corporeal being. Interestingly, the DVD of *Urban Legend* features a cracked mirror on its cover, with each of the mirror's sections reflecting one of the film's different characters. However, this take on the cracked mirror motif is confused. To be sure, the cracks refer to the film's violence; they also hint at the division between the characters, at how each is the victim of a different legend and, consequently, metaphorically exists in a different story than the other characters do.[56]

Since the mirror on the cover reflects several of the principal characters (Reese is missing), it as if the characters assemble before the camera's reflective gaze. For, when else would they all exist within the same reflective space? That the shattered mirror stands in for a camera here is apparent if the audience examines the eye in the center of the fractures. One may well surmise this eye is either the cinematographer's or the viewer's; the viewer, after all, can only look because the cinematographer has filmed the characters. When the viewer does look, however, the film's events play out. That is, by inserting the DVD into my player, I allow the film's reality to occur. I allow the events to fracture. The events contained within the movie do not become realities until I make it play on the screen.

Before the movie plays, the events have not happened, and so, have not encoded themselves into my (or the audience's) memories. Sensorially, they are inert, but possibilities. Those possibilities do not become actualities until the audience watches the movie unfold. And so, through this oblique technique, *Urban Legend*'s DVD cover denotes a truth of cinema: it is the viewer's gaze that fractures the narrative into its individual arcs. Any movie can play (or keep playing) even in the absence of any viewers. After all, who has not found someone (e.g., their grandfather) asleep in front of the television? Thus, a movie can unfold by itself, without an audience. However, as I established in the previous chapter, the point of fiction (film) is conveyed by cinema's reliance on directing the viewer's gaze, and so, for its narrative to have any affect or effect, the film must, necessarily, have an audience. Someone must watch as the movie's events unfold.

Conversely, on *Split*'s theatrical poster, it is not the viewer who fractures Kevin's self. This poster shows a man, Kevin, casting several shadows from the back toward the front of the poster (i.e., toward the observer). A light sits somewhere behind him, beyond what the viewer can perceive, and it scatters the shadows of his fractured self out across the ground. By looking at the different shadows, one can wonder about how "Kevin" leads multiple lives, has multiple inner selves, including The Beast, who occupies a privileged position as the foremost shadow, the foremost of Kevin's selves. Accordingly, these two images, *Urban Legend*'s DVD cover and *Split*'s theatrical poster, reveal different perspectives on the nature of the fractured self: unlike *Urban Legend*, which requires an audience to fracture it, in *Split*, it is not the observer who fragments Kevin's being.

In contrast, *Split*'s Blu-ray cover depicts a cracked mirror that aligns more closely to *Urban Legend*'s cover than to its own theatrical poster. On the Blu-ray cover, the central version of Kevin, the James McAvoy who stares at the viewer from the cover's left-hand side, remarkably remains intact. Despite the fissures curving their way through the glass, his image is whole. Off to the side, though, one can see images of some of his different selves, represented in different sections of the broken glass. Because these different versions of Kevin are thus subordinate to the largest version of him, the cover focuses not on the viewer's ability to fracture either a narrative or character, but rather on the different "selves" that every member of the audience contains within themselves. Kevin stares out at the audience, at us, and his proximity to the cover's front implies he may be the one breaking the glass. Here, Kevin is the powerful character: his personalities can split themselves, as the movie shows when Dennis and Patricia manifest The Beast with Hedwig's help.

What is interesting is that, in an initial reading, one might think the film suggests there is no self. After all, Kevin has 24 personalities, and so, 24 different selves existing simultaneously within the same body. Yet, there is still a self here. It is a multiple self, to be sure, and it lacks a central identity, but there is still a being here with some control over itself. Notice, for instance, how Kevin retains power on the Blu-Ray's cover and how the various shadows trace back to a single origin point on the theatrical poster. *Split*, therefore, provides a way of considering *our* cultural conceptions of the self, including the philosophical concept of diachronic unity, the feeling that, despite the changes we experience over time, there is still an "I" underneath it all, a being to whom all the experiences happen.[57]

Additionally, *Split* seems to challenge diachronically unified ideas of the self because the different personalities do not share memories: there does not seem to be much unifying them except a thin membrane of flesh containing all of them within a single entity. For most intents and purposes, they are different people, and hence, the "I" remains elusive. Yet the case is not so simple, as Anil Ananthaswamy writes: "There is still an 'I' that is suffering from schizophrenia, is depersonalized, is dealing with autism, is ecstatic, disowns body parts, has out-of-body experiences, loses its narrative, and even denies its own existence."[58]

To be clear, schizophrenia and D.I.D. are different, but Ananthaswamy's observation suggests that there may still be an "I" underneath Kevin's 24 personalities. Right now, philosophers and neuroscientists remain divided on the question of whether a self exists.[59] By challenging the notion of the self and, so, inciting its audience to contemplate whether there is a unifying "I" to Kevin, *Split* makes us, the audience, consider this question about the (non) existence of the self with which scholars are wrestling.

Split also foregrounds another aspect that we, as spectators, need to ponder over: our minds' ability to alter external reality. Dr. Fletcher, for instance, notes that D.I.D. patients (within the film) can have major physiological differences between their personalities. One personality, she says, can have high cholesterol while the others do not. One of Kevin's personalities is even a weightlifter who is physically stronger than the other personalities are. And The Beast takes these differences to the logical extreme by having superpowers when the other personalities do not. Dr. Fletcher uses these differences to posit that, in *Split*, the D.I.D. patient (McAvoy's character, in this case) has unlocked the mind's potential to alter the body, that is, external reality.

She further questions whether this hidden ability of the mind might be the explanation for supernatural phenomena. Indeed, in the film, it appears to be: because Dennis and Patricia believe The Beast exists within Kevin's body, they are able to think a supervillain into existence.[60] This notion, of Dennis and Patricia conjuring another personality into existence, is interesting, for it shows seemingly real effects of what was once a fantasy. Furthermore, there are several other films which demonstrate some version of this notion.

Section Four: Mental Projections: When Emotions Become Monsters

Where Dennis and Patricia actively work to bring The Beast into reality, other films depict the mind (sub-consciously) moving its phantoms into existence. For instance, consider 1982's *The Entity*, directed by Sidney Furie and starring Barbara Hershey. Hershey plays Carla Moran, an overworked single mother of three, whose life becomes upended when an unseen assailant sexually assaults her. This assailant is the eponymous entity, which attacks Carla repeatedly. It almost crashes her car while she is driving, and it rapes her on multiple occasions.

On finding her medical doctors' advice unhelpful, she seeks help from a group of parapsychologists (researchers of the paranormal). The parapsychologists create a replica of Carla's house so they can trap the entity and freeze it with liquid helium. The entity, however, breaks free of the ice and continues to haunt Carla. Finally, she confronts the entity herself and moves to a new state. The film's closing text informs the audience that Carla continues to experience the attacks, albeit fewer of them, and with less severity.

The Entity is a relatively obscure film seemingly tailor made for a psychoanalytic reading. It foregrounds its protagonist's trauma and treats the trauma as a distinct being, an external, objectively existing—albeit invisible—specter. Carla tells her doctors about her life: her father molested her, her first love (her son Billy's father) died young, and her daughters' father abandoned her. Her medical doctors take this history and construct a diagnosis that would make Freud proud: they believe her history of lacking sexual agency is now manifesting psychosomatically. But these doctors are only half right. The psychological treatment they prescribe does not help Carla in the slightest because the entity *is* an actual entity. Carla's mind is not warping her body; it is warping reality. It is only when Dr. Sneiderman sees the entity encased in ice that he realizes he and his medical colleagues were wrong to dismiss Carla's insistence that the entity exists.

Yet, the entity's external existence does not completely invalidate the doctors' diagnosis, for they are still correct in considering Carla's psychology responsible for her attacks. None of this, of course, exonerates the entity itself from being a vile rapist, but this analysis does explain why the entity's torment of Carla has a sexual nature. Carla lives alone with her three children, and, despite being in her early thirties, she has a teenage son (Billy), who looks just like his father, Carla's first love. When Carla describes one of the rape scenes, she says she felt three entities: two smaller ones who forcibly spread her legs and a larger one who assaulted her. As her doctors note, the number and size of the entities align with those of Carla's children: two young (and small) daughters and one teenaged son. Dr. Sneiderman takes this evidence and outright suggests Carla has incestuous desires for her son.

Disturbing as it is (Carla angrily dismisses it), this explanation makes sense. Billy's close resemblance to his father plus his proximity to his mother's age renders the logical leap a small one. That one of her assaults even mirrors her family's structure further reinforces this diagnosis. Earlier versions of the film's script went even further and moved the incestuous undertones from sub-text to actual text: originally, the film was to include a sequence in which Carla fantasizes about having sex with Billy.⁶¹ However, the film's creators cut that scene from the final version for obvious reasons. The sub-text, however, the skeleton of that excised scene, remains.

The film's opening follows Carla through the end of her day. She rushes from work to night school and then back home, where she checks on her kids. Carla lives a frantic life, and, though she handles her workload as well as anyone can, it, in conjunction with her earlier trauma and difficult history, creates a recipe for disaster. And this disaster takes place in the form of the entity. Carla's brain can no longer grapple with all the weight it carries, and so, her forbidden desires break out of her mind and manifest themselves in the physical world. The cut scene—in which Carla sexualizes her son—is a moment of her mind acting on her body. When one fantasizes sexually, one's mind is constructing a favorable fiction, one it designs to arouse the fantasizer.

The projection of Carla's desires into the external world, therefore, becomes a perverse and ironic twist on the idea of the sexual fantasy. She can no longer consciously construct a fiction that safely enacts her desires. Instead, her sub-conscious contrives a being who enacts those desires upon her as if they were never hers to begin with. Though this may seem far-fetched, it really is not: one needs only to recall something they wish they had not thought or felt or desired, to understand how Carla becomes distant from that which her subconscious has manufactured.

This occurrence—of a feeling or thought that one would rather forget—is the phenomenon of intrusive thoughts.⁶² A thought is intrusive when it is unwanted and when it seems to force itself to the forefront of the thinker's mind. In Carla's case, however, the intrusive thought breaks not just into the forefront of the mind but also onto the surface and into the depths of the human body. Thus, the film offers a disturbing reading of how thoughts and psychological baggage can develop a life of their own. It concretizes the psychological to prompt the audience into examining some of their most unpleasant inner sensations.

For a non-sexualized view of the same subject, consider *The Babadook* (2014, directed by Jennifer Kent). In this movie, single mother Amelia Vanek (Essie Davis) struggles to raise her son Samuel, who was born the day her husband—and Samuel's father—Oskar, died. Amelia struggles with grief over Oskar's death as well as with Samuel's behavioral problems. Both these issues get worse when Amelia reads a book called *Mister Babadook* to Samuel, who becomes terrified of the creature. Meanwhile, Amelia begins to experience strange occurrences, and she destroys the book only to find it returned to her doorstep, unharmed but more vicious than before. Eventually, she confronts the Babadook, at which point it flees into her basement. The film's ending reveals Amelia keeps the Babadook locked down there and now has a happier life with Samuel.

Critics tend to read *The Babadook* as a metaphorical story about grief.[63] Amelia refuses to acknowledge her grief over Oskar's death, and this refusal causes the resulting psychological baggage to fester into an infection and then manifest in the Babadook itself.[64] Her problem is opposite to Nancy's: whereas Nancy (from *A Nightmare on Elm Street*) has to learn to stop tackling her problems head on, Amelia has to learn to face her issues lest they become worse. The *Mister Babadook* picture book points out how ignoring the Babadook will only make him stronger, and the same is true of grief, of trauma.[65] Refusing to acknowledge one's problems makes it more difficult to solve said problems.

Thus, even though their methods of doing so are vastly different, *The Babadook* and *The Entity* tell similar stories. The protagonists of both films experience hauntings from manifestations of their psychological trauma, and neither Amelia nor Carla defeats their trauma; they cannot erase the past or its effects on them. Instead, they learn to live with weakened versions of their traumas. At the end of *The Babadook*, Amelia still has the creature, her grief, tucked away in her basement (symbolically, the recesses of her mind), and she must attend to it occasionally. Her grief will always be with her because she will always feel Oskar's absence. Similarly, at the end of *The Entity*, Carla still experiences attacks. Her trauma and difficult life are still with her, but she has come to terms with them and refused to let them define her.

While both films have something of a happy ending, their protagonists remain tormented, albeit to far lesser degrees than they initially were. There may, however, be cause for greater hope. A little-known Australian film, *Visitors*, offers a similar story structure with a much more upbeat conclusion. Released in 2003, *Visitors* is the final film by its director, Richard Franklin. It stars Radha Mitchell as Georgia Perry, who, at 25, is trying to be the youngest woman to solo-sail around the world. Nearing the end of her journey, she finds herself becalmed in the Indian Ocean with no company other than her cat, Taco.

Georgia informs the audience via voiceover that she found the "line between dreams and reality start[ing] to … blur" while she sat in the ocean.[66] Georgia, as the film soon discloses, is losing her grip on reality: she speaks to Taco and even hears him talk back—in a deep, masculine voice—when he accuses her of letting spirits onto the ship. And, indeed, Georgia gets visions of people from her life back in Australia. Her lover, Kai, seemingly visits her, and she also sees her mother, who committed suicide after Georgia set sail. The mother's spirit blames Georgia for her, the mother's, suicide, and Georgia wrestles with her feelings of guilt over her relationships with her mother and her fiancé Luke, who is cheating on Georgia with Georgia's sponsor.

Georgia's visions become increasingly violent, because of which she has a harder time coping with them as well as her guilt over her mom's death and her strained relationship with Luke. Then, she gets a vision of her father's ghost, whose appearance suggests he has died back home. Her father's spirit comforts her and tells her she must stop blaming herself. Buoyed by her deceased dad's support, Georgia resolves herself to push the unwelcome visitors from her boat. She sets the boat ablaze, sheltering herself and Taco in the safety of the hull. Thus, she banishes the ghosts and completes her voyage back to Australia.

Passing her starting point, she successfully becomes the youngest woman to solo-sail around the world, whereupon she turns her boat around and surprises the crowd by sailing back out into the ocean. The crowd retrieves a message Georgia throws into the water, and Luke finds it contains her engagement ring. Back on the ship, Georgia tells Taco they are sailing to Auckland, where her former lover Kai now resides. Taco does not reply. Upbeat music plays, and the sun shines down as Georgia sets sail for her new home, leaving her past behind.

Visitors draws together the various threads I have explored throughout this volume. The first is the interdiction. Taco plays the role of the harbinger, warning Georgia to not let the spirits in: "You let one on board, next thing...."[67] He also upbraids Georgia for killing "an albatross."[68] Earlier, when Georgia is on deck (before talking to Taco), she finds a black bird (either a raven or a crow) tangled in some rope. She tries to save it, but the bird struggles out of her hands, falls into the ocean, and drowns. Taco's dubbing the bird an albatross signals his belief Georgia has brought bad luck upon herself. In maritime folklore, it is bad luck to kill an albatross.[69]

Likewise, per the lore, it is bad luck to change a boat's name. Georgia herself expresses concern when Luke and her sponsor rename her yacht from Leander to Monné. Leander is a figure from Greek mythology, who swims across a strait every night to visit his love. Conversely, Monné is the company sponsoring Georgia. The name change mirrors the shift in Georgia's mission. When she departs, Georgia is sailing away from—but then back to—her love, Luke. But Luke is unfaithful to Georgia and has sexual relations with her sponsor from Monné. The boat's name, therefore, becomes an inescapable reminder of her fiancé's infidelity: she is no longer sailing back to her would-be husband, but instead toward a home from which she feels alienated.

In each of these instances, Georgia violates an interdiction: she lets the sponsor and Luke change the boat's name despite her misgivings; she allows the specter of Kai onto the boat despite Taco's warnings; and she kills the bird. In the last instance, however, one must note she was trying to save the bird, and, also, that it was not an albatross. Yet, as a raven or crow, the bird may have been a symbol of bad luck even before she accidentally killed it. In mythology, killing an albatross brings bad luck upon the one who committed the crime, but in contrast, the mere presence of a raven or crow can be an omen of ill-fate.

Along with its inclusion of interdictions and their violations, *Visitors* also revisits some of the other threads I discussed in earlier chapters. For one, it destabilizes both the viewer and Georgia, as it becomes increasingly difficult to differentiate fiction from reality in the narrative. The yacht's pitching and yawing mirrors the story's destabilizing effect, as it moves between Georgia's current voyage and the life she had (before embarking on the voyage) back in Australia. Consequently, it becomes the viewers' responsibility to piece together the order in which these events occurred, while also questioning if some of the events depicted actually happened or not (e.g., when Georgia encounters—or merely believes she encounters—the pirated tanker).

Though she runs into the pirates several times, it is not entirely clear how much of her experiences are real. Her friend (on a nearby ship) informs her his ship's radar has detected no such vessel, yet her visions of the pirates become increasingly violent and outlandish. When the pirates board her yacht and attempt to abduct her, they also shoot through the hull, causing the yacht to take on water. Then, they drag her onto the deck, but she struggles free and dives into the ocean. When she resurfaces, the fog bank that previously surrounded her ship has returned: the pirates are gone, the hull intact.

Here, the viewer must also consider how even though Georgia's dreams make her question what is real, they also afford her the opportunity to begin solving her personal problems. Like Nancy, Georgia receives pointed advice she must follow if she wishes to (successfully) overpower—and subdue—the world of dreams that threatens to consume her. Namely, to escape the fog and finish her journey, Georgia must overcome her guilt. Throughout the film, she negotiates her guilt with the eponymous visitors, who force her to confront her lingering anxieties and her feelings of having failed the people in her life. Most notably, the ghost of Georgia's mother hounds her and holds Georgia responsible for her mother's death by suicide.

The flashbacks Georgia experiences reveal to the audience that she placed her mother in a mental institution because the latter incessantly threatened suicide and even attempted it several times. Georgia's mother, ergo, blames her daughter for both her detainment and depression, and erroneously lays the guilt for her suicidal impulses at her daughter's feet.

And the mother's ghost takes matters even further by compelling Georgia to commit suicide herself: she slaps Georgia and later slashes Georgia's wrist with a razor blade—the same method Georgia's mother used to kill herself.

In contrast, her father's spirit provides a counterpoint to his ex-wife's (her mother's) assaults. Whereas her mother asks her, "Real? What's real," and goads Georgia into further doubting her own sanity and, perhaps, even to killing herself, her father tries to help her.[70] He contradicts the mother's ghost and tells her: "Just stop blaming yourself. If you don't get rid of [the ghosts], they'll sure as hell get rid of you."[71] Later, Georgia's friend on the other boat tells her—via radio—that she needs to "unload some of this shit," referring to her psychological baggage.[72] To phrase it in a different manner, both her father and her friend give her license to discharge her feelings of guilt, and she listens to them. When Luke (whom she resents for his infidelity, but also feels guilty toward due to her own unfaithfulness) informs her he is sending a search and rescue for her—thus terminating her voyage and forcing her back to the mainland—she stands up to him. She states she will resist any attempt to get her off the boat and goes further in asserting herself: "On this piece of fiberglass, I am God Almighty."[73]

This assertion, in turn, brings fire. Georgia uses a flare gun to shoot one of the spirits; and when this action does not remove the ghosts, she rigs the boat with containers of fuel and sets it ablaze while the various spirits wander above and below deck. The claim that one is God (especially from a person living in a Judeo-Christian nation such as Australia) can bring forth fire in two forms: either as punishment (via hell fire) or as confirmation (via holy fire). In the film, it comes as confirmation, as banishing the spirits affirms Georgia's power over her boat and life. Here, one should note that the fire, obviously, does not confirm she *is* God; rather, it ratifies her ability to defeat the spirits plaguing her as well as her ability to use fire to cleanse. Symbolically, she is ridding herself of her baggage: she is absolving herself of not only her fear of pirates, but also spiders (represented by the large sea spiders clinging to the boat's underside).

Nevertheless, her mother's spirit continues to haunt her even after the inferno, probably because Georgia's relationship with her mother is the strongest source of her guilt. Thus, Georgia must release her mother's spirit, not through force, but rather by facilitating understanding and reaching absolution thereby. Georgia, therefore, lets go of her guilt over not being able to help her mom, and even refuses her mother's final invitation for her to commit suicide. Affirming her desire to live, she sets her mother at peace and resolves herself to finish the journey. The light into which her mom disappears suggests Georgia has put her mother at peace, finally achieving what she failed to do when her mother was still alive.

Georgia gets a second chance, and she uses it to succeed. She lays her mom to rest, burns away her fears of spiders and pirates, and even finds the strength to leave the cheating fiancé she is not entirely sure she loves ("… pretty sure I love him").[74]

All these incidents, these obstacles Georgie needs to combat and conquer, indicate Georgia's psychological baggage is among the film's foremost concerns. When the movie opens, Georgia is becalmed in a fog bank. Here, she can no longer run from her problems. One could construe Georgia's solo-sailing voyage as, in part, an attempt to flee from her troubles. When she can no longer sail, however, those troubles stick with her, a sticking which consequently forces her to confront her issues, just like her friend and dad tell her to do. In kicking the corpse of one of the spirits off the yacht's deck, she is casting her troubles away from her and into the ocean's vast emptiness.

Like Carla and Amelia (from *The Entity* and *The Babadook*, respectively), Georgia must face her troubles to solve them. Unlike Carla and Amelia, however, she completely frees herself of her issues. Through this contrast, *Visitors* suggests that, unlike trauma or grief, guilt may be surmountable. By forgiving herself and leaving her troubled relationship behind, Georgia can begin anew. The film indicates as much via the sunshine and music in Georgia's final scene as well as via Taco's refusal to speak; now, he is a cat once more, and not a harbinger.

In a dark contrast, however, where Carla, Amelia, and Georgia all overcome (to one extent or another) their psychological issues, 2002's Japanese film *Ju-On: The Grudge* (*Ju-On*) renders emotions more insidious and inescapable, thereby emphasizing their omnipresence and ability to consume. Directed by Takashi Shimizu, this film tells (non-linearly) the story of a haunted house in Tokyo and the curse the house lays on visitors. The film first shows Rika (Megumi Okina) going to the house to care for an elderly woman. Rika quickly falls prey to the curse, however, when she encounters the spirit of a young boy, Toshio. There on, the film follows a variety of interlocking characters who encounter the curse and its expanding influence. Once the house curses someone, they cannot escape it, and the site of their death becomes cursed like the original house. At the film's end, Rika's ghost awakens as she becomes akin to *Ju-On*'s antagonistic spirits.

Ju-On, therefore, portrays its curse, the titular grudge, as inescapable. Not only does the film show every protagonist succumbing to the curse, but *Ju-On*'s opening text informs the audience: "Ju-On: The curse of one who dies in the grip of powerful rage. It gathers and takes effect in the places that person was alive. Those who encounter it die, and a new curse is born."[75] Thus, *Ju-On* focuses on an emotion the other films in this chapter do not focus on: rage. Importantly, rage, as *Ju-On* portrays it, is powerful enough to transcend time, space, and even death. In doing so, rage creates a cycle akin to that of the life cycle. The rage curses others, who then curse others in turn, causing the rage to slowly spread (i.e., reproduce).

Moreover, the film illustrates the curse playing out across history: it depicts when Izumi, who, as a teenage schoolgirl, has a vision of her father at the haunted house, and also when her father has a vision of a teenage Izumi as well, several years before. In this moment, the two share visions of each other, indicating they are looking across the span of years. Pivotally, Izumi's father died when she was a young girl. And so, here, her father receives a vision of Izumi's future, and Izumi receives a vision of her father's past. That they can do this suggests both their deaths (results of their respective visits to the haunted house) were predetermined. They could not escape their fates, a fact the film further underscores by ensuring that not a single protagonist manages to escape.

Additionally, when Izumi dies, her face appears beside her father's face in her family's shrine, which demonstrates the familiar cycle of life, reproduction, and death playing out across a family's history. In this case, however, the film connects rage to this cycle, implying one can spread not only their genes, but also their emotions across several generations. *Ju-On* is a liminal horror film, ergo, because it depicts emotions directly altering external reality when they should (ideally) have no power to do so.

Furthermore, it locates these emotions in the gothic space of a haunted house that somehow stands apart from the city around it. This phenomenon manifests, for instance, in how every character who approaches the house (other than its occupants) appears to be apprehensive about doing so and how, as the story progresses, the house takes on a greater mythos. Indeed, Izumi goes there because it has become infamous as the local haunted house, a space in which the dead can supposedly interact with the world of the living, a space, therefore, that is liminal.

Moreover, *Ju-On* preys on fears of generational scarring, whereby a parent infects their child with their own personal problems. An angry parent vents their wrath around (or at) their child, and that child consequently becomes an angry parent themselves, thereby perpetuating a cycle of rage that grows alongside their family tree. By collapsing a linear sense of time, *Ju-On* makes clear how a child and parent can share emotions: in this case, fear. As her father feared the haunted house, Izumi learns to fear the spirits with which the house infects her. Izumi, therefore, cannot escape her family's history, both in a genetic and an emotional sense.

Thus, all four films in this section—*The Entity*, *The Babadook*, *The Visitors*, and *Ju-On: The Grudge*—essentially revolve around the notion that the mind has the power to warp one's experienced reality. Though this is a powerful statement regarding fiction's ability to modify the world, it is also accurate. In offering a bleak portrayal of emotions' power, *Ju-On* resonates with the real-life experiences of those who find their emotions unshakable, even all-consuming. Such is the plight of those with psychosomatic disorders, whose emotions (inscrutable as they may be) alter their physiology.[76] And yet, the mind can do more than merely alter reality. It can, in a sense, *build* reality.

Seven

Powers of Belief
How the Mind Writes Reality

Doors are tricky: everyone—people, characters, audiences—uses them, shuts them, and even locks them "securely," but even so, everyone is aware, in some part of their mind, that doors are but flimsy barriers, breachable in a multitude of ways. The doors—the borders—between mind, reality, and fiction are easily permeable too: though one may use various apparatuses to distinguish between their mental world, the real world, and the world of fiction, these worlds can, nonetheless, overlap and even meld into each other, thereby becoming indistinguishable. The audience—we—inherently (though maybe, in some instances, unintentionally) believe in (un)real phenomena such as myths, legends, magic, and monsters, and it is this belief that lends power to the stories, the fictions, we create. Belief, in other words, shapes reality.

Stories that bend the line between the real and the imagined are not as fanciful as one might imagine them to be. Rather, such stories align with people's implicit (and sometimes explicit) superstitions, thereby exploiting the unconscious openings (e.g., doubts) in their minds, regardless of how informed or fortified they believe their minds to be. Such openings, or gaps, are innate to people's minds, and concrete evidence cannot always overcome them; instead, the slightest suggestion or inclination towards the mystical, the magical, or the unreal can seep through these openings and even broaden them, based on one's own nature(s), predispositions, and anxieties.

These gaps, once people—we—notice them, reveal the porous, non-binary boundary between reality and fiction, a boundary that is, as this chapter's title suggests, not as fixed as most tend to believe. Rather, superstitions and implicit (sometimes, even sub-/un-conscious) belief in magic evince how many often fail to understand their own views. To clarify and elaborate on this: we, as a species, blur the line between fiction and reality every day, often without realizing it. And, though it might seem far-fetched, this obfuscation takes the form of an (often) unconscious belief in magic.

That is to say, it is primarily belief that invites in—and further encourages—the warping of fiction and reality: one's conscious (or even unconscious and unintended) faith in the supernatural, in the unreal, opens the door for this obfuscation to take place, and even develop to the extent that the two distinct states of being become indistinguishable from one another. And, as I have evidenced throughout this book, horror fiction is perfectly suited for demonstrating this phenomenon of reality-fiction distortion, manipulation, and obscuration.

To explicate how one's predispositions, nature(s), and anxieties propagate belief in the unreal (or the supernatural), and so, cause fiction and reality to become indistinct, take an everyday example: that of daily rituals. Regardless of whether one feels compelled to establish their control—or the security of their being—through these daily rituals, the fact is people often engage in some routine, some activities, almost religiously. For instance, one may feel compelled to double or triple check the locks on the door while leaving, or arrange their belongings in a certain pattern identifiable only to them, or, even feel the need to "knock on wood" every time something good happens (to them, or in their lives), so as to not "jinx" it.

Some might regard these actions as mere evidence of one's quirks or habits, or even instances of obsessive-compulsive disorder. These dismissals, however, do not account for—or negate—the heart of the issue: that performing these activities is often necessary for one's sense of well-being, which reflects the underlying anxieties one feels and experiences. That is to say, those who find their underlying anxieties driving them will frequently develop little rituals that, to their rational selves, may not always make sense, but that they nevertheless repeat, day in and day out, for a host of logically inexplicable reasons (such as maybe to induce a false sense of security, or maybe as an attempt to safeguard their well-being).[1] These activities are modern-day superstitions: they are little rituals some believe (no matter how much their rational mind protests) can change the outcome of events that usually—and even decidedly—occur independent of them.[2]

Consequently, it is unsurprising that the role of rituals in assuaging anxieties is well-established in critical discourse. Renowned scholar Joseph Campbell argues: "The function of ritual, as I understand it, is to give form to human life...."[3] Campbell further asserts: "All life is structure."[4] Thus, rituals are central to human society in that they provide its members—us—with a necessary structure. Likewise, rituals are also central to the horror genre. Stephen King, for instance, describes horror as a ritualistic outpouring of negative emotions that helps the audience (or the readers) feel whole again when the story is over.[5] In the light of such a ubiquitous context, horror becomes a ritualized exorcism of our collective (i.e., societal) demons. Accordingly, to watch a horror movie is to participate in one such ritual, and, just as rituals are a key competent of horror, they are also a key component of magic.

When discussing magic and the occult, J. Lawton Winslade writes that "magic consists of acts that are ritual performances enacted to achieve specific results ... words do not 'do something' just by being uttered. They must be vibrated, chanted, ritualized."[6] In other words, magic involves multiple components, including the ritual itself and the spoken word. Here, I make the leap to words (or, specifically, the spoken word) because they are more intrinsically tied to magic. That is, even though one can acknowledge one's rituals are absurd, they will, nevertheless, regard the very notion of using words to modify the external world as even stranger still.[7]

Despite perceiving such a usage of words as strange, people frequently use their words to (try to) modify their external reality. To find evidence for this, one needs only think about all the times they have yelled (or witnessed someone else yelling) at the screen, while watching a football or basketball game, in an effort to make the athletes play a certain way. Similarly, one may have shouted (or witnessed others shouting) at fictional characters on the big screen, cautioning them to the danger awaiting them, or reprimanding them for not acting in a particular manner. Films, too, demonstrate this unwitting tendency, as is evident in *Scream*, wherein Randy shouts a warning to Jamie Lee Curtis's character from *Halloween* (which is playing on the TV). As I explicate in Chapter 2, Randy's warning in that scene is ironic. In most cases, however, especially in real life, people are usually in earnest when they call out to the characters on TV screens or on computer desktops.

To the purely rational person, all these acts of talking to people on screen or to fictional characters might seem just as absurd as the rituals described earlier (e.g., knocking on wood and double- or triple- checking door locks). Not only that, but to a person who operates purely on rationale and logic, these acts of talking might seem even more absurd. But, just as people (audiences as well as characters) repeat rituals, they also mutter things under their breath, hoping to thereby influence the outcome of an event, an outcome that is otherwise out of their hands. And this, in a nutshell, and at its most fundamental level, is magic.

The idea that one can say certain words, do things a certain way, and thus change the course of events without directly interfering with them, is sorcery of the first degree. And it is here that irony strikes, because if people are asked if they actually believe in magic, most would say "no." Moreover, if prodded, these same people may well disclose that they follow some superstitious rituals, or that they have talked to a screen, even if unintentionally. However, they would not consider these actions to be "magic."

The issue here is that people—we—implicitly believe reality is unfixed.[8] This belief is usually implicit, but as I have shown, many people have some level of belief in magic, though few would probably admit to it if asked outright. This is to say people can (and often do) harbor a belief their rational mind rejects. But belief is nothing if not stubborn. A striking example of this stubbornness is evident in the placebo effect: The phenomenon whereby firmly believing something will help can cause that thing to help, even if there is, otherwise, no sound medical reason it should.

Research also demonstrates that the placebo effect works even if people are aware they are taking a placebo.[9] Consequently, once people leave this door open, they (inadvertently and unconsciously) permit belief and magic to begin influencing them. Accordingly (and ironically), once someone opens the door by believing in something (superstition, placebo, or magic) and hoping it can help them, they are also leaving the door open and inviting in monsters.[10] As fictional works evince, belief is powerful.

Indeed, Candyman enters, or more accurately, smashes in through this opening, and so does the grither. The latter comes from an episode of *Tales from the Darkside*, entitled "Seasons of Belief." "Seasons of Belief" is a short story by Michael Bishop, adapted for television by Michael McDowell, as an episode of *Tales from the Darkside* (the only episode from the series I discuss in this volume). "Seasons of Belief" depicts two parents attempting to entertain their children around Christmas time. To do so, the parents begin telling a story; the audience, by this point, are aware the two parents have a penchant for improvising fanciful tales, even adding details to each other's fabricated stories.

For example, when the father discusses Santa Claus, the mother chimes in with comments about Mrs. Claus's favorite recipe, which, the mother claims, Mrs. Claus got from Eleanor Roosevelt.[11] In this vein of fabrication, the father agrees to tell a scary story for the two children, Stefa and Jimbo.[12] He begins a tale about a creature he names "the grither."[13] Here, I will reiterate that the father is making up this fiction spontaneously, even as he narrates it.

The grither, the father states, hates his name being said aloud—so much so, in fact, that this being is, according to the parents, heading toward their home at that very moment, enraged at the mere mention of his name. The parents, however, stop telling the story when Stefa becomes too upset for them to continue. And yet, the story's conceit is that the only way to protect oneself from the grither's rage, once one has spoken his name, is to finish the story. But the parents never finish the story—the story they themselves fabricated on the fly. At the end of the episode, both the parents are killed when two large hands (which, per the parents' descriptions, look remarkably like the hands of the grither) reach in through their living room windows and snap their necks.

The grither is an odd case in that, unlike any other monster I have discussed so far, he seemed to have no existence before people began believing in him. When the parents begin their story, it is clear they are improvising. This is evident, for instance, when the kids challenge them about the creature's theme song and they ad-lib "Oh I am the grither" to the tune of "O, Come All Ye Faithful." The parents are talented at improvisation, but the important fact is that they *are* improvising. It is clear they have not come across this particular fiction before; and, though they are merely imagining it, their made-up creature kills them.

Here, belief emerges as the key factor, the source of the grither's power.

The grither's arms retract through the family's windows after murdering Stefa and Jimbo's parents. From left to right, the characters are the mother (Margaret Klenck), Stefa (Jenna von Oy), and the father (E.G. Marshall). The grither is a practical effect ("Seasons of Belief," directed by Michael McDowell. Laurel Entertainment, Inc., 1986).

The episode is, after all, entitled "Seasons of Belief." The tale is a mere fiction to the parents, both of whom do not believe in it. However, their daughter, Stefa, does, and so much so that she insists her parents finish the story, but they never do. The literary source of this episode, Bishop's short story, is clear on this point: "For Stefa believed in the grither, and what she believed in could certainly do her harm, couldn't it?"[14] Subsequently, when the grither shows up, neither Jimbo nor Stefa is surprised: "But because they weren't a bit surprised, Stefa and Jimbo didn't even scream."[15] This is, perhaps, an alternative reading, as one could argue the grither is powered not by Stefa's belief, but rather by having been named. Both explanations are plausible, and the episode does not give a definitive answer. In either case, nevertheless, the audience must confront an unreal creature becoming real simply because it has been named or believed in. Words, consequently, become creators.[16]

This analysis, however, leaves out a key issue—that of disbelief. In fact, disbelief may be more central to this tale than belief is. The episode opens with the family finishing dinner; as they discuss Santa Claus, the father says it is wicked to disbelieve in Santa. Upon this statement, the camera cuts to the other room, wherein the toy train at the base of the Christmas tree sparks and falls over. This event foreshadows the episode's paranormal elements as well as the danger inherent to disbelieving. And the parents' song further reinforces this danger, as it declares the grither wants "To keep you from taking his name in vain."[17]

Though they disbelieve in Santa, the children clearly believe in the grither, and that his name should not be taken in vain. Subsequently, they both shout "no" when their father interrupts the story to answer the phone, a fateful choice for him.[18] That disbelief governs this fatal choice is apparent in the parents' lack of belief in the story. The father, the one who chastised his children earlier for not believing in Santa, repeats their argument against the Christmas icon back to them, by telling them that, like Santa, the grither does not exist.

This ironic reversal of belief proves to be his undoing, for immediately after this the grither kills the father and mother. The episode consequently implies that the grither does not tolerate disbelief. The source material (Bishop's story), on the other hand, presents the disbelief differently, as the father's disbelief is less ironic but still present. Rather than finish the clearly improvised story, he says: "I hope neither of you believes in the grither.... Because if you don't believe in what isn't, it can't do you any harm."[19]

It is, therefore, an open question as to whether the grither can harm the family solely because of the children's belief. Belief may, after all, be incidental. Whereas the parents do not believe in the grither, the children clearly do, and, as noted earlier, Stefan and Jimbo are not surprised when the grither arrives to punish them. This, however, is where Bishop's story ends, and, as a result, the audience never learns whom, exactly, the grither kills. That is to say, though the grither only kills the parents in the television episode, in Bishop's story, he may kill the entire family, only the parents, or only the children.

The story does not disclose any murders at its end, and, so, the audience cannot quite ascertain whether it, indeed, was belief that lent power to the creature and gave it life. Here, I suppose one could also argue the creature existed already, and that the father simply had the bad luck to fabricate an accurate story about a dangerous being. This scenario, however, seems very unlikely, but, then again, so does everything else about "Seasons of Belief." Thus, the audience must determine, by—and for—themselves, what they wish to believe or disbelieve.

Unlike Bishop's story and its corresponding series episode, *Candyman* is explicitly about belief. The question of faith pervades the film, wherein faith is the source of Candyman's power. In fact, the film's central conflict revolves around this notion of belief. Helen, for instance, begins the film a skeptic, and, like most horror film protagonists, she questions the existence of the horrors she will experience, thereby putting herself in danger. In fact, she is so confident in her disbelief that she ventures into Cabrini-Green despite the real-life danger there; further, her confident disbelief is strong enough that she summons Candyman himself.[20]

Significantly, she and Bernadette begin the ritual to summon him because they question the belief: "You don't believe in that nonsense, do you?"[21] Like so many adolescents have, they perform the ritual on an unstated dare, each silently pushing the other to prove, by performing the ritual, that she does not believe in the legend. If this is the game, then Helen wins: Bernadette chickens out, but Helen finishes the ritual by saying Candyman's name the requisite fifth time.

Candyman himself, however, does not appear until over 40 minutes into the film. He shows up not only after Helen has completed the ritual, but also after her actions have led to the arrest of the man masquerading as Candyman.[22] Moreover, he informs her: "You were not content with the stories, so I was obliged to come. I am the writing on the wall, the whisper in the classroom. Without these things, I am nothing. So now, I must shed innocent blood."[23]

From this, the audience can infer Candyman manifested not only because Helen was looking for him, and not only because she summoned him, but also (and most importantly), because she raised doubts about him, his very existence. After the criminal's arrest, Helen tells Jake that the criminal "took [Candyman's] name so he could scare us."[24] However, this criminal, the pretend Candyman, was doing more than just inspiring fear: he was keeping the legend of the real Candyman alive. Thus, after one "Candyman" is jailed, the other has to come, lest his legend die, and the proof for this lies in Candyman's candor about his nature and his reliance on belief, both of which he himself reinforces later on, when he tells Helen to "Believe in [him]."[25]

Candyman, consequently, wants people innately convinced about his existence so they will, in turn, convince others, thereby providing fuel for his legend to survive. In fact, maintaining others' belief in him is his primary goal throughout the film, and this becomes apparent when he tries to make Helen believe, as well as when he makes overt references to ensuring that the people in Cabrini-Green continue to regard his legend as credible: "Your disbelief destroyed the faith of my congregation. Without them, I am nothing.... Your death will be a tale to frighten children.... Come with me and be immortal."[26] With this declaration, Candyman himself admits that he is, in fact, a "rumor."[27]

Candyman, therefore, occupies a liminal space of existence: he is a legend, a story, and yet he can reach out and kill people, and he does so, primarily, to maintain his existence through his story. Per his own admission, he needs belief to exist, and Candyman's legend simultaneously embodies him and provides him with a means of life beyond death. Should the story die, he would too. That is to say, *Candyman* portrays a story that directly alters reality, and this, in turn, negates and obfuscates the preconceived border between reality and fiction.

Clive Barker further develops this point in "The Forbidden," wherein Candyman says to Helen: "I am rumor. It's a blessed condition, believe me. To live in people's dreams; to be whispered at street-corners; but not have to *be*" (emphasis Barker's).[28] Thus, both "Seasons of Belief" and *Candyman* are difficult; they both lack definitive answers to many of the questions they raise.

What, exactly, is the grither? Did it already exist? How did the people of Cabrini-Green know when to light their bonfire? With regard to this last point, in particular, Barker makes an interesting claim in his short story: when Helen is musing, Barker writes, "Perhaps (why did she sense this?) the terminology of verifiable truth was redundant here; perhaps the final answer to his question was not an answer at all, only another question."[29] That is to say: the stories may, therefore, be purposefully ambiguous and difficult to interpret. This, in turn, ensures the audience remains engaged in the act of hunting for truth in a sea of stories.

When one quests after the truth behind a legend, one can often be only so certain; and as both "The Forbidden" and *Candyman* reveal, Candyman himself is the source of his stories. That is, not only did he exist prior to any corresponding fictions, but he also propagated his fictions himself, by compelling people to believe in the legend of the Candyman. When one blends fact with fiction, one also raises the question of "truth" in the narrative, thereby giving birth to a quest. Helen's quest is trying to uncover the truth behind the legend of Candyman (in the story, she is concerned with murders and does not hear that name until meeting the being himself), and she ultimately does.

The quest for truth and the line between fiction and reality are part and parcel. These stories, consequently, inform their audience (within the movie as well as outside of it) about what happens when one quests after truth; this, of course, is in addition to telling the audience what truth is and, so, trying to scare them. What this means, to paraphrase simply, is that as is the case with so many questions, the central question that I focus on also has many answers.

When one combines the audience's implicit belief in magic with the motif of characters birthed or sustained by beliefs, one begins to realize that authors/creators are not inventing new terrors, but are, rather, twisting and exaggerating existing ones. That is, Bishop, McDowell, and Rose do not invent the notion that belief is powerful. Instead, they borrow a trend from history, a fact from psychology, and then stretch it to its horrific extreme.

If one were to analyze this phenomenon (like I do), one would realize these authors, through their stories, have shed light on the very real dangers of belief. While the grither and Candyman might not come and attack someone in real life (like you and me), one's own psyche is strong enough that it can prey upon their belief(s) and thus cause them harm. This, in brief, is the nocebo effect: when one believes something will hurt them or make them sick, it may well do so, even if there is not a shred of actual, biological, reason behind it.[30] The nocebo effect, in other words, is the placebo effect's lesser-known, evil twin. And despite a potential lack of popular knowledge of the nocebo effect, many still seem to realize (implicitly) that their beliefs, their thoughts as well as intangible phantoms, can hurt them and cause irreparable harm.

But this is only the negative side. If belief can hurt, it can also help. Indeed, both effects appear in *A Nightmare on Elm Street*, which, like *Candyman*, is a dream-like film. As I discussed in chapter five, *A Nightmare on Elm Street* was, in fact, originally supposed to be a single nightmare, with Nancy dreaming the entire film.[31] However, Craven and the film's producer, Robert Shaye, battled over this and ultimately settled on the current ending.[32] Before reaching the end (i.e., throughout the film), Nancy struggles against Freddy and against her overarching dream.[33] The two struggles are, of course, intertwined, and Nancy must receive some pointed advice from her boyfriend, Glenn, and mother, Marge, before she can accomplish this task.

Glenn informs Nancy about the Balinese way of dreaming: he claims they turn their backs on the dream monsters to defeat them. When Nancy asks about the people who do not turn their backs, he says: "Well, I guess those people don't wake up to tell what happens."[34] In this same vein, her mother tells her the following: "You face things. That's your nature. That's your gift. But sometimes you have to turn away too."[35] Glenn and Marge, consequently, lay out an explicit framework for Nancy, a game plan she has to follow to finally defeat Freddy and, so, end the nightmare on Elm Street. Furthermore, the advice Glenn and Marge offer is ironic. Note, for instance, that Marge contrasts Nancy's typical strategy—of facing challenges directly—by recommending that she "turn away."[36]

This strategic shift may remind one of the two contrasting Biblical edicts of "an eye for an eye" and "turn the other cheek." In this case, Marge claims (and the audience later learns) that the latter is preferable. Yet, this move contradicts typical horror movie strategies. The contradiction becomes apparent when one compares Nancy to, say, Sidney from *Scream*. Like most "final girls," Sidney triumphs not from facing away from her fears but rather by attacking (i.e., facing her fears). Nancy, on the other hand, must do the opposite.

This is an interesting subversion of the typical horror trope. Horror is often criticized for having weak characters and even being misogynistic. The final girl trope can work—to some extent—toward ameliorating this critique, as characters like Nancy are strong and resourceful. Nancy is, after all, self-sufficient. And despite her being intelligent enough to seek help from others (like her father and Glenn), she ultimately must defeat Freddy by herself. To do so, she tries to fight; that is, Nancy appropriates the strategies typical of the "final girl[s]." But all of her booby traps fail, and she wins not because she retaliates against Freddy by forcing him to suffer the damage he has brought to others (in the spirit of "an eye for an eye"), but because she can turn her back on him and so obliterate his source of power.

This, evidently, is a moment of faith for Nancy: to turn her back on Freddy, a nightmare demon who has killed her mother, boyfriend, and friends, she has to trust that the advice Marge and Glenn gave her is correct; she has to trust that this strategy can succeed where all others have failed. Imagine if Freddy did not rely on her fear for his power. If the scenario were such, the scene would end not with Freddy disappearing, but rather with Nancy being eviscerated. However, Freddy depends on Nancy's fear; thus, she has to trust, and have faith. In this case, it is harder for her to not fight.

To simply turn her back on the horror is difficult for her, but she does turn around, and, so, she wins. In other words, Nancy defeats Freddy with belief. She believes the advice she received is correct, that she finally has the answer. And herein lies the irony: it is ironic that Nancy's culmination of belief is not in her ability to fight, but in her not needing to fight. This is also a shift for Nancy's character, a move away from her typical strategy, as described by her mom.

A Nightmare on Elm Street, therefore, strives to hit the audience where it hurts. It seeks to remind them of their scariest moments while growing up: those dark nights when every creak was a demon, every shadow a monster, when imaginations ran wild, and when they believed in these nightmares. The film targets memories the audience may have, of their childhood fear of the night, wherein their parents were incapable of helping them, but their boogeymen, their demons, could haunt their dreams and hurt them. This is true for the film's characters as well.

Nancy's mother, Marge, gives her some sound advice, but this is only after Marge has spent most of the film buried in a vodka bottle and burying the truth. She hides Freddy's identity from Nancy; had Marge come clean sooner, she would have saved her daughter from much trouble. Nancy's father is likewise unhelpful, deflecting blame onto Nancy when he uses her as bait to lure out Rod. Meanwhile, Glenn's father appears only toward the climax, and his sole contribution to the story is to thwart Nancy's attempts to save Glenn's life. Parents in this film are useless.[37] And is that not the greatest fear for a young child: that the people whom the child trusts to offer protection from the world will be incapable of doing so?

Freddy, therefore, embodies the link between fear and belief. The two are united in him, and it is through him the audience realizes that for one to feel fear, one must also believe. Compare, for instance, the changes that occur in Nancy over the course of the film's narrative: she goes from screaming, "It's only a dream!"[38] to telling Freddy at the film's climax, "I take back every bit of energy I ever gave you. You're nothing. You're shit."[39]

The two are separated by experience, the former early in the film, after Tina's death, and the latter at the film's end. The first is the fearful, desperate scream of someone making a faithless assertion: Nancy hopes that proclaiming her nightmare to be a mere dream will end it, but it is clear that she is afraid and her faith shaken. On the other hand, at the film's climax, Nancy asserts herself calmly and through gritted teeth: here, she is confident, and her words carry weight. Instead of betraying her fear, her voice and demeanor now scream conviction. Belief is necessary for fear, but also for its absence. If Nancy believes Freddy can harm her, if she fears him, then he can, in fact, harm her. But once she believes he cannot, once she no longer fears him, he loses his teeth.

Belief, therefore, acts as a double-edged sword for both the characters and the audience. It can hurt, conjuring up the childhood fears we would rather keep buried, or summoning entities to enact horrible vengeance on us. Simultaneously, it can also turn the tables on these horrors. If belief is a weapon Candyman can use against other characters, it is also a weapon other characters can use against him. For real-life analogs to belief's double-edged nature, take, first, the nocebo effect: how one's belief can harm them in real-life. Then, take, second, the more famous placebo effect: how one's belief can help them.

The case, then, cannot be taken as for or against belief itself. Rather, belief occupies both states at once, straddling the boundary between positive and negative, the helpful and the harmful. It is belief's inherently liminal existence that makes it perfect for my discussion of liminality in horror: regardless of its nature, belief indelibly alters reality. When one fears something, it automatically becomes something worthy of fear. Contrarily, when one dismisses something, it becomes dismissible. In real-life, there are limits to how far belief can modulate reality. Pretending one has a million dollars in a bank account will not make those dollars manifest, for example. Nevertheless, belief's ability to warp reality is far stronger than many realize, a fact toward which horror films have long obliquely hinted.

This variation—that results from belief's liminality—connects to my earlier averment, that the border between fiction and reality is not fixed (as people often think it is), but rather, is somewhat permeable. The thoughts— of both real audiences and fictional characters—can alter reality, making fiction fact (to a degree). That is to say, the border between the two is innately porous, and it is this foundational porousness that comes into play in one's intrinsic, often unrealized, belief in magic. People—both audiences and characters—generally retain a rudimentary belief in magic despite their empirical consciousness, and this mixture, consequently, homogenizes through the alteration of one's external reality.

Therefore, to reiterate a point I made earlier, the distinctions between fiction and reality are permeable not only in the world of fiction, but also in *our*—my, as well as your—world of corporeal existence. Though there may not be a real-world Candyman, his story is perhaps closer to truth than most would like to believe, and belief, as I illustrated, proves to be an ideal point for the amalgamation of the real and the fictional, and also for toying with the boundary between the two. It is due to this conscious, unconscious, subconscious, obfuscation that I challenge the typically held binary view of reality.

The "fictions" our minds invent, as Phillips and Craven note, clearly have an impact on us: their effects are very real. In a similar vein, the dreams one's mind conjures while asleep are also real in a sense. That is to say, dreams exist in a liminal space between reality and fiction. They are fictional insofar as one's mind creates them, but they are real in that they actively shape one's corporeal existence as well as the world around them, by influencing one's actions, thoughts, emotions, and behavior (among other consequences). Here, I will clarify that this is a nuanced position: I do not mean to argue that the beings from one's nightmares can kill them, as does Freddy, or spring out of one's dreams and into the external world. But what I assert is that one's fictions, one's stories, conceived both consciously and sub/unconsciously, are more real than people generally credit them for being.

The reader may find it striking, for instance, that both *Scream* and *A Nightmare on Elm Street* are based on real-life events, the former on the Gainesville Ripper and the latter on a rash of strange deaths.[40] Wes Craven says he derived the idea for *A Nightmare on Elm Street* from stories in the *Los Angeles Times*. The *Times*, he said, reported that some young Asian men had died in their sleep. One of these men had told his parents he was afraid to sleep, and he died when he finally did lose consciousness. His parents then found a coffee pot hidden in his closet, hooked up with an extension cord, and they found the sleeping pills his father had given him, hidden in the room.[41]

The detail of the hidden coffee pot is evident in *A Nightmare on Elm Street*, as Nancy employs a similar tactic in her quest to stay awake. From Craven's account, what happened here, then, was an attempt to create a story around a real-life horror. This strategy, on the one hand, is a control mechanism, but on the other, it acknowledges both the power of fiction and the dubiousness of trying to create a hard line between tale and truth. As the unfortunate example above suggests, beliefs can kill.[42]

Craven's account—of what he was inspired by—is terrifying. If true, it might be the scariest thing I have ever heard. However, I have been unable to substantiate it: I searched through the *Times*'s online archive but could not find the story Craven refers to. And I am not the only one. Adam Bulger, a journalist for *Van Winkle's*, has also combed through the archives to no avail.[43] Due to this unyielding scavenger hunt for the tale, Bulger argues that Craven likely misattributed the story to the *Times* and that he mistakenly came to believe the details he had invented for the script had come from the news.[44] Bulger's assessment seems probable, and it also tracks with my argument that human memories are flawed.

I say this because, while scavenging for this elusive article, I put in a research order with the *Times*'s archive department and asked them to find Craven's story. The archivist found three articles, none of which verified Craven's account. One was of him recounting the story but failing to mention either the *Times* or the coffee pot.[45] That this article was an interview Craven did with the *Times* seems to support Bulger's position. The other two articles did concern sleep deaths but were from 1983 and later. Since *A Nightmare on Elm Street* released in 1984, and it took three years for the script to be picked up, it is reasonable to suppose the script for the film was complete by some time in 1981.[46,47] And so, these last two articles about sleep-deaths are unhelpful, for, from the dates of their publication, it is apparent they could not have been the inspiration behind Craven's *A Nightmare on Elm Street*.

My argument and discussion, however, do not actually need Craven's account. They are valid independent of it, because many Asian-American men did, in fact, die in their sleep through the late 70s and early 1980s. They died seemingly without explanation, with deaths peaking in 1981, at a rate equivalent to the five leading causes of natural death of American men in the same age group.[48] This phenomenon became known as Sudden Unexpected Nocturnal Death Syndrome (SUNDS), and it was very real. Note, then, that regardless of whether Craven's recollection corresponds to an identifiable journalistic account, he created an iconic horror film based on a real series of unexplained events. This, in turn, ties into horror's ability to help people (audiences and characters) control and contextualize their fears. Even Freddy Kruger is less scary than SUNDS, for this latter phenomenon—of people dying, apropos of nothing—in their sleep—is terrifying and can actually happen.[49]

It gets worse, however, because these deaths were not just particular to Asian-American men; they were particular to Hmong men (an ethnic group from Laos) who had emigrated to the United States. The Hmong, moreover, had a strong cultural belief in nightmares. They believed that evil spirits would pay nocturnal visits to those who failed their cultural and religious obligations and weigh upon them and, possibly, kill them after repeated visits.[50] This belief the Hmong held about nightmares aligns with the symptoms of SUNDS with frightening parallelism: "The symptoms of SUNDS-related events clearly mirror the features of the nightmare as it has been known across cultures and throughout history."[51] Eventually, the medical community would de-mystify SUNDS with Brugada syndrome—a heart disorder with a genetic component; and this diagnosis would help explain SUNDS's prevalence among a single ethnic group.[52]

Notice, here, that I wrote "help explain." Per the Centers for Disease Control: "Only in times of unusual stress and possibly in conjunction with other, as yet undefined factors are these people at risk of developing abnormal electrical impulses in the heart that result in ventricular fibrillation and sudden death."[53] I discussed the nocebo effect earlier, the mind's ability to make harmful something that would not be otherwise. Here, Shelley Adler argues for taking the nocebo a step further, and making deadly that which, otherwise, would not be. The CDC believed that a trigger was necessary to set off the underlying heart condition among the Hmong men. That trigger, Adler argues, is their nightmares, which are tied to their powerful cultural beliefs:

> It is my contention that in the context of severe and ongoing stress related to cultural disruption and national resettlement ... and from the perspective of a belief system in which evil spirits have the power to kill men who do not fulfill their religious obligations, the solitary Hmong man confronted by the numinous terror of the night-mare (and aware of its murderous intent) can die of SUNDS.[54]

This illustrates, once again, the dangers of belief. In this case, one's belief can allow nightmares, previously only *thought* to be lethal, to *actually become* lethal, as they raise that person's stress levels enough to trigger underlying heart conditions.[55]

Moreover, Adler's position does have additional scientific backing. First, cultural beliefs and practices can shape other phenomena, including schizophrenia, whose symptoms vary by culture.[56] Second, previous research has supported the notion that nocebos can kill. For instance, Chinese-Americans afflicted with disease, who maintain strong beliefs in traditional Chinese medicine—and are born in birth years conventionally regarded as unlucky—die an average of five years earlier than others with the same disease who were born in different years (i.e., ones not considered unlucky).[57] This is to reiterate that whether or not Craven's recollection is strictly accurate, the reality behind *A Nightmare on Elm Street* is terrifying, for it reinforces the reality that one's beliefs can kill them.

Furthermore, the phenomenon of giving up provides additional evidence for belief's capacity to kill. Dr. John Leach, a researcher at the University of Portsmouth, has found that: "Psychogenic death is real. It isn't suicide, it isn't linked to depression, but the act of giving up on life and dying usually within days, is a very real condition often linked to severe trauma."[58] This, in turn, validates that belief has the power to modulate the reality *we*—as audiences and characters—experience: it can either help us via the placebo effect or hurt us via the nocebo effect, and at times, it can also kill us. Thus, the monsters that haunt our dreams and manifest in our stories have more power over us than we would like to believe. Subsequently, the refrain that a story is just that, or that a movie is but a movie, is nothing but a vain attempt at shutting the door on real-life terrors that spring forth from our imaginations. We create our own monsters, but this is not a power we fully control.

I claim this power is beyond control—either yours or mine—because it *is*. Recall, for instance, how placebos work even if one is aware that they are placebos. The same, unfortunately, may be true for the nocebo. If, as I have argued, a person does not get to choose all their beliefs, then skepticism is an imperfect shield against fiction's powers. Ergo, horror fiction can hurt us—its intended audience—even if we are cognizant about its fictional nature. Moreover, some may be more susceptible to this deleterious effect than others are.

In chapter six, I mentioned the phenomena of intrusive thoughts—unwanted thoughts that invade the forefront of a person's mind like a monster smashing through the boundary between the conscious and unconscious minds. What I left out, however, was that intrusive thoughts appear to be more common in those with high activity in the language regions of their brains.[59]

And so, those prone to spinning tales, or otherwise using language, more often than the typical person does, may find themselves more susceptible to fictions intruding into their reality. Though these fictions (intrusive thoughts) are not necessarily dangerous like the nocebo effect is, their link to language suggests those who immerse themselves in fiction may find fiction harder to escape than other people do.

Nonetheless, the odds of fictions harming a person are slim. These cases are extreme, and I have used them especially for the purpose of showcasing fiction's abilities; the reader, however, would do well to remember that those abilities rarely take the kind of monstrous forms they did for Hmong men in 1980s America. As I discussed in chapter three, not all stories have as much truth associated with them as *A Nightmare on Elm Street* does.

For a further example, consider *The Entity*, which, like *A Nightmare on Elm Street*, is supposedly based on a true story. Doris Bither claimed to have experienced the events portrayed in the film, including three unseen beings raping her, and her account formed the foundation for Frank De Felitta's 1978 book *The Entity*, upon which the film is based and from which it gets its title.[60] Here, an astute reader might notice that, going against academia, I have just cited *Wikipedia* as my source. This is because there are no credible sources documenting Bither's claims. After searching—at first, cursorily, and then thoroughly—I have failed to uncover any sources more credible than those displayed on the aforementioned Wikipedia page. Therefore, I cannot even begin to substantiate Bither's story: her account, if true, would be astounding and, moreover, possible proof of the paranormal. Regardless, the suspicious—and debatable—nature of *The Entity* evinces that not all liminal horror films carry the same amount of truth.

Though the degrees of truth might vary, it, nevertheless, stands to reason that belief plays a dominant role in both *The Entity* and *A Nightmare on Elm Street:* maybe the reality grounding the former cannot be verified, but the purported truth of the latter remains just as horrifying and just as liminal. And this interwoven function of truth and belief brings me to my final point: that of the mind's powers beyond belief. While this may seem farfetched, the notion that one's emotions can gain external—and independent—existence manifests in several films I have discussed, including *The Entity*, *The Babadook*, *Visitors*, and *Ju-On*.

A similar phenomenon can occur in real-life, wherein people's emotions can warp their bodies, and cause them to suffer from psychosomatic disorders. On this subject, neurologist Suzanne O'Sullivan writes: "Because psychosomatic symptoms arise in the subconscious, their manifestation depends on what else lives there. Our subconscious is filled with memories, with past experience of illness, what we know about the body, and what lessons life has taught us."[61] This indicates, thereby, that the mind's ability to warp reality exists outside of belief: the mind conjures vivid fictions, and these fictions alter one's experience of their corporeal existence. If one believes their fictions can kill them, said fictions will begin to acquire power. Contrariwise, even if one does not think thus, does not put much stock in their fictions, the fictions themselves can effect changes in one's bodies, whether prominent or benign.

Reality, consequently, is complicated, as I have evinced through horror's liminality. We—as both characters and spectators—wish to vehemently believe that we know exactly who we are, and with as much force, we wish to reaffirm that our memories of our experiences—and our notions of the world around us—are accurate. As I have illustrated, however, the truth is far more complex. People are inherently very complicated, from presenting different versions of themselves and, possibly, possessing multiple consciousnesses.

And in accordance with this (often un/sub-conscious) multiplicity of one's "selves," one's reality is blurred and multiple as well. As a result, unitary truths are lost behind legends and flawed recollections, and generally, the human psyche hates this lack of unison: people try to grasp for certainty in an inherently uncertain world. Here, I will remind the reader that fear, either superficial or innate, arises from a lack of control. To curtail that fear, the human psyche automatically resorts to creating stark boundaries to quantify what is real, and what is not. These boundaries, though, are every bit as flawed and arbitrary as the biases that color an individual's personal narratives and render their personal realities subjective. What one thinks—or presumes—is reality, often is not, for the objective truth is generally mislaid beneath one's subjective beliefs.

The notion of objective truth, therefore, is essentially debatable, for "objectivity," in reality, is mutable. Though my claim might seem controversial, my analyses so far corroborate it. People, for instance, claim dreams are fake, and yet dreams can overflow into the waking state, going so far as to even kill the dreamer. Similarly, we—as writers, readers, characters—are inclined to claim (our) stories are not real, yet these same stories capture reality, externalize our fears, and, like dreams, affect us. True, these tales might not be real in the strictest sense; if they were, the grither would probably have killed quite a few people (including myself) by now.

Nevertheless, the fictions we birth are real in the sense that they contain the power to modify external reality. Remember, for instance, that the father from "Seasons of Belief" tells his children that what they do not believe in cannot hurt them; Stefa does believe and, therefore, knows that she can get hurt.[62] I present these examples here to reaffirm that though Freddy or the grither may not be real, they are not real *yet*: the moment one begins to believe in them, these fabricated monsters can affect changes (like paranoia, fear, and night terrors).

This, in turn, renders less useful the comfortable (and comforting) categories of the real and fake. Moreover, with the introduction of belief into the picture, the notion of "reality" becomes further subjective, for not everyone experiences the same corporeality. A "real" example for this is that the Hmong men died from their nightmares, but most people did/do not. This, in turn, reinforces (once more) that when one believes something is real, it becomes real for them, but not necessarily for everyone else.

Consequently, the question that ultimately remains—and defines—liminality in horror, is also the one I have addressed variedly, and numerously, so far: why do horror fictions incessantly simulate—and so, encroach upon—reality? The obvious reason, of course, is because they want to scare us. The more intrinsic and crucial reason, however, is that horror stories want to open their audience's—our—eyes to the subjective, fictional, liminal nature of the *constructs* of "truth" and "reality." This objective, in turn, makes the lessons horror fictions impart more powerful. Fiction, in general, makes us confront reality vicariously.[63]

Horror, with its exceptional ability to leave lasting scars, is uniquely suited to making us face uncomfortable truths, and brave them; in this case, this truth is that one's reality is usually not what one believes it to be. If the fictions we create *are* to teach us about reality, horror is the logical choice: for the masters of horror (some of whose works I have discussed) have shown us the truth psychologists and philosophers already knew: that these stories are not so far-fetched but rather reflective of reality as it is, not as we wish it to be.

Afterword

Fiction's very existence blurs reality. That is, for the line between fiction and reality to ever become unclear, there must be something we—as creators, characters, and spectators—construe as "unreal." Imagine two people in a world where fictions do not exist discussing whether something is real. The scenario makes no sense. This colloquial example is to say, therefore, that for us to even ask whether something is real, we need a conception that there is such a thing as "unreal," as fiction. Liminal horror, consequently, highlights a fundamental fact about fiction's very nature. And another fact about this nature is that fiction defines reality.

As established, in a world without fictions, it would be nonsensical to ask if something is real. Notice, though, that this nonsense goes both ways: in such a world, you could not ask if something is unreal, and you could not ask if something is *real*. If the category of "unreal" seems incomprehensible, then so does the category "real." Thus, in this case, opposites define one another: fiction is requisite for understanding reality, and reality is requisite for understanding fiction. It is in the convergence of these two states—of fiction and reality—that liminality (as I have discussed it) exists, and it is the collision between these two states, and the dynamics of their ebbs and flows, wherefrom the liminal horror film springs.

Because we use stories to navigate our daily lives, and because even our memories are stories themselves, we cannot escape fiction. Fiction is, therefore, part of our reality. Consciously or not, we revert to fictions to explain our world as well as comprehend our daily lives. As such, liminal horror films provide a useful lens through which to recognize the necessity of fiction in analyzing reality. That is, because one cannot escape fiction, their attempts to define reality will always be tinged with fiction. Fiction and reality, therefore, combine in an indelible blend. Furthermore, new research reveals that it is possible not just for two spectators to perceive the same event differently, but also for them to perceive that same event as two distinct events (i.e., for each spectator to perceive an entirely different occurrence). This research suggests, at the quantum level, there may not be a single, objective reality at all.[1]

If individuals adopt an empiricist mindset, they will have to maneuver around their personal biases and subjectivities, even as their memories spin fictional yarns about their activities. Fiction, thereby, arouses abjection. Per Kristeva, abjection is a feeling arising from an encounter with an Other, particularly an Other coming from within oneself.[2] For example, to vomit would be to experience abjection, for seeing the vomit would collapse one's sense of self as they have now confronted the truth about the strange "Other" inside of them, an "Other" that is them and yet not them. Because abjection breaches the body's boundaries, it challenges our conceptions of corporeal reality and takes us back to those first moments when, as infants, we first defined ourselves in contrast to the Others we pre-linguistically rejected. An encounter with the abject, therefore, entails the death and consequent resurrection of the self, the ego.[3]

As with vomit, so too with fiction. While we may deny fiction's power, we may find ourselves in abject horror when we realize our "objective" assessments are fictitious and that we are too. This revelation can be difficult to accept, but whether one accepts or rejects it will not change its stark reality. Ultimately, the "Other" (in this case, fiction) remains part of one's self whether one wants to accept it or not. And thus, the point remains that fiction helps us define ourselves, by being both a part of us and yet somehow apart from us.

As such (and as this volume has shown), liminal horror remains an area ripe for study. Indeed, recent technological advancements have made this topic especially relevant and interesting. With the advent of medium-obfuscating works such as *Black Mirror*'s Netflix film *Bandersnatch* (2018), in which viewers decide the course of the narrative, horror is poised to increasingly blur the boundary between the real and the fictional. As media becomes more and more interactive, the screen will become a weaker and weaker boundary between fantasy and real-life. Furthermore, with both the *Scream* and *Candyman* franchises expecting theatrical releases of their new films soon, one can be sure the liminal horror film will continue, thereby making room for it to develop exponentially in both popular and critical conversations.

Chapter Notes

Epigraph

1. Beckett Mufson, "13 Wes Craven Quotes Remember the Original Master of Horror," *Vice*, August 14, 2015, https://creators.vice.com/en_uk/article/13-wes-craven-quotes-remember-the-original-master-of-horror.

Preface

1. Victor Turner, "Liminal to Liminoid, in Play, Flow, and Ritual: An Essay in Comparative Symbology," *Rice University Studies* 60, no. 3 (1974): 59–60, https://scholarship.rice.edu/bitstream/handle/1911/63159/article_RIP603_part4.pdf?sequence=1&isAllowed=y.
2. *Ibid.* 77.

Introduction

1. Alexandra Heller-Nicholas, *Found Footage Horror Films: Fear and Appearance of Reality* (Jefferson, NC: McFarland, 2014), 6.
2. William Egginton, "Reality is Bleeding: A Brief History of Film from the 16th Century," *Configurations* 9, no. 2 (2001): 207.
3. *Ibid.* 198.
4. *Ibid.* 191–192.
5. *Ibid.* 191.

Chapter One

1. Robin Wood, "An Introduction to the American Horror Film," in *American Nightmares: Essays on the Horror Film* (Festival of Festivals, 1979), 14.
2. Noël Carroll, *The Philosophy of Horror* (New York: Routledge, 1989), 16.
3. David. J. Russell, "Monster Roundup: Reintegrating the Horror Genre," in *Refiguring American Film Genres: Theory and History*, ed. Nick Browne (Berkeley, CA: University of California Press, 1998), 241.
4. Carol J. Clover, *Men, Women, and Chainsaws: Gender in the Modern Horror Film* (Princeton, NJ: BFI, 1992), 35.
5. M. H. Abrams, *A Glossary of Literary Terms*, 7th ed. (Orlando, FL: Harcourt Brace College Publishers, 1999), 111.
6. Kendall R. Phillips, *Dark Directions: Romero, Craven, Carpenter, and the Modern Horror Film* (Carbondale and Edwardsville, IL: Southern Illinois UP, 2012), 73–74.
7. *Ibid.* 74.
8. Judith Halberstam, *Skin Shows: Gothic Horror and the Technology of Monsters* (Durham, NC: Duke UP, 1995), 179.
9. This list of the gothic's elements comes from Charlene Bunnell's "The Gothic: A Literary Genre's Transition to Film" in *Planks of Reason*, edited by Barry Keith Grant (82).
10. "Inspired by the true story of the most prolific serial killer in history," Primeval Poster (#1 of 2), December 15, 2006, Movie Poster.
11. Phillips, *Dark Directions*, 73–74.
12. Charlene Bunnell, "The Gothic: A Literary Genre's Transition to Film," in *Planks of Reason*, edited by Barry Keith Grant (Metuchen, NJ: Scarecrow Press, 1984), 82.
13. Tracie D. Lukasiewicz, "The Parallelism of the Fantastic and the Real: Guillermo del Toro's *Pan's Labyrinth/El Laberinto del fauno* and Neomagical Realism," in *Fairy*

Tale Films: Visions of Ambiguity, ed. Pauline Greenhill and Sidney Eve Matrix (Boulder, CO: University Press of Colorado, 2010), 64.
 14. Jon Thiem, "The Textualization of the Reader in Magical Realist Fiction," in *Magical Realism: Theory, History, Community*, ed. Lois Parkinson Zamora and Wendy B. Faris (Durham, NC: Duke University Press, 1995), 238.
 15. Tzvetan Todorov, *The Fantastic: A Structural Approach to a Literary Genre*, Transl. Richard Howard (Cleveland, OH: The Press of Case Western Reserve University, 1973), 43–47.
 16. *Scream*, directed by Wes Craven (1996; New York: Dimension Films, 1997), DVD.
 17. Stephen King, "What's Scary," foreword in *Danse Macabre* (New York: Gallery Books, 2010), xii.

Chapter Two

 1. For a thorough and enlightening discussion of found footage horror films, please see Alexandra Heller-Nicholas's *Found Footage Horror Films: Fear and the Appearance of Reality*.
 2. Available in Heller-Nicholas' *Found Footage Horror Films*.
 3. *Ibid*. 95.
 4. *Ibid*.
 5. *Blair Witch* is not alone in this. The Italian film *Cannibal Holocaust* had a similar marketing gimmick. The director, however, ended up in legal trouble when some believed he had, in fact, killed the actors on camera, and he was forced to reveal the illusion. "Cult-Con 2000," in *Cannibal Holocaust*, directed by Ruggero Deodato (1980; Rome: United Artists Europa, 2000), DVD.
 6. King, *Danse Macabre*, xiv.
 7. *Ibid*.
 8. Joshua Klein, "Interview—The Blair Witch Project," Web.Archive, The A.V. Club, July 22, 1999, https://web.archive.org/web/20150121163922/http://www.avclub.com/article/the-blair-witch-project-13607.
 9. *Found Footage Horror Films* 26.
 10. *Ibid*. 4.
 11. *Found Footage 3-D*, directed by Steven DeGennaro (2016; Austin, TX: Shudder, 2016), https://www.shudder.com/movies/watch/found-footage-3d-2d-version/430c8b6074b30e71.
 12. *Ibid*.
 13. *Ibid*.
 14. *Ibid*.
 15. *Ibid*.
 16. *Ibid*.
 17. *Ibid*.
 18. *Ibid*.
 19. *Ibid*.
 20. *Ibid*.
 21. Julia Kristeva, *Powers of Horror: An Essay on Abjection*, Transl. Leon S. Roudiez (New York: Columbia University Press, European Perspectives, 1980), 1.
 22. Carol J. Clover coined the term "final girl" in her seminal work *Men, Women, and Chainsaws*. I direct the reader to her for a thorough and enlightening discussion of gender in horror films.
 23. *Scream*.
 24. *Ibid*.
 25. Terry Kirby, "Video Link to Bulger Murder Disputed," *Independent*, November 26, 1993, http://www.independent.co.uk/news/video-link-to-bulger-murder-disputed-1506766.html.
 26. *Scream*.
 27. Valerie Wee, "The Scream Trilogy, "Hyperpostmodernism," and the Late-Nineties Teen Slasher Film," *Journal of Film and Video* 57, no. 3 (2005): 55–57.
 28. *Scream*.
 29. *Ibid*.
 30. *Ibid*.
 31. *Ibid*.
 32. *Ibid*.
 33. Clover, *Men, Women, and Chainsaws*, 32.
 34. *Ibid*.
 35. "Urban Legend," *Merriam-Webster*, Accessed March 10, 2020, https://www.merriam-webster.com/dictionary/urban%20legend.
 36. Linda Dégh and Andrew Vazsonyi, "Does the Word "Dog" Bite? Ostensive Action: A Means of Legend-Telling." *Journal of Folklore Research* 20, no. 1 (1983): 6.
 37. *Urban Legend*, directed by Jamie Blanks (1998; Los Angeles: TriStar Pictures, 1999), DVD.
 38. The "headlight initiation" myth is as follows. Driving alone at night, a motorist notices that a car in the opposite lane does not have its headlights on. Being a good Samaritan, the motorist flashes their headlights to warn the other driver to turn theirs on. Instead, the other driver turns their car around, follows the motorist, and murders

them. It turns out that the other driver's initiation into a gang was contingent upon their killing the first person to flash their headlights at them.

39. Mikel J. Koven, *Film, Folklore, And Urban Legends* (Lanham, MD: The Scarecrow Press, 2008), 108.

40. *Urban Legend*.

41. *The House That Dripped Blood*, directed by Peter Duffell (1971; Shepperton, United Kingdom: Amicus Productions, 2003), https://tubitv.com/movies/272775/the-house-that-dripped-blood?start=true.

42. *Ibid.*

43. *Ibid.*

44. *Darna Zaroori Hai*, directed by Sajid Khan, et al. (2006; Mumbai: K. Sera Sera Productions, 2006), https://www.amazon.com/Darna-Zaroori-Hai-Amitabh-Bachchan/dp/B081D9L7NY.

45. *Ibid.*

46. *Ibid.*

47. *Ibid.*

48. Phillips, *Dark Directions*, 73–74.

49. *Sinister*, directed by Scott Derrickson (2012; Santa Monica, CA: Alliance Films, 2013), DVD.

50. Jeff Saporito, "'What is the history of the Bughuul demon in "Sinister" and "Sinister 2"?,' Screenprism, Accessed March 2020, http://screenprism.com/insights/article/what-is-the-history-of-the-bughuul-demon-in-sinister-and-sinister-2. I have been unable to find this post.

51. Leviticus. *Bible*.

52. Sam Faulkner, "Interview with Sinister writer C. Robert Cargill," Web.Archive, Screengeek, October 8, 2012, https://web.archive.org/web/20121111060203/http://www.screengeek.co.uk/features/article/interview-sinister-writer-c-robert-cargill.

53. *Dictionary of Deities and Demons in The Bible*, 2nd ed., ed. Karel Van Der Toorn, Bob Becking, and Pieter W. Van Der Horst (Grand Rapids, MI: William B. Eerdmans Publishing Company, 1999), 583.

54. *Coming Soon*, directed by Sophon Sakdapisit (2008; Bangkok: GMM Thai Hub), DVD.

55. Clover, *Men, Women, & Chainsaws*, 23.

56. *Coming Soon*.

57. *Ibid.*

58. See: Adam Lovasz, "'Would you like to meet a ghost?': Repetition and spectral posthumanism in Kiyoshi Kurosawa's *Kairo*," *Horror Studies* 9, no. 2 (2018): 249–263. Giles A. Viennot, "*Kairo (Pulse,* Kurosawa, 2001) and Kairos: Postmodern Japanese Computer Culture, Memory and Entropy," in *Memory in World Cinema: Critical Essays*, transl. James H. Membrez, ed. Nancy J. Membrez (Jefferson, NC: McFarland, 2019), 173–186.

59. Viennot, "*Kairo*," 180.

60. The film does not make it entirely clear what world the dying characters enter. Here, I have dubbed it the "ghostly realm," but one could argue these characters are entering a digital space, and *Pulse* itself does little to provide the audience a key to the film's largely indecipherable elements.

61. *Pulse*, directed by Kiyoshi Kurosawa (2001; Chiyoda, Tokyo, Japan: Toho, 2006), DVD.

62. *Ibid.*

63. *Masters of Horror*, season 1, episode 8, "Cigarette Burns," directed by John Carpenter, aired December 16, 2005, on Showtime, https://tubitv.com/tv-shows/286426/s01-e08-cigarette-burns?start=true.

64. *Ibid.*

65. *Ibid.*

66. *Ibid.*

67. *Ibid.*

68. *Ibid.*

69. *Ibid.*

70. *Ibid.*

71. *Antrum: The Deadliest Film Ever Made*, directed by David Amito and Michael Laicini (2018; Brooklyn: Else Films, 2019), https://tubitv.com/movies/530312/antrum-the-deadliest-film-ever-made?start=true.

72. *Ibid.*

73. The brazen bull is a type of torture and execution device in which a person is locked inside a metal statue overtop a fire and then roasted to death as the statue heats up from the flames.

74. *Antrum.*

75. *Ibid.*

76. *Ibid.*

77. "Nicole Tompkins," Backstage, Accessed August 2020, https://www.backstage.com/u/Nicole-Tompkins/.

78. *Antrum.*

79. Leila Chaieb, et al., "Auditory Beat Stimulation and its Effects on Cognition and Mood States," *Frontiers in Psychiatry* 6, no. 70 (2015), https://www.ncbi.nlm.nih.gov/pmc/articles/PMC4428073/.

80. *Antrum.*

81. *Videodrome*, directed by David Cronenberg (1983; Los Angeles: Universal Pictures, 1999), DVD.
82. *Ibid*. Quotd. in Clover, *Men, Women, & Chainsaws*, 197.
83. Julien LeBourdais, "McLuhan: Now The Medium Is The Massage," *The New York Times*, Accessed February 20, 2020, https://www.nytimes.com/1967/03/19/archives/mcluhan-now-the-medium-is-the-massage.html.
84. *Videodrome*.
85. DVDs and Blu-rays did not exist during *Videodrome*'s production, hence my assertion that VHS tapes are the best format.
86. Technically, Bughuul enters a projection and not a screen in *Sinister*, but the effect and implications are the same.
87. This is a common criticism. Noël Carroll tackles it, for instance, though he points out that some horror stories are outright progressive. See: Carroll, *Philosophy of Horror*, 196–197. Stephen King, *Danse Macabre* (New York: Gallery Books, 2010), 41.
88. Thomas Marksbury, Personal Conversation, February 17, 2020.
89. *Videodrome*.
90. *Scream*.

Chapter Three

1. *Scream 2*, directed by Wes Craven (1997; New York: Dimension Films, 1998), DVD.
2. *Scream*.
3. Wes Craven directed the first four *Scream* films.
4. *Scream 4*, directed by Wes Craven (2010; New York: Dimension Films, 2011), DVD.
5. *Ibid*.
6. The film is based on Clive Barker's short story "The Forbidden," which is set in England rather than Chicago. Thus, many of the film's central tensions (e.g., race) are not present in the source material but rather unique to its American adaptation.
7. Cabrini-Green was notorious, both in the film and real-life, for being crime-ridden and dangerous. The mayor of Chicago famously spent some time living there, attempting to dispel its notorious mystique. See: Chris Jones, "Jane Byrne's move into Cabrini-Green is the subject of a new play. But the stunt's history 'depends on whom you ask,'" *Chicago Tribune*, February 27, 2020, https://www.chicagotribune.com/entertainment/theater/chris-jones/ct-ent-jane-byrne-cabrini-green-0301-20200227-ivj4syzdwzbqrc4opembeflyge-story.html.
8. The ritual to summon Candyman is like the real-life Bloody Mary legend, in which repeating "Bloody Mary" the requisite number of times in front of a mirror will summon her spirit. In fact, monster-in-mirror legends are their own topic worthy of study. For one such discussion, see: Elizabeth Tucker, "Ghosts in Mirrors: Reflections of the Self," *Journal of American Folklore* 118, no. 468 (2005): 186–203.
9. *Candyman*, directed by Bernard Rose (1992; Culver City, CA: TriStar Pictures, 1993), DVD.
10. Here, I omit other films I discussed in chapter 2 because they are less akin to *Candyman* than *The Ring* is.
11. Staci Poston Conner points out that undeath is a liminal state between living and dying in her essay "Liminal Figures in Poe's 'Bernice' and Gilman's 'The Giant Wistaria'" (1).
12. Stephen King, "The Importance of Being Bachmann," in *The Bachman Books: Four Early Novels by Richard Bachman, author of The Regulators* (Plume, 1996), 1.
13. *Ibid*. 2.
14. *Ibid*.
15. *Ibid*.
16. *The Dark Half*, directed by George Romero (1993; Los Angeles: Orion Pictures, 1994), DVD.
17. The author does not recommend this and is not liable for any ensuing damages.
18. Tucker, "Ghosts in Mirrors," 187.
19. *Ibid*. 190.
20. *Ibid*.
21. *Ibid*. 196–97.
22. *Ibid*.
23. Laura Wyrick, "Summoning Candyman: The Cultural Production of History," *Arizona Quarterly: A Journal of American Literature, Culture, and Theory* 54, no. 3 (1998): 89–117.
24. *Ibid*. 95–96.
25. *Ibid*. 97.
26. *Ibid*. 89–117.
27. *The Dark Half*.
28. None of this is to say that Helen is in anyway responsible for her husband's

infidelity. Trevor, alone, is responsible, and culpable, for his behavior. Rather, my point is that Helen lacks power in her relationship with Trevor, who clearly does not see her as an equal.

29. Wyrick, "Summoning Candyman," 89–117.
30. *Candyman*.
31. Ibid.
32. *Wes Craven's New Nightmare*, directed by Wes Craven (1994; Burbank, CA: New Line Cinema, 1995), DVD.
33. Ibid.
34. King, *Danse Macabre*, 13. Morris Dickstein similarly observes: "Going to horror films is a way of neutralizing anxiety by putting an aesthetic bracket around it" (69).
35. King, *Danse Macabre*, 6.
36. Ibid.
37. *Nightmares in Red, White, & Blue*, directed by Andrew Monument (2009; Lux Digital Pictures), https://tubitv.com/movies/15641/nightmares-in-red-white-and-blue?start=true.
38. Mufson, "13 Wes Craven Quotes."
39. Paul Schwenger, *At the Borders of Sleep: On Liminal Literature* (Minneapolis, MN: University of Minnesota Press, 2012), 85.
40. *Wes Craven's New Nightmare*.
41. *Never Sleep Again: The Elm Street Legacy*, directed by Daniel Farrands and Andrew Kasch (2010; 1428 Films, 2010), DVD.
42. Ernst Cassirer, *Language and Myth* (New York: Dover Publications, 1946), 6.
43. Ibid. 7.
44. *The Texas Chainsaw Massacre*, directed by Tobe Hooper (1974; Bryanston Distributing Company, 1984), https://tubitv.com/movies/499404/the-texas-chain-saw-massacre?start=true.
45. *The Texas Chainsaw Massacre*, directed by Marcus Nispel (2003; Burbank, CA: New Line Cinema, 2004), DVD.
46. John Bloom, "They Came. They Sawed," *Texas Monthly*, November 2004, https://web.archive.org/web/20111017042555/http://www.texasmonthly.com/2004-11-01/feature6-2.php.
47. Mike Mendez, "Tobe Hooper "Masters of Horror" part 1," YouTube, 2008, https://www.youtube.com/watch?v=AebBisE5ZE. This video depicts an interview with director Tobe Hooper, in which he notes the film's relative lack of blood.
48. *Celluloid Crime of the Century: The Last House on the Left*, directed by David Gregory (2003; Los Angeles: American International Pictures, 2003), DVD.
49. Ibid.
50. "Inspired by the true story of the most prolific serial killer in history."
51. Michael McRae, "Gustave, the Killer Crocodile—Update," *National Geographic Adventure Magazine*, August 2008.
52. The British government's official report on Shipman's crimes (cited below) notes that investigators have confirmed Shipman murdered 215 people. This number of confirmed victims ranks Shipman as possibly the single most prolific serial killer in history. Dame Janet Smith, "The Shipman Inquiry: Third Report." Crown Copyright, 2003, https://assets.publishing.service.gov.uk/government/uploads/system/uploads/attachment_data/file/273227/5854.pdf.
53. McRae, "Gustave."
54. Ibid.
55. Ibid.
56. Ibid.
57. "Inspired by the true story of the most prolific serial killer in history."
58. "Man remanded on suspicion of infamous unsolved triple murder from 1960," *Helsingin Sanomat*, Accessed September 2020, https://web.archive.org/web/20070930082146/http://www2.hs.fi/english/archive/news.asp?id=20040405IE7. *Helsingin Sanomat* is Finland's most widely circulated newspaper. The above link is for an archived version of a story the paper's international section did on the Lake Bodom murders.
59. *Lake Bodom*, directed by Taneli Mustonen (2016; Helsinki: Don Films, 2016), https://www.shudder.com/movies/watch/lake-bodom/4cc1126e0653ef59.
60. Ibid.
61. Ibid.
62. "Court finds Gustafsson not guilty of 1960 Bodom Lake triple murder," Web. Archive, *Helsingin Sanomat*, 2005, https://web.archive.org/web/20070628204433/http://www.hs.fi/english/article/Court%20finds%20Gustafsson%20not%20guilty%20of%201960%20Bodom%20Lake%20triple%20murder/1101981204857.

Chapter Four

1. See: Clover, *Men, Women, & Chainsaws*, 35.

2. The slasher genre includes such entries as *Halloween, Friday the 13th,* and *Black Christmas.* It also includes this volume's central texts *A Nightmare on Elm Street, New Nightmare,* and *Scream.*

3. Slasher films are sometimes mocked for how their ostensibly human killers act. These murderers, despite having no explicit supernatural powers, seem to be able to teleport, magically appearing in front of characters who were running far faster than the killer. Just before the killer catches up to the victim, the victim often trips and falls. While somewhat realistic in many circumstances, this stumble became frequent enough to be mocked. The killer, moreover, would somehow survive assaults that would kill a normal person. These films also have the unfortunate distinction of punishing sexually active young adults with death. One can often predict which characters will die merely by noting which ones the audience sees having sex.

4. Abed, a particularly media savvy character from the sitcom *Community,* makes this observation when criticizing one of his friend's Halloween stories. He tells her that her story was ineffective because the characters made choices the audience would not make. He then proceeds to tell a horror story with completely rational characters, which likewise proves ineffective. Audiences, this example shows, want characters who are believable and yet flawed enough to allow the story to progress. A slasher film where no one gets attacked is no fun. "Horror Fiction in Seven Spooky Steps." *Community,* season 3, episode 5, 27 October 2011.

5. *Scream.*

6. Eyes on Cinema, "Wes Craven 'Scream' interview-A Confused, Cynical Generation Looking for Essential Truth," YouTube, April 13, 2015, https://www.youtube.com/watch?v=un1arjkK3VI. This video depicts an interview with Wes Craven as he discusses horror films and *Scream.* See also: Morris Dickstein, "The Aesthetics of Fright," in *Planks of Reason,* ed. Barry Keith Grant (Metuchen, NJ: Scarecrow Press, 1984), 70.

7. *Scream.*

8. *Ibid.*

9. *Ibid.*

10. Gregory Currie, "Both Sides of the Story: Explaining Events in a Narrative," *Philos Stud: Philosophical Studies* 135, no. 1 (2007): 49.

11. *Scream.*

12. *Ibid.*

13. The *Nightmare* franchise has an interesting relationship with reality throughout its run. In the original film, Freddy does not want to be pulled into reality; doing this is Nancy's idea, and it helps her remove Freddy's power. And in *Freddy vs Jason,* Freddy is noticeably weaker after the protagonist, Laurie, pulls him into the real world, thereby forcing him to fight Jason Vorhees without the use of his dream powers. In the second *Nightmare,* however, Freddy actively tries to enter the real world, just as he does in *New Nightmare. New Nightmare* is not canon for the franchise, however, and the second film notably departs from its predecessor and is something of a black sheep for the franchise.

14. *Wes Craven's New Nightmare.*

15. *Never Sleep Again: The Making of A Nightmare on Elm Street.*

16. *Ibid.*

17. *Ibid.*

18. *Ibid.*

19. *Ibid.*

20. Angela Ndalianis, *The Horror Sensorium: Media and the Senses* (Jefferson, NC: McFarland, 2012), 172. Quoted in: Heller-Nicholas, *Found Footage Horror Films,* 101.

21. The film is confusing to write about. There are two Robert Englunds here (and indeed two Heather Langenkamps and two of every actor). One is the real-life Robert Englund, the actor you might meet on the street or whenever you have a casting call for a creepy character. He plays two versions of Freddy Kruger in the film. The other Englund is the character. Englund plays a fictional version of himself, a version who has also played the fictional Freddy. The "real" Freddy, likewise played by the real Englund, is set apart from this "fictional" Freddy, the one from the films, and the one the film itself acknowledges as fictional.

22. Of course, self-awareness serves many functions. It is also funny. But this volume can only consider the "why" for one genre, so for the purpose of comedy, I am afraid the reader will have to look elsewhere.

23. Conor McPherson, "The Weir," in *The Weir, and Other Plays* (New York: Theatre Communications Group, 1999), 33.

24. *Ibid.*
25. *Ibid.* 58–59.
26. *Ibid.* 58.
27. *Ibid.*
28. For this point, I must credit Dr. Shoshana Milgram Knapp.
29. Egginton, "Reality is Bleeding," 218.
30. "Wes Craven 'Scream' interview-A Confused, Cynical Generation Looking for Essential Truth."
31. Egginton, "Reality is Bleeding," 218.
32. Phillips writes, "The appearance of the nocturnal world's uncanny creatures forces upon both the protagonist and the viewer a space for reflection about those norms that underlie regular understandings" (75).
33. "Wes Craven 'Scream' interview-A Confused, Cynical Generation Looking for Essential Truth."
34. *Scream.*
35. "David Cronenberg," BrainyQuote, 2017, https://www.brainyquote.com/quotes/quotes/d/davidcrone158502.html.
36. Hidden Clips, "Wes Craven Interview (screamography)," YouTube, May 26, 2015, https://www.youtube.com/watch?v=_zmo9fGtcVE&t=1203s. This video depicts an interview with Wes Craven.

On a similar note, Dennis Giles observes that horror films offer their audience a safe outlet, a "well-defended fantasy" (Giles 39).

37. "Wes Craven Interview (screamography)."
38. See: Carroll, *Philosophy of Horror*, 196–197. King, *Danse Macabre*, 41.
39. One might make the argument that other genres fit this bill, that, perhaps fiction is didactic. Indeed, Jonathan Gottschall writes that "Fiction is, on the whole, intensely moralistic" (Gottschall 130). I believe there is a case to be made here, though it is beyond this book in scope. Nevertheless, even if all fiction is didactic by nature, that does not refute my arguments about horror and the specific lessons it teaches. Rather, it just broadens our analysis of fiction as a whole. For more on fiction's ability to instruct, see Bruno Bettelheim's *The Uses of Enchantment*, page 4.
40. On this topic, and considering Gottschall's quotation, I believe we should distinguish didacticism from moralism. Certainly, all moralistic tales are didactic, but not all didactic tales are necessarily moralistic.
41. Jonathan Gottschall, *The Storytelling Animal: How Stories Make Us Human* (Boston: Houghton Mifflin Harcourt, 2012), 4.
42. *Ibid.* 32.
43. Clover, *Men, Women, & Chainsaws*, 10.
44. Mikel J. Koven, "The Terror Tale: Urban Legends and the Slasher Film," *Scope: An Online Journal* (2003): 1, https://www.nottingham.ac.uk/scope/documents/2003/may-2003/koven.pdf.
45. Jan Harold Brunvand, *The Vanishing Hitchhiker: American Urban Legends & Their Meanings* (New York: W.W. Norton and Company, 1981), 10.
46. *Ibid.*
47. Koven, "The Terror Tale: Urban Legends and the Slasher Film," 6. See also: Daniel R. Barnes, "Interpreting Urban Legends," in *Contemporary Legend: A Reader*, edited by Gillian Bennett and Paul Smith (New York: Garland Publishing Inc., 1996), 1–16.
48. *Friday the 13th,* directed by Sean S. Cunningham (1980; Hollywood: Paramount Pictures, 1980), DVD.
49. *Urban Legend.*
50. *Ibid.*
51. "Judith," Disney, Accessed March 2020, https://family.disney.com/baby-names/baby-girl-names/meaning-of-judith/.
52. Jack Zipes, *The Irresistible Fairy Tale: The Cultural and Social History of a Genre* (Princeton, NJ: Princeton UP, 2012), 14.
53. "Rosemary," Web. Archive., Australian War Memorial, Accessed March 2020, https://web.archive.org/web/20131219155712/https://www.awm.gov.au/commemoration/customs/rosemary.asp. In fiction, see also: Scene 13 of William Shakespeare's *Hamlet.*
54. *Pan's Labyrinth,* directed by Guillermo Del Toro (2006; Madrid: Telecinco Cinema, 2007), DVD.
55. Jack Zipes, "*Pan's Labyrinth* (*El laberinto del fauno*) (review)," *Journal of American Folklore* 121, no. 480 (2008): 238.
56. Laura Hubner, "*Pan's Labyrinth*, Fear and the Fairy Tale," in *Fear Itself: Reasoning the Unreasonable*, ed. Stephen Hessel and Michèle Huppert (Amsterdam: Rodopi, 2010), 43; Zipes, "*Pan's*," 238. Gema Navarro Goig and Francisco Javier Sánchez-Verdejo Pérez, "Echoes of Fairy Tales: Fantasy and Everyday Horrors in Guillermo del Toro's Filmography," in *Contemporary Fairy Tale Magic: Subverting Gender and Genre*, ed. Lydia Brugué and

Auba Llompart (Amsterdam: Brill, 2020), 139.

57. Phillips, *Dark Directions*, 73–74.

58. Lukasiewicz 61; Hubner, "Fear and the Fairy Tale," 43; Goig and Perez, "Echoes of Fairy Tales," 138; Zipes, *"Pan's,"* 237.

59. Hubner, "Fear and the Fairy Tale," 44.

60. *Pan's Labyrinth.*

61. *In the Mouth of Madness*, directed by John Carpenter (1994; Burbank, CA: New Line Cinema, 1995), DVD.

62. Garth Jowett and James M. Linton, *Movies as Mass Communication* (Newbury Park, CA: Sage Publications, 1989), 91.

63. *Videodrome.*

64. *Ibid.*

65. Quoted in: Jennifer Ouellette, *Me, Myself, and Why: Searching for the Science of Self* (New York: Penguin Books, 2014), 158.

Chapter Five

1. E.B. Gurstelle and J.L. de Oliveira, "Daytime Parahypnagogia: a state of consciousness that occurs when we almost fall asleep," *Medical Hypotheses* 62, no. 2 (2004): 166–168.

2. *Ibid.*

3. *Ibid.* 166–167.

4. *A Nightmare on Elm Street*, directed by Wes Craven (1984; Burbank, CA: New Line Cinema, 1985), DVD.

5. *Ibid.*

6. I am not alone in this belief. Indeed, Heather Langenkamp has said, "...with the ending we have now, it doesn't quite make sense" (*Never Sleep Again: The Elm Street Legacy*).

7. I will discuss the ending at length later. For now, the curious reader should know Craven and producer Robert Shaye argued about the film's ending before settling on the current version (*Never Sleep Again: The Making of a Nightmare on Elm Street*).

8. *A Nightmare on Elm Street.*

9. Langenkamp wanted to keep the tongue prop afterward (*Never Sleep Again: The Elm Street Legacy*).

10. Thomas Metzinger, *The Ego Tunnel: The Science of the Mind and the Myth of the Self* (New York: Basic Books, 2009), 139.

11. *A Nightmare on Elm Street.*

12. On this point, I credit Dr. Shoshana Milgram Knapp, as she offered the interpretation to me.

13. Egginton, "Reality is Bleeding," 207–229.

14. *Scream.*

15. For a similar point in a discussion about rape in horror films, see: Count Jackula, "I Spit on Your Grave," YouTube, TheCountJackulaShow, 2015, https://www.youtube.com/watch?v=ZRlbB-jDS5U&list=PL7ykZa907Km5Ca3NPoAVmOkzh_cSM1qsf&index=19.

16. "Nightmare, n. and adj.," *OED*, September 2003, http://www.oed.com.ezproxy.lib.vt.edu/view/Entry/127012?rskey=zJDXaw&result=1&isAdvanced=false#eid.

17. *Ibid.*

18. Patrick McNamara, *Nightmares* (Westport, CN: Praeger, 2008), 22.

19. Of course, conflict is central to all stories. I will show, however, that nightmares have a unique sort of conflict, that of self versus self.

20. McNamara, *Nightmares*, 46.

21. *Ibid.*

22. *Ibid.* 136–137.

23. *Ibid.* 138.

24. *Ibid.* 94–95.

25. *Ibid.* 22.

26. I mean this in the psychological context. In the films, Freddy absolutely threatens characters' lives.

27. For historical context about the painting and its situation in the gothic genre, please see Martin Myrone's essay "Fuseli to Frankenstein: The Visual Arts in the Context of the Gothic." Myrone situates the painting nicely in the genre, but this discussion, while interesting, is outside my scope.

28. In "Fuseli's *The Nightmare*: Somewhere between the Sublime and the Ridiculous," Christopher Frayling points out that Fuseli was interested in dreams but that *The Nightmare* was unique in that it did not, as most paintings of the time did, invoke a particular dream reference (11;13). Instead, *The Nightmare* gives us a common, universal occurrence, acutely felt by many.

29. Thomas A. Green, *Folklore: An Encyclopedia of Beliefs, Customs, Tales, Music, and Art.* 1st ed., vol. 1 (Santa Barbara, CA: ABC-CLIO, 1997), 588.

30. Most links found through a cursory Google search will take you to paranormal websites. Nevertheless, the scholarly source in the earlier footnote should assuage skeptical readers.

31. Christopher Frayling, "Fuseli's The

Nightmare: Somewhere between the Sublime and the Ridiculous," in *Gothic Nightmares: Fuseli, Blake and the Romantic Imagination*, ed. Martin Myrone (London, United Kingdom: Tate Publishing, 2006), 12.

32. I want to be clear that I am not trying to say that my interpretation, my pointing out that Fuseli is treating a real-world phenomenon relevant to nightmares then and now, is the only valid one for the painting. Myrone points out in *"The Nightmare: Fuseli and the Art of Horror"* that the painting is often interpreted sexually. This interpretation, while outside this section's range, is compatible with my own reading. See Myrone's "Fuseli to Frankenstein: The Visual Arts in the Context of the Gothic."

33. The monster is the amalgamation of all the central characters' worst fears. For Mary, the monster is her stillborn child come to life.

34. Schwenger, *At the Borders of Sleep*, 85.

35. Ibid.

36. For argument's sake, I am going to treat *A Nightmare on Elm Street* as if the planned ending were preserved. Different stylistic elements support this choice. Even scenes when Nancy is supposedly awake contain blurring, which denotes dream scenes (see the bridge scene). As the film blurs the line between dream and real-life, the film's narrative becomes blurred, and I believe Craven made this choice intentionally to make the entire film dream-like as if it were, as he intended, just a dream.

37. Here, when I say Mary "breaks out," I mean that she awakens from the nightmare's literal space. She does not, however, escape the nightmare's influence, whereas Nancy arguably does, if we accept the original ending.

38. McNamara, *Nightmares*, 5.

39. *A Nightmare on Elm Street*.

40. Ibid.

41. *Gothic*, directed by Ken Russell (1986; Vestron Pictures, 1987), https://tubitv.com/movies/154228/gothic?start=true.

42. Ibid.

43. Ibid.

44. *A Nightmare on Elm Street*.

45. To further highlight the connection between these works, I should mention that *The Nightmare* features prominently in *Gothic*. A copy of the painting hangs over the fireplace in Mary's room, and she experiences a version of the painting in a nightmare within her overarching nightmare. Thus, the connection between these two works is explicit as well as thematic in that Russell intentionally invokes and even recreates (updates, perhaps) Fuseli's work.

46. *Celluloid Crime of the Century*.

47. In *Freddy vs Jason*, one character (Mark) screams out "Somebody please wake me up!" when he realizes he is in a nightmare with Freddy. No one does, and he dies.

48. *Never Sleep Again: The Making of A Nightmare on Elm Street*, directed by Jeffrey Schwarz (2006; Burbank, CA: New Line Cinema Entertainment, 2006), DVD.

49. To the producers' credit, the *Nightmare on Elm Street* series has been very successful, and Freddy Kruger is a horror icon. Theirs was a shrewd business decision.

I believe the last scene is meant to be perplexing, as it is nearly impossible to tell whether it is a nightmare or real-life. On the one hand, this lack of distinction is helpful for our purposes. On the other, it makes the scene difficult to read, and many, including myself, have struggled with it. Its inclusion does not work particularly well within the narrative, and it even seems to override Nancy's victory.

50. McNamara, *Nightmares*, 5.

51. *Jacob's Ladder*, directed by Adrian Lyne (1990; Culver City, CA: TriStar Pictures, 1998), Blu-ray.

52. Given his poignant advice and guidance to a dying man hesitating to move on, one might also consider Louie a psychopomp, a guide for the dead and dying.

53. As I noted before, Nancy's triumph may only be ostensible. Regardless of whether she actually escapes the nightmare, Nancy's apparent victory relies on her using the advice Glen and Marge gave her. And so, my point stands about the similarity between her and Jacob's actions.

54. *Jacob's Ladder*.

55. Ibid.

56. Ibid.

57. Ibid.

58. Stephen Saito, "TIFF '15 Interview: AKIZ on the Creative Awakening of 'Der Nachtmahr,'" Moveablefest, October 2, 2015, https://moveablefest.com/akiz-der-nachtmahr/.

59. *Der Nachtmahr*, directed by Achim Bornhak (2015; Berlin: Bon Voyage Films, 2016), https://www.amazon.

com/Nightmare-Nachtmahr-Kim-Gordon/dp/B078NLMSHP/ref=sr_1_1?crid=3PQJGZPTSCPU8&dchild=1&keywords=der+nachtmahr&qid=1605515517&s=instant-video&sprefix=der+nacht%2Cinstant-video%2C202&sr=1-1.

60. Chaieb, et. al, "Auditory Beat Stimulation."

61. Dickstein, "The Aesthetics of Fright," 67.

62. "Who can have sex with whom and from what age?," Zanzu, Accessed August 2020, https://www.zanzu.de/en/rights-and-law/your-rights/age-of-consent/.

63. "The '4 D's' of Abnormality," IvyLearn, Ivytech, Accessed August 2020, https://ivylearn.ivytech.edu/courses/740586/pages/the-4-ds-of-abnormality.

64. *Der Nachtmahr.*

65. *Ibid.*

66. The following article observes the tendency of dreams to incorporate external stimuli: Anthony Bloxham and Simon Durant, "The effect of external stimuli on dreams, as assessed using Q-Methodology," *Journal of Dream Research* 7, no. 2 (2014): 129–140. http://eprints.lincoln.ac.uk/id/eprint/17791/1/17791%2015754-39669-4-PB.pdf.

67. Roger Ebert, "Paperhouse," RogerEbert, March 31, 1989, https://www.rogerebert.com/reviews/paperhouse-1989.

68. Zsolt Györi, "'Animals Rule!' Timothy Conquered': Escape, Capture, and Liminality in Werner Herzog's Grizzly Man," *Hungarian Journal of English and American Studies, HJEAS* 21, no. 1 (2015): 96.

69. *Horsehead*, directed by Romain Basset (2014; Paris: HorseHead Pictures, 2015), https://tubitv.com/movies/547374/horsehead?start=true.

70. *Ibid.*

71. Carl Jung, *Modern Man in Search of a Soul*, Transl. W.S. Dell and Cary F. Baynes (San Diego: Harcourt Inc., 1933), 23–27.

72. Bruno Bettelheim, *The Uses of Enchantment: The Meaning and Importance of Fairy Tales* (New York: Vintage Books, 1989), 173; Zipes, *The Irresistible Fairy Tale*, 142.

73. *Ibid.*

74. *Horsehead.*

75. *Ibid.*

76. *Ibid.*

77. Ursula Voss, et al., "Lucid Dreaming: A State of Consciousness with Features of Both Waking and Non-Lucid Dreaming," *Sleep* 32, no. 9 (2009): 1191–1200, https://www.ncbi.nlm.nih.gov/pmc/articles/PMC2737577/.

78. Michael Barson, "William Castle: American director," Britannica, *Britannica*, Accessed October 2020, https://www.britannica.com/topic/House-on-Haunted-Hill.

Chapter Six

1. See: Mark Sanderson, *Don't Look Now* (London: British Film Institute, 1996).

2. Here, I thank Dr. Thomas Marksbury for pointing these themes out to me when my own assessment of the film overlooked them.

3. *All the Colors of the Dark*, directed by Sergio Martino (1972; Interfilm), DVD.

4. *Ibid.*

5. *Ibid.*

6. While *Halloween* (2018) is not as liminal as *Don't Look Now* or *All the Colors of the Dark*, it is still useful for exploring the role of misunderstanding in horror fiction, a trope this section's other two films speak to but do not explore in as great of depth. And so, I have included the newest *Halloween* here because it serves a valuable purpose even though it is not as liminal as most of the films this volume discusses.

7. *Halloween*, directed by David Gordon Green (2018; Los Angeles: Universal Pictures, 2018), DVD.

8. *Ibid.*

9. "Sartain Family History," Ancestry.com, Accessed February 2020, https://www.ancestry.com/name-origin?surname=sartain.

10. *Halloween.*

11. Alexandra Heller-Nicholas, *Suspiria* (Leighton Buzzard, United Kingdom: Auteur, 2015), 55.

12. *Ibid.* 59.

13. *Ibid.*

14. *Oculus*, directed by Mike Flanagan (2013; Los Angeles: Blumhouse Productions, 2014), DVD.

15. Don Kaye, "Interview: Oculus director Mike Flanagan," Den of Geek, April 14, 2014, https://www.denofgeek.com/movies/interview-oculus-director-mike-flanagan/.

16. Bunnell 82.

17. *Into the Mirror*, directed by Kim Sung-ho (2003; Seoul: Cinema Service), DVD.

18. Whereas Mary in *Gothic* also fails her quest, *Gothic* portrays both Mary and the monster still existing at the end of the film. Conversely, Wu fails by destroying (rather than reconciling with) one of his two halves.

19. In doing so, it resonates with Tucker's analysis of monsters in the mirror legends, and so, once more, the liminal horror film reflects and hyperbolizes real world phenomena.

20. *Scream*.

21. Here, I would like the reader to note that the exploration of this reality beneath the skin differs significantly when doctors conduct it. They use tools that allow them to see beyond the blood, such as suction, which drains the blood enough to provide a clear view of the tissues and layers underneath. Such an exploration, however, is not possible with the naked eye, unless the cut itself is deep enough to reveal either muscle or bone. Moreover, by extracting Casey's organs, Ghostface overcomes her blood's obfuscating effect.

22. Győri 96.

23. I will explore in-depth the topics of ritual and magic in the final chapter, when I discuss the role of belief in liminal horror films.

24. Ghislaine Boulanger, *Wounded by Reality: Understanding and Treating Adult Onset Trauma* (Mahwah, NJ: Analytic Press, 2007), 85.

25. Brigitte Peucker, "Herzog and Auteurism: Performing Authenticity," in *A Companion to Werner Herzog*, ed. Brad Prager (Hoboken, NJ: Wiley-Blackwell, 2012), 38.

26. Of course, all this applies to me, the author, as well. Brandon West, "Murky Waters: Loch Ness and Herzogian Notions of Truth," *The New Review of Film and Television*, forthcoming.

27. Roger Shattuck, *Forbidden Knowledge: From Prometheus to Pornography* (New York: St. Martin's Press, 1996), 166.

28. Ouellette, *Me, Myself, and Why*, 217.

29. Steven Novella, "Sleep and False Memory," *Neurologicablog*, July 24, 2014, https://theness.com/neurologicablog/index.php/sleep-and-false-memory/. Quoted in: Craig Good, "446: The Fallibility of Memory," December 23, 2014, in *Skeptoid*, produced by Skeptoid Podcast Media, podcast, http://skeptoid.com/episodes/4446.

30. Elizabeth F. Loftus, "Creating False Memories," *Scientific American* 277, no. 3 (1997): 70–75, http://staff.washington.edu/eloftus/Articles/sciam.htm.

31. Laura Spinney, "We can implant entirely false memories," *The Guardian*, December 3, 2003, https://www.theguardian.com/science/2003/dec/04/science.research1.

32. Good, "446: The Fallibility of Memory," *Skeptoid*.

33. Heller-Nicholas, *Found Footage Horror Films*, 168.

34. Ibid. 170.

35. See: Gottschall, *The Storytelling Animal*, 170.

36. Novella, "Sleep and False Memory."

37. Gottschall, *The Storytelling Animal*, 18.

38. Ibid. 149.

39. Ibid.

40. Fiction may have the ability to change our minds and affect us, but this does not undermine my point about reality being the scarier of the two. In some ways, fiction is the vehicle of reality, teaching us lessons it is probably better that we not learn the hard way.

41. Gottschall, *The Storytelling Animal*, 150.

42. Isaac Reed, "Why Salem Made Sense: Culture, Gender, and the Puritan Persecution of Witchcraft," *Cultural Sociology* 1, no. 2 (2007): 209–234. Reed is pushing for a more encompassing reading of the Salem Witch Trials, but he acknowledges that, prior to his article, sociological readings of the events tended to emphasize, among other facts, socioeconomic variables.

43. *Candyman*.

44. Ouellette, *Me, Myself, and Why*, 145.

45. Ibid. 161.

46. Gottschall, *The Storytelling Animal*, 96–99; R.W. Sperry, "Hemisphere Disconnection and Unity in Conscious Awareness," *American Psychologist* 23, no. 10 (1968): 726.

47. Gottschall, *The Storytelling Animal*, 103.

48. CGP Grey, "You Are Two," YouTube, May 31, 2016, https://www.youtube.com/watch?v=wfYbgdo8e-8.

49. Ibid.

50. Sperry, "Hemisphere Disconnection," 724. Since Grey's video released more than three decades after Sperry's Nobel Prize winning research, it is possible Grey bases his assessment on Sperry's experiments. Regardless of whether Grey has

directly consulted Sperry's research, however, the point stands that Sperry's argument predates Grey's.

51. Gottschall, *The Storytelling Animal*, 99.

52. Ouellette, *Me, Myself, and Why*, 259.

53. *Ibid.* 261.

54. While editing my manuscript for publication, I became aware of a growing field of criticism against how *Split* portrays the mentally ill as monstrous, and thereby perpetuates American society's stigma against mental illness. For clarity, I want to establish outright that *Split* is not an accurate portrayal of D.I.D. or its sufferers, and I do not condone vilifying the mentally ill or neurodivergent.

55. *Split*, directed by M. Night Shyamalan (2016; Los Angeles: Universal Pictures, 2017), DVD.

56. This division is imperfect. Natalie, Paul, Reese, and Brenda all exist within the same urban legend, and the characters' various arcs heavily overlap.

57. Anil Ananthaswamy, *The Man Who Wasn't There: Tales from the Edge of the Self* (New York: Dutton, 2015), 254.

58. *Ibid.* 255–256.

59. *Ibid.* 255.

60. *Split*.

61. Daniel Kremer, *Sidney J. Furie: Life and Films* (Lexington, KY: University Press of Kentucky, 2015), 271.

62. Hannah Reese, "Intrusive Thoughts: Normal or Not?: Am I a Terrible Person for Thinking That?," Psychology Today, October 24, 2011, https://www.psychologytoday.com/us/blog/am-i-normal/201110/intrusive-thoughts-normal-or-not. To be clear, though, experiencing an intrusive thought does not mean one sub-consciously wants to act on that thought. In fact, intrusive thoughts may stick around precisely because they are so unwanted that thinkers give them undue attention, thereby encoding them into memory. See: Martin Seif and Sally Winston, "Unwanted Intrusive Thoughts," Psychology Today, July 1, 2019, https://www.psychologytoday.com/us/blog/living-sticky-mind/201907/unwanted-intrusive-thoughts.

63. Paul Mitchell, "The Horror of Loss: Reading Jennifer Kent's The Babadook as a Trauma Narrative," *Atlantis Journal* 41, no. 2 (2019): 179–196.

64. *Ibid.*

65. *The Babadook*, directed by Jennifer Kent (2014; Toronto: Entertainment One, 2014), DVD.

66. *Visitors*, directed by Richard Franklin (2003; Melbourne, Victoria, Australia: Bayside Pictures, 2003), DVD.

67. *Ibid.*

68. *Ibid.*

69. See, for example, Samuel Taylor Coleridge's "The Rime of the Ancient Mariner."

70. *Ibid.*

71. *Ibid.*

72. *Ibid.*

73. *Ibid.*

74. *Ibid.*

75. *Ju-On: The Grudge*, directed by Takashi Shimizu (2002; Santa Monica, CA: Pioneer LDC, 2004), https://tubitv.com/movies/308306/ju-on-the-grudge?start=true.

76. K Kroenke and A D Mangelsdorff, "Common Symptoms in ambulatory care: incidences, evaluation, therapy, and outcome," *The American Journal of Medicine* 86, no. 3 (1989), Accessed October 2020, https://pubmed.ncbi.nlm.nih.gov/2919607/.

Chapter Seven

1. Just as not everyone is capable of being affected by horror films, I suspect there are some who have zero superstitions. Nevertheless, many, if not all, of us retain some rudimentary and possibly implicit belief in magic.

2. Many players of the *Dungeons & Dragons* roleplaying game are superstitious when it comes to their dice. They may put away dice that roll low and refuse to play with them, at least for that night. Of course, dice are random or at least mostly random, and just because a die rolls low a few times in a row does not mean it will continue to do so or that the player will have better luck with a different die. And yet, despite knowing and understanding this, many players opt for swapping dice out regardless. This is but one of many examples showing this superstitious ritual in action.

3. Joseph Campbell, *Myths to Live By* (New York: Penguin Compass, 1972), 44.

4. *Ibid.*

5. King, *Danse Macabre*, 12.

6. J. Lawton Winsdale, "Techno-Kabbalah: The Performative Language

of Magick and the Production of Occult Knowledge," *TDR: Drama Review* 44, no. 2 (2000): 98.

7. L.L. Bernard, "The Unilateral Elements in Magic Theory and Performance," *American Sociological Review* 3, no. 6 (1938): 775.

8. This implicit belief contrasts with our typical avowed belief that reality is, in fact, fixed. Despite our superstitions suggesting otherwise, we tend to say that we do not believe in these things, even though, as I have shown, we often do. Thus, I am addressing beliefs stated and unstated. Here, I have unearthed our unstated belief.

9. Mallika Marshall, "A placebo can work even when know it's a place," *Harvard Health Publishing*, Harvard, July 7, 2016, https://www.health.harvard.edu/blog/placebo-can-work-even-know-placebo-201607079926.

10. In *The Skeleton Key*, the main character, Caroline Ellis, played by Kate Hudson, struggles against some voodoo practitioners. At the end of the film, the villain gloats, telling Caroline that she, the villain, can only hurt Caroline because the latter now believes. The audience and Caroline thus learn that voodoo only works against believers, and the villain had to wait most of the film before moving against the protagonist because the protagonist was initially a skeptic.

11. *Tales from the Darkside*, season 3, episode 11, "Seasons of Belief," directed by Michael McDowell, aired on December 29, 1986, on CBS, DVD.

12. Unlike the kids, the parents remain unnamed. To a savvy horror viewer, this will likely foreshadow their fates.

13. According to the story, saying this being's name aloud is dangerous. Thus, I encourage the reader to read this section silently.

14. Michael Bishop, "Seasons of Belief," in *One Winter in Eden* (Sauk City, WI: Arkham House Publishers,1984), 51.

15. *Ibid*.

16. For a more thorough discussion of the subject, please see the work of German philosopher Ernst Cassirer, who writes of this at length in *Language and Myth*. Cassirer writes, "all verbal structures appear as *also* mythical entities, endowed with certain mythical powers, that the Word, in fact, becomes a sort of primary force, in which all being and doing originate" (emphasis Cassirer's) (45). He goes on to argue that names are endowed with power because they encapsulate one's individuality and become a sort of symbol for that individual being (51). His analysis should help us understand why beings like the grither and Candyman so jealously guard their names.

17. "Seasons of Belief," *Tales from the Darkside*.

18. *Ibid*.

19. Bishop, "Seasons of Belief," 51.

20. Helen is ambitious, and she enters Cabrini-Green also because she is driven to succeed in academia. There are, therefore, other motivations for her actions than mere disbelief in Candyman and the supernatural.

21. *Candyman*.

22. There is a criminal in Cabrini-Green who goes by the name "Candyman." He assaults Helen when she is visiting Cabrini-Green. When doing so, he explicitly references her search for him (*Candyman*).

23. *Candyman*.

24. *Ibid*.

25. *Ibid*.

26. *Ibid*.

27. *Ibid*.

28. Clive Barker, "The Forbidden," in *Books of Blood Volume 4–6*, vol. 5 (London: Sphere Books Limited, 2009), 33.

29. *Ibid*. 13.

30. Sara Planés, Céline Villier, and Michel Mallaret, "The nocebo effect of drugs," *Pharmacology Research & Perspectives* 4, no. 2 (2016), https://www.ncbi.nlm.nih.gov/pmc/articles/PMC4804316/.

31. *Never Sleep Again: The Making of A Nightmare on Elm Street*.

32. *Ibid*.

33. For the sake of argument, I am going to discuss the film as if the original ending were preserved. I believe many of the film's elements support this interpretation, as much of the film seems to take place in a dream, and it therefore follows that the film did, in fact, take place in a dream. The film's current ending seems to overturn Nancy's victory, but does not mesh well with the film's overall story.

34. *A Nightmare on Elm Street*.

35. *Ibid*.

36. *Ibid*.

37. Kyle Christensen, "The Final Girl versus Wes Craven's "A Nightmare on Elm Street": Proposing a Stronger Model of

Feminism in Slasher Horror Cinema," *Studies in Popular Culture* 51, no. 1 (2011): 35.
38. *A Nightmare on Elm Street*.
39. *Ibid*.
40. Kevin Williamson, the screenwriter for *Scream*, wrote the film's initial scene after seeing some news footage of the Ripper case. The Ripper murders occurred in 1990, and *Scream* was released in 1996 (*Behind the "Scream." Ultimate Scream Collection*).
41. *Never Sleep Again: The Elm Street Legacy*.
42. I do not mean to disrespect anyone's memory here. I am very sorry for the families and the young men affected.
43. Adam Bulger, "Sudden and Unexplained: The Sleep Deaths that Inspired Freddy Kruger," *Van Winkle's*, 30 October 2015, Accessed 7 September 2020, https://web.archive.org/web/20180417144220/https://vanwinkles.com/sudden-and-unexplained-the-sleep-deaths-that-inspired-freddy-krueger. *Van Winkle's* is now defunct, but archive.org has screen captures of the article from when the website was running.
44. *Ibid*.
45. Sean Mitchell, "A Gallery of Craven Images," *Los Angeles Times* (Los Angeles), November 18, 1989.
46. Larry Doyle, "Medical Experts Seek Clues to 'Nightmare Deaths' That Strike Male Asian Refugees," *Los Angeles Times* (Los Angeles), January 11, 1987. Karl Schoenberger, "Night Deaths of Asian Men Unexplained: Healthy Indonesians, Filipinos, Japanese Expire 'With a Snap,'" *Los Angeles Times* (Los Angeles), July 10, 1983.
47. *Never Sleep Again: The Elm Street Legacy*.
48. Shelley R. Adler, *Sleep Paralysis: Nightmares, Nocebos, and the Mind-Body Connection* (New Brunswick, NJ: Rutgers University Press, 2011), 94.
49. Again, I mean the utmost respect to those who were affected by this phenomenon. I am sorry for their losses.
50. Adler, *Sleep Paralysis*, 98–101.
51. *Ibid*. 95.
52. *Ibid*. 124–126.
53. Quoted in: Adler, *Sleep Paralysis*, 121.
54. *Ibid*. 130.
55. Here, Adler hyphenates the term "night-mare" to emphasize its roots. The earliest use of "nightmare" in English was defined as "A female spirit or monster supposed to settle on or produce a feeling of suffocation in a sleeping person or animal," in other words, a mare of the night (*Oxford English Dictionary*).
56. Anwesha Banerjee, "Cross-Cultural Variance of Schizophrenia in Symptoms, Diagnosis, and Treatment," *Georgetown University Journal of Health Sciences* 6, no. 2 (2012): 18–24. https://blogs.commons.georgetown.edu/journal-of-health-sciences/issues-2/vol-6-no-2-july-2012/cross-cultural-variance-of-schizophrenia-in-symptoms-diagnosis-and-treatment/. See also: Suzanne O'Sullivan, "When the Body Speaks," Psychology Today, January 2017, last reviewed September 7, 2019, https://www.psychologytoday.com/us/articles/201701/when-the-body-speaks.
57. Adler, *Sleep Paralysis*, 5–6.
58. "People can die from giving up the fight," Eureka Alert, September 27, 2018, https://www.eurekalert.org/pub_releases/2018-09/uop-pcd092018.php.
59. Simone Kühn, et al., "The neural representation of intrusive thoughts," *Social Cognitive and Affective Neuroscience* 8, no. 6 (2013): 688–693.
60. "Doris Bither Case," Wikipedia, Accessed March 2020, https://en.wikipedia.org/wiki/Doris_Bither_case.
61. Suzanne O'Sullivan, "When the Body Speaks."
62. Bishop, "Seasons of Belief," 51.
63. Gottschall, *The Storytelling Animal*, 52–63.

Afterword

1. Massimiliano Proietti, et al., "Experimental test of local observer-independence," *Science Advances* 5, no. 9 (2019), https://arxiv.org/abs/1902.05080.
2. Kristeva, *Powers of Horror*, 10–11.
3. *Ibid*. 10–35.

Bibliography

Primary Sources

Amito, David, and Michael Laicini, dir. *Antrum: The Deadliest Film Ever Made.* 2018; Brooklyn: Else Films, 2019. https://tubitv.com/movies/530312/antrum-the-deadliest-film-ever-made?start=true.
Barker, Clive. "The Forbidden," in *Books of Blood Volume 4–6*, vol. 5, 1–37. London: Sphere Books Limited, 2009.
Basset, Romain, dir. *Horsehead.* 2014; Paris: HorseHead Pictures, 2015. https://tubitv.com/movies/547374/horsehead?start=true.
Bishop, Michael. "Seasons of Belief," in *One Winter in Eden*, 43–51. Sauk City, WI: Arkham House Publishers, 1984.
Blanks, Jamie, dir. *Urban Legend.* 1998; Los Angeles: TriStar Pictures, 1999. DVD.
Bornhak, Achim, dir. *Der Nachtmahr.* 2015; Berlin: Bon Voyage Films, 2016. https://www.amazon.com/Nightmare-Nachtmahr-Kim-Gordon/dp/B078NLMSHP/ref=sr_1_1?crid=3PQJGZPTSCPU8&dchild=1&keywords=der+nachtmahr&qid=1605515517&s=instant-video&sprefix=der+nacht%2Cinstant-video%2C202&sr=1-1.
Carpenter, John, dir. *In the Mouth of Madness.* 1994; Burbank, CA: New Line Cinema, 1995. DVD.
Carpenter, John, dir. *Masters of Horror.* Season 1, episode 8, 2005, "Cigarette Burns." Aired December 16, 2005, on Showtime. https://tubitv.com/tv-shows/286426/s01-e08-cigarette-burns?start=true.
Christian, Roger, dir. *The Sender.* 1982; London: Kingsmere Productions, 1983. DVD.
Corillion, Jean-Michel, and Vincent Munié, dir. *Capturing the Killer Croc.* 2004; Arlington, VA: PBS Home Video, 2004. DVD.
Craven, Wes, dir. *A Nightmare on Elm Street.* 1984; Burbank, CA: New Line Cinema, 1985. DVD.
Craven, Wes, dir. *Scream.* 1996; New York: Dimension Films, 1997. DVD.
Craven, Wes, dir. *Scream 2.* 1997; New York: Dimension Films, 1998. DVD.
Craven, Wes, dir. *Scream 3.* 1999; New York: Dimension Films, 2000. DVD.
Craven, Wes, dir. *Scream 4.* 2010; New York: Dimension Films, 2011. DVD.
Craven, Wes, dir. *Wes Craven's New Nightmare.* 1994; Burbank, CA: New Line Cinema, 1995. DVD.
Cronenberg, David, dir. *Videodrome.* 1983; Los Angeles: Universal Pictures, 1999. DVD.
Cunningham, Sean S., dir. *Friday the 13th.* 1980; Hollywood: Paramount Pictures, 1980. DVD.
DeGennaro, Steven, dir. *Found Footage 3-D.* 2016; Austin, TX: Shudder, 2016. https://www.shudder.com/movies/watch/found-footage-3d-2d-version/430c8b6074b30e71.
Del Toro, Guillermo, dir. *Pan's Labyrinth.* 2006; Madrid: Telecinco Cinema, 2007. DVD.
Derrickson, Scott, dir. *Sinister.* 2012; Santa Monica, CA: Alliance Films, 2013. DVD.
Duffell, Peter, dir. *The House that Dripped Blood.* 1971; Shepperton, United Kingdom: Amicus Productions, 2003. https://tubitv.com/movies/272775/the-house-that-dripped-blood?start=true.

Bibliography

Flanagan, Mike, dir. *Oculus*. 2013; Los Angeles: Blumhouse Productions, 2014. DVD.
Foy, Ciaran, dir. *Sinister 2*. 2015; Los Angeles: Alliance Films, 2016. DVD.
Franklin, Richard, dir. *Visitors*. 2003; Melbourne, Victoria, Australia: Bayside Pictures, 2003. DVD.
Furie, Sidney J., dir. *The Entity*. 1982; Los Angeles: 20th Century Fox, 2005. Blu-ray.
Fuseli, Henry. *The Nightmare*. 1781. Painting, 40x50 (inches). Detroit Institute of Arts, Detroit.
Gillespie, Jim, dir. *I Know What You Did Last Summer*. 1997; Culver City, CA: Columbia Pictures, 1998. DVD.
Goddard, Drew, dir. *The Cabin in the Woods*. 2011; Santa Monica, CA: Lionsgate, 2012. DVD.
Gordon, Stuart, dir. *Dolls*. 1987; Los Angeles: Empire Pictures, 2005. https://www.amazon.com/Dolls-Guy-Rolfe/dp/B07HVP45FZ/ref=sr_1_1?dchild=1&keywords=Dolls+prime+video&qid=1605518897&sr=8–1.
Green, Adam, dir. *Hatchet*. 2006; Beverly Hills: Anchor Bay Entertainment, 2007. https://www.amazon.com/Hatchet-Joel-David-Moore/dp/B07VL64Q17.
Green, David Gordon, dir. *Halloween*. 2018; Los Angeles: Universal Pictures, 2018. DVD.
Gulager, John, dir. *Feast*. 2005; New York: Dimension Films, 2006. DVD.
Hooper, Tobe, dir. *The Texas Chainsaw Massacre*. 1974; Bryanston Distributing Company, 1984. https://tubitv.com/movies/499404/the-texas-chain-saw-massacre?start=true.
"Inspired by the true story of the most prolific serial killer in history." Primeval Poster (#1 of 2). December 15, 2006. Movie Poster.
Katleman, Michael, dir. *Primeval*. 2007; Burbank, CA: Buena Vista Pictures, 2007. DVD.
Kent, Jennifer, dir. *The Babadook*. 2014; Toronto: Entertainment One, 2014. DVD.
Khan, Sajid, et al, dir. *Darna Zaroori Hai*. 2006; Mumbai: K. Sera Sera Productions, 2006. https://www.amazon.com/Darna-Zaroori-Hai-Amitabh-Bachchan/dp/B081D9L7NY.
Kurosawa, Kiyoshi, dir. *Pulse*. 2001; Chiyoda, Tokyo, Japan: Toho, 2006. DVD.
Lopez, Alex Garcia, dir. *Chilling Adventures of Sabrina*. Season 2, episode 4, "Dr. Cerberus's House of Horror." Aired April 5, 2019, on Netflix. https://www.netflix.com/title/80223989?source=35.
Lovecraft, H.P. "Pickman's Model." 1927. Available at http://www.hplovecraft.com/writings/texts/fiction/pm.aspx.
Lyne, Adrian, dir. *Jacob's Ladder*. 1990; Culver City, CA: TriStar Pictures, 1998. Blu-ray.
Martino, Sergio, dir. *All the Colors of the Dark*. 1972; Interfilm. DVD.
McDonnell, B.J., dir. *Hatchet III*. 2013; Chicago, IL: Dark Sky Films, 2013. https://www.amazon.com/Hatchet-III-Rated-R-Version/dp/B00DOPU50S/ref=sr_1_1?dchild=1&keywords=Hatchet+III&qid=1605519882&s=instant-video&sr=1–1.
McDowell, Michael, dir. *Tales from the Darkside*. Season 3, episode 11, "Seasons of Belief." Aired on December 29, 1986, on CBS. DVD.
McPherson, Conor. "The Weir," in *The Weir, and Other Plays*, 1–72. New York: Theatre Communications Group, 1999.
Mustonen, Taneli, dir. *Lake Bodom*. 2016; Helsinki: Don Films, 2016. https://www.shudder.com/movies/watch/lake-bodom/4cc1126e0653ef59.
Nispel, Marcus, dir. *The Texas Chainsaw Massacre*. 2003; Burbank, CA: New Line Cinema, 2004. DVD.
Ottman, John, dir. *Urban Legends: Final Cut*. 2000; Culver City, CA: Columbia Pictures, 2001. DVD.
Øvredal, André, dir. *The Autopsy of Jane Doe*. 2016; New York: IFC Midnight, 2016. https://www.netflix.com/title/80022613.
Øvredal, André, dir. *Scary Stories to Tell in the Dark*. 2019; Santa Monica, CA: Lionsgate, 2019. DVD.
Roeg, Nicolas, dir. *Don't Look Now*. 1973; British Lion Films, 1980. DVD.
Romero, George, dir. *The Dark Half*. 1993; Los Angeles: Orion Pictures, 1994. DVD.
Rose, Bernard, dir. *Candyman*. 1992; Culver City, CA: TriStar Pictures, 1993. DVD.
Rose, Bernard, dir. *Paperhouse*. 1988; Stamford, Connecticut: Vestron Video, 1988. https://www.amazon.com/Paperhouse-Charlotte-Burke/dp/B00HSD0PKC.
Russell, Ken, dir. *Gothic*. 1986; Vestron Pictures, 1987. https://tubitv.com/movies/154228/gothic?start=true.

Sakdapisit, Sophon, dir. *Coming Soon*. 2008; Bangkok: GMM Thai Hub. DVD.
Shakespeare, William. *Hamlet*. 1601. Available at: http://shakespeare.mit.edu/hamlet/full.html.
Shapeero, Tristram, dir. *Community*. Season 3, episode 5, "Horror Fiction in Seven Spooky Steps." Aired October 27, 2011, on NBC. https://www.netflix.com/title/70155589?source=35.
Shimizu, Takashi, dir. *Ju-On: The Grudge*. 2002; Santa Monica, CA: Pioneer LDC, 2004. https://tubitv.com/movies/308306/ju-on-the-grudge?start=true.
Showalter, John F., dir. *Supernatural*. Season 6, episode 21, "Let it Bleed." Aired on May 20, 2011, on The CW. https://www.netflix.com/title/70143825?source=35.
Shyamalan, M. Night, dir. *Split*. 2016; Los Angeles: Universal Pictures, 2017. DVD.
Softley, Iain, dir. *Skeleton Key*. 2005; Los Angeles: Panorama, 2006. DVD.
Sung-ho, Kim, dir. *Into the Mirror*. 2003; Seoul: Cinema Service. DVD.
Verbinski, Gore, dir. *The Ring*. 2002; Los Angeles: DreamWorks Pictures, 2003. DVD.
Yu, Ronny, dir. *Freddy vs. Jason*. 2003; Burbank, CA: New Line Cinema, 2004. DVD.
Zuker, David, dir. *Scary Movie 3*. 2003; New York: Dimension Films, 2004. DVD.

Secondary Sources

Abrams, M. H. *A Glossary of Literary Terms*, 7th ed. Orlando, FL: Harcourt Brace College Publishers, 1999.
Adler, Shelley R. *Sleep Paralysis: Nightmares, Nocebos, and the Mind-Body Connection*. New Brunswick, NJ: Rutgers University Press, 2011.
Ananthaswamy, Anil. *The Man Who Wasn't There: Tales from the Edge of the Self*. New York: Dutton, 2015.
Banerjee, Anwesha. "Cross-Cultural Variance of Schizophrenia in Symptoms, Diagnosis, and Treatment." *Georgetown University Journal of Health Sciences* 6, no. 2 (2012): 18–24. Accessed November 2020. https://blogs.commons.georgetown.edu/journal-of-health-sciences/issues-2/vol-6-no-2-july-2012/cross-cultural-variance-of-schizophrenia-in-symptoms-diagnosis-and-treatment/.
Barnes, Daniel R. "Interpreting Urban Legends," in *Contemporary Legend: A Reader*, edited by Gillian Bennett and Paul Smith, 1–16. New York: Garland Publishing Inc., 1996.
Barson, Michael. "William Castle: American director." Britannica. *Britannica*. Accessed October 2020. https://www.britannica.com/topic/House-on-Haunted-Hill.
Behind the "Scream." Ultimate Scream Collection. 2006; New York: Dimension Home Video, 2006. DVD.
Bernard, LL. "The Unilateral Elements in Magic Theory and Performance." *American Sociological Review* 3, no. 6 (1938): 771–785.
Bettelheim, Bruno. *The Uses of Enchantment: The Meaning and Importance of Fairy Tales*. New York: Vintage Books, 1989.
Bloom, John. "They Came. They Sawed." *Texas Monthly*, November 2004. Accessed 7 September 2020. https://web.archive.org/web/20111017042555/http://www.texasmonthly.com/2004-11-01/feature6-2.php.
Bloxham, Anthony, and Simon Durant. "The effect of external stimuli on dreams, as assessed using Q-Methodology." *Journal of Dream Research* 7, no. 2 (2014): 129–140. Accessed October 2020. http://eprints.lincoln.ac.uk/id/eprint/17791/1/17791%2015754-39669-4-PB.pdf.
Boulanger, Ghislaine. *Wounded by Reality: Understanding and Treating Adult Onset Trauma*. Mahwah, NJ: Analytic Press, 2007.
Brunvand, Jan Harold. *The Vanishing Hitchhiker: American Urban Legends & Their Meanings*. New York: W.W. Norton and Company, 1981.
Bulger, Adam. "Sudden and Unexplained: The Sleep Deaths that Inspired Freddy Kruger." *Van Winkle's*, 30 October 2015. Accessed 7 September 2020. https://web.archive.org/web/20180417144220/https://vanwinkles.com/sudden-and-unexplained-the-sleep-deaths-that-inspired-freddy-krueger.
Bunnell, Charlene. "The Gothic: A Literary Genre's Transition to Film," in *Planks of Reason*, edited by Barry Keith Grant, 79–100. Metuchen, NJ: Scarecrow Press, 1984.
Campbell, Joseph. *Myths to Live By*. New York: Penguin Compass, 1972.

Bibliography

Carroll, Noël. *The Philosophy of Horror*. New York: Routledge, 1989.
Cassirer, Ernst. *Language and Myth*. New York: Dover Publications, 1946.
CGP Grey. "You Are Two." YouTube, May 31, 2016. https://www.youtube.com/watch?v=wfYbgdo8e-8.
Chaieb, Leila, et al. "Auditory Beat Stimulation and its Effects on Cognition and Mood States." *Frontiers in Psychiatry* 6, no. 70 (2015). Accessed October 2020. https://www.ncbi.nlm.nih.gov/pmc/articles/PMC4428073/.
Christensen, Kyle. "The Final Girl versus Wes Craven's *A Nightmare on Elm Street*: Proposing a Stronger Model of Feminism in Slasher Horror Cinema." *Studies in Popular Culture* 51, no. 1 (2011): 23–47.
Clover, Carol J. *Men, Women, and Chainsaws: Gender in the Modern Horror Film*. Princeton, NJ: BFI, 1992.
Conner, Staci Poston. "'Horror More Horrible From Being Vague, and Terror More Terrible From Ambiguity': Liminal Figures in Poe's 'Berenice' and Gilman's 'The Giant Wistaria.'" *The Edgar Allan Poe Review* 20, no. 1 (2019): 77–95.
Count Jackula. "I Spit on Your Grave." YouTube. TheCountJackulaShow, 2015. https://www.youtube.com/watch?v=ZRlbB-jDS5U&list=PL7ykZa907Km5Ca3NPoAVmOkzh_cSM1qsf&index=19.
"Court finds Gustaffson not guilty of 1960 Bodom Lake triple murder." Web. Archive. *Helsingin Sanomat*, 2005. Accessed September 2020. https://web.archive.org/web/20070628204433/http://www.hs.fi/english/article/Court%20finds%20Gustafsson%20not%20guilty%20of%201960%20Bodom%20Lake%20triple%20murder/1101981204857.
Currie, Gregory. "Both Sides of the Story: Explaining Events in a Narrative." *Philos Stud: Philosophical Studies* 135, no. 1 (2007): 49–63.
"David Cronenberg." BrainyQuote, 2017. Accessed March 7, 2017. https://www.brainyquote.com/quotes/quotes/d/davidcrone158502.html.
Dégh, Linda, and Andrew Vazsonyi. "Does the Word 'Dog' Bite? Ostensive Action: A Means of Legend-Telling." *Journal of Folklore Research* 20, no. 1 (1983): 5–34.
Deodato, Ruggero, dir. "Cult-Con 2000." *Cannibal Holocaust*. 1980; Rome: United Artists Europa, 2000. DVD.
Dickstein, Morris. "The Aesthetics of Fright," in *Planks of Reason*, edited by Barry Keith Grant, 65–78. Metuchen, NJ: Scarecrow Press, 1984.
Dictionary of Deities and Demons in The Bible, 2nd ed. Edited by Karel Van Der Toorn, Bob Becking, and Pieter W. Van Der Horst. Grand Rapids, MI: William B. Eerdmans Publishing Company, 1999.
"Doris Bither Case." Wikipedia. Accessed March 2020. https://en.wikipedia.org/wiki/Doris_Bither_case.
Doyle, Larry. "Medical Experts Seek Clues to 'Nightmare Deaths' That Strike Male Asian Refugees." *Los Angeles Times* (Los Angeles), January 11, 1987.
Ebert, Roger. "Paperhouse." RogerEbert, March 31, 1989. https://www.rogerebert.com/reviews/paperhouse-1989.
Egginton, William. "Reality is Bleeding: A Brief History of Film from the 16th Century." *Configurations* 9, no. 2 (2001): 207–229.
Eyes on Cinema. "Wes Craven 'Scream' interview-A Confused, Cynical Generation Looking for Essential Truth." YouTube, April 13, 2015. https://www.youtube.com/watch?v=un1arjkK3VI.
Farrands, Daniel, and Andrew Kasch, dir. *Never Sleep Again: The Elm Street Legacy*. 2010; 1428 Films, 2010. DVD.
Faulkner, Sam. "Interview with *Sinister* writer C. Robert Cargill." Web.Archive. Screengeek, October 8, 2012. https://web.archive.org/web/20121111060203/http://www.screengeek.co.uk/features/article/interview-sinister-writer-c-robert-cargill.
"The '4 D's' of Abnormality." IvyLearn. Ivytech. Accessed August 2020. https://ivylearn.ivytech.edu/courses/740586/pages/the-4-ds-of-abnormality.
Frayling, Christopher. "Fuseli's *The Nightmare*: Somewhere between the Sublime and the Ridiculous," in *Gothic Nightmares: Fuseli, Blake and the Romantic Imagination*, edited by Martin Myrone, 9–22. London, UK: Tate Publishing, 2006.

Giles, Dennis. "Conditions of Pleasure in Horror Cinema," in *Planks of Reason*, edited by Barry Keith Grant, 38–52. Metuchen, NJ: Scarecrow Press, 1984.

Goig, Gema Navarro, and Francisco Javier Sánchez-Verdejo Pérez. "Echoes of Fairy Tales: Fantasy and Everyday Horrors in Guillermo del Toro's Filmography," in *Contemporary Fairy Tale Magic: Subverting Gender and Genre*, edited by Lydia Brugué and Auba Llompart. Brill-Rodopi, 138–147. Amsterdam: Brill, 2020.

Good, Craig. "446: The Fallibility of Memory." Produced by Skeptoid Podcast Media. *Skeptoid.* December 23, 2014. Podcast. http://skeptoid.com/episodes/4446.

Gottschall, Jonathan. *The Storytelling Animal: How Stories Make Us Human.* Boston: Houghton Mifflin Harcourt, 2012.

Graham, Loren. "The Power of Names: In Culture and In Mathematics." *American Philosophy Society* 157, no. 2 (2013): 229–234.

Green, Thomas A. *Folklore: An Encyclopedia of Beliefs, Customs, Tales, Music, and Art.* 1st ed., vol. 1. Santa Barbara, CA: ABC-CLIO, 1997.

Gregory, David, dir. *Celluloid Crime of the Century: The Last House on the Left.* 2003; Los Angeles: American International Pictures, 2003. DVD.

Gurstelle, E.B., and J.L. de Oliveira. "Daytime Parahypnagogia: A State of Consciousness That Occurs When We Almost Fall Asleep." *Medical Hypotheses* 62, no. 2 (2004): 166–168.

Györi, Zsolt. "'Animals Rule! Timothy Conquered': Escape, Capture, and Liminality in Werner Herzog's Grizzly Man." *Hungarian Journal of English and American Studies, HJEAS* 21, no. 1 (2015): 83–101.

Halberstam, Judith. *Skin Shows: Gothic Horror and the Technology of Monsters.* Durham, NC: Duke University Press, 1995.

Heller-Nicholas, Alexandra. *Found Footage Horror Films: Fear and Appearance of Reality.* Jefferson, NC: McFarland, 2014.

Heller-Nicholas, Alexandra. *Suspiria.* Leighton Buzzard, United Kingdom: Auteur, 2015.

Hidden Clips. "Wes Craven Interview (screamography)." YouTube, May 26, 2015. https://www.youtube.com/watch?v=_zmo9fGtcVE&t=1203s.

"Horror, n." *OED.* http://www.oed.com.ezproxy.lib.vt.edu/view/Entry/88577?rskey=GlNT3D&result=1&isAdvanced=false#eid.

Hubner, Laura. "*Pan's Labyrinth*, Fear and the Fairy Tale," in *Fear Itself: Reasoning the Unreasonable*, edited by Stephen Hessel and Michèle Huppert, 43–62. Amsterdam: Rodopi, 2010.

Jones, Chris. "Jane Byrne's move into Cabrini-Green is the subject of a new play. But the stunt's history 'depends on whom you ask.'" *Chicago Tribune*, February 27, 2020. https://www.chicagotribune.com/entertainment/theater/chris-jones/ct-ent-jane-byrne-cabrini-green-0301-20200227-ivj4syzdwzbqrc4opembeflyge-story.html.

Jowett, Garth, and James M. Linton. *Movies as Mass Communication.* Newbury Park, CA: Sage Publications, 1989.

"Judith." Disney. Accessed March 2020. https://family.disney.com/baby-names/baby-girl-names/meaning-of-judith/.

Jung, Carl. *Modern Man in Search of a Soul.* Translated by W.S. Dell and Cary F. Baynes. San Diego: Harcourt Inc., 1933.

Kaye, Don. "Interview: Oculus director Mike Flanagan." Den of Geek, April 14, 2014. https://www.denofgeek.com/movies/interview-oculus-director-mike-flanagan/.

King, Stephen. *Danse Macabre.* New York: Gallery Books, 2010.

King, Stephen. "The Importance of Being Bachmann," in *The Bachman Books: Four Early Novels by Richard Bachman, Author of The Regulators.* Plume, 1996.

King, Stephen. "Rest Stop," in *Just After Sunset*, 141–167. New York: Pocket Books, 2008.

King, Stephen. "What's Scary," foreword in *Danse Macabre*, xi-xxxi. New York: Gallery Books, 2010.

Kirby, Terry. "Video Link to Bulger Murder Disputed." *Independent*, November 26, 1993. http://www.independent.co.uk/news/video-link-to-bulger-murder-disputed-1506766.html.

Klein, Joshua. "Interview—The Blair Witch Project." Web.Archive. The A.V. Club, July 22, 1999. https://web.archive.org/web/20150121163922/http://www.avclub.com/article/the-blair-witch-project-13607.

Koven, Mikel J. *Film, Folklore, And Urban Legends.* Lanham, MD: Scarecrow Press, 2008.
Koven, Mikel J. "The Terror Tale: Urban Legends and the Slasher Film." *Scope: An Online Journal* (2003). Accessed October 2020. https://www.nottingham.ac.uk/scope/documents/2003/may-2003/koven.pdf.
Kremer, Daniel. *Sidney J. Furie: Life and Films.* Lexington, KY: University Press of Kentucky, 2015.
Kristeva, Julia. *Powers of Horror: An Essay on Abjection.* Translated by Leon S. Roudiez. New York: Columbia University Press, European Perspectives, 1980.
Kroenke, K., and A. D. Mangelsdorff. "Common Symptoms in Ambulatory Care: Incidences, Evaluation, Therapy, and Outcome." *The American Journal of Medicine* 86, no. 3 (1989). Accessed October 2020. https://pubmed.ncbi.nlm.nih.gov/2919607/.
Kühn, Simone, et al. "The Neural Representation of Intrusive Thoughts." *Social Cognitive and Affective Neuroscience* 8, no. 6 (2013): 688–693.
LeBourdais, Julien. "McLuhan: Now The Medium Is The Massage." *The New York Times.* Accessed February 20, 2020. https://www.nytimes.com/1967/03/19/archives/mcluhan-now-the-medium-is-the-massage.html.
Leviticus. *The Bible.*
"Liminal Time in Monster Literature." *Children's Literature Association Quarterly* 29, no. 3 (2004): 217–227.
Loftus, Elizabeth F. "Creating False Memories." *Scientific American* 277, no. 3 (1997): 70–75. Accessed October 2020. http://staff.washington.edu/eloftus/Articles/sciam.htm.
Lovasz, Adam. "'Would you like to meet a ghost?': Repetition and Spectral Posthumanism in Kiyoshi Kurosawa's *Kairo.*" *Horror Studies* 9, no. 2 (2018): 249–263.
Lukasiewicz, Tracie D. "The Parallelism of the Fantastic and the Real: Guillermo del Toro's *Pan's Labyrinth/El Laberinto del fauno* and Neomagical Realism," in *Fairy Tale Films: Visions of Ambiguity,* edited by Pauline Greenhill and Sidney Eve Matrix, 60–78. Boulder: University Press of Colorado, 2010.
"Man remanded on suspicion of infamous unsolved triple murder from 1960." *Helsingin Sanomat.* https://web.archive.org/web/20070930082146/http://www2.hs.fi/english/archive/news.asp?id=20040405IE7. Accessed September 2020.
Marksbury, Thomas. Personal Conversation. February 17, 2020.
Marshall, Mallika. "A placebo can work even when you know it's a placebo." *Harvard Health Publishing.* Harvard, July 7, 2016. https://www.health.harvard.edu/blog/placebo-can-work-even-know-placebo-201607079926.
McNamara, Patrick. *Nightmares.* Westport, CT: Praeger, 2008.
McRae, Michael. "Gustave, the Killer Crocodile—Update." *National Geographic Adventure Magazine,* August 2008.
Mendez, Mike. "Tobe Hooper "Masters of Horror" part 1." YouTube, 2008. https://www.youtube.com/watch?v=Ae-bBisE5ZE.
Metzinger, Thomas. *The Ego Tunnel: The Science of the Mind and the Myth of the Self.* New York: Basic Books, 2009.
Mitchell, Paul. "The Horror of Loss: Reading Jennifer Kent's *The Babadook* as a Trauma Narrative." *Atlantis Journal* 41, no. 2 (2019): 179–196.
Mitchell, Sean. "A Gallery of Craven Images." *Los Angeles Times* (Los Angeles), November 18, 1989.
Monument, Andrew, dir. *Nightmares in Red, White, & Blue.* 2009; Lux Digital Pictures. https://tubitv.com/movies/15641/nightmares-in-red-white-and-blue?start=true.
Mufson, Beckett. "13 Wes Craven Quotes Remember the Original Master of Horror." *Vice,* August 14, 2015. https://creators.vice.com/en_uk/article/13-wes-craven-quotes-remember-the-original-master-of-horror.
Myrone, Martin. "Fuseli to Frankenstein: The Visual Arts in the Context of the Gothic," in *Gothic Nightmares: Fuseli, Blake and the Romantic Imagination,* edited by Martin Myrone, 31–42. London, United Kingdom: Tate Publishing, 2006.
Ndalianis, Angela. *The Horror Sensorium: Media and the Senses.* Jefferson, NC: McFarland, 2012.
"Nicole Tompkins." Backstage, Accessed August 2020. https://www.backstage.com/u/Nicole-Tompkins/.

"Nightmare, n. and adj." *OED*, September 2003. http://www.oed.com.ezproxy.lib.vt.edu/view/Entry/127012?rskey=zJDXaw&result=1&isAdvanced=false#eid.

Novella, Steven. "Sleep and False Memory." *Neurologicablog*. July 24, 2014. https://theness.com/neurologicablog/index.php/sleep-and-false-memory/.

O'Sullivan, Suzanne. "When the Body Speaks." Psychology Today, January 2017, last reviewed September 7, 2019. https://www.psychologytoday.com/us/articles/201701/when-the-body-speaks.

Ouellette, Jennifer. *Me, Myself, and Why: Searching for the Science of Self.* New York: Penguin Books, 2014.

"People can die from giving up the fight." Eureka Alert, September 27, 2018. https://www.eurekalert.org/pub_releases/2018-09/uop-pcd092018.php.

Peucker, Brigitte. "Herzog and Auteurism: Performing Authenticity," in *A Companion to Werner Herzog*, edited by Brad Prager, 35–57. Hoboken, NJ: Wiley-Blackwell, 2012.

Phillips, Kendall R. *Dark Directions: Romero, Craven, Carpenter, and the Modern Horror Film.* Carbondale: Southern Illinois University Press, 2012.

Planés, Sara, Céline Villier, and Michel Mallaret. "The nocebo effect of drugs." *Pharmacology Research & Perspectives* 4, no. 2 (2016). Accessed November 2020. https://www.ncbi.nlm.nih.gov/pmc/articles/PMC4804316/.

Proietti, Massimiliano, et al. "Experimental test of local observer-independence." *Science Advances* 5, no. 9 (2019). Accessed October 2020. https://arxiv.org/abs/1902.05080.

Reed, Isaac. "Why Salem Made Sense: Culture, Gender, and the Puritan Persecution of Witchcraft." *Cultural Sociology* 1, no. 2 (2007): 209–234.

Reese, Hannah. "Intrusive Thoughts: Normal or Not?: Am I a Terrible Person for Thinking That?" Psychology Today, October 24, 2011. https://www.psychologytoday.com/us/blog/am-i-normal/201110/intrusive-thoughts-normal-or-not.

"Rosemary." Web. Archive. *Australian War Memorial*. Accessed March 2020. https://web.archive.org/web/20131219155712/https://www.awm.gov.au/commemoration/customs/rosemary.asp.

Russell, David. J. "Monster Roundup: Reintegrating the Horror Genre," in *Refiguring American Film Genres: Theory and History*, edited by Nick Browne, 233–254. Berkeley, CA: University of California Press, 1998.

Saito, Stephen. "TIFF '15 Interview: AKIZ on the Creative Awakening of 'Der Nachtmahr.'" Moveablefest, October 2, 2015. https://moveablefest.com/akiz-der-nachtmahr/.

Sanderson, Mark. *Don't Look Now.* London: British Film Institute, 1996.

Saporito, Jeff. "'What is the history of the Bughuul demon in *Sinister* and *Sinister 2*?" Screenprism. Accessed March 2020. http://screenprism.com/insights/article/what-is-the-history-of-the-bughuul-demon-in-sinister-and-sinister-2.

"Sartain Family History." Ancestry.com. Accessed February 2020. https://www.ancestry.com/name-origin?surname=sartain.

Schoenberger, Karl. "Night Deaths of Asian Men Unexplained: Healthy Indonesians, Filipinos, Japanese Expire 'With a Snap.'" *Los Angeles Times* (Los Angeles), July 10, 1983.

Schwarz, Jeffey, dir. *Never Sleep Again: The Making of A Nightmare on Elm Street.* 2006; Burbank, CA: New Line Cinema Entertainment, 2006. DVD.

Schwenger, Paul. *At the Borders of Sleep: On Liminal Literature.* Minneapolis: University of Minnesota Press, 2012.

Seif, Martin, and Sally Winston. "Unwanted Intrusive Thoughts." Psychology Today, July 1, 2019. https://www.psychologytoday.com/us/blog/living-sticky-mind/201907/unwanted-intrusive-thoughts.

Shattuck, Roger. *Forbidden Knowledge: From Prometheus to Pornography.* New York: St. Martin's Press, 1996.

Smith, Dame Janet. "The Shipman Inquiry: Third Report." Crown Copyright, 2003. Accessed September 2020. https://assets.publishing.service.gov.uk/government/uploads/system/uploads/attachment_data/file/273227/5854.pdf.

Sperry, R.W. "Hemisphere Disconnection and Unity in Conscious Awareness." *American Psychologist* 23, no. 10 (1968): 723–733.

Spinney, Laura. "We can implant entirely false memories." *The Guardian*, December 3, 2003. https://www.theguardian.com/science/2003/dec/04/science.research1.

Thiem, Jon. "The Textualization of the Reader in Magical Realist Fiction," in *Magical Realism: Theory, History, Community*, edited by Lois Parkinson Zamora and Wendy B. Faris, 235–248. Durham, NC: Duke University Press, 1995.

Todorov, Tzvetan. *The Fantastic: A Structural Approach to a Literary Genre*. Translated by Richard Howard. Cleveland, OH: The Press of Case Western Reserve University, 1973.

Tucker, Elizabeth. "Ghosts in Mirrors: Reflections of the Self." *Journal of American Folklore* 118, no. 468 (2005): 186–203.

Turner, Victor. "Liminal to Liminoid, in Play, Flow, and Ritual: An Essay in Comparative Symbology." *Rice University Studies* 60, no. 3 (1974): 53–92. Accessed August 2020. https://scholarship.rice.edu/bitstream/handle/1911/63159/article_RIP603_part4.pdf?sequence=1&isAllowed=y.

"Urban Legend." *Merriam-Webster*. Accessed March 10, 2020. https://www.merriam-webster.com/dictionary/urban%20legend.

Viennot, Giles A. "*Kairo* (*Pulse*, Kurosawa, 2001) and Kairos: Postmodern Japanese Computer Culture, Memory and Entropy," in *Memory in World Cinema: Critical Essays*, translated by James H. Membrez, edited by Nancy J. Membrez, 173–186. Jefferson, NC: McFarland, 2019.

Voss, Ursula, et al. "Lucid Dreaming: A State of Consciousness with Features of Both Waking and Non-Lucid Dreaming." *Sleep* 32, no. 9 (2009): 1191–1200. Accessed October 2020. https://www.ncbi.nlm.nih.gov/pmc/articles/PMC2737577/.

"Was *Fargo* Based on A True Story?" Snopes, June 8, 1998. http://www.snopes.com/movies/films/fargo.asp.

Wee, Valerie. "The Scream Trilogy, 'Hyperpostmodernism,' and the Late-Nineties Teen Slasher Film." *Journal of Film and Video* 57, no. 3 (2005): 55–57.

West, Brandon. "Murky Waters: Loch Ness and Herzogian Notions of Truth." *The New Review of Film and Television*, forthcoming.

"Who can have sex with whom and from what age?" Zanzu. Accessed August 2020. https://www.zanzu.de/en/rights-and-law/your-rights/age-of-consent/.

Winsdale, J. Lawton, "Techno-Kabbalah: The Performative Language of Magick and the Production of Occult Knowledge," *TDR: Drama Review* 44, no. 2 (2000): 84–100.

Wood, Robin. "An Introduction to the American Horror Film," in *American Nightmares: Essays on the Horror Film*. Festival of Festivals, 1979.

Wyrick, Laura. "Summoning Candyman: The Cultural Production of History." *Arizona Quarterly: A Journal of American Literature, Culture, and Theory* 54, no. 3 (1998): 89–117.

Zipes, Jack. *The Irresistible Fairy Tale: The Cultural and Social History of a Genre*. Princeton, NJ: Princeton University Press, 2012.

Zipes, Jack. "*Pan's Labyrinth* (*El laberinto del fauno*) (review)." *Journal of American Folklore* 121, no. 480 (2008): 236–240.

Index

abject 22, 225
abnormality 143–144
Abrams, M.H. 11
All the Colors of the Dark 159–165, 168
Antrum: The Deadliest Film Ever Made 53–58, 63, 140
The Autopsy of Jane Doe 178–186, 189–190; *see also* Salem witch trials

The Babadook 198–199, 203–204, 222
binaural beats 55–56, 58, 140
Bither, Doris 221; *see also The Entity*
The Blair Witch Project 6, 16–18, 99
Brunvand, Jan Harold 107
Bughuul 36–42, 45–47, 71–73; *see also Sinister* and *Sinister 2*
Bulger, Adam 218
Bulger, James (murder of) 23, 61

The Cabin in the Woods 95
camera 16–17, 20, 27, 32, 34, 38, 43, 51, 53, 57, 82, 84, 96, 108, 110, 112, 155, 161–162, 169–170, 172, 185–186, 194, 211
Campbell, Joseph 207; *see also* ritual
Candyman 2, 69–71, 73–78, 128, 172–173, 189–190, 209, 212–214, 217, 225
Capturing the Killer Croc 86
Carpenter, John 50, 52, 104, 118–119, 121, 166
Carroll, Noël 9–10
Castle, William 156
Chilling Adventures of Sabrina 120
Cigarette Burns 50–58, 63
Clover, Carol J. 26, 106; *see also* final girl
Coming Soon 42–49, 58, 63
Craven, Wes 1, 8, 11, 14, 22, 24, 65, 78–80, 85, 94–96, 98–99, 103–106, 110, 126–127, 129, 131, 136–137, 214, 217–220
Cronenberg, David 58, 61–62, 104–105; *see also Videodrome*

The Dark Half 71–78, 138; *see also* King, Stephen
Darna Zaroori Hai 33–35
daytime parahypnagogia 125
Dolls 12–13, 110–114, 118
Don't Look Now 158–159, 165, 168

Ebert, Roger 147
Egginton, William 5–7, 17, 103–104
The Entity 196–199, 203–204, 221–222; *see also* Bither, Doris

fairy tales 13, 112–113, 116
the fantastic 1, 11, 13, 54, 88, 101, 169
Feast 95
final girl 10, 22, 27, 82, 94, 107, 215; *see also* Clover, Carol J
folklore 5, 27, 69, 75, 77, 100–101, 106–107, 114, 181, 200
"The Forbidden" 213
Found Footage 3-D 2, 18–22, 58, 63
Frayling, Christopher 132
Freud, Sigmund 197; *see also* psychoanalysis 75–76
Friday the 13th 24, 94, 98, 107, 129; day 33

gothic 11–14, 116, 156, 174, 204; film 131–137, 139, 146–147
Gottschall, Jonathan 5–7, 106, 188, 192
grither 209–214, 223

Halloween 23, 96, 98, 165–168, 208; day 4
hallucinations 43, 50–52, 55, 60, 123, 137, 143, 158, 169–171, 176, 178–179, 186–187
Hatchet 9–10
Hatchet III 10
Heller-Nicholas, Alexandra 5, 17–18, 22, 169, 188; *see also Suspiria*
history 6, 30, 53, 75, 77, 79, 85, 89, 91–92, 132, 152, 154–155, 166, 185, 189–190, 197–198, 204, 214, 219

Index

Horsehead 150–156
The House That Dripped Blood 30–33, 35
Hubner, Laura 116

I Know What You Did Last Summer 95
In the Mouth of Madness 118–122, 124, 145, 171
incest 154–155, 197
Into the Mirror 173–176
intrusive thoughts 198, 221
irony 1, 14, 20–21, 25, 32, 34, 44, 60, 76, 91, 94–99, 117, 148, 159, 162–163, 167, 171, 181, 183, 198, 208–209, 211, 215–216
isochronic tones 140

Jacob's Ladder 131, 137–139, 144, 146–147, 152
Jowett, Garth 121
Jung, Carl Gustav 3, 74–75, 152–153; *see also* psychoanalysis 75–76
Ju-on: The Grudge 203–205, 222

King, Stephen 15, 17, 71, 73–74, 77, 79, 103, 207; *see also The Dark Half*
Koven, Mikel J. 28, 107

Lake Bodom 89–93
The Last House on the Left 85, 136
liminality 1–9, 11–16, 41, 48, 50, 58–59, 65, 81, 93, 116, 122, 129, 150, 186, 217, 222–224
Linton, James M. 121
Loftus, Elizabeth F. 187
Lovasz, Adam 48–49, 58, 63; *see also Pulse* and *Kairo*
Lovecraft, H.P. 119–121, 171; *see also* "Pickman's Model"
lucid dreaming 128, 147, 150–152, 155

magic 7
magical realism 13–14
McLuhan, Marshall 59
McNamara, Patrick 130–131, 133, 136, 146; *see also* nightmares
memory 73, 119, 128, 149, 187–189
meta-fiction 14, 22, 52, 58, 79, 98, 120, 129, 141
mirror 31, 44, 70, 74–75, 77, 158, 169–178, 184–186, 189, 194–195, 197
Moloch 40–42

Der Nachtmahr 132, 139–145, 147, 155–156
Ndalianis, Angela 99
nightmare 1, 17, 39, 41, 47, 67, 98, 106, 126, 130–141, 143–146, 150–152, 156, 159, 161, 170, 214–216, 218, 220, 223; painting 131–132, 135, 137
A Nightmare on Elm Street 14, 78, 94, 103, 126–128, 130–131, 134–139, 143, 146–147, 149, 152, 175, 199, 201, 214–221
Nightmares in Red, White, and Blue 79
nocebo 214, 217, 219–221
Novella, Stephen 187–188

Oculus 169–172, 178–179, 185–186, 189–190
ostension 27–29, 35, 63, 108
Ouellette, Jennifer 186–187

Pan's Labyrinth 13–14, 114–118
Paperhouse 147–150, 165
Phillips, Kendall R. 11, 217
"Pickman's Model" 120; *see also* Lovecraft, H.P.
placebo 209, 214, 217, 220
Primeval 12–14, 85–89, 118
psychoanalysis 75–75; *see also* Freud, Sigmund and Jung, Carl Gustav
Pulse 48–49, 58, 63

The Ring 40–43, 45–49, 53, 58–60, 63, 70–73
ritual 2, 42, 54, 70, 74, 114, 163, 180–181, 207–208, 212
Russell, David J. 9–10

Salem witch trials 178, 189; *see also The Autopsy of Jane Doe*
Scary Movie 3 41–42
Scary Stories to Tell in the Dark 45–47, 49, 58–59, 63, 77–78
schizophrenia 196, 220
Schwenger, Paul 79, 133
Scream 2, 14, 22–25, 27–31, 33, 35, 39, 58, 60, 63, 65–69, 89, 94–99, 103–105, 107–108, 118, 129, 156, 158, 177, 182–183, 208, 215, 218, 225
Scream 2 65–68
Scream 3 65, 67–69, 77
Scream 4 67–69
The Sender 176–177, 183
Shattuck, Roger 186
Sinister 2, 35–43, 47–49, 58–60, 63, 71, 182; *see also* Bughuul
Sinister 2 37, 46; *see also* Bughuul
slasher 4, 10, 24, 26–27, 29, 66, 93–95, 97–98, 105, 107–108, 129, 166
Sperry, R.W. 192; *see also* split-brain surgery
Split 192–196
split-brain surgery 191–192; *see also* Sperry, R.W.
sublime 184
SUNDS 219–220
Supernatural 120

Suspiria 169–170; *see also* Heller-Nicholas, Alexandra

The Texas Chainsaw Massacre 26, 82–85, 89
Tucker, Elizabeth 74–75
Turner, Victor 2

Urban Legend 2, 22, 27–31, 33, 35–36, 39, 63, 69, 95, 108–110, 116, 118, 158, 182, 194–195; folklore 4, 27, 39, 44, 47, 100, 107–108, 110
Urban Legend: Final Cut 29–30, 39, 95

Videodrome 58–64, 123–124, 173
Viennot, Giles A. 48–49
Visitors 199–205, 222

The Weir 100–103, 106
Wes Craven's New Nightmare 78–81, 95, 98–100, 103, 129–130
Williamson, Kevin 22, 97
Wood, Robin 9
Wyrick, Laura 75

Zipes, Jack 112–113, 116

www.ingramcontent.com/pod-product-compliance
Lightning Source LLC
Chambersburg PA
CBHW021351300426
44114CB00012B/1178